Ubuntu® Certified Professional Study Guide

(Exam LPI 199)

Michael Jang

McGraw Hill

New York   Chicago   San Francisco   Lisbon   London   Madrid
Mexico City   Milan   New Delhi   San Juan   Seoul   Singapore   Sydney   Toronto

The McGraw·Hill Companies

Cataloging-in-Publication Data is on file with the Library of Congress

McGraw-Hill books are available at special quantity discounts to use as premiums and sales promotions, or for use in corporate training programs. To contact a special sales representative, please visit the Contact Us page at www.mhprofessional.com.

Ubuntu® Certified Professional Study Guide (Exam LPI 199)

1234567890   DOC DOC   0198

ISBN: Book p/n 978-0-07-159112-6 and CD p/n 978-0-07-159113-3
of set 978-0-07-159110-2
MHID: Book p/n 0-07-159112-5 and CD p/n 0-07-159113-3
of set 0-07-159110-9

Sponsoring Editor
Tim Green

Editorial Supervisor
Patty Mon

Project Manager
Harleen Chopra,
International Typesetting
and Composition

Acquisitions Coordinator
Jennifer Housh

Technical Editor
Elizabeth Zinkann

Copy Editor
Margaret Berson

Proofreader
Bev Weiler

Indexer
Karin Arrigoni

Production Supervisor
Jean Bodeaux

Composition
International Typesetting
and Composition

Illustration
International Typesetting
and Composition

Art Director, Cover
Jeff Weeks

For the young widows and widowers, may they find the courage to face their fears, to navigate their way through the pain, and to find hope for a brighter future.

ABOUT THE AUTHOR

Michael Jang (UCP, RHCE, LPIC-2, LCP, Linux+, MCSE) is currently a full-time writer, specializing in operating systems and networks. His experience with computers goes back to the days of jumbled punch cards. He has written other books on Linux certification, including *RHCE Red Hat Certified Engineer Linux Study Guide*, *Linux+ Certification Passport*, and *Sair GNU/Linux Installation and Configuration Exam Cram*. His other Linux books include *Linux Annoyances for Geeks*, *Linux Patch Management*, and *Mastering Fedora Core Linux 5*. He has also written or contributed to books on Microsoft operating systems, including *MCSE Guide to Microsoft Windows 98* and *Mastering Windows XP Professional, Second Edition*.

About the Technical Editor

Elizabeth Zinkann is a logical Linux catalyst, a freelance technical editor, and an independent computer consultant. She was a contributing editor and review columnist for *Sys Admin Magazine* for ten years. As an editor, some of her projects have included *RHCE Red Hat Certified Engineer Linux Study Guide*, *Linux+ Certification Guide*, *Mastering Fedora Core Linux 5*, *Linux Patch Management*, and *Write Portable Code*. She owns an iBook that thinks it's an UbuntuBook and is an avid digital photographer. In a former life, she also programmed communications features, including ISDN at AT&T Network Systems.

CONTENTS AT A GLANCE

CONTENTS

vii

ACKNOWLEDGMENTS

I personally would like to thank the following people:

My beautiful wife Donna—I love everything about you. I love your eyes, I love your smile, I love your heart. After the sadness we've shared, I'm thankful for every day I have with you. You've brought me hope, you've brought me love, you've brought me happiness. You've shown incredible patience as I write these books. Marrying you was the best decision I could ever have made. This book is also dedicated to your Randy and my Nancy, who brought us together from the hereafter.

The Ubuntu Community—With your efforts, Linux is now gaining market share and mind share with the eventual goal of overtaking Microsoft's market share in the server and the desktop operating system environments.

The Technical Editor—Elizabeth Zinkann is a magnificent editor and friend, someone who has taught me much about Linux in the real world, someone who has gently prodded me when my writing goes wrong.

All the incredibly hard-working folks at McGraw-Hill—Tim Green, Jennifer Housh, Harleen Chopra, Margaret Berson, Bev Weiler, and Karin Arrigoni for their help in launching a great series and being solid team players.

INTRODUCTION

L inux is thriving. The Ubuntu community has taken the lead in making Linux popular. IT departments will look toward Ubuntu Certified Professionals to make Linux work in real life.

When business, education, and governments are cost conscious, they move toward Linux. Even in times of economic strength, they want control of their operating systems. Ubuntu Linux saves money. The open source nature of Linux allows organizations to control and customize their operating systems.

If desired, commercial support is available from Canonical. Even with that support, Linux saves money, and provides a higher degree of control, when compared to Microsoft Windows.

Linux has proven itself in pressure-filled situations. The New York Stock Exchange is migrating to Linux. Major corporations, from Home Depot to Toyota, and governments such as Germany, the Republic of Korea, and Mexico are making the switch to Linux. When faced with a Microsoft audit for licenses, the Portland, Oregon school system switched to Linux. Major movie studios such as Disney and Dreamworks use Linux to create the latest motion pictures. IBM has invested billions in Linux—and frequently features Linux in its advertising. Even though Linux is freely downloadable, *Wall Street Technology* just reported that Linux server revenue in 2007 started approaching U.S. $8 billion, and is still gaining market share. Will the problems associated with Microsoft Vista motivate business to look more closely at Linux?

Ubuntu Linux and the Ubuntu Certified Professional exam are fairly new. But there's one telling report in *Enterprise Linux News*. Alfresco, an open source enterprise content management provider, suggests that Ubuntu now rivals Red Hat as the market leader in the Enterprise. I believe that Ubuntu will eventually also develop an Ubuntu Certified Engineer exam to rival the challenges associated with the Red Hat Certified Engineer exam.

To study for the UCP exam, you should have a network of at least two Linux or Unix computers. It's acceptable if these computers are on virtual machines such as VMware. You need to install Ubuntu Linux on at least one of these computers. That will allow you to configure Linux and test the results. After configuring a service, especially a network service, it's important to be able to check your work from another computer.

Who This Book Is For

This book is designed for those Linux professionals who want a tangible credential to prove their competence with Ubuntu Linux. As the exam is coupled with the LPI Level 1 exams from the Linux Professional Institute, it is also geared towards the "Junior Level Linux Professional." Comparable exams for other certifications suggest that level of competence is associated with at least two years of real-world experience.

To qualify as an UCP, you need to pass the Ubuntu Certified Professional exam—as well as the two LPI Level 1 exams.

The Ubuntu Certified Professional Exam LPI 199

The Ubuntu Certified Professional exam is based on your knowledge of *Ubuntu* Linux. Chapter 1 describes the basic options for downloads. In the following sections, I'll describe the basics of the Ubuntu Certified Professional curriculum, and what you can expect during the exam.

In This Book

The Ubuntu Certified Professional exam is designed to test candidate qualifications as Linux systems technicians and engineers. If you pass this exam, it's not because you've memorized a canned set of answers—it's because you have a set of Linux administrative skills and know how to use them under pressure, whether it is during an exam or in a real-world situation.

While this book is organized to serve as an in-depth review for the Ubuntu Certified Professional exam for both experienced Linux and Unix professionals, it is not intended as a substitute for Canonical courses, or more importantly, real-world experience. Nevertheless, each chapter covers a major aspect of the exam, with an emphasis on the "why" as well as the "how to" of working with and supporting Ubuntu Linux as a systems administrator or engineer. As the actual UCP curriculum is subject to change (www.ubuntu.com/training/certificationcourses/professional/curriculum), refer to the noted URL for the latest information.

Canonical says it's important to have real-world experience to pass their exam, and they're right! However, for the UCP exam, they do focus on a specific set of Linux administrative skills, as depicted in the UCP curriculum. This book is intended to help you take advantage of the skills you already have—and more importantly, brush up in those areas where you may have a bit less experience.

When logged in as a regular user, you'll see the prompt is slightly different; for user michael, it would typically look like the following:

```
michael@UbuntuGG:~$
```

As the length of this prompt would lead to a number of broken and wrapped code lines throughout this book, I've normally abbreviated this prompt as:

```
$
```

The Ubuntu Linux Exam Challenge

This section covers the reasons for pursuing industry-recognized certification, explains the importance of your UCP certification, and prepares you for taking the actual examination. It gives you a few pointers on how to prepare, what to expect, and what to do on exam day.

Leaping Ahead of the Competition!

The Ubuntu Linux's UCP certification exam includes a variety of questions. Most are multiple choice. Some are "fill in the blank"; others have multiple answers. The "fill in the blank" questions can be most challenging, as they often require commands with switches. You can get lucky with multiple-choice questions. But if you don't know a command in depth, including the switches needed to administer different systems, you won't answer those questions correctly.

e x a m

⚙ a t c h   *The UCP exam is an* *Ubuntu Linux exam. Knowledge of other* *Linux distributions such as Debian and* *Red Hat Linux is certainly helpful, as well* *as experience with services like Apache,* *Samba, NFS, DNS, and DHCP.*

Many of the questions are multiple choice, and may be familiar to those of you who have taken other certification exams. The following are two examples:

1. Which of the following repositories are not active in the standard Ubuntu /etc/apt/sources.list configuration file?

   A. Main

   B. Updates

   C. Backports

   D. Restricted

Answer C is correct; as noted in the comments to the /etc/apt/sources.list configuration file, the Backports repository is not active or searched by default.

Other questions may be *fill in the blank*. Correct spelling and syntax are required when you answer these questions. One example might be:

2. Type in the command that starts the GUI tool that can configure shared NFS directories. Do not include the full path to that command; assume that you've included a **sudo** in front of the command.

The command is **shares-admin**, which starts the Shared Folders tool, which can be used to configure shared NFS and Samba directories.

The level of difficulty is designed to be similar to the LPI Level 1 exams. While most UCP exams are given in a computer-based format, some organizations provide a "paper and pencil" option, which appear similar to standardized multiple choice exams such as the Scholastic Aptitude Test, with a line after each set of answers to accommodate fill in the blank questions.

Preparing for the UCP Exam

The best way to prepare for the UCP exam is to work with Ubuntu Linux. Install it on a computer (or virtual machine) that you don't need for any other purpose. Configure the services described in this book. Learn the commands described in the UCP curriculum (www.ubuntu.com/training/certificationcourses/professional/curriculum). Tinker with the options associated with the services described in the curriculum.

As you go through this book, you'll have the opportunity to install Ubuntu Linux several times. If you have more than one computer, you'll be able to install Ubuntu Linux over a network. And you should, as network installations are explicitly listed in the UCP curriculum. Then you can work with the different network services. Test out each service as you configure it, preferably from another computer on your network. Testing your work becomes especially important when you start working with the security features of Linux.

I prefer to test my systems on a virtual machine. When I do, problems don't affect my production systems. One freely available option that I use is VMware Server (www.vmware.com/products/server). If you're running an Ubuntu release through Gutsy Gibbon (7.10), VMware Server can also be installed from the Ubuntu partner repository, as listed in the /etc/apt/sources.list file.

Other options include Xen and the Kernel-based Virtual Machine systems. More information on making these options work is available from https://help.ubuntu.com/community/Xen and https://help.ubuntu.com/community/KVM, respectively.

Another guide to configuring Virtual Machines is freely available from McGraw-Hill. It's part of the *RHCE Red Hat Certified Engineer Study Guide*, available in PDF format from www.mhprofessional.com/downloads/products/0072264543/Virtual_Machine.pdf.

Signing Up for the UCP Exam

The UCP exam is available from Thomson Prometric (www.prometric.com) and Pearson VUE (www.vue.com) testing centers worldwide. It may also be available for reduced rates at events such as some of the Linux World Conference and Expos. It may also be available through some Linux user groups. As of this writing, the standard rate for the UCP exam is $100 in the United States of America.

The Ubuntu Certified Professional Exam LPI 199

There is little publicly written about the UCP exam. However, it is an exam associated with the Linux Professional Institute (LPI). As such, questions on the UCP exam are written in the same way as those you might see on the LPI Level 1 exams. A small number of questions on your exam may be there for evaluation purposes, and do not count toward grading your exam. When I took the exam, there were just under 50 questions, and the passing score is just over 50 percent.

There is a nondisclosure agreement (NDA) associated with the UCP exam. The time you take to read the NDA is counted against the time you have for the exam. As of this writing, the NDA is not publicly available.

Exam Readiness Checklist

The items in the Exam Readiness Checklist are based on the UCP curriculum available online at www.ubuntu.com/training/certificationcourses/professional/curriculum. It is subject to change at any time; coverage is current and complete as of this writing. Most of the items are covered in the noted chapters and sections. There may be exceptions, as listed in the "Inside the Exam" section in each chapter.

This table has been constructed to allow you to cross reference the official exam objectives with the objectives as they are presented and covered in this book. The checklist also allows you to gauge your level of expertise on each objective at the outset of your studies. This should allow you to check your progress and make sure you spend the time you need on more difficult or unfamiliar sections. References have been provided for the objective exactly as the vendor presents it, the section of the study guide that covers that objective, and a chapter and page reference.

TABLE I Coverage of the Ubuntu Certified Professional Curriculum

Exam Readiness Checklist

Certification Objective	Study Guide Coverage	Ch #	Pg #
Understand Ubuntu's Technical Infrastructure	A History of Ubuntu Releases A Variety of Ubuntu Resources	1	3 10
Source Help Through Support Resources	Ubuntu Support and More A Variety of Ubuntu Resources	1	13 10
Perform an Installation	Install Direct from the CD, Step by Step Review Automated Installation Files	2, 4	48 122
Configure Hardware	Configure Drives and Partitions Understand Basic Linux Hardware Compatibility Review Specialized Hardware Issues	2, 3	67 86 99
Configure Power Management	Explore Power Management Options	3	92
Understand Diskless Clients	Configure Servers for the Diskless Client Create the Diskless Client	4	135 141
Perform Ubuntu Package Management and Manage Repositories	Manage Individual Packages and More Review a Variety of Repositories Update and Manage Clients Create a Local Mirror	6	198 205 208 220
Manage Printers and Print Queues	Manage Print Queues Manage Printers	7	261 264
Install and Configure Local and Remote Printers	Work the CUPS Packages Configure Printers	7	236 245
Localise* the Operating System (*British spelling shown in the curriculum)	Configure Localization	8	278
Configure Ubuntu File System Security	Create Regular Users Set Up More Administrators Work the Shadow Password Suite	8	283 297 301
Configure Network Authentication for Clients	Configure Network Authentication for Clients	10	354
Configure Network Interfaces	Configure Network Interfaces	9	316
Configure Multiple Network Profiles	Set Up Network Profiles	9	338
Manage Network Filesystems	Set Up Network Filesystems	10	366
Configure GNOME	Configure the Desktop Environment	11	392
Configure GNOME Display Manager	Set Up the Display Manager	12	432
Configure Screen Features and Fonts	Manage Screen Features and Fonts	11	410
Configure Evolution Mail Client	Work with the Evolution E-mail Client	12	447

Tips for Succeeding on the Ubuntu Certified Professional Exam LPI 199

The UCP exam is tricky. Once you have the skills, the most important thing that you can take to the exam is a clear head. One hour can go quickly. If you're tired or frantic, you may miss the easy solutions that are often available. Get the sleep you need the night before the exam. Eat a good breakfast.

This book is not designed for beginners to Unix or Linux. The UCP exam is designed for Linux users with experience as a "Junior Level Linux Professional." For more information, see www.lpi.org/en/lpi/english/certification/the_lpic_program. To qualify as a UCP, you need to pass the LPI 199 exam, as well as the exams associated with the Linux Professional Institute Certification level 1 certification.

In Every Chapter

For this series, we've created a set of chapter components that call your attention to important items, reinforce important points, and provide helpful exam-taking hints. Take a look at what you'll find in every chapter:

- Every chapter begins with the **Certification Objectives**—the skills you need to master in order to pass the section on the exam associated with the chapter topic. The Objective headings identify the objectives within the chapter, so you'll always know an objective when you see it.

- **Exam Watch** notes call attention to information about, and potential pitfalls in, the exam. These helpful hints are written by authors who have taken the exams and received their certification—who better to tell you what to worry about? They know what you're about to go through!

exam

Watch *Of course, you can choose to download and install one of the variants of Ubuntu Linux, such as Kubuntu Linux or Xubuntu Linux. But remember the UCP Curriculum specifies only GNOME-based issues among available GUI tools.*

- **Practice Exercises** are interspersed throughout the chapters. These are step-by-step exercises that allow you to get the hands-on experience you need in order to pass the exams. They help you master skills that are likely to be an area of focus on the exam. Don't just read through the exercises; they are hands-on practice that you should be comfortable completing. Learning by doing is an effective way to increase your competency with a product.

on the **Job**

- **On the Job** notes describe the issues that come up most often in real-world settings. They provide a valuable perspective on certification- and product-related topics. They point out common mistakes and address questions that have arisen from on-the-job discussions and experience.

- **Inside the Exam** sidebars highlight some of the most common and confusing problems that students encounter when taking a live exam. These sidebars are designed to anticipate what the exam will emphasize—getting inside the exam will help ensure you know what you need to know to pass the exam. You can get a leg up on how to respond to those difficult-to-understand labs by focusing extra attention on these sidebars.

- **Scenario & Solution** sections lay out potential problems and solutions in a quick-to-read format.

- The **Certification Summary** is a succinct review of the chapter and a restatement of salient skills regarding the exam.

- ✓ The **Two-Minute Drill** at the end of every chapter is a checklist of the main points of the chapter. It can be used for last-minute review.

Q&A
- The **Self Test** offers multiple-choice, multiple-option, and "fill in the blank" questions designed to help test the practical knowledge associated with the certification exams. The answers to these questions, as well as explanations of the answers, can be found at the end of each chapter. By taking the Self-Test after completing each chapter, you'll reinforce what you've learned from that chapter.

- The **Lab Questions** at the end of the Self-Test section offer a unique and challenging question format that requires the reader to understand multiple chapter concepts to answer correctly. These questions are more complex and more comprehensive than the other questions, as they test your ability to take all the knowledge you have gained from reading the chapter and apply it to complicated, real-world situations.

Some Pointers

Once you've finished reading this book, set aside some time to do a thorough review. You might want to return to the book several times and make use of all the methods it offers for reviewing the material:

- *Reread all the Exam Watch notes*. Remember that these notes are written by authors who have taken the exam and passed. They know what you should expect—and what you should be on the lookout for.

- *Review all the Scenario & Solution sections* for quick problem solving.

- *Retake the Self-Tests*. Be aware that there are a number of "fill in the blank" questions on the Ubuntu Certified Professional exam.

- *Complete the exercises*. Did you do the exercises when you read through each chapter? If not, do them! These exercises are designed to cover exam topics, and there's no better way to get to know this material than by practicing. Be sure you understand why you are performing each step in each exercise. If there is something you are not clear on, reread that section in the chapter.

1

Ubuntu Community Resources

U

buntu Linux has come a long way in the past four years, since its initial release back in 2004. It has clearly become the most popular Linux distribution. While it probably is not the leader in revenue, it is beginning to push its way into the enterprise.

Its mission may be best expressed by Ubuntu's Bug #1, entitled "Microsoft has a majority market share." With the decision of Dell to sell computers preloaded with Ubuntu Linux, it appears that Linux, specifically Ubuntu Linux, now has a chance in the consumer marketplace. Will Ubuntu advance Linux to the point where regular consumers consider it as an alternative to Microsoft Windows? Only time will tell. But to get to this point, Ubuntu needs a community infrastructure; in other words, it needs more Linux administrators like yourself who specialize and are certified in the Ubuntu Linux distribution.

The Ubuntu Certified Professional (UCP) exam is targeted at the junior-level system administrator. Along with the Linux Professional Institute Level I exams, the UCP exam, as described at www.ubuntu.com/training/certificationcourses, is designed to demonstrate a candidate's ability to

- Configure a network of Ubuntu systems
- Understand security and package management fundamentals
- Perform key maintenance tasks

As a test of system administrative skills, the UCP goes beyond the skills associated with the Ubuntu Desktop Courses under development. As discussed in the Introduction, and based on the Ubuntu Professional Curriculum at www .ubuntu.com/training/certificationcourses/professional/curriculum, this book starts with a detailed analysis of the Ubuntu Community; an in-depth understanding of hardware, installation, and maintenance requirements; knowledge of routine administration tasks; the ability to configure networking and network services; and some know-how in configuring the GNOME Desktop Environment.

While the focus is on GNOME, short for the GNU Network Object Model Environment, other desktop environments are available for Ubuntu Linux. However, the UCP requirements specify GNOME among the major Linux desktops.

on the
job

Linux includes a number of so-called recursive acronyms, such as GNU, which stands for "GNU's not Unix." This is a jab of many Linux geeks at the standard way of doing things.

INSIDE THE EXAM

Understand Ubuntu's Technical Infrastructure (121.1)

An understanding of Ubuntu's Technical Infrastructure may not directly affect what you know about Linux or even Ubuntu's GUI tools. But the technical infrastructure provides a common language for most Ubuntu experts, helping us describe the breadth of what's available with this distribution. Furthermore, it is part of the UCP Curriculum, and therefore something you need to study for the UCP exam. In this chapter, you'll learn about every aspect of the technical infrastructure, at least as listed in the official curriculum.

A few elements listed in the UCP curriculum in this category are covered in other chapters. For example, repository-based elements such as Universe, Multiverse, and Backports are covered in Chapter 6. Installation-related terms such as standard, supported, and germinate are covered in Chapter 2 and Chapter 4.

Source Help Through Support Resources (121.2)

Ubuntu support resources are also a part of the UCP curriculum. As listed, they include community help pages, the Ubuntu Wiki, and Ubuntu's Malone bug-tracking system. These are the support resources used by experts and regular users alike to share and diagnose problems, as well as solutions.

Ubuntu Linux would not be possible without the efforts of Mark Shuttleworth or the backing of his private company, Canonical, Ltd.

This chapter focuses on Ubuntu community resources. While little of this chapter is directly related to Linux commands or graphical tools, it is still an important step in understanding *Ubuntu* Linux. And as these are topics from the UCP curriculum, they are fair game for the UCP exam.

CERTIFICATION OBJECTIVE 1.01

A History of Ubuntu Releases

Ubuntu Linux is based on the developmental packages of Debian Linux. As Debian development has proceeded, Ubuntu has taken advantage of these developments, with releases on a regular six-month cycle. While most Ubuntu support is community-based, Canonical also offers paid commercial support.

There are a number of variations on Ubuntu Linux, including variations based on desktop- and server-based packaging. New releases, of course, are available by download. To help make Ubuntu accessible in areas without high-speed connections, Ubuntu releases are also available through the ShipIt and the Freedom Toaster programs.

exam

Ⓦatch   *While subsections such as "Ubuntu Release History," "ShipIt," and "Freedom Toaster" may seem technically trivial, they do come directly from the UCP Curriculum, and are therefore fair game for UCP exam questions.*

Debian Foundation

Ubuntu Linux built its distribution on the work of the Debian Foundation. This is permissible and perhaps even encouraged as Debian Linux packages are available for all under the GNU General Public License (GPL). Furthermore, there are a number of Debian developers who are now working on Ubuntu Linux. Mark Shuttleworth, the owner of Canonical, the company behind Ubuntu Linux, has stated that "every Debian developer is also an Ubuntu developer."

Debian Linux releases are built on free software. The Debian Free Software Guidelines (DFSG) mean that Debian Linux allows free redistribution, releases all source code, allows modification and derived works, and more. For more information, see www.debian.org/social_contract.

One controversial decision by Ubuntu developers is the default installation of "non-free" drivers. As such drivers do not conform to accepted open source licenses, they are shunned by some Linux users, including a number of Debian developers. It means the standard installation of Ubuntu Linux is not completely open source. However, they do promote a Linux distribution that "just works," which, in my opinion, has greatly enhanced the popularity of Ubuntu Linux.

A second decision that has simplified Ubuntu's task is its list of supported architectures. While Debian Linux supports 11 architectures (and is working on 4 others), Ubuntu limits its releases to 2 architectures: 32-bit and 64-bit Intel/AMD systems. It's even simpler now, as Ubuntu officially supported the PowerPC architecture through Edgy Eft (6.10). Official Ubuntu Server support for Sun SPARC processors ended with the Gutsy Gibbon release. This decision limits the amount of work that has to be done in building packages—and more importantly, limits the number of platforms (and associated hardware) that have to be tested and proven for each release.

on the
ⓙob   *Ubuntu Linux continues to be ported to several other platforms, including the PowerPC, the IA-64, even the PlayStation 3. But these platforms are not supported. For a current list of available ports for various Ubuntu releases, see http://cdimage.ubuntu.com/ports/releases/.*

As Ubuntu Linux does not support as many architectures as Debian, Ubuntu also has more flexibility with its releases.

Since the primary developers do not have to build and test packages for as many architectures, the development task is much simpler.

The first Ubuntu Linux release, code-named Warty Warthog, was based on the development (unstable) branch of Debian Linux, then known as Debian Etch. Warty Warthog was released in October of 2004. Current Ubuntu Linux releases continue to incorporate Debian unstable packages during the development cycle for new releases.

Ubuntu Release History

As of this writing, Ubuntu has just completedwork on its eighth release, code-named Hardy Heron. The developers behind the Ubuntu project try to release new versions of its distribution on a six-month cycle, every April and October. The existing and known planned releases of Ubuntu Linux are as described in Table 1-1.

As shown in Table 1-1, Ubuntu Linux has been released on a regular basis. A couple of these releases have long-term support (LTS), described in the following section. Incidentally, the version number is based on the release year and month; for example, Ubuntu Gutsy Gibbon is designated as version 7.10, as it was released in the year 2007, during the *10th* month (October).

Regular releases (other than those designated as LTS) are supported for 18 months. So as this book goes to print, the releases marked with asterisks in Table 1-1 are no longer supported by Canonical.

TABLE 1-1	Code Name	Version	Comments
Ubuntu Linux Releases	*Warty Warthog	4.10	The first Ubuntu Linux release, October 2004
	*Hoary Hedgehog	5.04	Released April 2005
	*Breezy Badger	5.10	Released October 2005
	Dapper Drake	6.06	First Long Term Support release, June 2006
	*Edgy Eft	6.10	Released October 2006
	Feisty Fawn	7.04	Released April 2007
	Gutsy Gibbon	7.10	Released October 2007
	Hardy Heron	8.04	Second Long Term Support release, April 2008
	Intrepid Ibex	8.10	Planned release, October 2008

Support Levels

As suggested in Table 1-1, there are regular and LTS releases. Regular releases are supported for 18 months. LTS releases are supported for three years on the desktop, and five years on the server. Security and feature updates for packages are available via automated update systems, described in more detail in Chapter 6.

Commercial support is also available from Canonical for the noted periods. For more information, see http://www.ubuntu.com/support/paid.

Consistent Schedules

Ubuntu has committed to release a new version of its distribution every six months. It has missed this commitment only once, for the first LTS release, Dapper Drake. It has also committed to make LTS releases every two years. With the commitments made by Ubuntu, older releases have already lapsed to an unsupported status.

Ubuntu-Based Releases

By default, Ubuntu Linux includes the GNOME desktop environment. Canonical also now releases variants based on the KDE and Xfce desktop environments, known respectively as Kubuntu and Xubuntu. Gobuntu is a variant that does not include any proprietary software. Ubuntu Server Edition is its own variation. Canonical also releases variations for the educational and multimedia markets, known respectively as Edubuntu and Ubuntu Studio. ImpiLinux is a variant of Ubuntu, released by

TABLE 1-2	Linux Distributions Released by Companies Backed by Mark Shuttleworth	
Name	**Default GUI Desktop**	**Comments**
Ubuntu	GNOME	Baseline Ubuntu desktop distribution
Kubuntu	KDE	Ubuntu desktop distribution with the K Desktop Environment (KDE)
Xubuntu	Xfce	Ubuntu desktop distribution with the Xfce Desktop Environment
Gobuntu	GNOME	Limited to open source software
Ubuntu Studio	GNOME	Focused on the multimedia enthusiast
ImpiLinux	GNOME	Released by ImpiLinux, based on Ubuntu; a separate company also owned by Mark Shuttleworth

a different company, also mostly owned by Canonical founder Mark Shuttleworth. See Table 1-2 for more details on these Ubuntu-based releases.

These distributions are generally not mutually exclusive. For example, you can install the KDE desktop environment on the standard Ubuntu Linux distribution, and the GNOME desktop environment on Kubuntu Linux.

Most Ubuntu and Ubuntu-based distributions include more than just open source software. As suggested earlier, they includes "non-free" software, such as drivers for graphics cards for which reliable open source alternatives are not available. In those cases, the source code may not be released by the developers and is therefore not freely available. Often, these packages are included with Ubuntu Linux because they provide the only way for Ubuntu to work with some video cards, wireless devices, and more.

As most of Ubuntu and related variations are released under the GPL, others are free to use the source code to create their own Linux distributions. And a number of organizations have done so. At the time this chapter was drafted, there were 20 such Ubuntu-based derivatives, several of which are listed in Table 1-3. These distributions are released by companies or organizations not sponsored by Mark Shuttleworth.

Desktop and Server Releases

Ubuntu Linux is known for its performance on the desktop. To help Canonical push into the enterprise, it developed (and continues to develop) Ubuntu Server Edition with a different set of defaults optimized for the server. But as it uses the same repositories as the regular Ubuntu distributions, you can install GUI desktops on Ubuntu Server, and server services on Ubuntu desktops.

TABLE 1-3	Ubuntu Derivative	Comments
A Few Ubuntu Linux Derivatives	Fluxbuntu	Lightweight; uses Fluxbox window manager; uses only "free software."
	Freespire	Released by Linspire, formerly known as Lindows; was, until recently based on Debian Linux.
	gNewSense	Uses only free software; endorsed by the Free Software Foundation.
	Gnoppix	Live CD distribution, based on Debian Linux; similar to Knoppix, except with the GNOME desktop. The Ubuntu web site lists Gnoppix as "derived from Ubuntu."
	Guadalinex	Promoted by the Andalucia autonomous community of Spain.
	LinuxMint	Focused on a more elegant desktop environment.
	Mythbuntu	Ubuntu-based distribution that incorporates the MythTV application for digital multimedia.

The default Ubuntu Server installation does not include a GUI. It is designed for easy installation and configuration of major services. It secures all unused TCP/IP ports by default; it includes a Linux/Apache/MySQL/PHP (LAMP) installation option; it also provides thin client support based on the work of the Linux Terminal Server Project (LTSP).

Based on the freedom provided by open source licenses, Ubuntu Server includes a number of features from other Linux distributions such as the Fedora Directory Server and Novell's AppArmor.

A Focus on GNOME

The original Ubuntu Linux release included the GNOME desktop environment by default. The Ubuntu development team includes several major GNOME developers. As of this writing, the "About Ubuntu" page at www.ubuntu.com/aboutus specifies

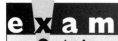

exam

🕅 a t c h   I personally prefer the KDE desktop, but use GNOME frequently. As the UCP requirements include several references to GNOME tools (and none to KDE or Xfce-based tools), you should install the GNOME desktop to help you study for the exam.

that Canonical staff include team leaders from the GNOME community. While they also now have leaders from the KDE desktop community, there is no doubt that their GUI roots are in GNOME. While derivatives such as Kubuntu and Xubuntu include other desktop environments, the focus of Ubuntu development and desktop advances is based on GNOME development.

Getting a New Release with ShipIt

ShipIt is Ubuntu's free CD distribution and shipping service, which allows anyone to request and receive physical copies of the Ubuntu Linux distribution by postal mail. As of this writing, there is no charge for the service. As these CDs are currently shipped from Europe, delivery to North America and other continents may take several weeks or more. The ShipIt option is currently available only for Ubuntu, Kubuntu, and Edubuntu variants. While Canonical does sell DVDs for a nominal fee, it also has plans to include DVDs as a ShipIt option sometime in the future.

Of course, ISO files for all Ubuntu releases are available for download. It is a practical option for anyone with a high-speed connection. ISO files can then be used by standard Linux and Microsoft Windows software to burn bootable CDs and DVDs. Some systems such as VMware can read ISO files directly as virtual CD/DVD drives.

Unfortunately, not everyone has a high-speed connection. As of this writing, nearly 50 percent of U.S. Internet users still connect from their home computers via telephone modem. High-speed connections are also less common in some of Ubuntu's target markets, such as South Africa.

on the
job

I once tried to download the CD for a different Linux distribution via telephone modem. Not only did it tie up my home telephone line; after three days, the download was corrupt and unusable.

Copying Releases with the Freedom Toaster

The Freedom Toaster was developed with backing from Mark Shuttleworth as a vending-machine-style dispenser of free digital products, including Ubuntu Linux. It's a practical alternative in areas with few high-speed connections or CD/DVD writers. As of this writing, Freedom Toasters are available only in the Republic of South Africa.

Identifying the Current Release

On any installed version of Ubuntu Linux, the easiest way to identify the current release is from the /etc/lsb-release file. It's a text file; on my Dapper Drake system, this file includes the following information:

```
DISTRIB_ID=Ubuntu
DISTRIB_RELEASE=6.06
DISTRIB_CODENAME=dapper
DISTRIB_DESCRIPTION="Ubuntu 6.06.1 LTS"
```

The same information is also available in the output to the **lsb_release -a** command.

CERTIFICATION OBJECTIVE 1.02

A Variety of Ubuntu Resources

The Ubuntu Technical Infrastructure includes a variety of resources. Financial support comes from Canonical, as the private corporate backer of the Ubuntu project. As a project that relies on decentralized input, community documentation is constantly evolving through the Ubuntu Wiki.

Launchpad is Canonical's proprietary platform for hosting open source projects, bug tracking, and more. Ubuntu software is organized in repositories. And with Ubuntu's commitment to regular releases, they have a well-defined development cycle.

Backed by Canonical

Canonical, Ltd. is a private company founded by Mark Shuttleworth to promote certain free software projects, including Ubuntu Linux. With fewer than 200 employees in about 20 countries, many of whom are dedicated to their global support functions, they rely heavily on input from the open source community, including current UCPs.

on the job

In contrast to Canonical's 200 employees, Red Hat has over 2000 employees; Microsoft has around 80,000 employees.

Shuttleworth was the founder of Thawte, which created digital certificates. As he sold it to VeriSign in 1999 for over $500 million, it's reasonable to assume that he has the financial stability to see Ubuntu through some level of growth.

The Ubuntu Wiki

With its worldwide community of developers, the Ubuntu Wiki at http://wiki.ubuntu.com is one way in which development and documentation is organized. The current version of this wiki illustrates how resources and teams are organized, lists community councils and boards, cites current Ubuntu events, and notes a list of releases.

Anyone with a Launchpad account has the permissions to edit most of the Ubuntu Wiki. Just be aware that any edits you make will be associated with your account (and perhaps IP address), so poor or malicious edits may be tracked back to you.

Launching Pads

Launchpad is a platform for developing free software. Ironically, it is also a proprietary platform; it is one of the current ways Canonical makes money. It provides services to people and companies who develop their own Linux distributions based on Ubuntu. Launchpad provides several services, as described in Table 1-4.

Any user can sign up for a Launchpad account; all that's required is a valid e-mail address. Launchpad is constantly changing. As of this writing, Launchpad has a new release every four weeks.

Free and Restricted Repositories

Ubuntu software is organized in several different repositories. Some contain only free software; others contain software that is not released under an open source license or for which source code is not available. With Ubuntu's roots in Debian Linux and

TABLE 1-4	Launchpad Components
Launchpad Component	**Comments**
Bazaar	Source code management using the Bazaar version control system; intended as an alternative to two other version control systems: CVS (Concurrent Versions System) and Subversion (SVN)
Bugs	A bug tracker, also known as Malone
Blueprints	A specifications tracker for documenting new software features
Translation	A community development tool for human language translation, also known as Rosetta
Answers	A community-developed knowledge base
Soyuz	A tracker for Linux distributions registered in Launchpad

the help of many community and third-party developers, there is a larger universe of available packages stored in other repositories.

Additional repositories are dedicated to bug fixes, security updates, and backports. For every repository where source code is available, there is a companion repository for source code packages. For more information on available Ubuntu repositories and how they are managed, see Chapter 6.

The Ubuntu Development Cycle

With Ubuntu's regular six-month release cycle, Ubuntu developers don't take a lot of breaks. Timely development depends on a certain sequence of events, some of which are outside of Ubuntu's control. Like other Linux distributions, Ubuntu depends on the work of other open source projects, such as GNOME. In fact, the Ubuntu release cycle is designed to incorporate the latest GNOME release.

Early in the first month of the release cycle, there is an "all-hands" summit, where specifications are developed. Specifications are finalized by the end of that first month, and the first experimental release is made, also known as an "Alpha" release. If you're interested in the day-by-day progress, "daily builds" are often available on downloadable ISO files.

Before I continue, I should explain the so-called "Alpha" and "Beta" releases. Alpha and Beta are terms associated with developmental software. For most software, the distribution of an Alpha release is limited to testers and developers within the company or organization. Beta releases come later and are intended for testing by advanced outside users. For Ubuntu Linux, Alpha and Beta releases are publicly available. In fact, most developmental Ubuntu Linux releases are Alpha releases; current Ubuntu Linux cycles include only one Beta release. In any case, neither Alpha nor Beta release software should be used on production computer systems.

Other major milestones include:

- Debian Import Freeze; until this milestone, new packages are frequently imported from the Debian Linux unstable (development) repository.
- Feature Freeze; at this point, developers stop introducing new features, and focus on bug fixes.
- User Interface Freeze; at this point, changes to the look, feel, and functionality of the GUI and related applications are frozen.
- Beta Freeze; after this point, package changes are further limited to minimize the risk of package dependency issues.
- Beta Release; at this point, real-world testing is encouraged.

- Documentation String Freeze; basic documentation is no longer changed after this time. Done concurrently with the Beta Freeze to allow time for translations.
- Non-Language Pack Translation Freeze; certain items especially related to GUI icons and menus must be translated and input to packages manually.
- Kernel Freeze; final date for new kernel updates.
- Release Candidate; a production quality pre-release.
- Final Release

Exceptions may be made after each freeze milestone, when the Ubuntu teams feel the exceptions are justified and do not impact the schedule. However, Ubuntu did delay their first LTS release (Dapper Drake) by a couple of months to better ensure stability of that release.

Ubuntu development work for LTS releases may vary. For example, the Hardy Heron (8.04) development cycle assumed fewer new features; most of the development work for that release was focused on creating a more stable distribution.

The Ubuntu Dialect

While Ubuntu Linux is based on Debian Linux, Ubuntu has its own dialect, with terms not normally used in any other distribution. If you're more familiar with another Linux distribution such as Red Hat or SUSE Linux, you'll need to pay attention to the different key terms and support structures.

By the time you finish this book, you'll know at least the basics of all the terms listed in the UCP Curriculum, and will understand the purpose of everything from Soyuz to the kinds of packages included in the Multiverse repository.

CERTIFICATION OBJECTIVE 1.03

Ubuntu Support and More

While paid support is available through Canonical, several community-based alternatives are also available. The Ubuntu Fridge is a news site that covers Ubuntu community events. The Malone bug-tracking system helps developers cover all issues related to individual packages. The support system available to most Ubuntu users is community-based, and goes beyond the wiki described earlier.

Ubuntu News in the Fridge

The Ubuntu Fridge provides "news, grassroots marketing, advocacy, team collaboration, and great original content." Available at http://fridge.ubuntu.com, it's essentially a community news site, detailing release announcements, conference events, hot new features, project reports, and more. As with other aspects of Ubuntu's technical infrastructure, the Fridge is listed as part of the UCP Curriculum, and therefore a basic understanding of the Fridge is fair game on the UCP exam.

Closely related to Ubuntu News from the Fridge are Ubuntu Security Notices (USN). As security issues often require updates, more information is available in Chapter 6.

Ubuntu Rosetta Translations

Rosetta is the Launchpad translations tool, available at https://launchpad.net/rosetta. It's an open source human-language translation tool. Like other machine translation tools, it can be considered a starting point in software translations; but machine translations are still far from perfect. For this reason, the Non-Language Pack Translation Freeze described earlier in this chapter provides additional time for developers to check and correct the work of Rosetta.

Bugsy Malone Bug Reports

The Ubuntu bug tracker, part of the Launchpad platform, is known as Bugsy Malone. It goes beyond standard user reports to collect information from the system with the bug. First implemented for Gutsy Gibbon (7.10), Malone includes a GUI-based tool to assist in bug reporting. More important for the administrator, and therefore also for the exam, is the command-line version of this tool, which is the ubuntu-bug script.

on the
(i)ob

When reporting a bug, use the tools available to search for existing bug reports. If you add credible new information to an existing bug report, it's more likely that Ubuntu developers will pay attention to the report and address it sooner.

Normally, the script is run against a specific package; for example, the following command files a bug against the Samba package:

```
# ubuntu-bug -p samba
```

The **ubuntu-bug** command requires the GUI and Internet access, as it next opens a browser to access Bugsy Malone via Launchpad. When the **ubuntu-bug** command is run by itself, it assumes you want to file a bug against the general distribution. If you don't have the **ubuntu-bug** command, you may need to install the apport package.

If you're using Ubuntu Linux Feisty Fawn (7.04), don't use **bug-buddy** unless you know what you're doing. In fact, if you run a command like this:

```
$ sudo bug-buddy --package=somepackagename
```

a bug report is immediately added to the GNOME bug list at http://bugzilla.gnome.org. A developer then has to take the time to evaluate the bug. Please don't file unnecessary bugs. The volunteers who have to read them don't normally have the time to waste.

However, if you're in the GNOME desktop environment through Ubuntu Edgy Eft (6.10), the **bug-buddy** command opens the Bug Buddy tool shown in Figure 1-1.

Take a look at the five different categories of bugs available; for more information, see Table 1-5.

After Edgy Eft, the process associated with the **bug-buddy** command changed. But the categories described in Table 1-5 are an excellent way to think about bugs, when you've found a new problem and feel the need or duty to report it.

FIGURE 1-1

Bug Buddy

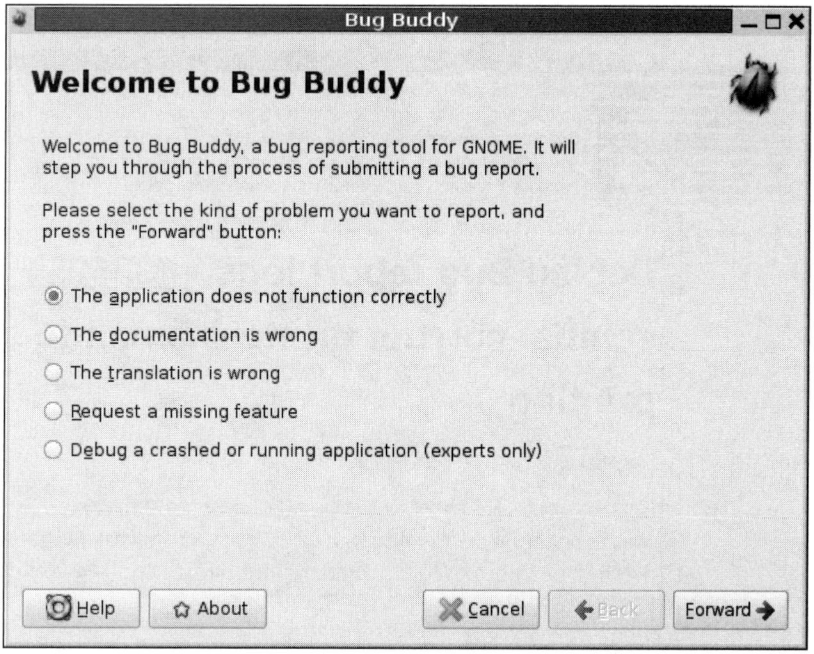

Bug Buddy

Welcome to Bug Buddy

Welcome to Bug Buddy, a bug reporting tool for GNOME. It will step you through the process of submitting a bug report.

Please select the kind of problem you want to report, and press the "Forward" button:

◉ The application does not function correctly

○ The documentation is wrong

○ The translation is wrong

○ Request a missing feature

○ Debug a crashed or running application (experts only)

⊙ Help   ☆ About   ✖ Cancel   ← Back   Forward →

TABLE 1-5 Ubuntu Bug Report Categories

Ubuntu Bug Category	Comments
The Application Does Not Function Correctly	May apply to any application
The Documentation Is Wrong	Documentation isn't always kept up to date, or may not yet exist
The Translation Is Wrong	Generally applies to non-English documentation or GUI labels
Request A Missing Feature	Practical changes have a better chance of being adapted
Debug A Crashed Or Running Application	Requires a crashed application or core dump

One useful option for finding bugs is the **reportbug-ng** command, installed from the package of the same name. When this command is run in the GUI, it opens a Reportbug NG tool as shown in Figure 1-2. I used "samba" as a search term, and found a list of current and resolved bugs, listed by severity. Note the additional information for the highlighted report.

FIGURE 1-2

Reportbug
NG Tool

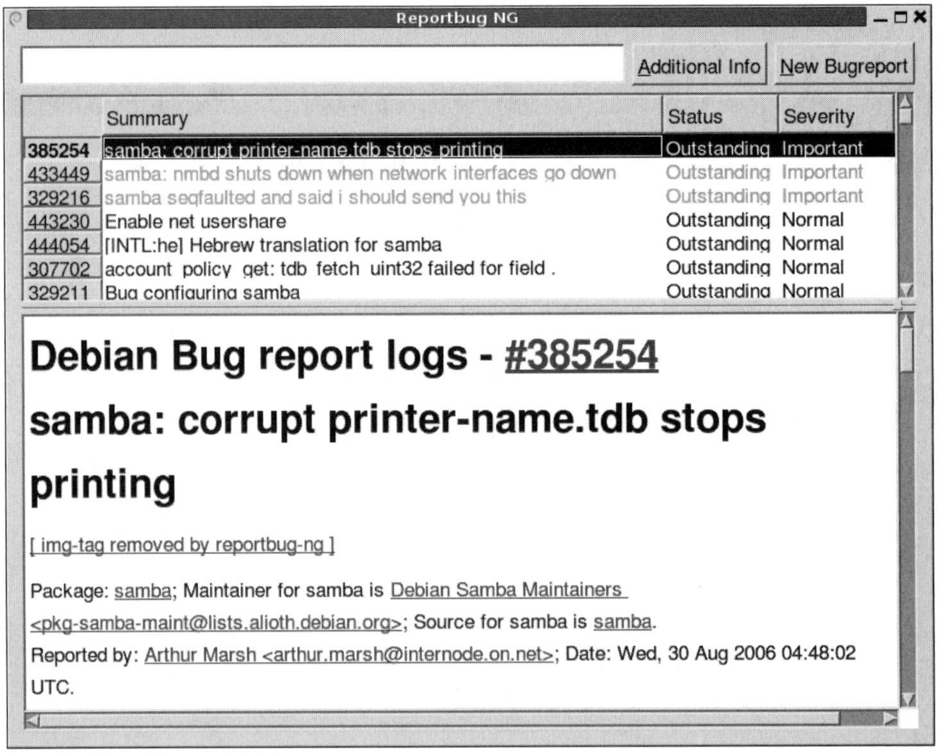

Reportbug NG

	Summary	Status	Severity
385254	samba: corrupt printer-name.tdb stops printing	Outstanding	Important
433449	samba: nmbd shuts down when network interfaces go down	Outstanding	Important
329216	samba seqfaulted and said i should send you this	Outstanding	Important
443230	Enable net usershare	Outstanding	Normal
444054	[INTL:he] Hebrew translation for samba	Outstanding	Normal
307702	account policy get: tdb fetch uint32 failed for field .	Outstanding	Normal
329211	Bug configuring samba	Outstanding	Normal

Debian Bug report logs - #385254

samba: corrupt printer-name.tdb stops printing

[img-tag removed by reportbug-ng]

Package: samba; Maintainer for samba is Debian Samba Maintainers <pkg-samba-maint@lists.alioth.debian.org>; Source for samba is samba.

Reported by: Arthur Marsh <arthur.marsh@internode.on.net>; Date: Wed, 30 Aug 2006 04:48:02 UTC.

Standard Bug Reports

Of course, it's also possible to file a bug report "the old-fashioned way." The standard bug-reporting system is available through the Launchpad at www.launchpad.net. Click on the bug icon (or navigate directly to https://bugs.launchpad.net). If you haven't logged in already, you're prompted to use your Launchpad account. Find and click the Report A Bug icon.

You're then taken to the Launchpad Bug Tracker, also known as Malone. At this point, you should be able to specify the Distribution, Package, and Project. Once appropriate information is entered, Launchpad compares your report to existing bug reports, to help you see if your problem has already been reported. Note the variety of distributions that can be reported; even Linux distributions associated with other companies, such as Fedora, SUSE, and Mandriva are also covered.

If you decide that the bug report is unique, you can then describe the problem in more detail, and specify whether you believe the problem is a security issue.

Community Help

Three categories of Ubuntu-based community help are available: mailing lists, IRC-based chat rooms, and message boards. These areas go over and above what can be found in the Ubuntu Wiki described earlier.

Mailing Lists

To subscribe to an Ubuntu mailing list, navigate to https://lists.ubuntu.com/, select a list, and sign up using your e-mail address. Some of the mailing lists may require moderator approval. As described in Table 1-6, mailing lists are available in 11 different categories.

Personally, I subscribe to several Ubuntu lists, in digest mode, which groups messages together. Otherwise, I'd be overwhelmed by the amount of traffic. I'll come back to this issue in Chapter 12, in the "Work with the Evolution E-mail Client" section.

IRC Chat Rooms

One venue that can sometimes connect users who provide real-time help is the IRC (Internet Relay Chat)-based discussion area. As the Ubuntu chat rooms are often crowded with dozens users or more, be focused and polite with your questions. If you

TABLE 1-6	Mailing List Category	Comments
	Ubuntu Announcements	Limited to distribution release announcements
Ubuntu Mailing List Categories	Announcement Lists	Forums for various Ubuntu project announcements from source code (Bazaar) to news and security announcements
	Community Support	Basic community support mailing lists, divided by derivative (Ubuntu, Kubuntu, Edubuntu, Ubuntu Studio, Xubuntu, and the Launchpad)
	Development Lists	Discussion forums for software development in a wide range of areas
	Bug Lists	Groups for bugs in different categories, including kernels, desktops, and accessibility
	Package Upload and Automatic Notification	Notification groups for changes, organized primarily by distribution release
	Loco Teams	Geographic-specific Ubuntu user groups
	Localization Lists	Groups primarily for translators
	Other Projects and Groups	Miscellaneous lists
	Bazaar-Related Lists	Discussions related to Ubuntu and related source code
	Storm	A single list associated with the Storm Object Relational Mapper (STORM)

don't get the response you need, it's quite possible that the problem is more suited to a mailing list or message-board type discussion.

If you choose to look for help via IRC, the Ubuntu IRC council has created a code of conduct, available as part of the Ubuntu Wiki at https://wiki.ubuntu.com/IrcGuidelines.

Ubuntu Message Boards

The main Ubuntu message boards are available at http://ubuntuforums.org/. They're organized into a number of categories, from "Absolute Beginner Talk" to functionally based discussions on everything from games to virtualization.

As of this writing, Launchpad accounts aren't recognized on Ubuntu message boards, so before posting, you'll have to register separately at http://ubuntuforums.org/register.php. Whether you use a message board or a mailing list is often a matter of personal taste—or where you get the best answer.

Support Subscriptions

Canonical provides commercial support for Ubuntu, as enterprises especially want access to professional support beyond what can be provided by a community. Enterprises who are converting from Microsoft Windows often want real-time paid support available. As Ubuntu Linux is also an alternative to Red Hat Enterprise Linux, enterprises who consider changing distributions want at least a similar level of subscription-based support.

While the focus is on the server, Canonical provides enterprise-level support for desktops, servers, thin clients, and more. For more information, including pricing and service level agreements, see www.canonical.com/services/support.

CERTIFICATION SUMMARY

The topics in this chapter are only loosely related to the tips and techniques associated with installing, configuring, and managing Ubuntu Linux. However, they come directly from the UCP Curriculum, specifically 121.1, "Understand Ubuntu's technical infrastructure," and 121.2, "Source help through support resources."

Ubuntu's technical infrastructure takes us from its beginnings in the Debian Linux unstable repository, through its release history, regular and LTS support levels, and regular six-month release schedules. While the UCP is explicitly focused on the GNOME desktop environment, there are variants for other desktop environments, such as Kubuntu for KDE desktop environment users. Canonical, Ubuntu's sponsor, also has different releases customized for the desktop and server. Canonical also encourages sharing through the ShipIt and Freedom Toaster programs.

A variety of support resources are available, courtesy of Mark Shuttleworth and Canonical. The Ubuntu Wiki and Help sites provide user and Ubuntu-official documentation. The Launchpad provides a platform for bug reporting, open source infrastructure projects, Ubuntu derivatives, and more. New resources are associated with key milestones in the Ubuntu development cycle.

✓

TWO-MINUTE DRILL

Here are some of the key points from the certification objectives in Chapter 1.

A History of Ubuntu Releases

❑ The first Ubuntu Linux release was based on the development repositories of the Debian Linux distribution; Ubuntu limits the number of architectures.

❑ Ubuntu Linux has already released a number of versions, from Warty Warthog through the latest LTS release, Hardy Heron.

❑ Canonical supports standard Ubuntu releases for 18 months. It supports LTS releases for three years on the desktop and five years on the server.

❑ Canonical releases Ubuntu Linux on a regular six-month cycle.

❑ Canonical has released a number of Ubuntu variants, including Kubuntu, Xubuntu, and Gobuntu; other organizations have released more variants such as ImpiLinux and Freespire.

❑ Ubuntu now has different releases customized for desktop and servers.

❑ The focus of Ubuntu is on GNOME, which is also reflected in part of the UCP Curriculum.

❑ New releases of Ubuntu are available for download; they're also available as physical CDs via Ubuntu's ShipIt program.

❑ Canonical is promoting the Freedom Toaster as a distribution system for freely available digital media such as Ubuntu Linux.

❑ The current release of an Ubuntu distribution can be identified in the /etc/lsb-release file.

A Variety of Ubuntu Resources

❑ Financial backing for Ubuntu comes from Canonical and Mark Shuttleworth.

❑ The Ubuntu Wiki provides a community documentation forum.

❑ Canonical uses the proprietary Launchpad system to promote open source infrastructure projects.

❑ Ubuntu packages are organized in free and restricted repositories such as Ubuntu main and Ubuntu restricted, Universe and Multiverse.

❑ Ubuntu has a language all of its own beyond the idiosyncrasies of Linux.

Ubuntu Support and More

❑ Ubuntu Linux includes a variety of community and commercial support resources.

❑ The latest Ubuntu news is available in "The Fridge" at http://fridge.ubuntu.com.

❑ The Rosetta component of Launchpad provides machine-based human language translation, which then must be painstakingly checked by Ubuntu and volunteer developers.

❑ Bug reports include system data courtesy of Bugsy Malone, associated with the **ubuntu-bug** command.

❑ Community help is available through a variety of mailing lists as well as http://help.ubuntu.com.

❑ For those who need it, Canonical offers paid support for Ubuntu. Canonical has targeted this support to enterprise customers.

SELF TEST

The following questions will help you measure your understanding of the material presented in this chapter. Read all the questions carefully, as there may be more than one correct answer. Some questions are "fill in the blank" and normally require an exact answer. Choose all correct answers for each question.

A History of Ubuntu Releases

1. Which of the following repositories was used to create the first Ubuntu Linux distribution?
   A. Ubuntu Main
   B. Ubuntu Multiverse
   C. Debian Stable
   D. Debian Unstable

2. Which of the following releases has Canonical committed to support for three years? (Two answers are correct.)
   A. Gutsy Gibbon
   B. Dapper Drake
   C. Hoary Hedgehog
   D. Hardy Heron

3. If you see a release version 8.10, what is the release date?
   A. August 2010
   B. October 2008
   C. August 10, 2008
   D. There's not enough information.

4. Type in the complete path to the filename that identifies the installed version of Ubuntu Linux.

   _____

5. Which of the following projects support distribution of physical copies of Kubuntu Linux around the world?
   A. Launchpad
   B. ShipIt
   C. Dapper Drake
   D. Freedom Toaster

6. What's the main difference between Xubuntu and Ubuntu Linux?

    A. Ubuntu Linux provides a default KDE desktop environment; Xubuntu provides a default Xfce desktop environment.

    B. Ubuntu Linux provides a default GNOME desktop environment; Xubuntu provides a default KDE desktop environment.

    C. Ubuntu Linux provides a default Xfce desktop environment; Xubuntu provides a default GNOME desktop environment.

    D. Ubuntu Linux provides a default GNOME desktop environment; Xubuntu provides a default Xfce desktop environment.

7. Which of the following architectures is not supported on Ubuntu Linux as of the Gutsy Gibbon release?

    A. Intel 32-bit (and clones)

    B. PowerPC

    C. SPARC

    D. AMD-64 bit (and clones)

8. Which of the following is not an Ubuntu Linux release?

    A. Warty Warthog

    B. Gnu Generation

    C. Hardy Heron

    D. Hoary Hedgehog

9. Which of the following versions of Ubuntu is not released by Canonical?

    A. Kubuntu Linux

    B. Ubuntu Studio Linux

    C. Mythbuntu Linux

    D. Gobuntu Linux

A Variety of Ubuntu Resources

10. Which of the following characterizes a Multiverse repository?

    A. Packages with all free software; source code is available in all cases; packages are supported by Canonical

    B. Packages with proprietary software; source code is available in all cases; packages are supported by Canonical

C. Packages with proprietary software; source code is not generally available; packages are not generally supported by the Linux community

D. Packages with proprietary software; source code is generally available; packages are supported by the Linux community

11. Which of the following Launchpad projects supports third-party derivatives of Ubuntu Linux?

A. Soyuz

B. Bazaar

C. Malone

D. CVS

12. Which of the following types of milestones are used through most of an Ubuntu release cycle?

A. Alpha release

B. Beta release

C. Import Freeze

D. Release candidate

13. Which of the following venues is not used by the Ubuntu community for shared support?

A. http://wiki.ubuntu.com

B. Ubuntu mailing lists

C. Launchpad

D. Canonical support service

14. Where do regular Ubuntu users share information and document tips and tricks associated with this distribution? (Two answers are correct.)

A. https://wiki.ubuntu.com

B. The Fridge

C. https://help.ubuntu.com/community

D. www.canonical.com

Ubuntu Support and More

15. Type in the command that files a report to Ubuntu's Bugsy Malone system. Feel free to type in just the command, without the full path or switches.

_____

16. Which of the following items can you find in the Ubuntu Fridge?

A. Security notices

B. Bug fixes

C. Mailing list subscriptions

D. Ubuntu news

17. Where can you find the official releases of the Ubuntu Documentation Project?

A. www.launchpad.net

B. https://help.ubuntu.com

C. https://wiki.ubuntu.com

D. www.tldp.org

18. If you want access to the latest Ubuntu announcements, which of the following venues can help? (Two answers are correct.)

A. The USN

B. The Fridge

C. Launchpad

D. Ubuntu mailing lists

LAB QUESTIONS

The first lab is fairly elementary, designed to help you learn about Ubuntu's technical infrastructure. The second lab, similarly, is designed to help you learn about Ubuntu's support resources.

Lab I

Review the UCP curriculum, listed at www.ubuntu.com/training/certificationcourses/professional/curriculum. This lab will give you the opportunity to explore Ubuntu's technical infrastructure. For this lab, you'll need an e-mail address for a Launchpad account, as well as a browser. If you've already taken any of the steps in this lab, you're already on your way towards passing the UCP exam.

1. Review the Hardy Heron release schedule at https://wiki.ubuntu.com/HardyReleaseSchedule. Note the "Debian Import Freeze" milestone. Read https://help.ubuntu.com/community/DebianImportFreeze for more information.

2. Review https://help.ubuntu.com/community/CommonQuestions for Ubuntu releases and version numbers. Note the alternative method for identifying releases, using the **lsb_release -a** command.

3. Navigate to the home pages for Kubuntu (www.kubuntu.org), Edubuntu (www.edubuntu.org), and Xubuntu (www.xubuntu.org). Look through their web sites. Note how all advertise the same latest release as Ubuntu Linux.

4. Review The Fridge (http://fridge.ubuntu.com) to see how it is like a magazine and blog for the latest news on Ubuntu.

5. Go to the Launchpad site at www.launchpad.net. If you haven't already done so, register for a Launchpad account. You'll need an e-mail address for this purpose. Look through the major options available at the Launchpad site.

6. Review the ShipIt site at https://shipit.ubuntu.com. Note how you can order Ubuntu Linux CDs with a Launchpad account. Navigate to the companion sites for Kubuntu and Edubuntu. What about Xubuntu? Can you use ShipIt for this distribution variant?

7. Read the Freedom Toaster web site at www.freedomtoaster.org. Note its intent, and the country where Freedom Toasters are located.

8. Navigate to the Canonical web site at www.canonical.org. As of this writing, Canonical's mission is on its home page. Read it.

9. Review the Ubuntu Wiki at https://wiki.ubuntu.com. As of this writing, one of the "teams" is an Engineer Certification team, which is intended as Ubuntu's equivalent to the Red Hat Certified Engineer.

10. Navigate to the download site for Ubuntu Linux at www.ubuntu.com/getubuntu/download. Review available options for the Desktop and Server edition, as well as the variety of available locations.

Lab 2

This lab will give you the opportunity to explore what the UCP curriculum really means when it says "Source help through support resources."

1. Explore the Ubuntu Team Wiki at https://wiki.ubuntu.com. If you want to contribute to the Wiki, read the link to the Ubuntu Code of Contact at www.ubuntu.com/community/conduct.

2. Pay attention to the "How To Get Help" page at https://help.ubuntu.com/community/ HowToGetHelp. Note the many community venues available for help and support.

3. Try the Ubuntu Malone bug-reporting tool. If you're using Ubuntu Linux Edgy Eft (6.10) or before, try the **bug-buddy** command in the GUI. If you're using a more recent release, try the **ubuntu-bug -p** *packagename* command.

4. Review the Ubuntu help pages at https://help.ubuntu.com. The official Ubuntu documentation is sometimes not updated when new releases are made. If you see a link to "Community Docs" or "User Documentation," try them out. See if they're more up to date.

SELF TEST ANSWERS

A History of Ubuntu Releases

1. ☑ **D.** The Debian Unstable repositories were used by the developers of Ubuntu to create their first distribution release—it's still used today early in the development process of each new release.

    ☒ As there was no Ubuntu Main or Multiverse repository before there was an Ubuntu release, answers **A** and **B** are both wrong. As Ubuntu developers did not work from the Debian stable repositories, answer **C** is also wrong.

2. ☑ **B and D.** As both Dapper Drake and Hardy Heron releases have long-term support, Ubuntu is supporting both releases for three years on the desktop—and five years on the server.

    ☒ As other releases are supported for 18 months on the desktop and server, answers **A** and **C** are both wrong.

3. ☑ **B.** Per Ubuntu conventions, Ubuntu Linux 8.10 is associated with a release in October 2008.

    ☒ As the other answers don't correspond to Ubuntu release-numbering conventions, answers **A**, **C**, and **D** are all incorrect.

4. ☑ **/etc/lsb-release.** The standard file that contains the Linux distribution version name and number is /etc/lsb-release.

    ☒ Don't confuse the /etc/lsb-release file with the alternatives associated with other Linux distributions such as /etc/redhat-release on Red Hat–based systems.

5. ☑ **B.** The ShipIt project supports the distribution of physical CDs of Kubuntu, Ubuntu, and Edubuntu Linux around the world.

    ☒ While Launchpad does a lot for Ubuntu Linux and derivatives, it does not enable the distribution of physical installation CDs, so answer **A** is wrong. As Dapper Drake is the code name for a specific Ubuntu distribution and is not directly related to CD sharing, answer **C** is also wrong. While the Freedom Toaster is intended to help distribution of Ubuntu Linux and variants, it is currently limited to South Africa, so answer **D** is also wrong.

6. ☑ **D.** The default Ubuntu Linux GUI desktop environment is GNOME; the default Xubuntu desktop environment is Xfce.

    ☒ While it's possible to install any of the supported desktops on Ubuntu, Kubuntu, and Xubuntu, there is only one default GUI desktop for each of these variants; therefore answers **A**, **B**, and **C** are all incorrect.

7. ☑ **B.** While the PowerPC architecture was formerly supported by Ubuntu, formal support on new releases ended with the Feisty Fawn 7.04 release.
   ☒ While it's true that Ubuntu architecture support is limited, the limits do include standard 32-bit and 64-bit CPUs on the desktop and SPARC CPUs for the server. Therefore answers **A**, **C**, and **D** are all incorrect. Incidentally, Gutsy Gibbon was the last release with support for SPARC CPUs.

8. ☑ **B.** The Gnu Generation is not an Ubuntu Linux release.
   ☒ As Warty Warthog, Hardy Heron, and Hoary Hedgehog are official Ubuntu Linux releases, answers **A**, **C**, and **D** are all incorrect.

9. ☑ **C.** While the Mythbuntu Linux distribution is clearly based on Ubuntu, it is not released by Canonical.
   ☒ As Kubuntu Linux, Ubuntu Studio Linux, and Gobuntu Linux are all now standard Ubuntu releases, they are all released by Canonical, Ltd. Therefore answers **A**, **B**, and **D** are all incorrect.

A Variety of Ubuntu Resources

10. ☑ **C.** The Multiverse repository is dedicated to software not released by nor supported by Ubuntu that also does not conform to open source licensing. Such packages rarely include public releases of the source code.
    ☒ As Multiverse packages do not generally include "free software," answer **A** is wrong. As the Multiverse repositories do not include support by Canonical, answer **B** is also wrong. As the source code for Multiverse repository packages is rarely made available, answer **D** is also incorrect.

11. ☑ **A.** The Soyuz component of the Launchpad allows third-parties to use the Launchpad platform to help develop derivatives of Ubuntu Linux.
    ☒ As the Bazaar is Ubuntu's Revision Control System and CVS stands for the similar Concurrent Versions System, answers **B** and **D** are both wrong. As Malone is Ubuntu's bug-tracking system, answer **C** is also incorrect.

12. ☑ **A.** The most common milestone in an Ubuntu development schedule is the Alpha release. Just be aware that Alpha releases are not stable enough for testing by anyone but developers.
    ☒ There is typically only one Beta release during the Ubuntu development cycle, therefore, answer **B** is incorrect. The "Import Freeze" could apply to Debian packages, GNOME packages, or packages from other outside sources. As that is not well defined and outside of Ubuntu's control, answer **C** is also wrong (but not by much). As there is only one release candidate, typically about a week before the final release, answer **D** is also wrong.

13. ☑ **D.** The Canonical support service is a paid service.

☒ The Ubuntu Wiki, mailing lists, and Launchpad are all used by the community for shared support; therefore, answers **A**, **B**, and **C** are all incorrect.

14. ☑ **A and C.** The wiki and community help sites are two locations where users share information and document tips and tricks.

☒ The Fridge is an Ubuntu news site. The Canonical web site is a corporate web site; therefore, answers **B** and **D** are both incorrect.

Ubuntu Support and More

15. ☑ **ubuntu-bug** Be aware that the **reportbug-ng** tool is just a search tool. While there is a focus on the GNOME desktop environment, the focus for UCP-quality administrators is on command-line tools.

16. ☑ **D.** The Ubuntu Fridge is primarily an Ubuntu news site.

☒ While it's possible that the Ubuntu Fridge includes references to security notices and bug fixes, there are other tools, namely USN and Bugsy Malone, which are dedicated to this purpose. Therefore, answers **A** and **B** are wrong. As individual mailing list subscriptions are unrelated to Ubuntu news, answer **C** is also wrong.

17. ☑ **B.** The Ubuntu Documentation Project publishes their work at http://help.ubuntu.com.

☒ While the Launchpad (www.launchpad.net) and the Ubuntu Wiki do contain user-created documentation, that is not an official release of the Ubuntu Documentation Project; therefore, answers **A** and **C** are both incorrect. While www.tldp.org is the web site of the Linux Documentation Project, that's a separate group from Ubuntu, and therefore answer **D** is also wrong.

18. ☑ **B and D.** The Fridge and the appropriate announcements mailing list are the best places to look for the latest Ubuntu announcements.

☒ While the USN lists (remember, USN stands for Ubuntu Security Notices) do contain some announcements, they're mostly limited to security issues, therefore answer **A** is not quite correct. Launchpad is generally not used as an announcements platform; therefore answer **C** is also wrong.

LAB ANSWERS

Lab 1

The intent of Lab 1 is to familiarize you with the items associated with the UCP Curriculum Item 121.1, "Understand Ubuntu's Technical Infrastructure." A few of the items listed in the UCP curriculum are covered in other chapters. For example, detailed information on repositories such as Universe and Multiverse are covered in Chapter 6. Some installation-related items such as "minimal" and "boot" are covered in Chapter 2.

As up-to-date information may vary, there is no "right" answer in this lab. But you do need to be familiar with the terms and associated web sites to cover these exam topics.

Lab 2

The intent of Lab 2 is to familiarize you with the items associated with the UCP Curriculum Item 121.2, "Source help through support resources." As up-to-date information may vary, there is no "right" answer in this lab. But you do need to be familiar with the terms and associated web sites to cover these exam topics.

2

Installing Ubuntu

This chapter is focused on the local Ubuntu installation process. There are a number of ways to install Ubuntu: from within the workstation loaded from the Live CD, directly from the alternate CD, or even from within Microsoft Windows. While the steps are similar for the Ubuntu Server, the default server installation doesn't even include a GUI.

The Ubuntu test drive takes advantage of its Live CD capabilities. As such, you can boot a complete Ubuntu Linux operating system from the CD without affecting anything on the local hard drive. It can help you determine whether Ubuntu Linux detects your hardware, at least in the default configuration. Once satisfied, you can start the Ubuntu installation process directly from the workstation as loaded from the Live CD.

Perhaps the key part of the installation process relates to decisions on hard drive configuration. The variety of filesystem formats, as well as choices associated with Redundant Array of Independent Disks (RAID) and logical volume management (LVM), may be bewildering to those not yet initiated. These options are not available as of this writing through the Live CD.

If you want to follow along in this chapter, you'll need to download a Live CD, an Alternate CD, and an Ubuntu Server installation CD. You may also choose to download the Ubuntu Linux DVD. The Live DVD has the functionality of the three Ubuntu Linux CDs (Live, Alternate, and Server), and can be used as a substitute for any of these options throughout the chapter.

As Ubuntu releases change, the installation steps may vary. For the purpose of this chapter, I use Ubuntu Gutsy Gibbon (7.10). If you install Linux from a different Ubuntu Linux release, there may be significant differences in what you see when compared to this chapter. As the UCP exam is not version-specific, use the latest available version of Ubuntu Linux. If you're studying with more than one version, study the common elements.

There are a number of step-by-step instructions listed in this chapter. The actual steps vary by Ubuntu Linux release, whether you're installing from the Live, Alternate, or Server CD, and even if you're installing in normal or expert mode. Related questions, especially those associated with network installations, are covered in Chapter 4.

INSIDE THE EXAM

Perform an Installation (122.1)

As suggested in the UCP curriculum, "candidates should have a thorough understanding of the installation process on i386 architecture." To provide that understanding, you'll explore all types of local installations in this chapter. Once you've analyzed this chapter, you'll also "be able to differentiate between server and desktop installation types" in some detail.

While the Ubuntu text-based installer shares the same structure as the Debian Linux installer, the UCP exam is an *Ubuntu* Linux exam. Once you learn how to install from the Alternate and Server CDs, you'll have a good idea of how to install Ubuntu Linux.

The automated "preseed" system and network-related installation issues in this part of the curriculum are covered in Chapter 4. But first, for those of you less experienced with large downloads, I present a primer to downloading Ubuntu Linux CDs.

CERTIFICATION OBJECTIVE 2.01

Download the Ubuntu Linux Installation CDs

First, this section is not directly related to the UCP exam. There is no evidence from the UCP curriculum or outlines that you need to know how to download and write the Ubuntu Linux CDs during the exam.

Nevertheless, you need the Ubuntu Linux distribution to prepare for the UCP exam, and this section focuses on steps you need to take to download and use the relevant media. Yes, such CDs are available using the ShipIt program described in Chapter 1, but the mailing time can take weeks.

An Overview of the Download Process

Whether you download the Live CD, the Alternate CD, the Ubuntu Server CD, or the DVD, the basic download process is the same and follows these basic steps:

1. Select a variant to download.
2. Find the download server with ISO files.
3. Proceed with the download, using a high-speed connection.

An ISO file is the Linux standard format for downloads customized for burning onto CD/DVD media. It's recognized by standard CD/DVD-writing applications on both Linux and Microsoft Windows. While the acronym is not important, ISO files do have .iso extensions.

Downloads of CD- and especially DVD-length ISO files are not practical without a high-speed connection. (I once tried downloading a Red Hat installation CD over a telephone modem. After three days, the download file was corrupt and unusable.) If you don't have a high-speed connection, a couple of options are described in Chapter 1. The ShipIt program at https://shipit.ubuntu.com supports requests for a small number of copies of the Ubuntu Linux desktop installation CD. As of this writing, that web page also includes links to online retailers where CDs and DVDs can be purchased.

The Download Process

The download process for Ubuntu Linux is straightforward. As of this writing, the starting point is www.ubuntu.com/getubuntu/download. Generally, it provides a choice—the latest release and the latest available long-term support (LTS) version. Just remember, as with all web site options, change happens frequently, so use these steps as a guide, not as gospel. The choices are in five categories:

1. Select either an Ubuntu Desktop or Server edition.

2. Choose an appropriate release. The LTS version is often more appropriate for production systems.

3. Make sure to select an appropriate architecture. Default Ubuntu Linux installations are available for standard 32-bit and 64-bit systems. Ubuntu Server installations are also available for the Sun SPARC architecture through the Gutsy Gibbon release. If you have another architecture, it's not supported by Ubuntu, but a port may be available in a subdirectory of http://cdimage.ubuntu.com/ports/releases/.

4. You also have to choose between the Live and Alternate CD. The Alternate CD is available from the noted web site by using the check box labeled "Check here if you need the alternate desktop CD."

5. Choose a download location. Generally, it's best (and fastest) to download from a mirror site geographically closer to you. Try the link associated with the "complete list of download locations"; it may help find mirrors for alternate downloads such as DVDs and BitTorrent peer-to-peer downloads.

e x a m

Of course, you can choose to download and install one of the variants of Ubuntu Linux, such as Kubuntu Linux or Xubuntu Linux. But remember the UCP Curriculum specifies only GNOME-based issues among available GUI tools.

Burning from the ISO File

Once the download is complete, you can then use a Linux command such as **cdrecord**, a GUI tool such as GnomeBaker, K3b, or even many Microsoft Windows–based tools to write the ISO file to appropriate blank CDs or DVDs. The use of GUI tools to write ISO files to CDs (or even DVDs) is fairly trivial, so I do not cover the details in this book. Of course, it requires hardware that can write to said media. Just look for the menu command that writes the ISO file directly to the CD or DVD.

An Alternative to Burning

If you have a virtual machine system such as VMware, Xen, or KVM (Kernel Virtual Machine), it may not even be necessary to write the ISO file to a CD/DVD drive. This is a handy option for developers. Sometimes I download and test the "Daily Build" of the latest version of Ubuntu Linux—and as that changes on a daily basis, I don't want to have to write this data to a CD/DVD every time. The Daily Build is available from http://cdimage.ubuntu.com/daily/current/.

CERTIFICATION OBJECTIVE 2.02

Take the Ubuntu Test Drive

One of the appealing elements about Ubuntu Linux is that it allows you to test the operating system without installing anything on a computer hard drive. All that's needed is a system that will boot from a local CD/DVD. We'll describe the boot process, the look and feel of Ubuntu Linux as it's booted from the Live CD, and the installation process available from the Live CD screen.

While it's certainly possible to configure or even boot Ubuntu Linux from other media such as a USB device or external drive, that requires a BIOS that can detect such media.

The Live CD

To make full use of a Live CD, you need a system that can boot from this media. On most PCs, it's possible to configure the BIOS (Basic Input/Output System) menu to boot from the CD/DVD drive. On many PCs, it's possible to boot directly from the CD/DVD drive without changing the BIOS menu; just press a key such as F12 or ESC during or just after the PC's power-on self-test (just after the PC is powered on) for a menu of boot options. Due to the wide variety of available BIOS menus and boot menus, it's not practical to explain how this works in greater detail.

If the PC successfully boots from a Live CD or DVD, it'll display the screen shown in Figure 2-1. If you don't take any action within 30 seconds, it'll automatically start the first option: "Start Or Install Ubuntu." If you're using the Live CD, it'll boot a complete and functional version of Ubuntu Linux. Because this is being done from the CD/DVD drive, it will be slower than a standard operating system boot from a hard drive.

FIGURE 2-1

Live CD boot
screen

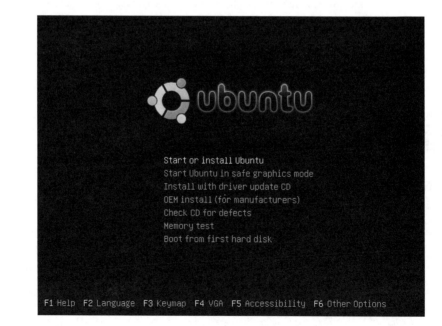

on the **!** job

Starting with the Hardy Heron (8.04) release, the default boot option from the Live CD/DVD is "Try Ubuntu Without Any Change To Your Computer."

For more information on other options available from the Live CD boot screen, see the next section. Obviously, booting a complete operating system from a CD/DVD drive takes more time than a boot from a hard drive. In many cases, the system may appear to "lock" for a few minutes. In one case, it took about 10 minutes to boot the Live CD—even though it was direct from an ISO file. So be patient, unless you see messages that clearly indicate a problem.

Once the boot process is complete, the Ubuntu Linux Live CD displays a fully functional GNOME desktop environment, with 1680 × 1050 resolution. I've changed it to 800 × 600 resolution for Figure 2-2.

Naturally, the default Live CD desktop is simple; the two icons are almost self-explanatory. The Examples icon opens the Nautilus file manager with a group of examples. The Install icon starts the installation process from the Live CD, which will be described in more detail later in this chapter in the section "Install Direct from the CD/DVD, Step by Step."

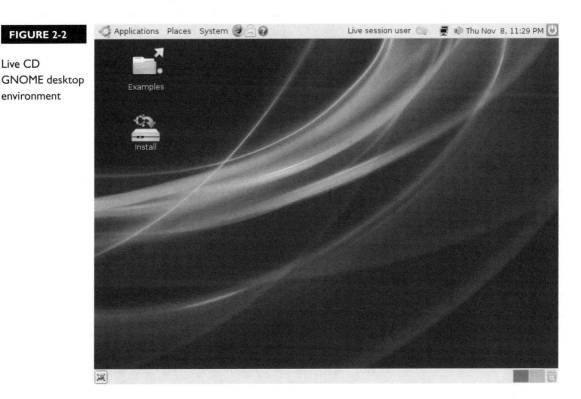

FIGURE 2-2

Live CD GNOME desktop environment

The menus are also fully functional; available software is fairly complete. Even the OpenOffice.org suite is available when you click Applications | Office. The GUI-based administration tools are available from the System | Administration submenu. If the installation process properly detects your hardware, you may be able to connect to the Internet, even through a wireless connection.

Basic text consoles are also available; for access, press CTRL-ALT-FX where X is between 1 and 6. The default user name is *ubuntu*; it is not password protected in the Live CD. Administrative commands can be run by prefacing them with the **sudo** command; passwords are not required for administrative access in the Live CD either.

Options Within the Installation CD

When you boot the Live CD (or any other Ubuntu installation CD/DVD), press a key (other than a function key or ENTER) within 30 seconds. Then you can follow along with the discussion in this section. Most of the options discussed here also apply to the first screen shown when booting from other Ubuntu CDs.

As shown earlier in Figure 2-1, there are two sets of options available from the menu, which boots from the Live CD. There are the direct options available in the middle of the screen, starting with Start Or Install Ubuntu. And then there are the function keys, briefly labeled at the bottom of the screen.

These options may appear only when booting from one or more of the CDs or the DVD; the operation of each function key varies slightly by media. The options for releases other than Gutsy Gibbon may vary.

Installation CD Boot Options

There are several options available in the middle of the installation CD boot screen. The options vary depending on whether you're booting from the Ubuntu Live CD, the Ubuntu Live DVD, the Alternate CD, or the Server CD. If you're using a Live CD or DVD, the first option boots into the Ubuntu Live CD desktop. The first option, with a different name, boots into the standard text installation program from other Ubuntu Linux installation CDs. For a summary of each option, see the following descriptions.

Start or Install Ubuntu   Available only from the Live CD/DVD, this option boots the preconfigured Ubuntu Linux operating system directly from the CD/DVD media. Once the preconfigured GUI Ubuntu Linux desktop loads onto the system, you can then start the installation process directly from the graphical desktop screen, as described earlier in the "Take the Ubuntu Test Drive" section.

Start Ubuntu in Safe Graphics Mode   Similar to the Start or Install Ubuntu option, except it forces booting of the preconfigured Ubuntu Linux desktop with the generic standard of the Video Electronics Standards Association, more commonly known by its acronym, VESA. Some users may recognize VESA as another name for Super VGA (Video Graphics Array) mode, and it is associated with the **xforcevesa** option.

Install in Text Mode   This option is the default with the Alternate CD; it starts the text-mode installation process, which will be described later in the section "Install Direct from the CD/DVD, Step by Step." This option is also available when booting from the Live DVD.

Install to Hard Disk   The Install to Hard Disk option is listed only when booting from the Ubuntu Server CD. In fact, it's the only installation option available when booting from that CD. It's equivalent to the Install in Text Mode option, and is detailed later in this chapter in the "Install Direct from the CD/DVD, Step by Step" section. But as you'll see, it supports additional server-specific configuration options.

If you're booting from the Ubuntu DVD, this option is equivalent to the "Install a Server" option.

Install with Driver Update CD   Neither Linux or Microsoft Windows supports all current computer hardware. If there's a hardware problem during the installation process, and there's a Linux-capable driver available on a separate CD, this option can help. It starts the text-mode installation process, prompting for a Driver CD at the appropriate time.

OEM Install (For Manufacturers)   This option installs Ubuntu with the oem-config-prepare package, which supports a customized installation suitable for computers (such as some Dell systems) on which Ubuntu Linux is preinstalled. OEM stands for Original Equipment Manufacturer, and is associated with the companies that build and sell PCs, for consumers as well as businesses.

Install a Command-Line System   The Command-Line System option does not include any packages associated with configuring a local GUI or graphical desktop environment. All a server needs is a command-line interface. It's best to configure such from the Server CD, as an installation from the Alternate Installation CD does not provide access to preconfigured groups of server packages.

Check CD for Defects The Check CD for Defects option does not install anything on your system; it loads a minimal amount of software required to check the integrity of the CD or DVD. It does take a few minutes; if successful, it'll display the following message:

```
Check finished: no errors found
```

Rescue a Broken System Most administrators don't use the Rescue a Broken System option, as booting the Live CD starts a fully functional copy of Ubuntu Linux, without mounting any partitions on local hard drives. But if necessary, rescue mode is available from the Alternate and Server CDs.

From the DVD, rescue mode is available from the **boot:** prompt, accessible by pressing the ESC key. Just type **rescue** at the prompt and press ENTER.

Memory Test The Memory Test option runs a local memtest86 program to check the status of current RAM. This program can take an hour or more to complete. Some version of this program is also available from many modern BIOS menus.

From the DVD, this option is available from the **boot:** prompt, accessible by pressing the ESC key. Just type **memtest** at the prompt and press ENTER.

Boot from First Hard Disk If you already have an operating system installed on the first local hard disk, this option bypasses any Ubuntu Live CD or installation program functionality, and looks for whatever program currently resides in that hard disk's master boot record (MBR). This option is currently not available from the Ubuntu Live DVD.

Installation CD Function Keys

There are also several function keys listed at the bottom of the Ubuntu Linux boot screen, which I describe in Table 2-1. Here's a hint for you—to review the command options associated with the menu choices just described, press the F6 key, *once*. Command-line boot options appear (and the F6 option disappears).

As described in Table 2-1, the F1 key opens a submenu of help screens, also accessible via Function key, as shown in Figure 2-3. Don't confuse these function key *help* options in Table 2-2 with the function key options described in Table 2-1.

TABLE 2-1	Function Key	Description
Ubuntu Boot CD Function Key Options	F1	Opens a menu of help screens, with options associated with F1 through F10, described in Table 2-2.
	F2	Accesses available installation languages; installation proceeds with that language by default. Nearly 60 human languages are available for Ubuntu Linux.
	F3	Allows selection of a keyboard keymap, mostly associated with country-specific keyboards.
	F4	Supports installation in different modes; the options vary with installation media.
	F5	Provides accessibility options for specialized situations such as Braille terminals and onscreen keyboards.
	ESC	An undocumented option that accesses the **boot:** prompt. See the installation options described in Table 2-2 for available options.

FIGURE 2-3

Ubuntu Installation boot screen Help menu

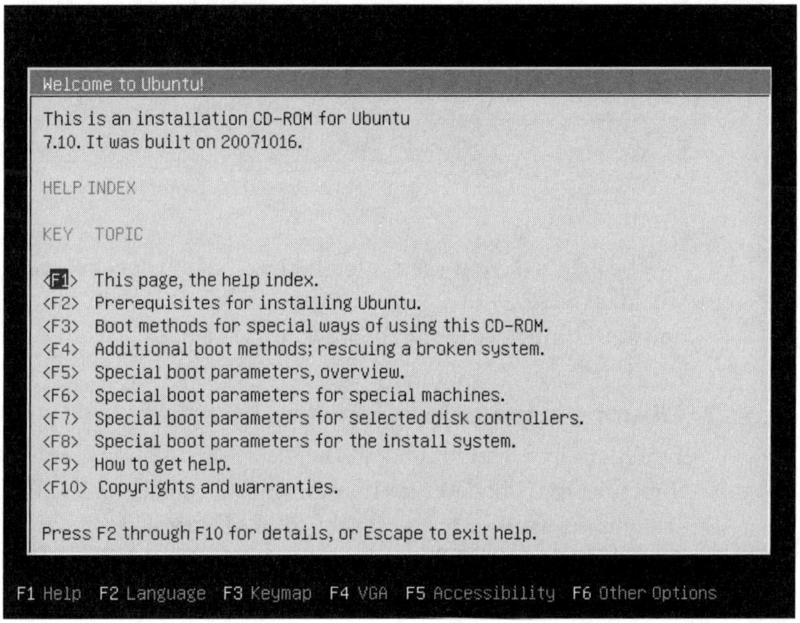

```
Welcome to Ubuntu!

This is an installation CD-ROM for Ubuntu
7.10. It was built on 20071016.

HELP INDEX

KEY  TOPIC

<F1>  This page, the help index.
<F2>  Prerequisites for installing Ubuntu.
<F3>  Boot methods for special ways of using this CD-ROM.
<F4>  Additional boot methods; rescuing a broken system.
<F5>  Special boot parameters, overview.
<F6>  Special boot parameters for special machines.
<F7>  Special boot parameters for selected disk controllers.
<F8>  Special boot parameters for the install system.
<F9>  How to get help.
<F10> Copyrights and warranties.

Press F2 through F10 for details, or Escape to exit help.

F1 Help  F2 Language  F3 Keymap  F4 VGA  F5 Accessibility  F6 Other Options
```

TABLE 2-2	Function Key	Description
Ubuntu Boot CD Help Options	F1	Returns to the help index.
	F2	Lists basic prerequisites; 32MB of RAM is required to use the installer. More is necessary for Ubuntu Linux even in most text-mode installations, but those are requirements beyond that of the installer. It also lists a requirement for at least 2GB for a desktop or 400MB for a server installation.
	F3	Describes different boot methods, associated with the **boot:** prompt accessible by pressing the ESC key, as described earlier. Not all options are available from all Ubuntu CD or DVD boot media. The default is with the **install** command. If you type in **expert**, that starts the installation in expert mode. There are also two text-mode installations available; **cli** and **cli-expert**. The **rescue** option starts rescue mode.
	F4	Notes the rescue mode, available by typing in **rescue** at the **boot:** prompt.
	F5	Provides an overview of other boot parameters that you might include in the installation process.
	F6	Suggests basic hardware boot parameters.
	F7	Suggests boot parameters associated with SCSI drives.
	F8	Includes more suggested hardware-related boot parameters.
	F9	Lists generic help suggestions available at www.ubuntu.com.
	F10	Notes the basic Ubuntu copyrights and warranties.

The help screens suggest other boot command options, such as **acpi=off**, which would boot using the previous command such as **install**, with Advanced Configuration and Power Interface (ACPI) hardware disabled.

Ubuntu Installation from the Live CD

By definition, Ubuntu Linux installation from the Live CD is a GUI-based installation from the GNOME desktop environment. It assumes a valid Internet connection and IP addresses assigned from a local DHCP (Dynamic Host Configuration Protocol) server. The Live CD GUI screen associated with the Gutsy Gibbon release is shown

The Ubuntu GUI
installation starts

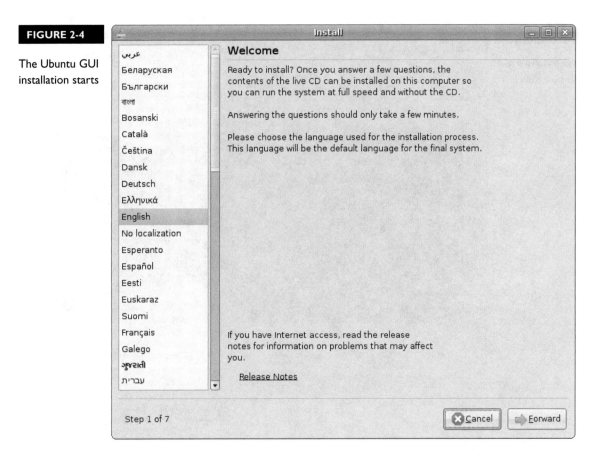

earlier in Figure 2-2. Now click the Install icon to start the installation process as
shown in Figure 2-4.

Select a language; it'll continue to be used through the installation and become
the default for the GUI and command line after installation is complete.

Now click Forward to open the Where Are You window (see Figure 2-5). In this
window, select the time zone where the system is located, and select Forward to
continue.

The Where Are
You window

In the Keyboard Layout screen that follows in Figure 2-6, select the nationality and style associated with your keyboard; I have a standard U.S. English keyboard. If uncertain, test your keyboard in the text box. When satisfied, click Forward to continue.

Next, you can prepare disk space. For the purpose of this section, use the Guided option, which automates the partitioning process, and click Forward to continue. For more information on the manual option, including how you can configure different partitions, read the Configuring Drives section later in this chapter.

FIGURE 2-6

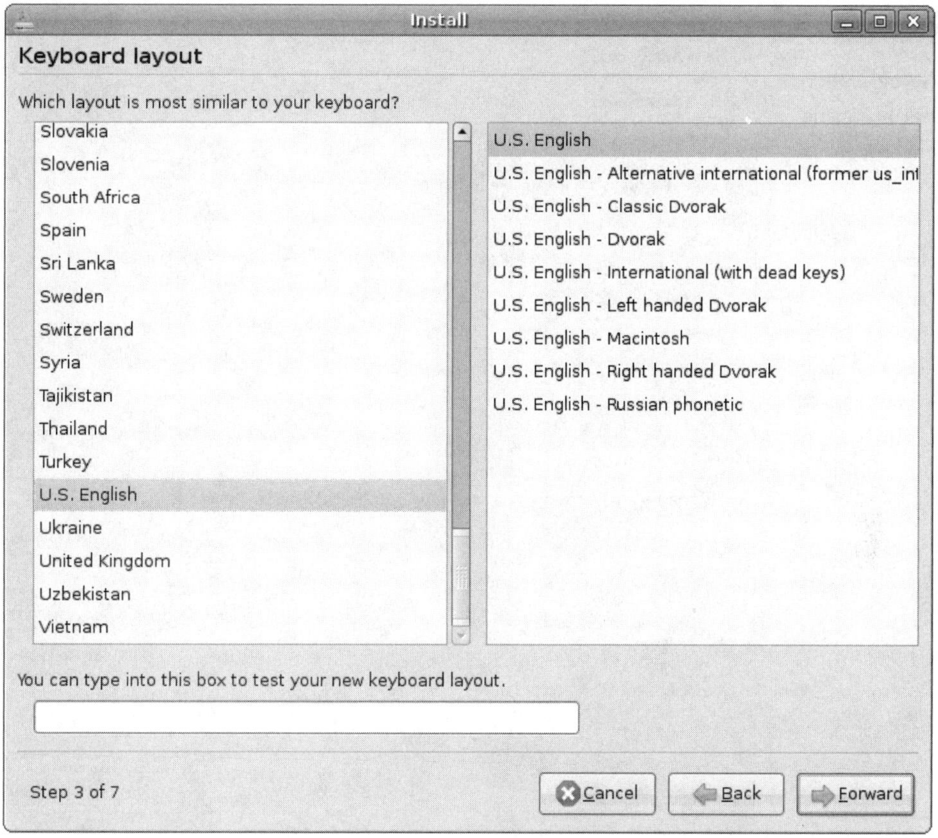

The Keyboard
Layout window

FIGURE 2-6

The Keyboard
Layout window

Now in the Who Are You screen shown in Figure 2-7, select a name for the default user account and computer hostname. If you're not familiar with Ubuntu Linux, the installation program doesn't manage the root user password. Ubuntu Linux administration is done with the **sudo** command, where the first account has **sudo** privileges, as discussed in Chapter 8.

Finally, there's the Ready to Install screen shown in Figure 2-8, which summarizes the choices you've made, as well as the default partitions. Even though the partitions are listed as SCSI devices, they're actually on a SATA hard drive. In Linux, SCSI

FIGURE 2-7

The Who Are You
user/hostname
window

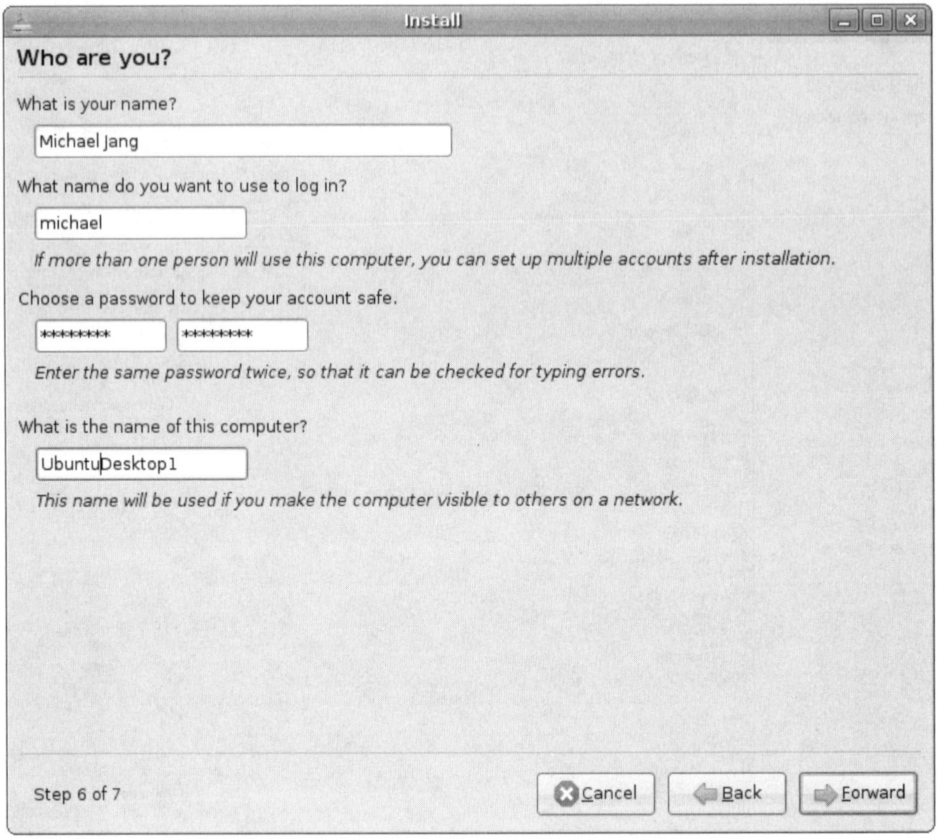

and SATA hard drive device names follow the same format; for example, the first partition on the first SATA or SCSI hard drive is /dev/sda1.

Figure 2-8 also shows the Advanced Options window, which opened when I clicked the Advanced button in the Ready to Install screen. It suggests that the boot loader is installed by default on the first available hard drive (hd0). I select OK to exit the Advanced Options window, and click Install to start the actual installation process.

You'll see messages that display the progress of the installation. In most cases, you won't have to do anything. Installation proceeds based on packages available from the

FIGURE 2-8

The Ready to
Install window

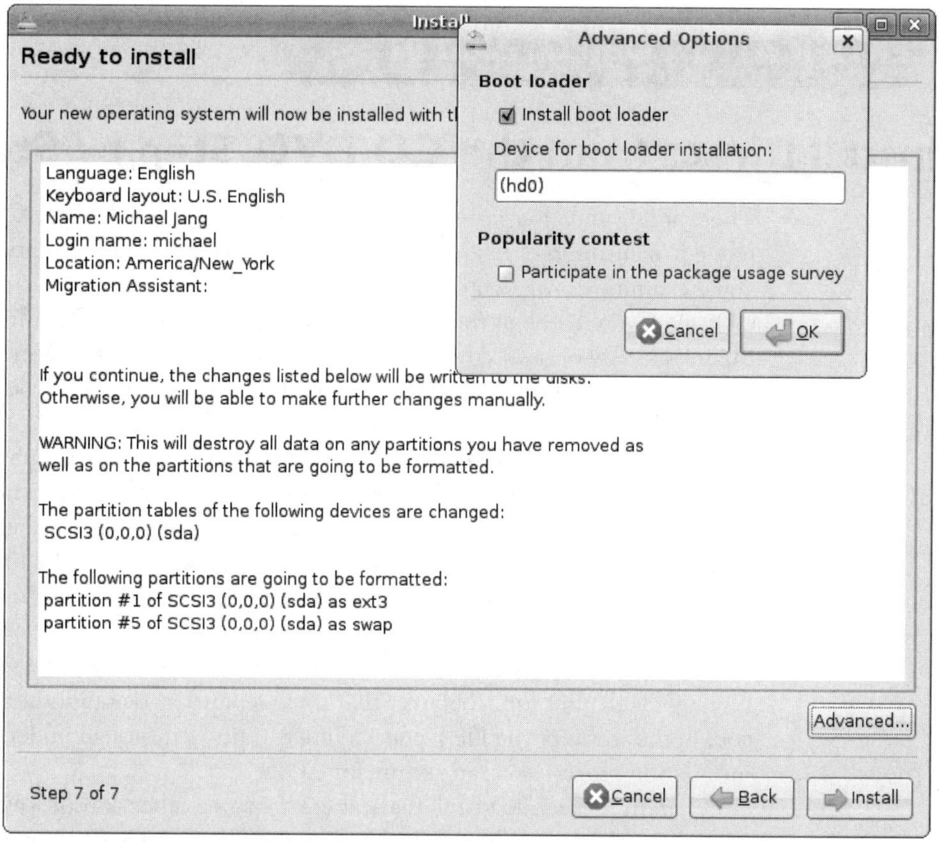

Live CD/DVD and possibly packages in default repositories, discussed in Chapter 6. The installation depends on the speed of the Internet connection and related hardware issues.

Once installation is complete, you're given a choice on whether to continue running the Live CD/DVD or immediately proceed to reboot the system. Naturally, if you've set the BIOS menu to boot first from the CD, you'll have to either change the BIOS menu again or remove the CD/DVD when rebooting.

CERTIFICATION OBJECTIVE 2.03

Install Direct from the CD/DVD, Step by Step

There are several alternatives available to installing from the Live CD. All but one relate to some form of text or low-resolution console-based installation. In order, you'll examine how to start the text-mode installation process from the Alternate CD. Then you'll look at the differences when you select the OEM Install (For Manufacturers) option. Afterwards, you'll examine a Microsoft Windows XP system, where you can install Ubuntu Linux directly from there. Finally, you'll see how to install Ubuntu Server.

I'll describe a standard **text** installation from the Alternate CD, as well as an **expert** installation from the Server CD. Of course, you can also **install** using the defaults associated with that CD. These options are in bold, as you can put any of them into effect from some of the Ubuntu Linux boot media. The first three steps in the next section show how you can access the boot: prompt and choose one of these options.

There are many similarities between each of these installations; some repetition is unavoidable. But I'm a believer that some repetition is appropriate, as it can help you, in the words of the UCP curriculum, to gain "a thorough understanding of the installation process on i386 architecture."

When in text-mode installation, there are three other consoles available. The second and third consoles, accessible with the ALT-F2 and ALT-F3 key combinations, are available for text console commands. The fourth console, available with the ALT-F4 key combination, lists messages associated with the installation process and can sometimes help you diagnose a problematic installation without having to restart the installation from scratch. You can then return to the text-mode installation screen with the ALT-F1 key combination.

on the job *The following sections do not describe exact steps, and may vary depending on hardware and selected options. In fact, if you click Go Back at certain points, you'll see different steps when compared to what's described in this chapter. If in doubt, the default option is most likely acceptable; but proceed at your own risk.*

Text-Mode Installation from the Alternate CD

The Live CD doesn't include a text-mode installation option, unlike the Alternate CD or the Ubuntu Server CD. Depending on whether you've installed Ubuntu Linux or some other distribution on this system, the steps may vary slightly. I describe steps I've found that work on both the Alternate CD and Live DVD for the Gutsy Gibbon release. As they say, your mileage may vary (YMMV)—in other words, the steps you take may vary with different releases. As suggested earlier, I can't cover every scenario. Now to proceed with installation, take the following steps:

1. To access text-mode installation, boot from the CD. When you see the screen shown in Figure 2-1, press ESC.

2. The Ubuntu installer should present a message: "You are leaving the graphical boot menu and starting the text-mode interface. Click OK to continue."

   At this point, the following prompt should appear in a single line atop a black screen:

   ```
   boot:
   ```

3. This is the "boot prompt," where you can enter some of the options described earlier in this chapter. In this case, to start the installation process directly, type **install** and press ENTER.

   This starts the text-mode installation process shown in Figure 2-9, where you can select the language used during the installation process. There are no buttons to click. Just press the appropriate arrow, PAGEUP, PAGEDOWN, and TAB keys.

exam

Ⓦatch   **The Ubuntu Linux Installer, in text-mode installations, borrows heavily from the Debian Linux installer.**

4. Select the desired language and press ENTER to continue. That language becomes the default for the text and any GUI systems that may be subsequently installed.

on the Ⓙob   *At any time during the text-mode installation process, you can access a higher-level menu. To do so, select Go Back and press ENTER. You may need to repeat several times, to get to the Ubuntu Installer Main Menu screen.*

5. Next, choose the country, territory, or area where the target system resides, and press ENTER.

```
┌──────────────────┤ [!!] Choose language ├──────────────────┐

  Please choose the language used for the installation process. This
  language will be the default language for the final system.

  This list is restricted to languages that can currently be displayed.

  Choose a language:

              Albanian              - Shqip                       ↑
              Arabic                - عربي
              Basque                - Euskaraz
              Belarusian            - Беларуская
              Bosnian               - Bosanski                    ▮
              Bulgarian             - Български
              Catalan               - Català
              Chinese (Simplified)  - 中文(简体)
              Chinese (Traditional) - 中文(繁體)
              Croatian              - Hrvatski
              Czech                 - Čeština
              Danish                - Dansk
              Dutch                 - Nederlands
              English               - English                     ↓

     <Go Back>

 <Tab> moves between items; <Space> selects; <Enter> activates buttons
```

6. You can then choose to try to have Ubuntu detect a keyboard automatically; if it fails, you're prompted to type some keys. If you want to try this out, select Yes and press ENTER. I personally prefer the manual configuration option, so I select No and press ENTER to continue.

7. Then I can select a keyboard from one of several dozen national and related origins. Make a selection, and press ENTER to continue.

8. Next, as shown in Figure 2-10, you get to choose the specific keyboard associated with the selected country, territory, or area. After making a choice, press ENTER to continue.

9. Next, enter an appropriate hostname for the system. The default is *ubuntu*; if you've installed Ubuntu Linux on more than one system, make sure to change the name. When ready, press ENTER to continue.

10. Next, the installation program takes us to one of five partitioning options, as shown in Figure 2-11. (There may be more or fewer options, depending on the previous hard drive configuration.)

11. In the previous section where Ubuntu Linux was installed from the GUI installation program on the Live CD, there were only two options available. In text mode, it's possible to let the Ubuntu Installer guide the process with an LVM configuration—or even an encrypted LVM configuration. I selected "Guided—use entire disk and set up LVM," and pressed ENTER.

FIGURE 2-10

Selecting from available U.S. Keyboard Layouts

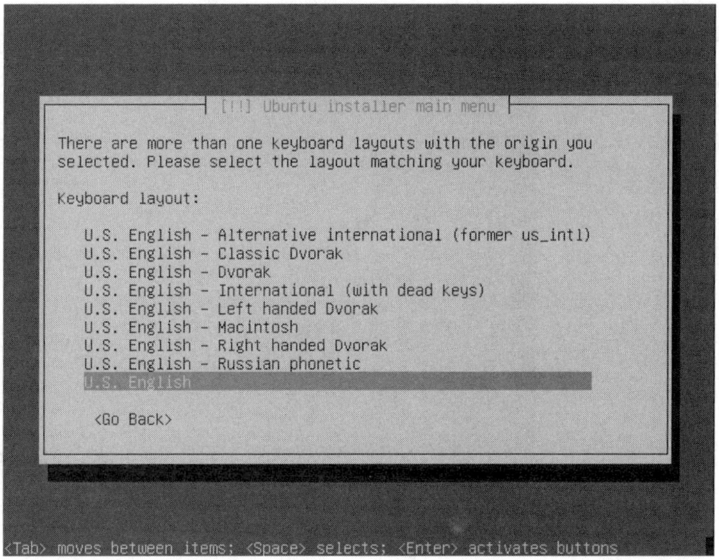

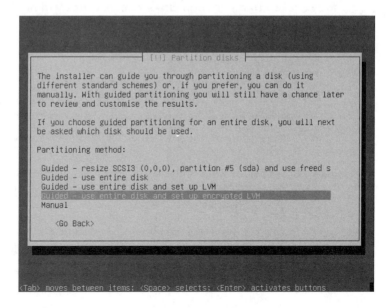

```
                    ┤ [!!] Ubuntu installer main menu ├
    There are more than one keyboard layouts with the origin you
    selected. Please select the layout matching your keyboard.

    Keyboard layout:

       U.S. English - Alternative international (former us_intl)
       U.S. English - Classic Dvorak
       U.S. English - Dvorak
       U.S. English - International (with dead keys)
       U.S. English - Left handed Dvorak
       U.S. English - Macintosh
       U.S. English - Right handed Dvorak
       U.S. English - Russian phonetic
       U.S. English

       <Go Back>
```
```
<Tab> moves between items; <Space> selects; <Enter> activates buttons
```

12. If there's more than one physical hard drive available, you'll get to choose; if there's only one, just select the default, and press ENTER, to get to the screen shown in Figure 2-12.

13. If you selected encryption, you'll get to enter a passphrase twice.

FIGURE 2-11

Partitioning disks with LVM options

```
                    ┤ [!!] Partition disks ├
    The installer can guide you through partitioning a disk (using
    different standard schemes) or, if you prefer, you can do it
    manually. With guided partitioning you will still have a chance later
    to review and customise the results.

    If you choose guided partitioning for an entire disk, you will next
    be asked which disk should be used.

    Partitioning method:

      Guided - resize SCSI3 (0,0,0), partition #5 (sda) and use freed s
      Guided - use entire disk
      Guided - use entire disk and set up LVM
      Guided - use entire disk and set up encrypted LVM
      Manual

       <Go Back>
```
```
<Tab> moves between items; <Space> selects; <Enter> activates buttons
```

FIGURE 2-12

Ready to write
partition scheme
to disk

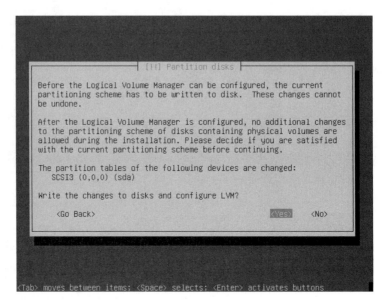

14. Review the changes; if they conform to the desired configuration, select Yes
    and press ENTER. The Ubuntu installer proceeds to format and create the
    configured logical volume(s).

on the
job
If the partition options in step 14 are not what's desired, select Go Back.
You're taken to a Partition Disks screen, which will be described in the
"Configure Drives and Partitions" section.

15. Select an appropriate time zone; choices for U.S. time zones are limited to
    those available in U.S. states and territories. If the system is located elsewhere
    (the installation could be in a remote location such as an embassy on another
    continent), you'll have to change the time after installation is complete.

16. Now you get to choose whether the local hardware clock is or should be set
    to UTC, which is for our purposes, the same as Greenwich Mean Time or
    U.S. military Zulu time. Select Yes unless the system is in a dual-boot config-
    uration with an operating system such as Microsoft Windows. Make a choice
    and press ENTER.

17. In the next few steps, you'll set up one standard user account. In this step,
    enter the full name (and/or any other identifying information) of the user and
    press ENTER.

18. Based on the name entered in the previous step, the installer suggests a user-
    name. Accept or substitute and press ENTER to continue.

19. Next, you'll get to create a password for the user. After pressing ENTER, you'll get to confirm that password. When you press ENTER again, the installation process starts.

20. The process takes some time. If you're not using the Ubuntu DVD, a network connection is required. At some point, you may be prompted for information on any proxy server that may be regulating connections from the LAN to the Internet. The process may take some time. If you want to monitor the process, press ALT-F2 to access a console, ALT-F4 to access system messages. When ready, press ALT-F1 to return to the installation screen.

21. Now configure desired video modes. Current versions of Ubuntu Linux include options for regular and widescreen format monitors/screens such as 1280 × 800. As shown in Figure 2-13, selected video modes are marked with an asterisk. When you've completed your choices, press TAB until the Continue option is highlighted, and then press ENTER.

22. The software installation process continues, until completion. Again, it takes some time, so be patient. When the process is complete, it provides a message to that effect, including a suggestion to remove any installation media. Do so, press TAB to highlight the Continue option as required, and then press ENTER.

23. Enjoy as Ubuntu Linux now boots onto your system! Remember the username and password created during the installation process, as that'll be required for the first login.

FIGURE 2-13

Available video modes

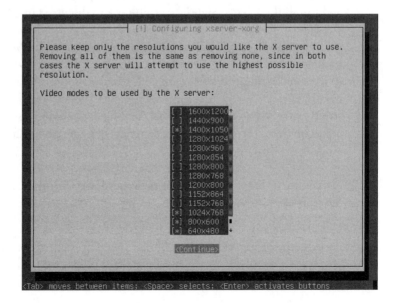

OEM Installation

As noted in Chapter 1, Ubuntu's bug number 1 is associated with Microsoft's majority market share. One of the barriers to entry associated with that bug is that Microsoft Windows is preinstalled on PCs when they are sold to consumers. The OEM Installation option is intended to help manufacturers customize an installation for sale to consumers.

To start the OEM installation process from the Desktop or Alternate installation CD, select the OEM Install (For Manufacturers) option. The basic steps are the same as the text-mode installation just described. There are two main differences:

1. There's a standard oem user; it's available to OEMs to prepare the system with the given password.

2. Next, there's the oem-config-prepare package and command. Once OEM customization is complete, the OEM can use this command to prepare a "for sale" configuration.

Of course, this configuration can be automated. Some options are discussed in Chapter 4. Other options are more straightforward, such as "ghosting," where the image of the desired configuration is copied to other systems. As ghosting works well when copied to other systems with identical configurations, it's well suited for manufacturers.

Although I was prompted for a password during the installation process, the first boot led directly to the GNOME desktop environment, without stopping at the GNOME display manager for a login screen. As an OEM, you may want to load and install the latest updates for customers, as discussed in Chapter 6 in the section "Update and Manage Clients."

When the GNOME desktop environment starts in OEM configuration, it includes an icon labeled "Prepare For Shipping To End User." This is a front end to the **oem-config-prepare** command, which requires the password used during the installation process. When run, it suggests that a reboot is required. Well, that's not strictly true. What I do is run the following commands to start the OEM system configuration process. The first command here moves to runlevel 1:

```
$ sudo init 1
```

And then this command restarts the runlevel with the GNOME desktop environment:

```
# init 2
```

Then the System Configuration tool starts, allowing you to select a default language, time zone, keyboard layout, and regular user. I don't go into any more detail as OEM installations are not listed in the UCP curriculum.

The Microsoft Windows Installer

You can even install Ubuntu Linux directly from within the Microsoft Windows operating system. Use the Live CD or DVD, and look for the wubi-cdboot.exe program. When started, it prepares the basic Ubuntu Linux installer for Microsoft Windows. Once loaded, it requires a Windows reboot before the installer can continue.

While WUBI is not currently supported by Ubuntu, I think it's a significant step towards Ubuntu Linux adoption by Microsoft Windows users.

There are a couple of major issues associated with WUBI. Loop-mounted disk files are sensitive to fragmentation, as Microsoft filesystems often break big files into a large number of disparate chunks. As the installed Ubuntu Linux system is used, data reads may jump from chunk to chunk. If there are too many jumps, the system is effectively unusable. A related issue is associated with compressed NTFS drives.

There's also a start.exe program available on the Ubuntu installation CD. It doesn't start the Ubuntu Linux installation. It opens up a special browser link, shown in Figure 2-14, which includes Ubuntu's Windows-to-Linux conversion documentation, as well as links to install a Microsoft version of the Firefox web browser, the Thunderbird e-mail tool, and the Abiword word processor.

FIGURE 2-14

The Ubuntu
start.exe program

Installing Ubuntu Server

The Ubuntu Server installation uses the same repositories as the Ubuntu Desktop. But there are differences. The installation CD includes fewer options. The kernel is optimized for servers. Linux/Apache/MySQL/Perl (or PHP or Python) installation support, known as LAMP, is available. The Ubuntu Server is also optimized for thin client support, using the work of the Linux Terminal Server Project (LTSP).

If you're installing an Ubuntu Server (and if you've read the chapter to this point), I assume you're something of an expert at the process, so I'll describe the current process associated with expert mode. To switch into expert mode from the Ubuntu Server installation CD, as shown in Figure 2-15, press F6 twice and select Expert Mode. (The Expert Mode option is not available from the DVD menu.)

Boot the installation program. It opens the main menu shown in Figure 2-16. To help you gain "a thorough understanding of the installation process on i386 architecture," we'll explore each of these options.

Choose Language

The Choose Language option allows you to choose the language used during the installation process, as well as the default language for the installation. If applicable, further steps support a customized locale, such as UK English or Canadian French. Detailed steps depend on the language and locale. You can choose an additional locale if and as desired. For more information on localization, see Chapter 8.

FIGURE 2-15

Ubuntu Server
Expert mode

Ubuntu Server
installer Main
menu

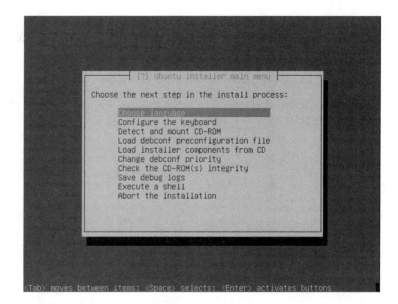

Configure the Keyboard

The Configure The Keyboard option supports the selection of one of a wide range (well over 100 at last count) of keyboard makes and models. If you don't see the right keyboard after making the selection, check appropriate documentation, which may give you hints on compatible keyboards. If all else fails, there are four generic keyboard options available.

Once a keyboard is selected, you can also select the national origin of the keyboard, which can be especially useful for those keyboards associated with multiple languages. Finally, you're allowed to select from available keyboard layouts. This is similar to steps 7 and 8 of the Text-Mode installation instructions described earlier. There are additional steps associated with the keyboard:

1. The next step allows you to configure a specialized key, as shown in Figure 2-17. The key combinations shown in the figure, when used in combination with preconfigured regular keys, can enter specialized characters such as accented letters or currency symbols. Make a selection and press ENTER to continue.

2. If you've configured a console with something other than Unicode fonts, you can select a "Compose Key" in the next step, to allow the use of multiple keys such as an ASCII key combination. Make a selection and press ENTER to continue.

3. This is followed by encoding options. The standard for U.S. English is UTF-8. There are a number of ISO encoding options as well; different ISO encodings

FIGURE 2-17

Ubuntu Server
specialty key
configuration

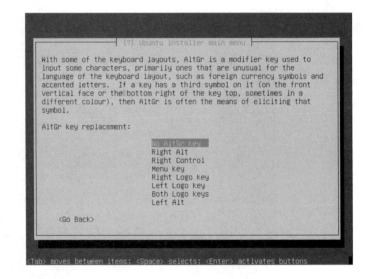

are associated with different European languages. Make a selection and press
ENTER to continue.

4. The next selection shown in Figure 2-18 allows selection of various language
character sets. Make a selection and press ENTER to continue.

5. Next, you can select a font for the console. VGA is sufficient for most applications. Make a selection and press ENTER to continue.

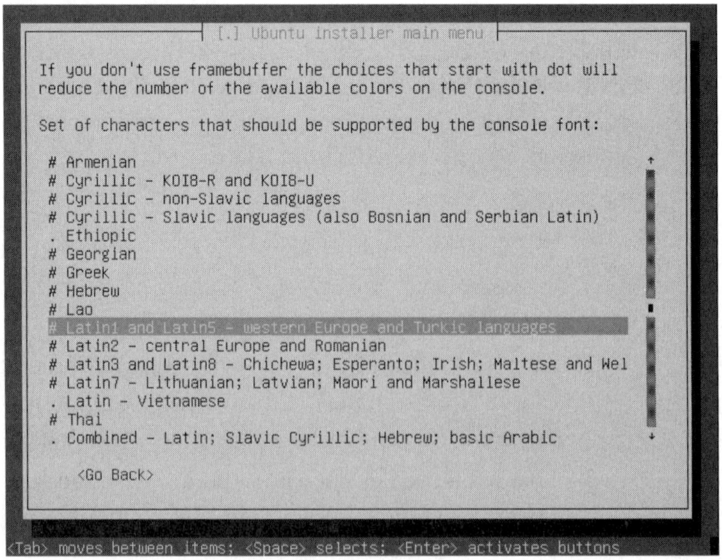

FIGURE 2-18

Ubuntu Server
specialty key
configuration

6. Now choose a font size; the default is 16. Make a selection and press ENTER to continue.

7. In this step, you can configure the virtual consoles. By default, there are six virtual consoles available, accessible when pressing CTRL-ALT-FX, where X is the virtual console number. That's expressed by the associated device files, /dev/tty[1-6]. Make any desired changes and press ENTER to continue.

Detect and Mount CD-ROM

The Detect and Mount CD-ROM section applies to similar media players, including CD and DVD read- and write-capable drives. Pay particular attention to this section, if you need any type of PC Card—even if it's not required for a CD/DVD drive. (Similar menu options are made available for other hardware when appropriate.) If you select this option from the main menu, the Ubuntu Installer navigates through the following steps:

1. First, the installer detects available hardware and configures required modules to load. Review the list, make any desired changes, and press ENTER to continue.

2. As some CD/DVD drives are associated with PC Card services, also known as PCMCIA (Personal Computer Memory Card International Association) cards, one step in this section supports the starting of PC Card services. For modern Linux distributions, it's also known as 32-bit Cardbus services. If these services are desired, select Yes and press ENTER to continue.

3. Some configuration options may be configured for PC Card services; the configuration is documented in the config.opts file. Add any special configuration options to the blank line in this step and press ENTER to continue.

4. The installer should now have enough information to detect the local CD/DVD drive; if successful, it will even list the label of any CD such as the Ubuntu Linux installation CD currently in the drive. Press ENTER to return to the main Ubuntu installer menu.

Load debconf Preconfiguration File

When you select the Load debconf Preconfiguration File option, this loads the Debian Configuration file from the installation CD/DVD. It's also known as a "preseed" file, with a .seed extension, in the CD/DVD preseed/ subdirectory. The selected preseed file depends on the installation CD and installation option. Available preseed files are discussed in Chapter 4.

When you select this option, the preseed file is loaded automatically, without prompting. Then you're taken back to the main Ubuntu installer menu.

Load Installer Components from CD

The Load Installer Components From CD option allows you to further customize the installation, with the options shown in Figure 2-19. As you can see from Table 2-3, the installer components provide considerable flexibility. You can make any or all of these options part of the Ubuntu installer; just use the arrow keys to select an option, and press the spacebar to activate or deactivate the option. Only then can you use any of these options during the installation process.

Choose desired components, press TAB until Continue is highlighted and press ENTER to continue. The additional highlighted components are loaded, expanding the menu as shown in Figure 2-20. Note the Download Installer Components option; it accesses a configured network installation mirror for additional options.

Installation details beyond this depth are beyond what would typically be seen during the LPI Level I exams, and are therefore beyond the scope of the UCP exam. Even if you make no optional selections after choosing the Load Installer Components from CD option, you still get an extended menu, as shown in Figure 2-21.

Detect Network Hardware

One of the expanded options is Detect Network Hardware, which supports network card detection. Select this option if you have a network card. If the network card is a special PC Card, you may need to specify a PCMCIA resource range. Once network hardware is detected, the installer returns to the main menu.

FIGURE 2-19

Additional
Ubuntu Installer
components

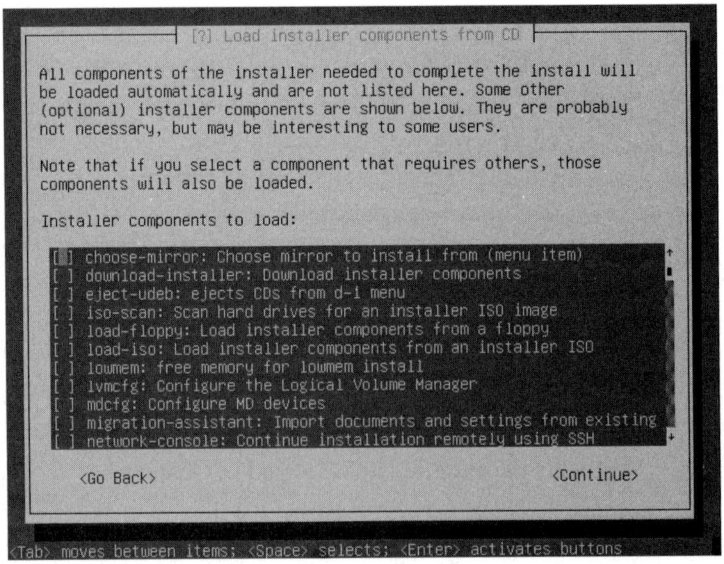

```
┌──────────────┤ [?] Load installer components from CD ├──────────────┐
│                                                                      │
│ All components of the installer needed to complete the install will  │
│ be loaded automatically and are not listed here. Some other          │
│ (optional) installer components are shown below. They are probably    │
│ not necessary, but may be interesting to some users.                 │
│                                                                      │
│ Note that if you select a component that requires others, those      │
│ components will also be loaded.                                       │
│                                                                      │
│ Installer components to load:                                         │
│                                                                      │
│  [ ] choose-mirror: Choose mirror to install from (menu item)        │
│  [ ] download-installer: Download installer components                │
│  [ ] eject-udeb: ejects CDs from d-i menu                            │
│  [ ] iso-scan: Scan hard drives for an installer ISO image           │
│  [ ] load-floppy: Load installer components from a floppy            │
│  [ ] load-iso: Load installer components from an installer ISO        │
│  [ ] lowmem: free memory for lowmem install                          │
│  [ ] lvmcfg: Configure the Logical Volume Manager                    │
│  [ ] mdcfg: Configure MD devices                                     │
│  [ ] migration-assistant: Import documents and settings from existing│
│  [ ] network-console: Continue installation remotely using SSH       │
│                                                                      │
│     <Go Back>                                       <Continue>        │
│                                                                      │
└──────────────────────────────────────────────────────────────────────┘
 <Tab> moves between items; <Space> selects; <Enter> activates buttons
```

TABLE 2-3	Component	Description
Optional Ubuntu Installer Components	choose-mirror	Supports downloading components from the mirror of your choice
	download-installer	Supports download of additional installation components
	eject-udev	Supports CD ejection; appropriate if multiple CDs are required
	iso-scan	Allows searching for ISO files with Ubuntu installer images
	load-floppy	Allows installation to load drivers from floppy disks
	load-iso	Supports component installation from CD information on an ISO file
	lomem	Configures the option to make additional memory available
	lvmcfg	Allows use of the Logical Volume Manager
	mdcfg	Supports configuration of Multi-Devices (MD), associated with RAID arrays
	migration-assistant	Supports the use of an existing system configuration
	network-console	Allows remote control of an installation using SSH
	oem-config-udeb	Enables the use of the OEM configuration assistant
	ppp-udeb	Enables the Point-to-Point Protocol daemon; for network installations, associated with DSL communications
	rescue-mode	Supports a minimal generic installation for rescue purposes

FIGURE 2-20

Completely expanded Ubuntu Installer menu

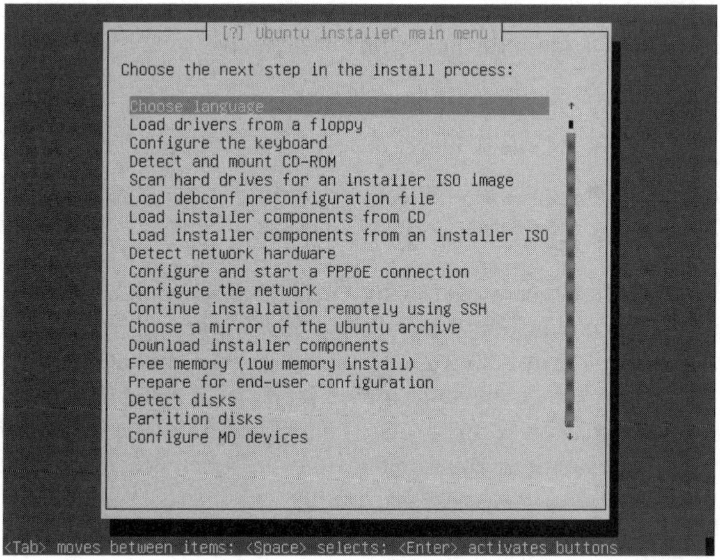

Modestly
expanded Ubuntu
Installer menu

```
                    [?] Ubuntu installer main menu

      Choose the next step in the install process:

        Choose language                                      ↑
        Configure the keyboard
        Detect and mount CD-ROM
        Load debconf preconfiguration file
        Load installer components from CD
        Detect network hardware
        Configure the network
        Detect disks
        Partition disks
        Configure time zone
        Configure the clock
        Set up users and passwords
        Install the base system
        Configure the package manager
        Select and install software
        Install the GRUB boot loader on a hard disk
        Install the LILO boot loader on a hard disk
        Continue without boot loader
        Finish the installation                              ↓

<Tab> moves between items; <Space> selects; <Enter> activates buttons
```

Configure the Network

After network hardware has been detected, the next logical step is to configure the
network. When this option is selected, the Ubuntu installer allows configuration via
an existing connected DHCP server or static configuration. If static configuration is
desired (the Ubuntu installer recognizes only IPv4 addresses), the installer prompts
you to enter the following information:

- IP Address
- Netmask (also known as a network mask or subnet mask)
- Gateway Address
- Name server (DNS) address

In either case, after an IP address is assigned, the installer prompts for a hostname.
Depending on the installation CD, the default hostname is ubuntu or ubuntuserver;
if you're installing more than one instance of Ubuntu Linux, make sure that the
hostname is different. It then prompts for a domain name; if there's an existing
DHCP server, any domain name assigned by the server is listed in the installer. You
can substitute the domain name of your choice.

on the **job**

Many home hardware routers include a DHCP server. If you want to assign a domain name for a LAN behind a firewall such as that common to many home hardware routers, I suggest example.com, example.net, or example.org. These names cannot be registered on the Internet and are therefore suitable for private home use.

Detect Disks

The Detect Disks option uses Ubuntu's detection tools to find connected hard drives. If the disk is connected through a PC Card controller, you may need to specify a PCMCIA resource range. Once appropriate media is detected, the installer returns to the main menu.

Partition Disks

When the Partition Disks option is selected, the Ubuntu installer allows you to let the installer provide a default partition configuration, or allows you to configure the partition in some detail. This option will be described in more detail later in the "Configure Drives and Partitions" section.

Configure Time Zone

When you select the Configure Time Zone option, the Ubuntu installer provides time zone options based on the language and country selected earlier in the Choose Language subsection. For example, if you've selected English in the United States, the Ubuntu installer provides options based on time zones associated with U.S. states and territories. If there is only one time zone associated with the language/country selection, the Ubuntu installer just requests confirmation.

on the **job**

If you're configuring Ubuntu Linux in a specialized situation, such as a U.S. embassy in a non-U.S. time zone, you'll need to configure the time zone after installation is complete.

Configure the Clock

When you select the Configure The Clock option, the Ubuntu installer prompts you to confirm or deny that the system clock is set to UTC; as noted earlier, equivalent to Greenwich Mean Time.

Set Up Users and Passwords

When you select the Set Up Users and Passwords option, the Ubuntu installer prompts for basic configuration settings of the local authentication database. This option includes several steps:

1. The first question is whether to enable the Shadow Password Suite. Modern Linux distributions use the Shadow Password Suite. For more information, see the section "Work the Shadow Password Suite" in Chapter 8. Choose Yes or No and press ENTER to continue.

2. The next question is whether to enable the root user to log in. Ubuntu Linux disables logins by the root user by default. This measure promotes security. Unless there's some other pressing need, select No and press ENTER to continue. (If you select Yes, jump to step 5.)

3. When prompted, type in the full name (and any other desired information for the first regular user). As this is comment information, it doesn't matter to Ubuntu Linux what is entered here. Press ENTER to continue.

4. Confirm or change the suggested username, and press ENTER to continue.

5. Type in the configured user's password, press ENTER, confirm the password, and press ENTER again. If the passwords match, you should be returned to the Ubuntu installer main menu.

Install the Base System

When you select Install The Base System, the Ubuntu installer starts loading packages from the CD and from remote networked repositories. It doesn't require additional input, but takes some time. When the process is complete, the installer should return you to the Ubuntu installer main menu.

Configure the Package Manager

When the Configure The Package Manager option is selected, the first step is to select a mirror. A CD can't contain all required packages for current Linux distributions, including Ubuntu Linux. If you accept the option to "Use A Network Mirror," take the following steps:

1. Choose either an HTTP or FTP connection for downloads, and press ENTER to continue.

2. Select an archive mirror country; if you have your own archive, scroll to the top of the list and choose the Enter Information Manually option, as shown in Figure 2-22. Make a choice and press ENTER to continue.

FIGURE 2-22

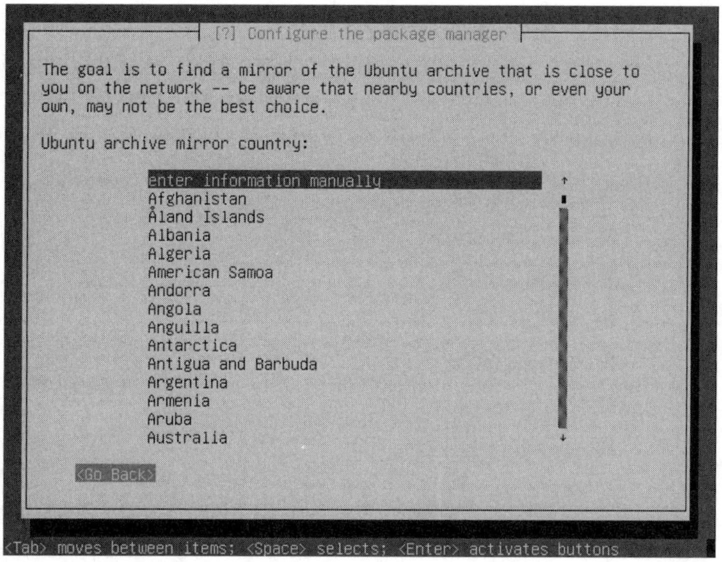

Select an Ubuntu
archive mirror
country.

```
┌───────────────┤ [?] Configure the package manager ├───────────────┐
│                                                                    │
│  The goal is to find a mirror of the Ubuntu archive that is close to│
│  you on the network -- be aware that nearby countries, or even your │
│  own, may not be the best choice.                                   │
│                                                                    │
│  Ubuntu archive mirror country:                                    │
│                                                                    │
│         ┌──────────────────────────────────────────────┐ ↑        │
│         │ enter information manually                     │ ▮        │
│         │ Afghanistan                                    │          │
│         │ Åland Islands                                  │          │
│         │ Albania                                        │          │
│         │ Algeria                                        │          │
│         │ American Samoa                                 │          │
│         │ Andorra                                        │          │
│         │ Angola                                         │          │
│         │ Anguilla                                       │          │
│         │ Antarctica                                     │          │
│         │ Antigua and Barbuda                            │          │
│         │ Argentina                                      │          │
│         │ Armenia                                        │          │
│         │ Aruba                                          │          │
│         │ Australia                                      │ ↓        │
│                                                                    │
│                          <Go Back>                                 │
│                                                                    │
└────────────────────────────────────────────────────────────────────┘
  <Tab> moves between items; <Space> selects; <Enter> activates buttons
```

on the **①ob**

For more information on repositories, see Chapter 6.

3. If you selected a country, accept the default archive mirror, or select Go Back
    to choose the Enter Information Manually option described in the previous
    step, which allows you to enter the URL to the desired mirror here.

4. If there's a Proxy Server that regulates access from the local network to the
    Internet, type in the URL and any required authentication/port information
    here, and press ENTER to continue.

5. The next four steps ask whether you want to enable access to various repositories:
    Ubuntu restricted, Universe, Multiverse, and Backports. Select Yes or No for
    each of these questions, and press ENTER to continue.

If you decline the option to "Use A Network Mirror," you're limited to the default
repository mirrors for security updates. When the process is complete, you should be
returned to the Ubuntu installer main menu.

Select and Install Software

Now that you've selected network repositories, the Ubuntu installer is ready for the Select And Install Software option. The Server installation CD supports the installation of several different groups of packages, including the following:

- DNS server
- LAMP server
- Mail server
- OpenSSH server
- PostgreSQL database
- Print server
- Samba file server

Make any desired selections, and then press ENTER to continue. Depending on what's selected, you may be prompted to add information such as a MySQL password. When the process is complete, you should be returned to the Ubuntu installer main menu.

Install a Boot Loader

You should select only one of the next three options:

- Install the GRUB boot loader on a hard disk.
- Install the LILO boot loader on a hard disk.
- Continue without boot loader.

GRUB and LILO are the two main options for Linux boot loaders. GRUB, the Grand Unified Bootloader, is the default for most Linux distributions. LILO, the Linux Loader, is the legacy bootloader, still used in a few situations such as some PowerPC and Itanium systems. If there's already a third-party bootloader on the local system, you can continue without installing a bootloader, if an appropriate entry is already configured in that third-party bootloader.

on the **!** **job** *The terms bootloader and boot loader are used interchangeably.*

Now you can select Finish The Installation. There are other options after this in the Ubuntu installer main menu, but they are not related to the installation. When Finish The Installation is selected, settings are saved. When you see the Installation Complete message, highlight Continue and press ENTER to reboot the system.

CERTIFICATION OBJECTIVE 2.04

Configure Drives and Partitions

Perhaps the most important part of the installation process is partition configuration. What you do depends on the number and size of available hard drives, as well as requirements for data redundancy and volume size flexibility. This section just covers how to configure partitions, logical volumes (LV), and software RAID arrays. But before creating and configuring a partition, it's important to understand the range of available filesystem formats.

on the *Job*

The terms filesystem and file system are interchangeable; a filesystem format is associated with disk-based filesystems.

In this section, I'll show you how to manually configure a 100MB /boot directory partition, a software RAID 1 array with 1GB of storage for the /home directory, and dedicate the remaining space as a logical volume for the rest of the top-level root (/) directory filesystem. I've created two 3GB virtual hard drives on a VMware server system for the purpose of this chapter.

Filesystem Formats

Linux is a clone of Unix. The Linux filesystems were developed from the Unix filesystems available at the time. The first Linux operating systems used the Extended Filesystem (ext). Just a few years ago, most Linux distributions formatted their partitions by default to the Second Extended Filesystem (ext2).

Most Linux distributions have moved to journaling filesystems, which have two main advantages. First, it's faster for Linux to check during the boot process. Second, if a crash occurs, a journaling filesystem has a log (also known as a journal) that can be used to restore the metadata for the files on the relevant partition.

There are a wide variety of filesystems available for Ubuntu Linux, a sample of which are included in Table 2-4. The list includes standard filesystems, as well as those with "journaling" features. The filesystems marked with an asterisk can be configured during the standard text-mode Ubuntu Linux installation process.

TABLE 2-4	Filesystem Type	Description
Some Linux Standard Filesystem Types	ext	The first Linux filesystem, used only on early versions of that operating system.
	* ext2 (Second Extended)	The standard filesystem for most Linux distributions until the early 2000s. Still a better option for smaller media such as floppy drives.
	* ext3 (Third Extended)	The ext3 filesystem is essentially ext2 with journaling.
	* JFS	IBM's journaled filesystem, commonly used in IBM enterprise servers.
	* ReiserFS	The Reiser File System is resizable and supports fast journaling. It's more efficient when most of the files are very small and very large. It's based on the concept of "balanced trees."
	* xfs	Developed by Silicon Graphics as a journaling filesystem, it supports very large files; as of this writing, xfs files are limited to 9×10^{18} bytes. Do not confuse this filesystem with the X Font Server; both use the same acronym.
	* swap	The Linux swap filesystem is associated with dedicated swap partitions. You've probably created at least one swap partition when you installed Linux.
	* FAT16, FAT32	These filesystems support formatting of filesystems that can also be read natively by Microsoft operating systems.
	ISO 9660	The standard filesystem for CD-ROMs. It is also known as the High Sierra File System, or HSFS, on other Unix systems.
	NTFS	The standard Microsoft filesystem for Windows NT through Vista; designed for username/password security. Ubuntu Linux now can read and write to NTFS systems.

Partitions

Now that you have a basic overview of available filesystems during the Ubuntu Linux installation process, we're ready to proceed to partitioning. At some step during the installation process, there will be an option to partition disks. When selected, it starts the Ubuntu installer partitioning tool. As with other parts of the Ubuntu installer, the steps and details vary with release and installation method, so these steps should be taken as guidelines, not exact instructions. This section assumes basic knowledge of partition types. For more information, see the "Work the Filesystem" section in Chapter 5.

At the appropriate time during the installation process, you'll see something like a Partition Disks option in the Ubuntu installer main menu. Select it, and it'll start the Ubuntu partitioner. Take the following steps:

1. Select the Manual partitioning method.

2. In the Partition Disks screen, you'll see detected drives. In this case, I see two detected SCSI drives, as shown in Figure 2-23.

3. When selecting a drive for the first time, the installer prompts you to create a new empty partition table. Select Yes and press ENTER to add the hard drive to the available space.

4. Now select the free space on an available drive and press ENTER. This opens a question on how to use the free space.

5. There are two options: You could create a new partition, or automatically create a partition using all available space. Let's create a new primary partition for the /boot directory. Such a partition typically contains 100MB. Select Create A New Partition and press ENTER.

6. Type in the desired new partition size. For a 100MB partition, type in **100M**. If you wanted a 1GB partition, type in **1G**. You can also allocate a percentage of the available free space, such as **20%**.

7. Select a Primary partition and press ENTER. (The alternative is a Logical partition.)

FIGURE 2-23

Configuring partitions

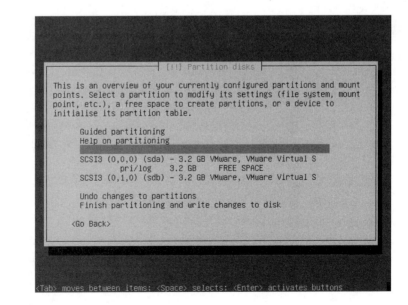

8. Locate the partition at the beginning of the drive and press ENTER; if you're using an older system, this ensures that the BIOS can find the Ubuntu boot files.

9. Now review available partition settings in the window shown in Figure 2-24. To change any of the settings, select it and press ENTER.

   Try different options. Select the Use As option, and review available filesystems, as described earlier in Table 2-4. Select Go Back and press ENTER.

10. Select the Mount Point option, choose the /boot directory, and press ENTER.

11. If the Bootable Flag option is off, select it and press ENTER. After a moment, it should appear as on.

12. Select Done Setting Up The Partition and press ENTER.

13. The partition you just created should now appear in the partition table. It won't be exactly 100MB, as hard disk cylinder boundaries aren't tidy in decimal terms. This is not a problem.

RAID

Now it's time to create a RAID array. I assume that you're still in the Partition Disk screens. To create a RAID 1 array of 1GB, which is a disk mirror, you'll need two partitions of 1GB each. On a production system, a software RAID array doesn't serve its purpose unless its created from partitions on different physical drives. However,

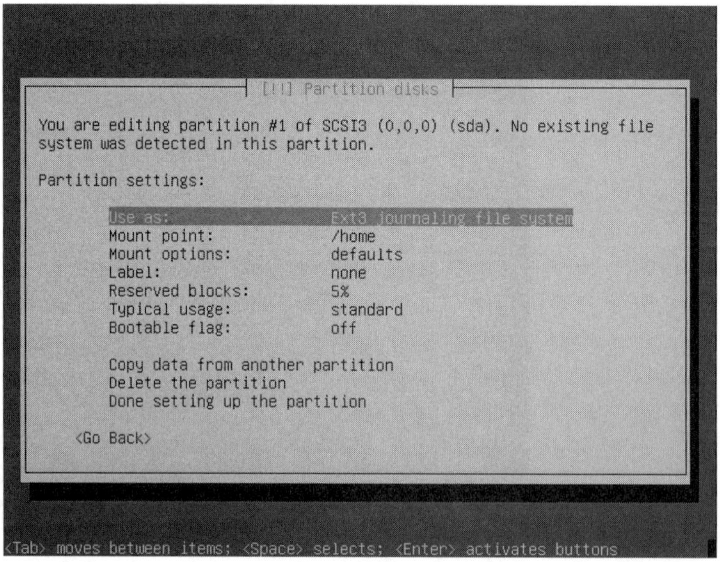

FIGURE 2-24

Configuring
partition settings

```
                  ┤ [!!] Partition disks ├

  You are editing partition #1 of SCSI3 (0,0,0) (sda). No existing file
  system was detected in this partition.

  Partition settings:

          Use as:                      Ext3 journaling file system
          Mount point:                 /home
          Mount options:               defaults
          Label:                       none
          Reserved blocks:             5%
          Typical usage:               standard
          Bootable flag:               off

          Copy data from another partition
          Delete the partition
          Done setting up the partition

      <Go Back>



  <Tab> moves between items; <Space> selects; <Enter> activates buttons
```

if you only have one drive, it's OK for test purposes to create two RAID partitions on the same drive. The primary purpose of this section is to learn, not to create a production system.

When you see a menu like that shown in Figure 2-23, select free space in one of the drives and press ENTER. Use the steps described in the previous section to create a new partition of 1GB. Change the filesystem format from ext3 to Physical Volume for RAID. Repeat the process to create a second 1GB partition on a different hard drive. You should now see an option in the partitioning menu. It'll be similar to Figure 2-23, but will show a Configure Software RAID option. Take the following steps:

1. Select the Configure Software RAID option and press ENTER; it should take you to a screen like that shown in Figure 2-25.

2. Accept the changes; select Yes and press ENTER. This will write the changes to the noted hard drives.

3. To create a software RAID array, you'll need to create a multidisk (MD) device. Select the Create MD Device option and press ENTER to continue.

4. Note the different available MD devices available; the Ubuntu installer currently supports configuration of RAID 0, RAID 1, and RAID 5 arrays. Select RAID 1 and press ENTER to continue.

FIGURE 2-25

Writing to
partition tables

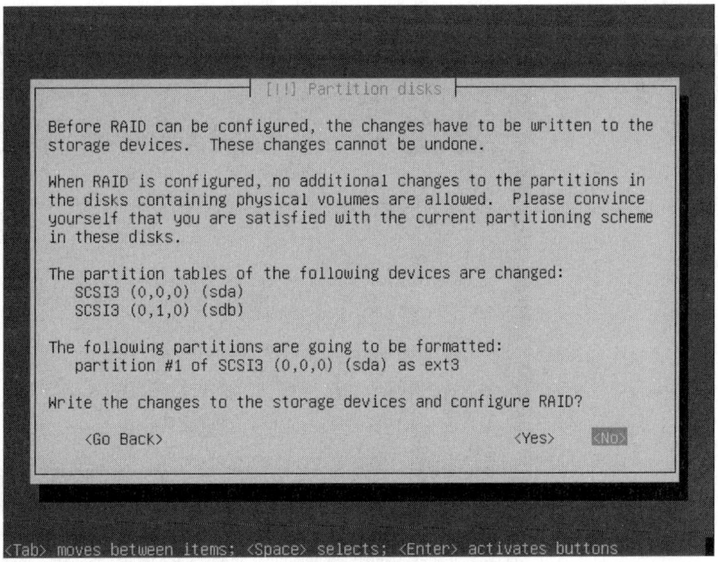

```
                        ┤ [!!] Partition disks ├
  ┌──────────────────────────────────────────────────────────────────┐
  │                                                                    │
  │ Before RAID can be configured, the changes have to be written to the │
  │ storage devices.  These changes cannot be undone.                  │
  │                                                                    │
  │ When RAID is configured, no additional changes to the partitions in │
  │ the disks containing physical volumes are allowed.  Please convince │
  │ yourself that you are satisfied with the current partitioning scheme │
  │ in these disks.                                                    │
  │                                                                    │
  │ The partition tables of the following devices are changed:        │
  │    SCSI3 (0,0,0) (sda)                                             │
  │    SCSI3 (0,1,0) (sdb)                                             │
  │                                                                    │
  │ The following partitions are going to be formatted:               │
  │    partition #1 of SCSI3 (0,0,0) (sda) as ext3                     │
  │                                                                    │
  │ Write the changes to the storage devices and configure RAID?      │
  │                                                                    │
  │    <Go Back>                                      <Yes>    <No>    │
  │                                                                    │
  └──────────────────────────────────────────────────────────────────┘

  <Tab> moves between items; <Space> selects; <Enter> activates buttons
```

5. Type in the number of active MD partition devices. A RAID 1 array requires two active partition devices, which should already be typed into the text box. Type in 2 if required and press ENTER.

6. If there are one or more spare partitions available, they can be allocated to this array for redundancy. If available, type in the number to allocate to the array (type in 0 if none are available), and press ENTER to continue.

7. Select at least two of the configured partitions for the MD device, and press ENTER to continue.

8. Back in the MD configuration menu, select Finish and press ENTER to continue. You should now see a menu similar to that shown in Figure 2-23, but with a configured RAID device. Select the RAID #1 device (assuming this is the only configured RAID device) and press ENTER.

9. Now you should be able to create RAID settings. Before the RAID array exists, the option as shown in Figure 2-26 may be a bit confusing; just highlight the Use As: Do Not Use option and press ENTER.

10. Select a format for the array; the format options (including the default ext3 format) are the same as a standard partition.

11. The next menu should confirm that you're editing "partition #1 of RAID1 device #0." Select the Mount Point setting and press ENTER.

FIGURE 2-26

RAID 1 partition settings

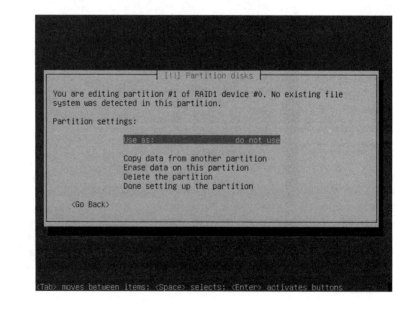

12. Select an appropriate mount point. Based on the requirements listed earlier, that mount point is the /home directory. Make the desired selection and press ENTER.

13. Assuming you're satisfied with the result, select the Done Setting Up The Partition option and press ENTER. The Partition Disks screen that appears should confirm your new RAID 1 array.

In the next section, we'll take this configuration and configure a logical volume from the remaining space on both hard drives, as shown in Figure 2-27.

Logical Volumes

In this section, we take the configuration from the previous section, and create an LV from the remaining space. The top-level root (/) directory will be mounted on that volume. Start from the configuration shown in Figure 2-27. To create the desired LV, take the following steps:

1. Select the available free space on the first hard drive and press ENTER.

2. Since we're using all remaining free space, select the Automatically Partition Free Space option and press ENTER. This should assign all remaining space on the drive to the new partition.

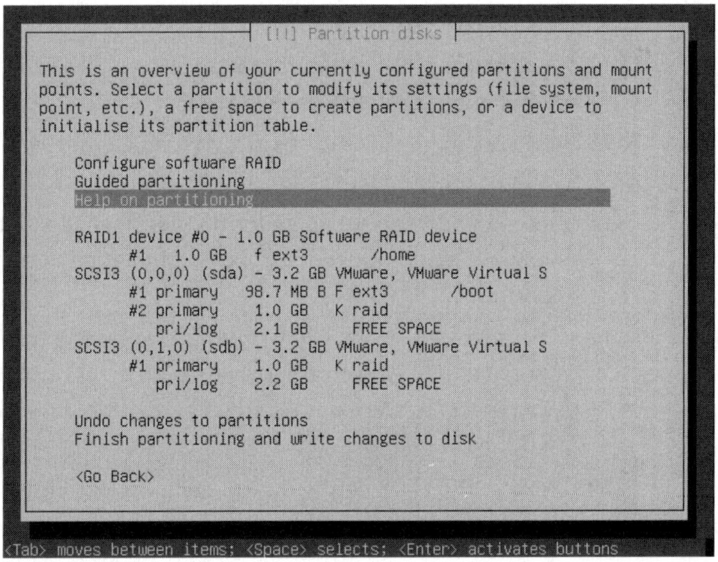

FIGURE 2-27

Partition configuration with RAID 1 array

```
─────────┤ [!!] Partition disks ├─────────

This is an overview of your currently configured partitions and mount
points. Select a partition to modify its settings (file system, mount
point, etc.), a free space to create partitions, or a device to
initialise its partition table.

    Configure software RAID
    Guided partitioning
    Help on partitioning

    RAID1 device #0 - 1.0 GB Software RAID device
        #1   1.0 GB   f ext3      /home
    SCSI3 (0,0,0) (sda) - 3.2 GB VMware, VMware Virtual S
        #1 primary  98.7 MB B F ext3      /boot
        #2 primary   1.0 GB   K raid
           pri/log   2.1 GB     FREE SPACE
    SCSI3 (0,1,0) (sdb) - 3.2 GB VMware, VMware Virtual S
        #1 primary   1.0 GB   K raid
           pri/log   2.2 GB     FREE SPACE

    Undo changes to partitions
    Finish partitioning and write changes to disk

    <Go Back>


<Tab> moves between items; <Space> selects; <Enter> activates buttons
```

3. Repeat steps 1 and 2 on the available free space on the second hard drive.

4. Select the partition just created on the first hard drive and press ENTER.

5. Select the Use As: Do Not Use option and press ENTER. This opens the standard list of available filesystem formats.

6. Select the Physical Volume For LVM option and press ENTER.

7. Select the Done Setting Up Partition option and press ENTER.

8. Repeat steps 4 though 7 for the partition created on the second hard drive.

9. Back in the Partition Disks overview menu, you should now see the free space—or at least most of the free space—from the hard drives allocated to LVs, as labeled by the **lvm** file format. You should also see the Configure the Logical Volume Manager option closer to the top of the menu. Make that selection and click ENTER.

10. If you've made recent changes (as described in the aforementioned steps), you'll be asked to review and confirm the changes. In that case, select Yes and press ENTER.

11. Review the current LVM configuration. Select Create Volume Group and press ENTER.

12. Enter an appropriate name for the new volume group. A descriptive name such as rootvol can be helpful. Type in a name and press ENTER to continue.

13. Select the LVs previously configured for the new volume group. Make the selections, click TAB to highlight Continue, and press ENTER.

14. Back in the LVM configuration menu, you'll see an option to Create Logical Volume. Select it and press ENTER.

15. If there's more than one existing volume group, select the one with the name you just used to create it in step 12, and press ENTER.

16. Enter an appropriate name for the new logical volume group. A descriptive name such as rootlogvol can be helpful. Type in a name and press ENTER to continue.

17. The next step allows you to enter a size for the new logical volume. It does not have to fill the entire logical volume; let's leave 256MB available for swap space. In the case described here, that leaves 3745MB available for the new logical volume.

18. Back in the LVM configuration menu, select Finish and click ENTER.

19. Back in the main Partition Disks menu, select the numbered LVM volume that was just created and press ENTER.

20. You can now configure the LV as part of a specific partition. Select the Use As: Do Not Use option and press ENTER.

21. Select a format for the LV; the format options (including the default ext3 format) are the same as a standard partition.

22. The next menu should confirm that you're editing "partition #1 of LVM VG rootvol LV rootlogvol." Select the Mount Point setting and press ENTER.

23. Select an appropriate mount point. Based on the requirements listed earlier, that mount point is the top-level root (/) directory. Make the desired selection and press ENTER.

24. Assuming you're satisfied with the result, select the Done Setting Up the Partition option and press ENTER. The Partition Disks screen that appears should confirm your new LV mounted on the top-level root (/) directory.

Once satisfied with the partition configuration (based on any or all of these sections), scroll down to the Finish Partitioning and Write Changes To Disk option. Press ENTER, which returns you to the Ubuntu installer main menu. Then proceed with the installation as described earlier.

CERTIFICATION SUMMARY

This chapter is focused on the Ubuntu Linux installation process. It's intended to provide a through understanding of the process from the Live CD and from the Alternate CD, as well as from the Server CD. It covers GUI installation from the operating system loaded from the Live CD, regular text installation from any of the CDs, as well as expert modes available from the Alternate or Server CD.

The Ubuntu Linux installer is based on the Debian Linux installer. It provides a high degree of flexibility from the boot CD. This chapter describes the step-by-step process associated with text and expert mode installation. It even describes the Microsoft Windows installer, which loads Ubuntu Linux as if it were a virtual machine.

Installation details associated with partitions, RAID, and LV are especially complex. The /boot directory should be mounted on a regular partition. RAID and LV can be configured as volumes for other directories.

✓ TWO-MINUTE DRILL

Here are some of the key points from the certification objectives in Chapter 2.

Download the Ubuntu Linux Installation CDs

❑ As this is not part of the UCP curriculum, there are no key points for this section.

Take the Ubuntu Test Drive

❑ A fully featured version of Ubuntu Linux can be loaded from the Live CD.
❑ The Live CD includes a full set of applications, including the OpenOffice.org suite.
❑ Access to the GUI installation tool is available from within the Live CD.

Install Direct from the CD/DVD, Step by Step

❑ Installation can be started directly from any of the installation CDs.
❑ Standard text installation requires Internet access (unless you use the installation DVD).
❑ The first installation screen just after booting provides a lot of flexibility.
❑ Expert installation modes also provide great flexibility.
❑ The Ubuntu Server installation supports the installation of a specialized kernel and suitable server services.

Configure Drives and Partitions

❑ Available hard drives can be configured into partitions.
❑ Linux directories can be mounted directly onto partitions.
❑ Partitions can be organized into RAID arrays.
❑ Partitions can be set up in LVs.

SELF TEST

The following questions will help you measure your understanding of the material presented in this chapter. Read all the questions carefully, as there may be more than one correct answer. Some questions are "fill in the blank" and normally require an exact answer. Choose all correct answers for each question.

Download the Ubuntu Linux Installation CDs

1. Which of the following CDs are *not* available for download?
   A. Ubuntu Linux Live CD
   B. Ubuntu Linux Alternate CD
   C. Ubuntu Linux Text CD
   D. Ubuntu Linux Server CD

Take the Ubuntu Test Drive

2. Which of the following desktop environments is associated with the Ubuntu Linux Live CD?
   A. None
   B. GNOME
   C. KDE
   D. Xfce

3. What is the name of the package associated with OEM installation? Do not include the version number or file extension.

   _____

4. The "UTC" associated with installation tools is associated with which of the following?
   A. All time in Ubuntu Linux should be set to UTC.
   B. As long as you have only Linux operating systems on the local computer, you should set the local hardware clock to UTC.
   C. It's only for Microsoft Windows.
   D. It's the designation associated with local time.

5. What would you do to boot from the Live CD into Ubuntu Linux text installation?
   A. Nothing. Installation automatically proceeds after 30 seconds.
   B. Select Start Ubuntu in Safe Graphics Mode.
   C. Press the ESC key and then press ENTER.
   D. It's not currently possible.

Install Direct from the CD/DVD, Step by Step

6. For a custom installation from the Ubuntu Alternate CD, how can you access Expert Mode?

    A. Press ESC and press ENTER.

    B. Select Install in Text Mode.

    C. Press F6 and type in **expert** at the end of the Boot Options line.

    D. Press F6 twice and select Expert Mode.

7. What command from the Ubuntu Live CD can start the installation program from within Microsoft Windows?

    A. Ubuntu.exe

    B. Start.exe

    C. wubi-cdboot.exe

    D. autorun.exe

8. Which of the following is not required if you're configuring a static network address, capable of connecting to the Internet, during the installation process?

    A. A DHCP server

    B. An IP address

    C. A network mask

    D. A DNS server address

9. Which of the following key combinations access messages during the installation process?

    A. ALT-F1

    B. ALT-F2

    C. ALT-F3

    D. ALT-F4

10. Which of the following services can be specifically included in the default installation process from the Ubuntu Server CD? (Two answers are correct.)

    A. OpenOffice.org Suite

    B. The Apache web server

    C. The DHCP server

    D. An e-mail server

Configure Drives and Partitions

11. Which of the following volumes is best suited for the /boot directory?

    A. A regular partition

    B. A logical volume

    C. A RAID array

    D. A combination of RAID and logical volumes

12. What is the standard filesystem format for Ubuntu Linux? Type in the answer.

_____

13. Which of the following volume types are associated with MD?

    A. A logical volume

    B. A regular partition

    C. A multidisk volume

    D. A RAID array

14. Which of the following filesystem formats can be read by both Ubuntu Linux and Microsoft Windows? (Two answers are correct.)

    A. ext3

    B. FAT32

    C. NTFS

    D. xfs

15. In a RAID 1 array, if you have three partitions available, how many partitions can be made active for the array?

    A. 0

    B. 1

    C. 2

    D. 3

16. From which of the following installation CDs can you *not* configure a RAID array?

    A. The Live CD

    B. The Alternate CD

    C. The Server CD

    D. The Installation DVD

LAB QUESTIONS

These two labs are designed to help you install Ubuntu Linux. It's most convenient if you've set up a virtual machine such as VMware or Xen. Step-by-step instructions are not provided, as the details are available in the body of the chapter. I assume you've downloaded the Ubuntu Linux Alternate and Server CDs. Both labs can also be run from the Ubuntu Linux DVD.

You'll need a hard drive with at least 5GB available. If you're using a physical system with no free partitions available, tools such as GParted on the Ubuntu Live CD can help. It can take the available free space from a partition formatted (and defragmented) to the NTFS or VFAT/FAT32 filesystems. Once free space is available on the hard drive, the Ubuntu installer can take over.

Lab 1

In this lab, you'll install an Ubuntu Linux desktop environment from the Ubuntu Linux Alternate CD. Install the desktop with the following partition scheme:

- A /boot directory with 100MB
- A swap partition with twice the space of available RAM (if you have more than 512MB of RAM, limit the swap partition to 1GB).
- The remaining space allocated to the top-level root (/) directory.

Lab 2

In this lab, you'll install an Ubuntu Linux server environment from the Ubuntu Linux Server CD. If there's more space available, preferably on multiple hard disks, make sure the RAID arrays are located on different hard drives. That is one reason why a virtual machine is more suitable; it's relatively easy to create different virtual hard drives.

Make sure to choose the LAMP option. Review the result, as it provides the Apache web server, the MySQL database service, and the Perl scripting language. If successful, you'll see configuration files in the /etc/apache2/, /etc/mysql, and /etc/perl directories.

SELF TEST ANSWERS

Download the Ubuntu Linux Installation CDs

1. ☑ **C.** There is no Ubuntu Linux Text CD.
   ☒ The Ubuntu Linux Live, Alternate, and Server CDs are available for download, therefore answers **A**, **B**, and **D** are all incorrect.

Take the Ubuntu Test Drive

2. ☑ **B.** The Ubuntu Linux Live CD loads the GNOME desktop environment.
   ☒ As there is a desktop environment associated with the Live CD, answer **A** is wrong. As the KDE and Xfce desktop environments are associated with the Kubuntu and Xubuntu Live CDs, and other releases are supported for 18 months on the desktop and server, answers **C** and **D** are both wrong.

3. ☑ **oem-config-prepare**
   ☒ The oem-config-prepare package provides the tools for OEM administrators to create a custom environment for preloading Ubuntu Linux prior to sale of the PC.

4. ☑ **B.** Unless there's an incompatible operating system such as Microsoft Windows, setting the hardware clock to UTC supports changes associated with Daylight Savings Time.
   ☒ As UTC is effectively Greenwich Mean Time, the Ubuntu system should not be set to UTC, unless of course the system is in that time zone. Therefore, answers **A** and **D** are both wrong. As Microsoft Windows can't handle UTC, answer **C** is also wrong.

5. ☑ **D.** Based on the current Ubuntu Live CD, there is no way to boot from that media into text installation.
   ☒ If you entered **expert** at the boot prompt, answer **A** would work. If the default were a text-based installation, such as from the Alternate or Server CD, answers **A** and **C** would work. But the media in the question is the Live CD, so those answers are incorrect. Safe Graphics Mode in a Live CD just loads the operating system from the CD in a less demanding graphics mode; therefore, answer **B** is also wrong.

Install Direct from the CD/DVD, Step by Step

6. ☑ **D.** Pressing the F6 key twice is the way to access the option for Normal mode and Expert mode.
   ☒ Pressing ESC accesses the **boot:** prompt. Answer **A** would work if you typed **expert** at the prompt. Install in Text Mode accesses the normal mode text installation, unless the actions associated with answer **D** are taken. Therefore, answer **B** is also wrong. The **expert** command at the end of the command line doesn't work, so answer **C** is also wrong.

7. ☑   **C.** The wubi-cdboot.exe program from the Live CD starts the Ubuntu Linux installation program from within Microsoft Windows.
☒   As the ubuntu.exe and autorun.exe programs don't exist on the Live CD, answers **A** and **D** are both wrong. As the start.exe program opens a documentation-related page, answer **B** is also wrong.

8. ☑   **A.** A DHCP server is not required if you're configuring a static network address. A DHCP server would automate this process, but sometimes static network addresses are preferred, such as for a DNS server.
☒   As an IP address and network mask are part of a static network configuration, answers **B** and **C** are wrong. As a DNS server address is required to allow communication on the Internet, answer **D** is also wrong.

9. ☑   **D.** The ALT-F4 key combination accesses messages during the Ubuntu Linux installation process.
☒   As the ALT-F1 key combination returns to the text-mode installation screen, answer **A** is incorrect. As the ALT-F2 and ALT-F3 key combinations access a command line, answers **B** and **C** are also incorrect.

10. ☑   **B and D.** The Apache web service is part of the LAMP package. Mail services can also be selected during the standard Ubuntu Server installation process.
☒   As the OpenOffice.org suite and DHCP server are not part of the service selection menu associated with the standard Ubuntu server installation process, answers **A** and **C** are both incorrect.

Configure Drives and Partitions

11. ☑   **A.** A regular partition is best suited for the /boot directory.
☒   As the /boot directory contains boot files, you don't want LVM or RAID problems to prevent a system from booting; therefore answers **B**, **C**, and **D** are all incorrect.

12. ☑   ext3 The standard filesystem format for many modern Linux distributions, including Ubuntu Linux, is the third extended filesystem, also known as ext3.

13. ☑   **D.** A multidisk volume is most closely associated with a RAID array, as that is how such arrays are organized.
☒   As logical volumes and regular partitions are not necessarily organized on multiple disks, they're not related to multidisk volumes, so answers **A** and **B** are wrong. As a multidisk volume by itself is not used, at least not without a RAID configuration, answer **C** is also wrong.

14. ☑ **B** and **C.** The FAT32 and NTFS filesystems are accessible from both current Ubuntu Linux and Microsoft Windows operating systems. Current Ubuntu Linux releases can both read and write to NTFS filesystems, courtesy of the ntfs-3g package.

☒ As the ext3 and xfs filesystems are not readable natively by current Microsoft Windows operating systems, answers **A** and **D** are both incorrect.

15. ☑ **C.** A RAID 1 array is a mirror of two partitions.

☒ While it's possible to include a third partition as a spare in a RAID 1 array, that partition is not active. Therefore, answers **A**, **B**, and **D** are all incorrect.

16. ☑ **A.** As the Live CD can't access text-mode installation, it does not have access to the RAID configuration tools accessible in that mode.

☒ As the Alternate and Server CDs as well as the DVD have access to text mode installation, it is possible to configure RAID when installing from noted media, therefore, answers **B**, **C**, and **D** are all wrong.

LAB ANSWERS

The one and only true measure of success in these labs—or any Ubuntu Linux installation—is a successful installation.

Lab 1

The intent of this lab is as practice installing Ubuntu Linux as a desktop. The installation from the Live CD is almost trivial; you can best learn the options available associated with an Ubuntu Linux installation using text mode. And for the desktop, that's available from the Alternate CD (or the DVD).

Lab 2

The intent of this lab is as practice installing Ubuntu Linux as a server. This requires the Server CD. The LAMP option is just a suggestion; practice installing various services (and reviewing associated files) can help you better understand the installation process.

3

Specialized Hardware and Power Management

I t's not even a bold statement any more: It's as easy to configure hardware for Linux as it is for Microsoft Windows. When you consider the problems associated with Windows Vista, some might suggest that Linux is now even more hardware-friendly. A quick look at the Hardware Abstraction Layer device manager will ease the fears of many Microsoft administrators.

Power management has matured in Ubuntu Linux. Advanced Power Management (APM) and Advanced Configuration and Power Interface (ACPI) are both well supported in the latest versions of Linux. If you know where to look, many details are available; hardware "events", such as the unplugging of a laptop system, are recorded in logs.

As you explore how hardware works with Linux, the devil is in the details. So we explore a variety of specialized hardware issues, ranging from SATA drives to wireless devices. As the UCP curriculum does go into some detail on these devices, expect a similar level of detail on the UCP exam.

CERTIFICATION OBJECTIVE 3.01

Understand Basic Linux Hardware Compatibility

Now it's time to explore in detail how Ubuntu Linux handles hardware. While some manufacturers now include their own Linux hardware drivers, most Linux hardware support is either part of the kernel (usually as modules) or is available from third parties.

Fortunately, a vast community of Linux users are hard at work producing Linux drivers and more, even distributing them freely on the Internet. If a certain piece of hardware is popular, you can be certain that Linux support for that hardware will pop up somewhere on the Internet and will be incorporated into various Linux distributions, including Ubuntu Linux.

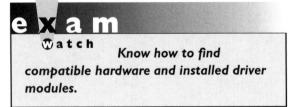

Know how to find compatible hardware and installed driver modules.

When a hardware component works with Linux, some Hardware Compatibility List (HCL), blog, user group, or message board documents the success. And with the development of the Hardware Abstraction Layer (HAL), compatibility is less of an issue.

INSIDE THE EXAM

Configure Power Management (122.3)

As suggested in the UCP curriculum, "candidates should be able to use, enable, and disable power management. This objective includes APM and ACPI power management schemes." To that end, we explore the files used to configure each of these schemes. As APM is, by and large, a legacy system today, the focus of this chapter is on ACPI.

Configure Hardware (122.2)

The configuration of current PC hardware goes hand-in-hand with power management. The UCP curriculum suggests that candidates need to know how to configure a wide variety of hardware devices. There are a variety of files and commands that can help you understand how hardware has been—and can be—detected.

Hardware Compatibility

Be careful when purchasing a new computer to use with Linux. Though Linux has come a long way the last few years, and you should have little problem installing it on most modern PCs, you shouldn't assume Linux will install or run flawlessly on *any* PC, especially if the PC in question is a state-of-the-art computer (though many, perhaps most, manufacturers seem determined to maintain good relationships with the Linux community). Laptops especially are often designed with proprietary configurations that work with Linux only after some reverse engineering. Perhaps the best way to test out a laptop is with a Live CD. If a retailer wants your business, they'll let you boot Ubuntu Linux on their computers.

Linux runs very well on lower-end computers. This is one of Linux's strong points over other operating systems, especially Microsoft Windows Vista. The Ubuntu Linux installer can even run fine on 32MB of RAM, although more is always better, especially if you want to run any graphical applications. And the latest versions of Linux do have limits; modern distributions, including Ubuntu Linux, don't run on anything less than a Pentium-class system.

For most hardware, the question is not one of compatibility, as the great majority of hardware is already there, especially with Ubuntu Linux. The question is one of licensing. Drivers included with the Linux kernel, whether they're embedded or loaded as modules, are open source drivers. But Ubuntu Linux includes restricted drivers, which are proprietary drivers for which source code is not publicly available. Security updates for such updates depend almost solely on the hardware manufacturer.

Linux Hardware Documentation

Many resources are available to help you select the best hardware for Linux. Thousands of Linux gurus who *might* be willing to help are available online via mailing lists, IRC rooms, and message boards. They document their experiences on wikis and blogs. Perhaps the most authoritative source for hardware is still the Linux Documentation Project (LDP). The LDP is a global effort to produce reliable documentation for all aspects of the Linux operating system, including hardware compatibility.

Linux Hardware Compatibility HOWTO

The Linux Hardware Compatibility HOWTO is a document listing most of the hardware components supported by Linux. It's updated frequently with the latest in newly supported hardware. To read this document, search for the Hardware-HOWTO at www.tldp.org.

Where appropriate, the Hardware-HOWTO includes links to existing individual hardware projects, such as the Linux USB project at www.linux-usb.org and a couple of major Linux laptop hardware projects at http://tuxmobil.org and www.linux-laptop.net.

Ubuntu Hardware Compatibility Lists

Ubuntu Linux is just building the infrastructure associated with a fully supported distribution. The HCLs associated with Ubuntu Linux are far from complete, and currently rely on community input and support. As of this writing, two of the most promising sites for an Ubuntu HCL are http://ubuntuhcl.org and https://wiki.ubuntu .com/HardwareSupport. While both sites use Ubuntu logos, they appear to be run by users, and rely on reports from people like yourself.

Plug and Play and the Hardware Abstraction Layer

Plug and play (PnP) refers to the ability of an operating system to allocate hardware ports or addresses automatically to specific devices such as hard drives, sound cards, or modems. Linux's ability to work with PnP devices is finally up to speed, courtesy of the Linux implementation of HAL. Conceptually different from the Microsoft version, HAL provides a constantly updated list of detected components. Ubuntu Linux can even automatically detect and mount the smart cards associated with digital cameras and fingerprint readers.

If you want to see the full list of detected hardware, run the **lshal** command. It's a long list, so you may need to pipe the output to a pager with a command like

```
$ lshal | less
```

which allows you to scroll through the output with PAGEUP and PAGEDOWN keys.

HAL and Hardware

The HAL layer is the communications layer between the operating system and the hardware. It provides a number of tools beyond just the **lshal** command for detected hardware. Some of the more important HAL commands are summarized in Table 3-1.

If there's any doubt about hardware compatibility, just one look at the HAL Device Manager in Figure 3-1 should set your fears to rest.

TABLE 3-1 HAL Commands	HAL Command or Service	Description
	hald	The HAL daemon
	dbus-daemon	The D-BUS (data bus) message bus service; links GNOME (and KDE starting with version 4.0) to hardware
	lshal	The command to list HAL detected devices; see the section "Understand Kernel Modules" for more detail
	udev	A dynamic device manager, which includes device files for only connected devices
	hal-device	A command similar to **lshal**; customized to provide information for hal-device-manager
	hal-device-manager	A command that opens a GUI view of detected devices
	hal-disable-polling	A method to disable (or re-enable) detection messages for removable hardware such as CD/DVD disks
	hal-find-by-capability	A command that searches through the **info.capabilities** flags in the output to the **hal-device** command; requires the **--capability** switch

HAL Device
Manager

Understand Kernel Modules

Most Linux systems, including Ubuntu Linux, use kernel modules. A kernel module
is not compiled directly into the kernel but instead operates as a pluggable driver
that can be loaded and unloaded into the kernel as needed. In most cases, the
process described in this section is automated, courtesy of HAL.

To have the kernel dynamically load and unload kernel modules as needed, the
kernel module loader is used to control the loading and unloading of modules.
The Ubuntu module list is simple and is stored in the /etc/modules file. When
appropriate, add the driver module names of your choice to this file.

Most hardware modules are automatically detected during the boot process. With
HAL, most hardware installed while Linux is running is also automatically detected.

If HAL doesn't work for a specific component (and that list of problems is shrinking quickly), you could issue the following command:

```
$ sudo depmod -a
```

This command scans available modules, finds dependencies for installed modules, and maps them out to a file (modules.dep). This command also creates a number of other files in the /lib/modules/`uname -r`/ directory. (The `**uname -r**` in the directory tree substitutes the version number of the kernel in the subdirectory).

Once the **depmod -a** module scan is complete, additional kernel modules can be loaded. If that module has dependencies, then all the needed modules will automatically load first.

To load a module, you can use the **modprobe** command with the name of a specific driver, like so:

```
$ sudo modprobe ipw3945
```

This command loads the Ethernet module for an Intel Wireless 3945 card common on many laptop systems. This wireless card requires the ieee80211 module to work properly. If **depmod** were run first (and the physical card were detected), then the ieee80211 module would have loaded automatically before the ipw3945 driver. If a dependency in the list fails during loading, then all dependent modules will be automatically unloaded. Again, this is just an example of a process that happens automatically on most Ubuntu Linux systems, courtesy of HAL.

Detailed module configuration options are separated into individual files in the /etc/modprobe.d directory.

To review loaded modules, you can type either

```
$ cat /proc/modules
```

or

```
$ lsmod
```

The **lsmod** command returns output that looks something like the following:

```
Module            Size   Used by
usb_storage        73024  0
ide_core          116804  1 usb_storage
libusual           18448  1 usb_storage
ipv6              273892  12
....
```

(Numerous entries omitted.)

```
. . . .
processor              32072   2 acpi_cpufreq,thermal
fan                     5764    0
fuse                   47124    3
apparmor               40728    0
commoncap               8320    1 apparmor
```

The module name is listed on the left, and its size is in the second column. The Used by column shows more detail on how the module is being handled. If there's a module name, such as apparmor, in the far right column, then the noted module, in this case commoncap, is a dependency of on apparmor.

CERTIFICATION OBJECTIVE 3.02

Explore Power Management Options

The Linux implementation of HAL supports the two basic computer power management standards, ACPI and APM. Among other things, both standards help manage PC power consumption. As such, they are important tools to extend the lifetime of battery-operated devices such as laptop computers. In server rooms, appropriate power management practices can lead to significant savings in electric and cooling bills.

Most PC manufacturers customize their power-saving features for Microsoft operating systems. On Linux systems, some customization may be required, especially for laptops. For this purpose, the experiences of others as documented on sites such as www.tuxmobil.org are most valuable.

Based on these experiences, Ubuntu Linux has customized their latest releases for features such as specialized Dell laptop buttons for the so-called ACPI-defined S states, described later in this chapter in the section "Review Specialized Hardware Issues."

The Ubuntu Linux power management packages that are installed depend on the hardware. I have a Ubuntu Linux Gutsy Gibbon desktop where both APM and ACPI support are installed, but only ACPI was installed on my Dapper Drake laptop system. Neither was installed by default on my Ubuntu server virtual machine.

Ubuntu Linux has taken the signals associated with specialized laptop buttons, which may hibernate, control volume, eject the CD, and more. Various laptops may use different signals for each of these functions. Ubuntu Linux has collected these signals, and has included brand-specific scripts to emulate the desired functionality when Linux is loaded.

on the **job** *Perhaps the biggest development in computer power management goes beyond APM and ACPI—it's virtualization. When several virtual machines are run on a single physical system, the power savings goes beyond what can be saved through ACPI.*

Advanced Power Management

While APM is still listed in the UCP curriculum, the latest Ubuntu releases no longer include default support for APM power management (though module-based support is available). The BIOS in current PCs also does not support APM. Both are required for APM to work. As APM is essentially obsolete, I would be surprised to see APM-related questions on future UCP exams. But as it is part of the UCP curriculum, it's still fair game. So let's explore the basics of APM.

First, APM is based on the apmd package. Once Ubuntu Linux is installed, you can install this package from the command line with the **sudo apt-get install apmd** command. It installs a standard service in the /etc/init.d directory, and should be active during a default boot. But APM may not be available locally if you see the following output to the **/usr/sbin/apmd** command:

```
No APM support in kernel
```

on the **job** *Administration is performed in Ubuntu Linux primarily from the regular account created during the installation process. The user who owns that account has administrative privileges; all he needs to do is preface any administrative commands with* sudo, *and then enter his own regular user password when prompted. For more information, see Chapter 8.*

APM actions are configured around power-related events. Default events are configured in the /etc/apm directory. They fall into several categories, as defined by the subdirectories described in Table 3-2.

However, while APM may be disabled for a system, it still may be enabled for a component such as a hard drive, which will be described shortly in the section "Review Specialized Hardware Issues."

Advanced Configuration and Power Interface

Unlike APM, ACPI puts the operating system in control of power management. It needs no specialized settings in the BIOS. It supports fine-grained power management of just about every appropriate component. ACPI is controlled by two services, the daemon (**acpid**) configured in the /etc/default/acpid configuration file (from the acpid package), and the support service package (acpi-support), which details available functionality.

Until the development of the hotkey-setup package, Linux's ability to respond to hot keys was limited. Hot keys on laptop systems are most frequently associated with laptop power management functionality.

One of the problems associated with ACPI is the different power events configured by different laptop and motherboard manufacturers. One way to review available power events is from the list of files installed from the acpi-support package. From the command line, you can review this list with the following command (if the package is installed):

```
$ dpkg -L acpi-support
```

Many of the files configured for ACPI are manufacturer-specific; some flexibility is required when reading these filenames, in light of recent changes in ownership, such as Lenovo's purchase of the IBM PC division, and the acquisition of Gateway by Acer.

The ACPI Service

The ACPI service is something of a controller to the ACPI detailed support files. The ACPI service itself is fairly easy to configure. The options in the /etc/default/acpid configuration file are straightforward. The first **OPTIONS** directive lists the default ACPI socket:

```
OPTIONS="-s /var/run/acpid.socket"
```

There are also two options for the **MODULES** directive. One specifies a list of modules to be loaded; the second has no limits. The first of the two directives is "commented out" with the hash mark (#). You could use hash marks to deactivate the second directive as well. Do not save the file with both directives activated, as they do not work together.

```
#MODULES="battery ac processor button fan thermal"
MODULES="all"
```

For troubleshooting, there's also an **acpi_listen** command. When run at the command line, it may appear to hang—but is actually listening for ACPI-related power events. If you're running a laptop system, connecting or disconnecting the system from AC power may result in an event like that shown here:

```
ac_adapter AC 00000080 00000000
```

As of this writing, power connection events are the only ones recorded directly by the ACPI daemon. The only event that is part of the acpid package is /etc/acpi/events/powerbtn. It refers to the shell script in the /etc/acpi/powerbtn.sh file, which has different responses depending on the desktop environment and current power status. This is the model upon which other ACPI support events are built.

ACPI Hardware Events

ACPI is flexible, and can help control more than just power events. Depending on the functionality built into the system, it can control a variety of events from brightness to zoom to wireless network activity.

Reading ACPI Event Files

There are a large number of ACPI event files, courtesy of the acpi-support package. The detailed configuration files, as shown in Figure 3-2, are listed in the /etc/acpi/events directory, and are usually manufacturer-specific.

The event filenames are somewhat descriptive; we describe some basic categories of events in Table 3-2. Each event file on the left column is in the /etc/acpi/events directory; each script in the right column is in the /etc/acpi directory.

TABLE 3-2	APM Event Directory	Event Type
APM Event Categories per /etc/apm	/etc/apm/event.d/	Regulates basic hardware, including hard drives, laptop mode (power/standby), and PPP connections
	/etc/apm/other.d/	Includes jobs that do not fit into other categories
	/etc/apm/resume.d/	Adds scripts to keep the hardware clock running, and load sound modules during resume events
	/etc/apm/scripts.d/	Includes scripts associated with suspend and resume events in the /etc/apm/suspend.d and /etc/apm/resume.d directories
	/etc/apm/suspend.d/	Adds scripts to stop the hardware clock, and unload sound modules during suspend events

FIGURE 3-2

ACPI events in
/etc/acpi/events

```
michael@UbuntuGG:~$ ls /etc/acpi/events/
ac                          lenovo-touchpad             thinkpad-thinklight
asus-a6u-touchpad           lidbtn                      thinkpad-thinkpad
asus-brightness-down        panasonic-brightness-down   thinkpad-volume-down
asus-brightness-up          panasonic-brightness-up     thinkpad-volume-up
asus-internet               panasonic-hibernatebtn      thinkpad-zoom
asus-lock                   panasonic-lockbtn           tosh-battery
asus-mail                   panasonic-mute              tosh-brightness-down
asus-media-eject            panasonic-sleepbtn          tosh-brightness-up
asus-media-next             panasonic-volume-down       tosh-hibernate
asus-media-play-pause       panasonic-volume-up         tosh-ibutton
asus-media-prev             powerbtn                    tosh-lock
asus-media-stop             sleepbtn                    tosh-mail
asus-touchpad               sony-brightness-down        tosh-media
asus-volume-down            sony-brightness-up          tosh-mute
asus-volume-mute            sony-eject                  tosh-next
asus-volume-up              sony-hibernate              tosh-play
asus-wireless               sony-mute                   tosh-prev
battery                     sony-sleep                  tosh-sleep
ibm-hibernatebtn            sony-volume-down            tosh-stop
ibm-lockbtn                 sony-volume-up              tosh-wireless
ibm-sleepbtn                thinkpad-brightness-down    tosh-www
ibm-videobtn                thinkpad-brightness-up      video_brightnessdown
ibm-wireless                thinkpad-cmos               video_brightnessup
lenovo-lockbtn              thinkpad-mute               videobtn
michael@UbuntuGG:~$ []
```

Read at least a few of the individual laptop event files. You'll see links to common manufacturer-independent scripts. For example, the **ibm-sleepbtn**, **panasonic-sleepbtn**, and **sony-sleep** events all link to the sleepbtn.sh script in the /etc/acpi directory.

Whenever there's an ACPI event, detailed log information is added to the /var/log/acpid file. You may see a series of messages; at this level, the three messages that matter are as follows:

```
[Tue Nov 20 09:01:32 2007] received event "battery BAT0 00000080 00000001"
[Tue Nov 20 09:26:06 2007] executing action "/etc/acpi/power.sh"
[Tue Nov 20 09:26:06 2007] action exited with status 0
```

This specifies the event, associated with the battery; the script that's executed, which affects the power; and the result—a status 0 message means that the script was executed successfully (a status 1 message would be an error).

Configuring ACPI Hot Keys

None of this works without a map—not a geographic map, but a file that associates the signals from a hot key to an ACPI support event described in the /etc/acpi/ support directory. Maps for various laptop manufacturers have been collected in the hotkey-setup package. To review the files in this package (assuming it's installed), run the following command:

```
$ dpkg -L hotkey-setup
```

ACPI Event	Event Type
ac	Records an AC adapter connection; uses the power.sh script
asus-*	Includes a series of events associated with Asus laptops
battery	Records a transfer from AC to battery power; uses the power.sh script
ibm-*	Includes a series of events associated with laptops associated with IBM; see also **lenovo-*** and **thinkpad-*** event files
lenovo-*	Includes a series of events associated with Lenovo laptops; other events may use **ibm-*** and **thinkpad-*** event files
lidbtn	Records the opening or closing of a laptop lid; normally moves away from the GUI
panasonic-*	Includes a series of events associated with Panasonic laptops
powerbtn	Reacts to the pressing of the power button; the powerbtn.sh script may initiate a shutdown, subject to GNOME (or KDE) settings
sleepbtn	Responds to a sleep mode activation; the sleep.sh script may change the power setting associated with hard drive spinning, subject to the gnome-power-manager (or **klaptopdaemon**)
sony-*	Includes a series of events associated with Sony laptops
thinkpad-*	Includes a series of events associated with Lenovo/IBM laptops; see also **ibm-*** and **lenovo-*** event files
tosh-*	Includes a series of events associated with Toshiba laptops
video_brightnessdown	Reacts to the standard signal to reduce brightness on laptops
video_brightnessup	Reacts to the standard signal to increase brightness on laptops
videobtn	Responds to the signal to toggle the backlight on the laptop screen

TABLE 3-3

ACPI Event Files in /etc/acpi/events directory

Most of the files from the hotkey-setup package are loaded in the /usr/share/hotkey-setup directory; a current list is shown in Table 3-3. As Ubuntu Linux improves, this list may grow.

As an example, take a closer look at the dell.hk file. It specifies specialized keycodes and their button combinations. For example, here's the directive that maps the keycode that ejects the CD/DVD drive:

```
setkeycodes   e009   $KEY_EJECTCD   # Fn+F10   EjectCD (e009)
```

The keycode, e009, is the signal received when the user presses the FUNCTION and F10 keys together on a Dell laptop system. It's mapped to the **KEY_EJECTCD** variable, which can also be found in the /etc/acpi/ejectbtn.sh script.

The basic configuration is driven by the **setkeycodes** command. It maps a key code from the laptop keyboard, in hexadecimal notation, with an event based on a variable. The default key code list is stored in the atkbd.hk file in the same directory. It lists all standard key mappings, such as the letter F to keycode 21. Many standard keycodes are "reserved" in this file, for customization through other files.

TABLE 3-4	Hotkey Setup File	Description
ACPI Event Files in /etc/acpi/events Directory	acer-aspire-1600.hk	Sets hotkeys for Acer Aspire 1600 series laptops
	acer.hk	Associates hotkeys for other Acer laptops
	asus.hk	Assigns hotkeys for Asus laptops
	atkbd.hk	Sets defaults for the keyboard
	clevo-dp500p.hk	Associates a key code for the Keynux Agora system by Clevo
	compaq.hk	Configures key codes for Compaq systems, now sold by HP
	default.hk	Lists key codes for laptops not configured by other files
	dell.hk	Configures specialized keys for Dell laptops, including Media Direct keys
	generic.hk	Lists key codes common to all laptops
	hp.hk	Sets hotkeys for HP systems; may work with compaq.hk
	hp-tablet.hk	Sets hotkeys for HP Tablet systems; also see hp.hk and compaq.hk
	hp-v2000.hk	Configures hotkeys associated with the Presario laptop model, first developed by Compaq
	ibm.hk	Associates highly customized keycodes for a variety of Thinkpad and Lenovo series laptops.
	key-constraints	Sets variables for standard keys, such as **KEY_ESC=1**
	lenovo.hk	Associates custom keycodes for Lenovo series laptops
	medion.hk	Configures custom keycodes for Medion laptops
	micro-star-infinity.hk	Sets hotkeys for the MSI MS-1035 laptop system
	samsung.hk	Sets hotkeys for Samsung systems
	toshiba-tablet.hk	Configures hotkeys for the Toshiba Portege tablet

CERTIFICATION OBJECTIVE 3.03

Review Specialized Hardware Issues

Just as the Linux ACPI system includes custom keycode signal configurations for different laptop manufacturers, the same system includes a number of custom configurations for different kinds of hardware. The smartmontools package can help monitor the health of attached hard drives. Serial ATA (SATA) drives emulate SCSI drives in some ways. ACPI S States are associated with power modes. Direct Memory Access (DMA) allows individual hardware systems to bypass the CPU. Wireless devices have been a special challenge for Linux. More challenges have been overcome with Bluetooth and infrared devices.

Smart Hard Disk Monitoring

Current versions of Ubuntu Linux include a hardware hard-disk monitor, based on the smartmontools package. At this time, it is focused on monitoring the health of local hard disks, based on the Self-Monitoring, Analysis, and Reporting Technology (SMART) system built into SATA, SCSI, and later-model IDE hard drives.

While monitoring is configurable in the /etc/default/smartmontools file, Ubuntu's default version of this file just contains default settings. The key command is **smartctl**. It's a rich command. Understanding every switch is beyond the scope of the UCP exam. You should be aware of the basics; for example, the following command lists all SMART report information on the first SATA (or SCSI) hard drive. The | **less** "pipes" the output to a pager (the **less** command), which you should already know at the UCP level of experience.

```
$ sudo smartctl -a /dev/sda | less
```

When I run this command on my laptop, I get a long output, which is the reason to pipe the output to the **less** command. It allows you to scroll through the output with the PAGEUP/PAGEDOWN and UP and DOWN ARROW keys. One excerpt from the output is shown in Figure 3-3.

Without getting into too many details associated with hard drive performance, the data shown in Figure 3-3 show that my laptop has run with this hard drive for 1807 hours, with a **Load_Cycle_Count** of 89070. Wait a second—the **Load_Cycle_ Count** variable is associated with load and unload cycles, as the drive is powered up and down. The specifications for the hard drive in question note that hard drives

FIGURE 3-3	Output from smartctl -a /dev/sda

ID#	ATTRIBUTE_NAME	FLAG	VALUE	WORST	THRESH	TYPE	UPDATED	WHEN_FAILED	RAW_VALUE
1	Raw_Read_Error_Rate	0x000f	100	253	006	Pre-fail	Always	–	0
3	Spin_Up_Time	0x0003	098	098	000	Pre-fail	Always	–	0
4	Start_Stop_Count	0x0032	100	100	020	Old_age	Always	–	349
5	Reallocated_Sector_Ct	0x0033	100	100	036	Pre-fail	Always	–	0
7	Seek_Error_Rate	0x000f	074	060	030	Pre-fail	Always	–	28080281
9	Power_On_Hours	0x0032	098	098	000	Old_age	Always	–	1807
10	Spin_Retry_Count	0x0013	100	092	034	Pre-fail	Always	–	0
12	Power_Cycle_Count	0x0032	100	100	020	Old_age	Always	–	334
187	Unknown_Attribute	0x0032	082	082	000	Old_age	Always	–	18
189	Unknown_Attribute	0x003a	100	100	000	Old_age	Always	–	0
190	Temperature_Celsius	0x0022	058	049	045	Old_age	Always	–	840564778
191	G-Sense_Error_Rate	0x0032	100	100	000	Old_age	Always	–	0
192	Power-Off_Retract_Count	0x0032	100	100	000	Old_age	Always	–	281
193	Load_Cycle_Count	0x0022	056	056	000	Old_age	Always	–	89070
194	Temperature_Celsius	0x001a	042	051	000	Old_age	Always	–	42 (Lifetime Min/Max 0/19)
195	Hardware_ECC_Recovered	0x0012	060	056	000	Old_age	Always	–	19460887
197	Current_Pending_Sector	0x0010	001	001	000	Old_age	Offline	–	4294967295
198	Offline_Uncorrectable	0x003e	001	001	000	Old_age	Always	–	4294967295
199	UDMA_CRC_Error_Count	0x0000	200	200	000	Old_age	Offline	–	0
200	Multi_Zone_Error_Rate	0x0032	100	253	000	Old_age	Always	–	0
202	TA_Increase_Count	0x0000	100	253	000	Old_age	Offline	–	0

may fail with a load cycle of over 600,000 cycles. I leave my laptop on most of the time, so it means my hard drive will fail in a couple of years. Others have reported more substantial problems. So we add the following On The Job:

on the **Job**

The default Ubuntu smartctl settings for several releases include aggressive power management settings for hard drives, which may quickly, exceed the cyclic lifetimes of many hard drives. For more information, see bug 59695 at https://bugs.launchpad.net.

The setting is based on and can be changed with the **hdparm** command, as described in the next section.

Hard Drives and CD/DVD Drives

Hard drives are the primary storage medium for current PCs. Until solid state drives become more popular, hard drives are a primary consumer of power. ACPI settings are often used to limit the power consumption of these drives. Before getting into power issues, let's review the following about CD/DVD and hard drives on Linux:

- The standard PC is configured to manage up to four IDE (Integrated Drive Electronics) hard drives, now known as PATA (Parallel Advanced Technology Attachment) drives.

- Newer PCs can handle more SATA (Serial ATA) drives.
- Depending on the SCSI (Small Computer Systems Interface) hardware, up to 31 different SCSI hard drives can be attached to a single system.

Although you can install Linux on USB (Universal Serial Bus) or IEEE 1394 (Institute of Electrical and Electronics Engineers standard 1394, also known as FireWire or iLink) hard drives, they only need to be powered when attached to the PC; thus, power consumption is not nearly as big of an issue with said drives. The same can be said for the older parallel port drives. Linux communicates with all of these drives through device files, as described in Table 3-5.

The **hdparm** command can help control a number of settings on CD/DVD and hard drives, including power consumption. While some of the options are designed for PATA/IDE drives, don't feel constrained by the old documentation, which suggests that it can't be used on SATA drives. To review current settings, run the following command (substitute /dev/hda for /dev/sda if the target is a PATA drive):

```
$ sudo hdparm -I /dev/sda | less
```

The output should show a lot of information about the target hard drive. It includes model information and configuration, including a lot of detail beyond the

TABLE 3-5	Media Device	Device File
Media Devices	Floppy drive	First floppy = /dev/fd0
	PATA (IDE) hard drive PATA (IDE) CD/DVD drive	First drive = /dev/hda Second drive = /dev/hdb Third drive = /dev/hdc Fourth drive = /dev/hdd
	SATA or SCSI hard drive SATA or SCSI CD/DVD drive	First drive = /dev/sda Second drive = /dev/sdb ... Twenty-seventh drive = /dev/sdaa and so on
	Parallel port drives	First drive = /dev/pd1 First tape drive: /dev/pt1
	USB drives	Uses SCSI /dev/sdx device files
	IEEE 1394 drives	Uses SCSI /dev/sdx device files
	Smart media cards	First card = /dev/mmcblk0p1 Second card = /dev/mmcblk0p2 and so on

scope of any Linux certification exam that I know. The excerpt from Figure 3-4 illustrates supported and enabled features associated with a local hard drive.

The list of supported features will vary by hard drive. Whether or not a feature is enabled depends on BIOS settings as well as any configuration in /etc/hdparm.conf. Of course, BIOS information is not Linux-specific and is therefore beyond the scope of this exam.

Let's examine the current performance of the drive, using basic disk and cached reads:

```
$ sudo hdparm -Tt /dev/sda
/dev/sda:
 Timing cached reads:   2340 MB in  2.00 seconds = 1171.98 MB/sec
 Timing buffered disk reads: 172 MB in 3.03 seconds = 56.76 MB/sec
```

If you have access to a drive of another of the three main types (SATA, SCSI, and PATA), run the preceding command on the other drive. Observe the differences.

In the previous section, we described a problem in which Ubuntu Linux cycles a hard drive too frequently. If, based on the aforementioned **smartctl** command, that situation applies to you, you can use the **hdparm** command to disable load cycling with the following command:

```
$ hdparm -B 255 /dev/sda
```

FIGURE 3-4

Hard drive
configured
features, per
hdparm

```
Commands/features:
        Enabled Supported:
           *        SMART feature set
                    Security Mode feature set
           *        Power Management feature set
           *        Write cache
           *        Look-ahead
           *        Host Protected Area feature set
           *        WRITE_BUFFER command
           *        READ_BUFFER command
           *        DOWNLOAD_MICROCODE
                    Advanced Power Management feature set
                    SET_MAX security extension
           *        48-bit Address feature set
           *        Device Configuration Overlay feature set
           *        Mandatory FLUSH_CACHE
           *        FLUSH_CACHE_EXT
           *        SMART error logging
           *        SMART self-test
           *        IDLE_IMMEDIATE with UNLOAD
           *        SATA-I signaling speed (1.5Gb/s)
           *        Native Command Queueing (NCQ)
           *        Phy event counters
                    Device-initiated interface power management
           *        Software settings preservation
           *        SMART Command Transport (SCT) feature set
        :□
```

Don't let the output message "setting Advanced Power Level level to disabled" confuse you. ACPI is still enabled, as long as appropriate packages are properly configured, as described earlier in the "Explore Power Management Options" section. To confirm, run the **hdparm -I /dev/sda** command again. The output should reveal the following (even if ACPI is active):

```
Advanced Power Management feature set
```

Since there is no asterisk in the left column, this feature is not enabled. When this feature is disabled, the hard drive does not power down even when the system is running on battery power. For a more measured result, you could try other settings by substituting a number between 1 and 254 for 255 in the **hdparm -B 255 /dev/sda** command.

To make sure this setting works the next time Linux is booted on my system, I added this command to the /etc/hdparm.conf configuration file. Following the format of the commented stanzas at the bottom of the file led me to create the following stanza with the required command (no space is required between the **-B** and the **255**).

```
command_line {
    hdparm -B255 /dev/sda
}
```

You don't need to reboot to test the result; just reload or restart the **hdparm** daemon:

```
$ sudo /etc/init.d/hdparm reload
```

DMA Speeds

In standard mode, a disk requires CPU attention for as long as it takes to transfer a file. If you're transferring a DVD-length ISO file, that can be a waste of resources. With appropriate DMA settings, a disk does not have to slow down when other systems require CPU attention.

This situation applies only to PATA/IDE drives. SATA drives are automatically configured to use DMA, so those are not a concern. SCSI drives already bypass the CPU via their own controller.

PATA/IDE drives may need to be configured to use DMA. To see if this is true, apply the **hdparm** command to the PATA/IDE device file in question. For example, when I ran the following command on my DVD drive

```
$ sudo hdparm /dev/hda
```

I get the following output, which tells me that DMA is already enabled for this drive.

```
using_dma     =  1 (on)
```

Of course, DMA can be disabled and enabled with the following commands:

```
$ sudo hdparm -d0 /dev/hda
$ sudo hdparm -d1 /dev/hda
```

If there's a performance issue with a hard drive or CD/DVD drive, run the **hdparm -Tt** command described earlier, and try enabling DMA. Then run the **hdparm -Tt** command again on the drive, and see if the transfer speeds have improved.

ACPI Power Management States

ACPI is associated with several power states, known as the "S" states. As listed in Table 3-6, they describe various states of power consumption for the CPU, RAM, and other components.

The states S1, S2, S3, and S4 are collectively known as a G1 "sleeping" state. To find available power states on the local system, run the following command:

```
$ grep S0 /var/log/dmesg
```

You should see output similar to the following,

```
[    1.900000] ACPI: (supports S0 S3 S4 S5)
```

unless you're running an older system with different power state signals, such as C0 and D0. Once sleep states are configured, they are stored in the /proc/acpi/sleep and /proc/acpi/wakeup files.

TABLE 3-6	ACPI "S" State	Description
ACPI "S" States	S0	The normal working state; also known as a G0 "working" state
	S1	Sleep mode, which maintains power to CPU and RAM; common option on older ACPI systems (also known as a G1 state)
	S2	Same as S1, except the CPU is unpowered (also known as a G1 state)
	S3	Standby/sleep mode where only RAM is powered (also known as a G1 state)
	S4	Hibernation mode; all RAM is stored in swap space before the system is powered down (also known as a G1 state)
	S5	Equivalent to the **halt** command; also known as a G2 "soft-off" state

USB and IEEE 1394 Devices

The UCP curriculum suggests that candidates need to know how to configure USB devices. As of this writing, it does not mention IEEE 1394 devices. In real life, most of these devices are already configured automatically by HAL, and all you need to do is recognize how such devices are configured. Connected USB devices are shown in the output to the **lsusb** command. For example, from the following output,

```
Bus 005 Device 004: ID 04e8:1623 Samsung Electronics Co., Ltd
Bus 005 Device 001: ID 0000:0000
Bus 003 Device 001: ID 0000:0000
Bus 002 Device 001: ID 0000:0000
Bus 001 Device 001: ID 0000:0000
Bus 004 Device 001: ID 0000:0000
```

I know there's some device connected to USB Bus 005. Additional information is available from the log files; if you've just connected the USB device, run the following command to determine which log files have the newest information:

```
$ ls -ltr /var/log
```

The log files at the end of the list that correspond approximately to the current time are the log files affected by the USB device, unless they're associated with some other process or job that was running at the same time.

The first appropriate messages in /var/log/syslog (which have a timestamp in the left column) reveal that the USB device is a storage device, and is configured with SCSI emulation. At the end of the file, I see the following message, which means the device was mounted as the /dev/sdc1 partition, for the current user, with a user ID of 1000.

```
Nov 21 15:21:10 UbuntuGG hald: mounted /dev/sdc1 on behalf of
uid 1000
```

The messages in /var/log/messages add information, such as the device model, drive size, write protection status, and filesystem format. The messages in /var/log/kern.log are similar, with an added warning about the state of the filesystem.

As there is no equivalent to **lsusb** for IEEE 1394 devices, the signals are more subtle, but are revealed in just as much detail in the log files. For example, when I attach my portable hard drive to an IEEE 1394 connection, a number of messages are sent to five different log files, as described in Table 3-7. They are ordered from oldest to newest, based on when IEEE 1394-related log messages are added to each file.

	/var/log File	Description
TABLE 3-7	debug	Adds several messages adding appropriate node(s) and devices
Log Files Affected by IEEE 1394 Connections	syslog	Includes node(s) with driver(s); detects and mounts configured partitions
	messages	Notes messages similar to /var/log/syslog
	kern.log	Notes messages similar to /var/log/syslog
	daemon.log	Document-specific mount commands

Wireless Variety

Ubuntu Linux has made significant progress with wireless network card drivers. Well, that's not strictly true, as their "progress" incorporates the hard work of many open source developers. They've also included non-open-source wireless device drivers made available by a number of manufacturers in appropriate "restricted" repositories. While Linux drivers aren't yet available for all wireless network cards, incredible progress has been made. And there are ways to use Microsoft Windows wireless drivers for those few cards where Linux drivers are not available.

on the *Job*

If you have one of the few wireless devices not yet recognized by Ubuntu Linux, the ndiswrapper packages can help. These packages include a "wrapper" that translates an installed Microsoft driver for Linux. For more information, see http://ndiswrapper.sourceforge.net. It may be available for some Ubuntu Linux releases; try the sudo apt-get install ndiswrapper-common command. I avoid it where there's a real Linux driver available; in my experience, the ndiswrapper packages lead to slower performance, and I don't want to depend on a Microsoft driver.

More information on wireless cards (and many other peripherals) is available in the output to the **lspci** command. For more information, use the **-v** and **-vv** switches. For example, the excerpted output from the **sudo lspci -v** command shown in Figure 3-5 tells me all I would need to know about the detected wireless device— if it weren't already automatically configured with the right driver.

Wireless network hardware also include a different series of commands. Basic wireless network management commands are described in Table 3-8.

One of my favorite commands searches for and returns a list of detected wireless networks. In this case, my wireless card is associated with the eth1 device; to find your wireless device(s), run the **iwconfig** command.

```
$ sudo iwlist eth1 scan
```

FIGURE 3-5

Excerpt of lspci
-v with detected
wireless network
card information

```
0c:00.0 Network controller: Intel Corporation PRO/Wireless 3945ABG Network Conne
ction (rev 02)
        Subsystem: Intel Corporation Unknown device 1020
        Flags: bus master, fast devsel, latency 0, IRQ 17
        Memory at efdff000 (32-bit, non-prefetchable) [size=4K]
        Capabilities: [c8] Power Management version 2
        Capabilities: [d0] Message Signalled Interrupts: Mask- 64bit+ Queue=0/0
Enable-
        Capabilities: [e0] Express Legacy Endpoint IRQ 0

michael@UbuntuGG:~$ []
```

Depending on where I am inside my home in a residential neighborhood, I've detected as many as 30 different wireless networks with this command. At this point, I may use the **iwconfig** command to connect to one of my wireless networks. But as this chapter is focused on hardware, I focus on a couple of hardware-related configuration options. First, when I have trouble configuring a connection to a specific access point, I look up the MAC (Media Access Control) hardware address of that access point—it should be in hexadecimal (base 16) notation. For example, for a MAC address of 00:14:D1:C0:36:44, I run the following command:

```
$ sudo iwconfig eth1 ap  00:14:D1:C0:36:44
```

on the **J**ob

To understand hexadecimal notation (base 16), first think of the standard base 10 decimal numbering system with 10 numbers, 0 through 9. As hexadecimal notation includes 16 numbers, letters are added as the last six numbers: 0, 1, 2, 3, 4, 5, 6, 7, 8, 9, a, b, c, d, e, and f. In this case, f in hexadecimal notation equals 15 in decimal notation.

TABLE 3-8

Wireless
Network
Management
Commands

Command	Description
iwconfig	Configures a specific card with network characteristics such as the ID, channel, encryption, transmitted power, and more
iwevent	Monitors the system for other wireless events
iwgetid	Identifies the wireless network ID, also known as the Extended Service Set ID (ESSID)
iwlist	Lists network interface data, such as channels, transmission power, and authorization keys
iwpriv	Configures detailed parameters; associated with **iwconfig**. I've never had to use the **iwpriv** command.
iwspy	Measures quality of wireless link information; an easier option is the information in the /proc/net/wireless file

The other hardware-related **iwconfig** option relates to transmission power. Standard transmission power is 15 decibels per milliwatt, or 15dBm. That's the maximum for many wireless cards. If your wireless card can handle more, data transfer rates might be helped by increasing that power; for example, for those cards which can handle it, the following command

```
$ sudo iwconfig eth1 txpower 20dBm
```

increases transmission power from the wireless card to 20dBm, if it's not beyond the capability of the wireless card.

Bluetooth Devices

Bluetooth is the low-power low-range standard for wireless communication. While it uses the same range of frequencies as standard wireless networks (as associated with the IEEE 802.11b/g standards), they don't interfere with each other due to different multiplexing schemes. Current versions of Bluetooth have a range of up to 10 meters and a speed of 3Mbps.

Bluetooth is configured first in the /etc/default directory. The latest Ubuntu Linux releases include basic Bluetooth settings in the /etc/default/bluetooth file; older releases configured it in the /etc/default/bluez-utils file. Detailed settings based on Bluetooth signals may be available in the /etc/bluetooth directory, with files briefly described in Table 3-9. Further details are beyond the scope of the UCP exam.

TABLE 3-9	/etc/bluetooth file	Description
Bluetooth Configuration Files	audio.service	Configures Bluetooth audio; requires either the bluez-btsco or bluetooth-alsa driver
	hcid.conf	Associated with the Host Controller Interface (HCI) daemon
	input.service	Works with input devices such as a mouse and keyboard
	network.service	Connects with Bluetooth-enabled network devices
	rfcomm.conf	Configures radio frequency communication (RFCOMM) service to emulate serial connections
	serial.service	Works with serial port–enabled devices

IrDA

IrDA refers to a standard of the Infrared Data Association. It's a protocol for data exchange based on infrared light transmission. While it was a common option on many systems in the late 90s through the first few years of this century, it's been supplanted by Wi-Fi and Bluetooth-based devices. But infrared devices still exist, and that category is listed in the UCP curriculum.

To configure an infrared device, install the irda-utils package with a command like **sudo apt-get install irda-utils**. Then basic options can be set up in the /etc/default/irda-utils configuration file. Just change the **DEVICE** and **SETSERIAL** directives to:

```
DEVICE="irda0"
SETSERIAL="/dev/ttyS1"
```

Next, open the associated modules configuration file, /etc/modprobe.d/irda-utils, and add the following directives, where the **nsc-ircc** driver enables ISA plug-and-play support:

```
alias irda0 nsc-ircc
options nsc-ircc dongle_id=0x09
```

Finally, add the following directive to the end of /etc/modules, which configures an infrared-friendly terminal connection:

```
ircomm-tty
```

Now restart the **irda-utils** service script in the /etc/init.d directory as follows:

```
$ sudo /etc/init.d/irda-utils restart
```

If your system has detected an infrared device, you should now be able to make use of the infrared and related terminal modules with the following commands:

```
$ sudo modprobe irda
$ sudo modprobe ircomm-tty
```

Review the result in loaded modules with the **lsmod | more** command. Assuming no error messages appeared when running the modprobe commands, you should now see the modules atop the list shown in the output to the **lsmod** command.

CERTIFICATION SUMMARY

This chapter is focused on how Ubuntu Linux works with hardware. It's intended to provide a basic overview of hardware compatibility issues, power management with APM and ACPI, and a compendium of specialized issues based on the UCP curriculum.

Basic hardware compatibility is well documented in the basic Linux HCL as well as emerging Ubuntu Linux hardware lists. Most hardware in Linux is now truly plug and play. Hardware events such as the unplugging of a battery-powered laptop system while Linux is running are recorded in different log files in the /var/log directory.

This chapter also covers a number of specialized hardware issues. Coverage is driven by the HAL device manager. ACPI S states are power states. DMA frees hardware from always using the CPU. There are similarities in the way SATA, SCSI, and PATA drives are handled. Connected USB devices are shown by the **lsusb** command. Wireless devices can be managed with a number of **iw*** commands. Bluetooth devices are configured in /etc/bluetooth files. Infrared devices, while less common, may still be used for a variety of interfaces.

✓ TWO-MINUTE DRILL

Here are some of the key points from the certification objectives in Chapter 3.

Understand Basic Linux Hardware Compatibility

❑ While Linux may be better than Microsoft operating systems in terms of hardware compatibility, don't assume that all hardware is compatible with Linux.

❑ Linux hardware documentation is available at www.tldp.org, www.ubuntuhcl.org, and www.wiki.ubuntu.com/HardwareSupport.

❑ HAL has delivered on the promise of plug and play for Linux.

❑ HAL includes several commands that detail hardware detection, including **lshal** and **hal-device-manager**.

❑ Detected hardware usually leads to automatic insertion of appropriate kernel modules.

Explore Power Management Options

❑ Two available power management options include APM and ACPI.

❑ APM does not work unless the BIOS supports it.

❑ ACPI is the current standard, configured in files in the /etc/acpi directory.

❑ Hardware events can be monitored through log files in the /var/log directory.

Review Specialized Hardware Issues

❑ The SMART system supports monitoring of hard disk health with commands like **smartctl**.

❑ There are three basic hard disk types: PATA, SATA, and SCSI. PATA, and to some extent, SATA disks can be managed with the **hdparm** command.

❑ DMA bypasses the CPU, which can be a bottleneck. Therefore, enabling DMA on hard drives and CD/DVD drives can result in faster access.

❑ ACPI S States correspond to various power states for the CPU and RAM.

❑ USB and IEEE 1394 data devices are detected as if they were SCSI drives.

❑ Wireless devices often rely on proprietary drivers.

❑ **iwconfig** can configure a connection to a router with a specific hardware address, or a transmission power level.

❑ Bluetooth uses short-range wireless devices; it's configured in the /etc/bluetooth directory.

❑ Infrared devices are line-of-sight connections configured in /etc/default/irda-utils, and are set up as a virtual serial port.

SELF TEST

The following questions will help you measure your understanding of the material presented in this chapter. Read all the questions carefully, as there may be more than one correct answer. Some questions are "fill in the blank" and normally require an exact answer. Choose all correct answers for each question.

Understand Basic Linux Hardware Compatibility

1. Which of the following systems or commands automate the hardware installation process in Linux?
   A. HCL
   B. lsmod
   C. HAL
   D. modprobe

2. Which of the following websites does not include hardware compatibility lists for Ubuntu Linux?
   A. www.tldp.org
   B. www.ubuntuhcl.org
   C. www.wiki.ubuntu.com/HardwareSupport
   D. www.tuxmobil.org

3. What command lists currently loaded modules? Type in the answer. Do not cite the full path.

   _____

Explore Power Management Options

4. If you see the following message, which of the following might be the problem? (Two answers are correct.)

   ```
   No APM support in the kernel
   ```

   A. APM module support has not been compiled into the kernel.
   B. The boot process doesn't support APM.
   C. The BIOS doesn't support APM.
   D. ACPI support is installed.

5. Which of the following directories is not associated with a standard APM configuration?
   A. /etc/apm/suspend.d
   B. /etc/apm/power.d

C. /etc/apm/scripts.d

D. /etc/apm/resume.d

6. Name two packages directly associated with ACPI support. Version numbers or .deb extension names are not required.

_____

_____

7. Which of the following directories configures ACPI responses to messages associated with certain buttons or switches?

A. /etc/acpi

B. /etc/acpi/messages

C. /etc/acpi/conf

D. /etc/acpi/events

8. In which of the following directories can you find scripts that execute commands based on ACPI messages?

A. /etc/acpi

B. /etc/acpi/messages

C. /etc/acpi/conf

D. /etc/acpi/events

9. Which of the following commands opens a GNOME tool that lists HAL characteristics for each detected hardware component?

A. **hal-device**

B. **hal-device-manager**

C. **hal-set-property**

D. **hald**

Review Specialized Hardware Issues

10. Which of the following commands lists available ACPI power states on a single line?

A. **dmesg**

B. **dmesg I grep ACPI**

C. **dmesg I grep ACPI I grep supports**

D. **dmesg I grep S0**

11. What command would list the SMART-monitored characteristics of a hard drive? Only the command (without switches) is required.

_____

12. What command lists detected USB devices? Only the command (without switches) is required.

_____

13. What command can control the transmission power of a wireless device? Only the command (without switches) is required.

_____

14. Which of the following commands activates the DMA channel for the DVD drive connected to an PATA controller?

    A. dmactl -d1 /dev/hdc

    B. hdactl -d1 /dev/hdc

    C. hdparm -d1 /dev/hdc

    D. hdparm -d0 /dev/sdc

15. In what directory would you find generic configuration files associated with hibernation? The BIOS does not support APM.

_____

16. Which of the following systems automatically detects infrared devices?

    A. APM

    B. HAL

    C. IrDA

    D. USB

LAB QUESTIONS

These two labs are designed to help you understand what happens when Ubuntu Linux detects hardware. It requires available "hot" plug-and-play hardware components such as those with USB or IEEE 1394 connections. Other connections may serve the purpose. While ideally this lab would use hardware that isn't automatically detected, hardware detection is now so good in Linux that few users have such hardware. These labs assume you have a USB key or some other USB storage device, configured with a format that can be recognized by Linux, with data. These labs are to be run consecutively. As Ubuntu Linux is constantly changing, what you see may vary.

Lab I

In this lab, you'll insert a USB key or some other USB storage device on a system with the Ubuntu Linux GNOME desktop environment.

    1. Start the system, and log in to the GNOME desktop environment.

    2. Insert a USB key into an available slot.

3. Observe that the USB key is mounted; Nautilus file manager window should be opened automatically. Be patient; this may take more than a few seconds.

4. Open a command-line terminal. Run the **mount** command. The mounted directory should be shown at the bottom of the list.

5. Run the **ls -ltr /var/log** command. What files were just updated? To cross-check against the current date and time, run the **date** command.

6. Run the **tail** command on some of these updated files. For example, to view the last 20 lines of /var/log/messages, run the **tail -n 20 /var/log/messages** command. Review the latest messages. Do you see messages associated with the recognition of your USB key?

7. Run the **sudo fdisk -l** command. The output should reveal the device shown in the output to the mount command.

Lab 2

In this lab, you'll remove the USB key inserted in Lab 1. You should still be in the GNOME desktop environment. Just wait a couple of minutes. Do not unmount the drive before removing the key.

1. Remove the USB key.

2. You may see a message in the lower-right corner. Why the warning?

3. Open a command-line terminal. Run the **mount** command. The formerly mounted directory should now not exist.

4. Run the **ls -ltr /var/log** command. What files were just updated? To cross-check against the current date and time, run the **date** command.

5. Run the **tail** command on some of these updated files. For example, to view the last 20 lines of /var/log/messages, run the **tail -n 20 /var/log/messages** command. Review the latest messages. Do you see messages associated with the removal of your USB key?

SELF TEST ANSWERS

Understand Basic Linux Hardware Compatibility

1. ☑ **C.** HAL, short for Hardware Abstraction Layer, automates the hardware detection process in Linux.

☒ The HCL is the hardware compatibility list; hardware on this list is not necessarily automatically detected. The **lsmod** command lists loaded modules. The **modprobe** command searches for available modules, and loads any that correspond to existing hardware. Therefore answers **A**, **B**, and **D** are all incorrect.

2. ☑ **D.** While the tuxmobil.org web site can help determine compatible hardware for Ubuntu Linux on mobile systems, it is not a hardware compatibility list.

☒ The www.tldp.org web site includes the work of the Linux Documentation Project, including the standard HCL; therefore, answer **A** is incorrect.. The www.ubuntuhcl.org web site as well as the noted wiki include emerging Ubuntu-specific HCLs; therefore , answers **B** and **C** are both incorrect.

3. ☑ **lsmod**

☒ The **lsmod** command lists all currently loaded modules.

Explore Power Management Options

4. ☑ **A and C.** Unless there's APM support loaded into the kernel, and specific support in the BIOS, APM support doesn't work, which can lead to the message as stated in the question.

☒ As the boot process might be interpreted to include the BIOS initialization process, this answer might be interpreted to include BIOS support for APM. But that's a stretch in my opinion; therefore, answer **B** is wrong. As ACPI installation does not preclude APM support, answer **D** is also wrong.

5. ☑ **B.** To understand the answer to this question, you should install the apmd package. Then you'll be able to see that there is no /etc/apm/power.d directory.

☒ As there are /etc/apm/suspend.d, /etc/apm/scripts.d and /etc/apm/resume.d directories installed with the apmd package, answers **A**, **C**, and **D** are all incorrect.

6. ☑ **acpi, acpi-support**, and **hotkey-setup** are all acceptable answers.

☒ This question is subject to interpretation. While other packages may require ACPI support to work, they don't meet the requirements of the question.

7. ☑ **D.** The /etc/acpi/events directory responds to messages associated with certain buttons or switches.

   ☒   While the /etc/acpi/events directory is a subdirectory of /etc/acpi, /etc/acpi/events is a better answer; therefore answer **A** is incorrect. As there are no /etc/acpi/messages or /etc/acpi/conf directories, answers **B** and **C** are both wrong.

8.   ☑   **A.** If you've read any of the files in the /etc/acpi/events directory, you'll know that they all refer to scripts in the /etc/acpi directory.
   ☒   As there is no /etc/acpi/messages or /etc/acpi/conf directories, answers **B** and **C** are both wrong. As the /etc/acpi/events directory responds to messages associated with certain buttons or switches, answer **D** is also wrong.

9.   ☑   **B.** The **hal-device-manager** command in the GUI opens the GNOME tool associated with hardware management.
   ☒   While the **hal-device** command is the front end to the **hal-device-manager**, it is itself a command-line tool, so answer **A** is incorrect. The **hal-set-property** command sets values associated with a hardware component; therefore, answer **C** is also wrong. As the **hald** command is the HAL daemon, answer **D** is also wrong.

10.   ☑   Answer **D** is correct. The grep command when applied to a file or output returns the line associated with the search term. S0 is the only search term associated with a known ACPI power state.
   ☒   The other answers include 2 or more lines from the dmesg output, also known as the kernel ring buffer. Therefore, answers **A**, **B**, and **C** are incorrect.

Review Specialized Hardware Issues

11.   ☑   **smartctl.** This command with the hard drive device lists SMART-monitored settings for that drive. For example, **smartctl -a /dev/hda** lists all SMART measures for the first PATA drive.

12.   ☑   **lsusb** This command lists USB connections, with connected hardware when available.

13.   ☑   **iwconfig.** This command, with the **txpower** switch, can control the transmission power of a wireless network card.

14.   ☑   **C.** The **hdparm** command controls hard drive parameters. The **-d1** switch activates DMA for the given drive.
   ☒   As there are no hdactl or dmactl commands, answers **A** and **B** are both incorrect. As the **-d0** switch turns off DMA (and /dev/sdc is a SCSI or SATA drive), answer **D** is also wrong.

15.   ☑   **/etc/acpi.** That directory includes generic configuration files associated with ACPI-based hibernation.

☒　There are a couple of hints in the question; since APM is not supported, the available power management system is ACPI. Generic configuration settings are located in the /etc/acpi directory; manufacturer-specific settings are stored in the /etc/acpi/events directory.

16.　☑　**B.** The Hardware Abstraction Layer is how Linux detects many hardware components, including infrared devices.

☒　As APM is not related to hardware detection, answer **A** is not correct. As IrDA is just the acronym for infrared devices, answer **C** is also wrong. As USB is just a connection, answer **D** is also wrong.

LAB ANSWERS

Remember, these labs are to be run in sequence.

Lab 1

The intent of this lab is to view the messages associated with HAL. The automounting of the USB key is secondary. Your review of the log messages created when inserting a USB device can help you learn more about how Linux uses plug and play.

Lab 2

The intent of this lab is the same as Lab 1; the only difference, assuming you've removed a USB key, is to make you aware of the data that might be lost unless you first run the **umount** command on the mounted drive.

4

Automated Installation and Diskless Clients

T o promote its place in the enterprise, Ubuntu Linux supports automated installations. Ubuntu developers have adapted Red Hat's Kickstart tools as well as Debian's preseed configuration system. Both options provide preconfigured answers to installation program requests, which allows an Ubuntu Linux installation to proceed automatically.

Closely related to automated installation is the concept of the diskless client. Both concepts require some of the same services, including DHCP and TFTP (Trivial File Transfer Protocol). You'll see how to configure these services, along with a NFS (Network File System) server. While the focus of this chapter is on automated installations and diskless clients, the lessons in this chapter can help you manage your network in other ways.

Ubuntu Linux's implementation of the diskless client is based in part on the work of the Linux Terminal Server Project (LTSP). A diskless client supports multiple terminals running from the same computer, connected via a higher-speed network. Incidentally, many of the steps required for the diskless client can also enable a remote network installation.

CERTIFICATION OBJECTIVE 4.01

Review Automated Installation Files

Automated installations require a file configured to provide answers to the Ubuntu installation program. When properly configured, all you need to do is boot to the installation screen, point to the appropriate file, and then walk away as the installation proceeds automatically. Ubuntu Linux provides two basic options for creating these automated installation files: preseed and Kickstart. Preseed is native to Debian, and Kickstart is native to Red Hat. As preseed is native to Debian and is more flexible, we analyze sample Preseed configuration files. As a GUI tool exists only for Kickstart, we analyze that tool as well.

As of this writing, the Ubuntu efforts to combine the best features of each automated installation system are associated with the Kickseed project. For the latest information, see https://launchpad.net/kickseed/.

INSIDE THE EXAM

Perform an Installation (122.1)

One of the installation options listed in the UCP curriculum is "preseed," which is the Ubuntu method for providing automated answers to the installation program. For completeness, we also present Ubuntu's adaptation of the Kickstart tool. While that is currently beyond the scope of the UCP curriculum, many Ubuntu developers seem to prefer Kickstart, so I would not be surprised to see it made part of the UCP exam in the near future.

Understand Diskless Clients (122.4)

Per the UCP curriculum, "Candidates will not be expected to implement a client." However, you should recognize basic configuration options associated with creating a DHCP server. If and when Canonical creates an Ubuntu Certified Engineer exam, I suspect that candidates will be expected to implement an LTSP client to qualify as an Ubuntu Certified Engineer.

The UCP curriculum specifically cites the /etc/init.d/dhcp3-server, the /etc/dhcpc/config, and /usr/sbin/dhcpd files. They're associated with the dhcp3-server, dhcpcd, and dhcp packages. The /etc/dhcpc/config filename is out of date, and has been replaced with the /etc/default/dhcpcd file in the latest versions of the dhcpcd package.

The UCP curriculum also specifies the /etc/hosts.allow configuration file, which is part of the tcp_wrappers security system.

Kickstart

Kickstart was originally Red Hat's solution for automated installation of Red Hat. It can now be configured for an installation of Ubuntu Linux. If you know Kickstart for Red Hat, Kickstart for Ubuntu should be easy for you. There are only slight differences, as described in this section.

The principles of Kickstart for Ubuntu and Red Hat are the same. All the questions asked during setup can be automatically supplied with one text file. Once the text file is configured, it's possible to set up nearly identical systems very quickly. Before using Kickstart on Ubuntu Linux, first install the applicable Kickstart configuration tool. One method uses the following command:

```
$ sudo apt-get install system-config-kickstart
```

One way to solidify your understanding of Kickstart is with the graphical Kickstart Configurator. When you experiment with this GUI tool, you can learn more about what happens in the Kickstart configuration file.

on the
Öob

For more information on Kickstart and the configuration file, see the RHCE Red Hat Certified Engineer Study Guide, **Fifth Edition.**

The Kickstart Configurator can only be started from the GUI. Open a command-line interface shell. Start the Kickstart Configurator with the **system-config-kickstart** command. If that command is not found, you'll need to run the installation command shown above to install the package of the same name. Alternatively, in the Ubuntu Linux desktop, choose Applications | System Tools | Kickstart. As Kickstart was developed by Red Hat, the menus are related to the Red Hat installation process. However, the basic elements of Red Hat and Ubuntu installations are sufficiently similar. The first screen, shown in Figure 4-1, illustrates a number of basic installation options.

FIGURE 4-1

The Kickstart
Configurator

As you can see, a number of options appear in the left pane, each associated with different Kickstart categories. To learn more about Kickstart, experiment with some of these settings. Use the File | Save command to save these settings with the filename of your choice, which you can then review in a text editor. Alternatively, you can choose File | Preview to see the effect of different settings on the Kickstart file.

The following sections provide a brief overview of each option shown in the left pane. One of the weaknesses of Kickstart on Ubuntu is the lack of a default configuration file for the current system; in other words, unlike on a Red Hat system, there is no anaconda-ks.cfg file or any other Kickstart file based on the local system as installed.

on the **job** *Ubuntu developers are working on a Kickstart tool to generate a file based on the current configuration; for more information, see bug 15156 at https://bugs .launchpad.net.*

Once the configuration is complete, click File | Save. Accept the default to save the settings in the ks.cfg file in the default user's home directory. If you're satisfied with this file, save it to an FTP or HTTP server. You can then access the ks.cfg file. For example, if you have the Alternate Installation CD (other Ubuntu boot CDs can be used), take the following steps:

1. Boot from the Alternate Installation CD.
2. Press the esc key. When prompted, click OK to start the text-mode interface.
3. When you see the **boot:** prompt, type **install** and the path to the Kickstart configuration file. For example, if it's the ks.cfg file, on an HTTP server with an IP address of 192.168.0.50, in the default directory, type the following:

```
boot: install ks=http://192.168.0.50/ks.cfg
```

Basic Configuration

In the Basic Configuration screen, you can assign settings for the following components:

- **Default Language** Assigns the default language for the installation and operating system.
- **Keyboard** Sets the default keyboard; also normally associated with language.

- ■ **Mouse**   Configures the pointing device; if in doubt or if the pointing device varies, the Probe For Mouse option may work.
- ■ **Emulate 3 Buttons**   Configures the left and right mouse buttons; when pressed simultaneously, it simulates the action of the middle mouse button.
- ■ **Time Zone**   Allows configuration of the time zone of the local system.
- ■ **Use UTC Clock**   Supports computers in which the hardware clock is set to the atomic realization of UTC, which corresponds closely to Greenwich Mean Time.
- ■ **Language Support**   Adds extra languages for configuration and installation.
- ■ **Target Architecture**   Helps customize a Kickstart file for different CPU architectures.
- ■ **Reboot System After Installation**   Adds the reboot command to the end of the Kickstart file.
- ■ **Perform System Installation In Text Mode**   Supports automated installation in text mode.
- ■ **Perform Installation In Interactive Mode**   Allows you to test the steps associated with a Kickstart-based installation.

Installation Method

The Installation Method options are straightforward. The Ubuntu version only supports new installations; it does not support the Red Hat options associated with upgrades. The installation method and associated entries are based on the location of the installation files. For example, if you select an FTP installation method, the Kickstart Configurator prompts for the name or IP address of the FTP server and the shared directory with the installation files. It also supports entries for an FTP username and password, if the FTP server does not support anonymous connections.

You can set up a Kickstart file to install Ubuntu Linux from a CD/DVD; a local hard drive partition; or an HTTP, NFS, or FTP Server.

Boot Loader Options

The next section lists boot loader options. The default boot loader is GRUB, which supports encrypted passwords for an additional level of security during the boot process.

Linux boot loaders are normally installed on the MBR (master boot record). If you're dual-booting Linux and Microsoft Windows with GRUB, you *can* set up the Windows boot loader (or an alternate boot loader such as Partition Magic or System Commander) to point to GRUB on the first sector of the Linux partition with the /boot directory.

Partition Information

The Partition Information options determine how this installation configures the hard disks on the affected computers. While it supports the configuration of standard and RAID partitions, it does not currently support the configuration of LVM groups. The Clear Master Boot Record option configures Kickstart to wipe the MBR from an older hard disk; in other words, it sets up the **zerombr yes** command in the Kickstart file.

on the Job

Don't use the *zerombr yes* ***option if you want to keep an alternate bootloader on the MBR such as Partition Magic or the NT Boot Loader.***

You can remove partitions depending on whether they've been created for a Linux filesystem. If using a new hard drive, you'll want to Initialize the Disk Label as well. Click the Add command; it opens the Partition Options dialog box. As you can see in Figure 4-2, this dialog box supports detailed configuration of each partition, per the following components.

FIGURE 4-2   Using the Kickstart Configurator to set up partitions

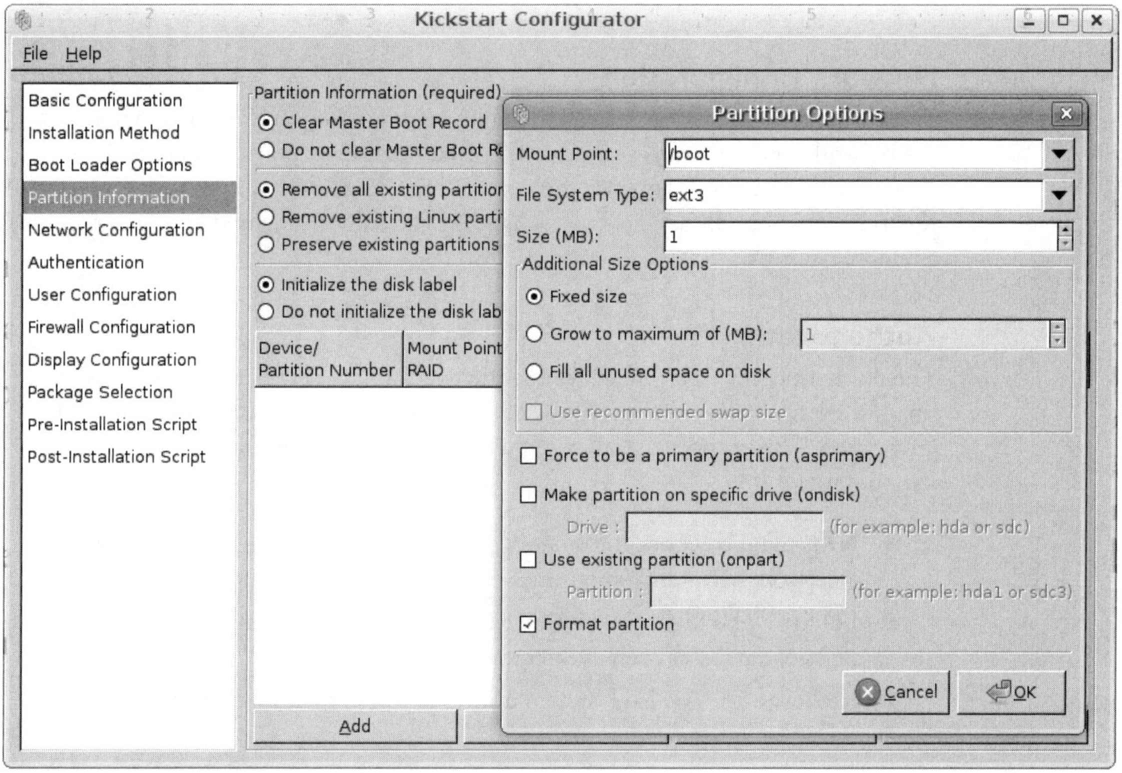

- **Mount Point** Assigns the directory where the configured partition is to be mounted.
- **File System Type** Sets the format for the configured partition.
- **Size** Configures a size for the partition.
- **Additional Size Options** Supports growable partitions to fill available free space on a hard drive. It can fill all available space; a swap partition can be configured to the recommended size, normally twice available RAM.
- **Force To Be A Primary Partition** Configures the partition as a primary partition on the hard drive.
- **Make Partition On Specific Drive** Assigns a drive device for the partition; required if there is more than one hard drive available. As of this writing, Kickstart on Ubuntu cannot be configured on more than one hard drive.
- **Use Existing Partition** Assigns a specific existing partition, based on the device filename.
- **Format Partition** Sets the configured partition to be formatted during the installation process.

Network Configuration

The Network Configuration section enables configuration of IP addressing on the network cards of a target computer. You can customize static IP addressing for a specific computer, or configure the use of a DHCP server. You can also make Kickstart look for a BOOTP server, which is a specially configured DHCP server on a remote network.

Authentication

The Authentication section lets you set up two forms of security for user passwords: Shadow Passwords, which encrypts user passwords in the /etc/shadow file, and MD5 encryption. This section also allows you to set up authentication information for various protocols:

- **NIS** The Network Information Service configures one login database for a network with Unix and Linux computers.
- **LDAP** The Lightweight Directory Assistance Protocol is used for certain types of databases such as directories.
- **Kerberos 5** The MIT system utilizes strong cryptography to authenticate users over a network.

- **Hesiod**   Associated with Kerberos 5.
- **SMB**   Samba (CIFS) allows configuration of your Linux computer on a Microsoft Windows-based network.
- **Name Switch Cache**   Associated with NIS for looking up passwords and groups.

While the options exist in the Kickstart configuration tool, the Ubuntu installer does not currently recognize the options associated with LDAP, Kerberos 5, Hesiod, or Samba authentication. Of course, this will hopefully change some time in the near future.

User Configuration

The User Configuration section supports options for the root account and an initial regular user. Ubuntu Linux disables the root account by default, and I think this is an excellent security option. But if you don't enable a root account, you'll need to configure an initial user in this screen. That user is allowed administrative root privileges by using his or her standard password.

Firewall Configuration

The Firewall Configuration section allows configuration of a default firewall for the subject computer. Generally, you'll want a firewall only for those computers that are connected to outside networks such as the Internet. This section allows the easy configuration of a firewall to permit access to trusted services on the local system, including HTTP, FTP, SSH, Telnet, and SMTP. If there are other services to be trusted, they can also be configured by TCP or UDP packet, along with the port number, as defined in the /etc/services configuration file.

Display Configuration

The Display Configuration section supports the configuration of the Linux GUI. While there is a lot of debate on the superiority of GUI-based versus text-based administrative tools, text-based tools are more stable. For this reason (and more), many Linux administrators don't even install a GUI. By default, neither a GUI nor the X Window System is installed on Ubuntu Server. However, if you're installing Linux on a series of computers, it's likely that most regular users who will want a GUI.

In this section are three tabs. Under the General tab, you can set a default color depth and resolution, indicate a default desktop (GNOME or KDE), configure the X Window System to start by default, and disable or enable the Setup Agent (the First Boot process). Under the Video Card and Monitor tabs, you can set Linux to probe the hardware or specify the hardware from a list.

Package Selection

In the Ubuntu Linux implementation of Kickstart, the Package Selection section allows you to choose whether the installation includes the Ubuntu Desktop or Kubuntu Desktop, which correspond to the GNOME and KDE desktop environments, respectively. Remember, the UCP curriculum is focused on the GNOME desktop environment.

Installation Scripts

You can add preinstallation and postinstallation scripts to the Kickstart file. Postinstallation scripts are more common, and they can help you configure other parts of a Linux operating system in a common way. For example, if you wanted to install a directory with employee benefits information, you could add a postinstallation script that adds commands such as **cp** to copy files from a network server.

The Preseed

To create a preseed file based on the current installation, you'll need commands available from the debconf-utils package. Assuming a system based on Gutsy Gibbon (7.10) or later, these instructions are based on a text-mode installation, which includes the installation-report package. If you don't have these options available, there's a compressed example-preseed.txt.gz available on the Ubuntu Linux installation CD/DVDs, in the doc/install/manual subdirectory.

While it's possible to set up a custom CD or local hard drive partition with preseed files, the simplest method in my opinion is based on a preseed file stored on a network server, such as a NFS. For detailed information on configuring NFS, see Chapter 10.

Using the Standard Preseed Configuration File

Let's start the analysis with the standard Preseed configuration file, available in the Ubuntu Linux installation CD/DVDs. Mount the drive. If you're in the GUI, the drive should be mounted automatically; otherwise, on the command line, mount the CD/DVD with the following command:

```
$ mount /dev/cdrom
```

This assumes the CD/DVD is inserted in the first available drive. (Some trial and error may be required if you have multiple CD/DVD drives.) Next, copy the example-preseed.txt.gz file to the current user's home directory.

The tilde (~) represents the home directory of the current user:

```
$ cp /media/cdrom/doc/install/manual/example-preseed.txt.gz ~
```

Navigate to your home directory and unzip the example Preseed configuration file:

```
$ cd ~
$ gunzip example-preseed.txt.gz
```

Let's analyze this file. It should now be available in your home directory in the example-preseed.txt file. The opening directives relate to localization, which encompasses language and keyboard selections. This first directive is associated with a U.S. English language installation and language configuration. Note how most directives in this file start with **d-i**, which is short for Debian Installer. The Ubuntu Installer is derived from and inherits many of the features of the Debian Installer, including various Preseed directives.

```
d-i debian-installer/locale string en_US
```

For alternative locales, see the /usr/share/i18n/locales directory. The following directives do not support automated detection (**boolean false**), and they specify a standard U.S. keyboard. If desired, you can uncomment the options associated with the 105-character keyboard, and the Dvorak option.

```
d-i console-setup/ask_detect boolean false
#d-i console-setup/modelcode string pc105
d-i console-setup/layoutcode string us
# To select a variant of the selected layout (if you leave this
# out, the
# basic form of the layout will be used):
#d-i console-setup/variantcode string dvorak
```

As for network configuration, the following directive automatically looks through active network interfaces, attempting configuration with DHCP. You can substitute a network device name such as *eth0* or *eth1* if desired.

```
d-i netcfg/choose_interface select auto
```

If you prefer a static network configuration, uncomment the following directives. Substitute the desired static network IP address, network mask, gateway, and DNS name server.

```
#d-i netcfg/disable_dhcp boolean true
#d-i netcfg/get_nameservers string 192.168.1.1
#d-i netcfg/get_ipaddress string 192.168.1.42
#d-i netcfg/get_netmask string 255.255.255.0
#d-i netcfg/get_gateway string 192.168.1.1
#d-i netcfg/confirm_static boolean true
```

Substitute desired options for host and domain names for *unassigned-hostname* and *unassigned-domain*:

```
d-i netcfg/get_hostname string unassigned-hostname
d-i netcfg/get_domain string unassigned-domain
```

Assuming you're in the United States of America, and are in range of the noted mirror site, the following settings need not change. However, if you prefer to connect to an FTP site, uncomment the first directive revise others as needed. Don't forget to substitute *ftp* for *http* in the other directives. And recognize that http.us.debian.org is not an Ubuntu mirror and needs to be changed appropriately:

```
#d-i mirror/protocol string ftp
d-i mirror/country string enter information manually
d-i mirror/http/hostname string http.us.debian.org
d-i mirror/http/directory string /ubuntu
d-i mirror/http/proxy string
```

The following directives specify the device for the hard drive to be partitioned; only one hard drive is supported through preseed. If you aren't using a SATA or SCSI drive, substitute accordingly:

```
d-i partman-auto/disk string /dev/sda
```

The standard partition configuration uses LVM; old LVM volumes are purged. (If you're comparing Kickstart and preseed, you'll note that Kickstart for Ubuntu does not currently support LVM.) Authorization to write LVM partitions is given, and the top-level root directory is configured in a single volume:

```
d-i partman-auto/method string lvm
d-i partman-auto/purge_lvm_from_device boolean true
d-i partman-lvm/confirm boolean true
d-i partman-auto/choose_recipe \
    select All files in one partition (recommended for new users)
```

on the **!** **ʘ**ob

I've added backslashes to a number of lines when I display directives in the Preseed configuration file. The backslash "escapes" the meaning of the RETURN key; in other words, Linux reads it as one line. It also helps with the formatting requirements of this series.

The following directives automatically write the changes to disk, without confirmation (as that's what's desired for an automated installation).

```
d-i partman/confirm_write_new_label boolean true
d-i partman/choose_partition \
        select Finish partitioning and write changes to disk
d-i partman/confirm boolean true
```

Time zone configuration is associated with UTC and a time zone location. If you don't want to use UTC, substitute *false* for *true*. If you're not in the Eastern time zone of the United States of America, you'll want to change the second directive to point to the appropriate file in the /usr/share/zoneinfo directory. For example, users in the Pacific time zone would substitute *US/Pacific* for *US/Eastern*:

```
d-i clock-setup/utc boolean true
d-i time/zone string US/Eastern
```

Default repositories are based on choices for localization. However, there are commented suggestions in the example-preseed.txt file that support access to additional repositories. The following may be the most troublesome part of the file, in terms of security. However, you do need to create some sort of password-protected account for each Ubuntu Linux installation. To create a regular account, uncomment appropriate directives. Substitute the desired username in the first directive for *ubuntu* and the password in clear text for *insecure*. There are options for MD5 encryption, which goes beyond the scope of the UCP curriculum.

```
#d-i passwd/username string ubuntu
#d-i passwd/user-password password insecure
#d-i passwd/user-password-again password insecure
```

Not all administrators want to associate a bootloader on the master boot record of the subject hard drive. Don't let the **only_debian** directive fool you; Ubuntu Linux is a derivative of Debian Linux. If you don't want to install GRUB to the MBR, suggested directives are in comments in this file.

```
d-i grub-installer/only_debian boolean true
d-i grub-installer/with_other_os boolean true
```

Now there's the basic functionality of the installation; the default, as suggested by the **ubuntu-desktop** directive, is a standard Ubuntu Linux desktop system. Self-explanatory options include kubuntu-desktop and xubuntu-desktop. The **lamp-server** directive configures an Ubuntu Linux server in the LAMP configuration; for Ubuntu Linux, LAMP is short for Linux, Apache, MySQL, and Perl.

For other systems, the "P" in LAMP may also stand for PHP or Python.

```
tasksel tasksel/first multiselect standard, ubuntu-desktop
```

If you want to include specialized packages, activate the following directive. The default includes the SSH server and utilities for building Debian packages from source code. Add or substitute package names as desired:

```
#d-i pkgsel/include string openssh-server build-essential
```

The following directive reboots the system. If you've configured an installation from a CD/DVD, and the BIOS menu is set to boot from that media, activate the directive that follows:

```
d-i finish-install/reboot_in_progress note
#d-i cdrom-detect/eject boolean false
```

While the Ubuntu installer often detects appropriate graphics drivers by default, there are commented options that suggest what you can do if there is a problem. And you may want to change the default mode for the monitor, as there are few where 1024×768 resolution is desired:

```
xserver-xorg xserver-xorg/config/monitor/selection-method \
      select medium
xserver-xorg xserver-xorg/config/monitor/mode-list \
      select 1024x768 @ 60 Hz
```

These are the basics of the example-preseed.txt configuration file. If you choose to work from that file, test it out. Make desired changes, and test it on a nonproduction system. Even if you choose to work from the standard file, a review of the next section, which uses configured parameters on a local system to create a custom preseed configuration file, can help guide what you do.

Creating a Preseed Configuration File

In this section, we'll customize a preseed configuration file from an Ubuntu Linux system installed in text mode. This assumes the installation added a couple of data files in the /var/log/installer/cdebconf directory. But that works only if the installation-report package is installed. And that package is not included unless you've installed Ubuntu Linux in text mode. While the system is not yet a reliable way to create a preseed configuration file, it is a useful way to learn more about automated installations in Ubuntu Linux.

You may also need to install the debconf-utils package, which will add a **debconf-get-selections** command in the /usr/bin directory. Once installed, you can create a Preseed configuration file using the following steps:

1. Run the **sudo debconf-get-selections --installer > local.seed** command. You can substitute the name of your choice for local.seed. This command takes information on installation options from the files in the /var/log/installer/ cdebconf directory.

2. Run the **sudo debconf-get-selections >> local.seed** command. This completes the configuration.

You'll also need a system based on an installation in the local system. But such options may lead to errors; when I ran these steps on my system, it included directives such as

```
d-i country-chooser/shortlist-zh_TW select TW
```

This suggests an installation associated with a system in Taiwan, which does not apply to me in the United States of America. However, the following could help me if I were configuring Ubuntu Linux on identical systems with widescreen monitors (or laptops):

```
d-i xserver-xorg xserver-xorg/config/display/modes \
    multiselect 1280x768
```

CERTIFICATION OBJECTIVE 4.02

Configure Servers for the Diskless Client

Linux is a multiuser, multitasking system. The latest PCs and networks can handle the processing requirements for several GUI terminals simultaneously. With a diskless client, you can configure terminals with old hardware. Diskless clients on a network all run programs from the same system. Diskless clients can be a convenience for the administrator, and a big cost saving for the organization.

But as diskless clients are not "dumb terminals," they do require a bit of infrastructure. While local graphics hardware (video card, appropriate monitor) is required to display a GUI, a local hard drive isn't even required. This works on a modern system assuming the network card and BIOS on the terminal are enabled with the Pre-boot eXecution Environment (PXE). DHCP services provide unique network addresses to each client. Trivial File Transfer Protocol (TFTP) servers share the files required to boot the diskless client over a network. Key files and directories such as user home directories can be shared efficiently from an NFS server. But be aware, as TFTP servers are inherently insecure, communication from outside networks to TCP/IP port 69 should be blocked.

One Ubuntu Linux implementation of diskless clients is based on the work of the Linux Terminal Server Project (LTSP). In fact, the command that installs the appropriate LTSP server package (ltsp-server-standalone) also installs the dhcp3-server package by default:

```
$ sudo apt-get install ltsp-server-standalone
```

Dynamic Host Configuration Protocol (DHCP) Services

A DHCP server automates the network configuration process for clients. In detail, DHCP allows a Linux computer to serve dynamic IP addresses. It supports the configuration of a range of IP addresses. It allows you to reserve a specific IP address, based on the hardware address associated with a client's network card. It can assign more information, such as the gateway and DNS IP address to every system that requests an IP address.

DHCP servers can simplify and centralize network administration if you're administering more than a few computers on a network. They are especially convenient for networks with a significant number of mobile users. Three DHCP-related files are cited in the UCP curriculum: /etc/init.d/dhcp3-server, /etc/dhcpc/config, and /usr/sbin/dhcpd. In the latest versions of Ubuntu, /etc/default/dhcpcd has replaced /etc/dhcpc/config. These files require the installation of the dhcp3-server, dhcpcd, and dhcp packages. Both dhcp3-server and dhcp are DHCP server packages, and generally won't be run simultaneously on the same system.

Just be aware that many users already have a configured DHCP service. Even home users may already have a DHCP server on the router that connects their home networks to the Internet. Multiple DHCP servers on a single network can lead to trouble. So it's best to deactivate other DHCP servers before testing the DHCP servers described here.

If you're configuring DHCP support for a remote network, you'll also want the bootp package, which configures appropriate BOOTP protocol configuration files. That protocol relays DHCP information to and from clients on remote networks.

The configuration files associated with both the dhcp3-server and dhcp packages use many of the same directives, so read both of the following subsections. While either package can be used to configure a DHCP server, the Ubuntu installation guide recommends using the dhcp3-server package for diskless clients.

The DHCP3 Server

First, review the configuration of the DHCP3 server. The default version of the configuration file, /etc/dhcp3/dhcpd.conf, does not configure any IP addresses. So if you try to activate the DHCP3 server without modifying the configuration file, the DHCP server won't assign any IP addresses. This section reviews default configuration directives, along with the directives you need to add to set up a DHCP3 server on a standard private IP version 4 network.

In the /etc/dhcp3/dhcpd.conf configuration file, Dynamic DNS updates are not enabled based on the following directive:

```
ddns-update-style none;
```

In the following directives, you should substitute the domain name for the local private network for example.org. You should also substitute the fully qualified domain name (FQDN) or, preferably, the IP address of the DNS servers for ns1.example.org and ns2.example.org:

```
option domain-name "example.org";
option domain-name-servers ns1.example.org, ns2.example.org;
```

IP addresses are leased for a certain number of seconds, before they have to be renewed. The lease time is as defined by the following directives: the **default-lease-time** is the standard, and the **max-lease-time** is the maximum before a renewal is required:

```
default-lease-time 600;
max-lease-time 7200;
```

By default, logging from this service is sent to the local system. Depending on the severity of the log, this directive means that DHCP server log messages are available in /var/log/debug and /var/log/messages, as defined in the /etc/syslog.conf configuration file.

```
log-facility local7;
```

Of course, you need to configure a system for some local network. The following stanza configures the DHCP server on the 192.168.0.0/255.255.255.0 network. It assigns IP addresses between 192.168.0.200 and 192.168.0.220, and specifies a gateway address of 192.168.0.1.

```
subnet 192.168.0.0 netmask 255.255.255.0 {
 range 192.168.0.200 192.168.0.220;
 option routers 192.168.0.1;
}
```

There are a number of other suggested options in comments. They provide hints for configuring the DHCP server for remote networks and reserved IP addresses, as well as allowing or denying DHCP access to a group of systems.

Once the configuration is complete, turn off any other DHCP services, and start this one with the following command:

```
$ sudo /etc/init.d/dhcp3-server start
```

Success or failure is logged in files such as /var/log/messages. Test this server from a remote client, with a command such as

```
$ sudo dhclient eth0
```

Then review the logs to see what happened, and then deactivate this DHCP server with the following command:

```
$ sudo /etc/init.d/dhcp3-server stop
```

If you deactivated other DHCP servers in this section, it's now okay to reactivate those servers.

The Regular DHCP Server

Now review the configuration of the regular DHCP server. The default configuration file, which is /etc/dhcpd.conf, does not configure any IP addresses by default. So if you try to activate the regular DHCP server without modifying the configuration file, the attempt will fail. This section reviews default configuration directives, along with the directives you need to add to set up a DHCP3 server on a standard private IP version 4 (IPv4) network.

Many of the directives are the same as that used in /etc/dhcp3/dhcpd.conf, so refer to the previous section for more information. One directive seen only in the /etc/dhcpd.conf file is the following, which sets the subnet mask for assigned DHCP addresses from this server. Generally, you'll want a bigger subnet mask, such as 255.255.255.0, for a bigger selection of IP addresses.

```
option subnet-mask 255.255.255.254;
```

The other basic options in this file use the same directives as /etc/dhcp3/dhcpd.conf. To test this DHCP server, take steps similar to those taken for the aforementioned DHCP3 server; the only "major" difference is the filename of the service script, /etc/init.d/dhcp.

Trivial File Transfer Protocol

There are several TFTP services available for Ubuntu Linux. The focus of this section is based on the tftpd-hpa package. It should be automatically configured. One message that you should see when installing the ltsp-server package at the beginning of the section relates to directives added to the /etc/inetd.conf configuration file. If you have a firewall on the local system, pay attention to the associated port number(s) listed in this file. Just remember, to test the TFTP service, you also need the tftp client package.

The simplest way to configure the TFTP service is through the /etc/default/tftpd-hpa configuration file. I use the following directives in my version of this file:

```
RUN_DAEMON="yes"
OPTIONS="-l -s /var/lib/tftpboot"
```

The directives are simple; the first is almost self-explanatory as it runs the /usr/sbin/in.tftpd daemon. The second feeds command-line options to the daemon. As can be verified with the in.tftpd man page, these options run the server in stand-alone mode, using the /var/lib/tftpboot directory as the root directory for clients. The information from this file is fed to the associated start script, /etc/init.d/tftpd-hpa.

Configuring a Network Installation

Much of this chapter is associated with the configuration of a diskless client. But configuring a network installation requires many of the same steps. The only difference is based on the files associated with the TFTP server. If you've downloaded an ISO file associated with an Ubuntu installation CD or DVD, all you need to do is mount that file on the TFTP directory. For example, the following command mounts the DVD on the appropriate TFTP directory:

```
$ sudo mount -o loop ubuntu-7.10-dvd-i386.iso /var/lib/tftpboot/ubuntu
```

Create the noted mount directory if needed. Make sure the TFTP and DHCP3 servers described earlier are active. Boot the system where you want to install Linux over a network using the PXE environment described shortly, and it will boot the installation CD/DVD over the network.

If you don't want to install Ubuntu Linux over a network, ignore this section. But remember, network installation is part of the UCP curriculum and therefore is fair game for the exam.

NFS Sharing

Thin clients prior to Ubuntu Gutsy Gibbon rely on remote access with an NFS server. While there are alternatives, the standard is the NFS kernel server. That and associated packages can be installed with the following command, which also installs other packages as required, such as portmap and nfs-common:

```
$ sudo apt-get install nfs-kernel-server
```

While the LTSP software automatically creates an NFS share, you do need to know how to share directories using NFS. And that information is available in Chapter 10.

PXE Booting

Modern diskless clients require some sort of network boot card. Many modern systems configure access to the PXE environment through the boot menu. As there are a wide variety of options for the boot menu, we do not describe them here. If available, the option should be listed in your computer's hardware documentation. If the PXE environment is selected, it should show messages such as

```
Network boot from some network card

CLIENT MAC ADDR: 00 0C 39 40 4E EA
GUID: 564DFD09-31C9-77F0-ED6C-CE86DA304EEA
DHCP:
```

If the LTSP client is properly configured on the server, the client PXE environment should automatically detect the DHCP server, along with the client files as configured. However, this may not work before related commands are run to create a diskless client template, as described in the next section.

If PXE booting is not available on the desired client's network card or BIOS, it's possible to create a boot CD or floppy that simulates the PXE boot process. For more information, see www.rom-o-matic.net.

Create the Diskless Client

Ubuntu Linux relies on the work of the LTSP (www.ltsp.org) for diskless clients. The previous section described the component servers, DHCP, TFTP, and NFS. Ubuntu relies on the advantages of the Initial RAM disk filesystem, also known as initramfs, to simplify the loading of LTSP for diskless clients. But to set up an actual diskless client, you need the commands associated with the ltsp-server and ltsp-server-standalone packages. You can then create the files for the terminal server, and configure a special DHCP server to support access from remote PXE clients.

Take care to avoid blockage by firewalls. One option for firewalls is created with the **iptables** command; to review a currently configured **iptables**-based firewall, run the **iptables -L** command. A second option works with TCP-based services, known as TCP wrappers; it's configured through the /etc/hosts.allow and /etc/hosts.deny configuration files, as listed in the UCP curriculum.

e x a m

ⓦatch *Understand the importance of the Initial RAM Disk filesystem, also known as initramfs, in the boot process.*

Security by tcp_wrappers

When a system receives a network request for a service, it passes the request on to tcp_wrappers. This system logs the request and then checks its access rules. If there are no limits on the particular host or IP address, tcp_wrappers passes control back to the service.

The tcp_wrappers system only controls those services which use TCP network packets as defined in /etc/services. When I review this file, I note that TCP packets only affect NFS communication, in this case on port 2049. But that's sufficient to regulate access to diskless clients.

```
nfs     2049/tcp
```

The key files are /etc/hosts.allow and /etc/hosts.deny. The philosophy is fairly straightforward: users and clients listed in hosts.allow are allowed access; users and clients listed in hosts.deny are denied access. As users and/or clients may be listed in either files, the tcp_wrappers system takes the following steps:

1. It searches /etc/hosts.allow. If tcp_wrappers finds a match, it grants access. No additional searches are required.

2. It searches /etc/hosts.deny. If tcp_wrappers finds a match, it denies access.

3. If the host isn't found in either file, access is automatically granted to the client.

You can use the same access control language in both /etc/hosts.allow and /etc/hosts.deny to tell tcp_wrappers which clients to allow or deny. The basic format for commands in each file is as follows:

```
daemon_list : client_list
```

The simplest version of this format is

```
ALL : ALL
```

This specifies all services and makes the rule applicable to all hosts on all IP addresses. If you set this line in /etc/hosts.deny, access is prohibited to all services. However, you can create finer filters. For example, the following line in /etc/hosts.allow allows the client with an IP address of 192.168.1.5 access to NFS:

```
nfs : 192.168.1.5
```

The same line in /etc/hosts.deny would prevent the computer with that IP address from using NFS to connect to your system. You can specify clients a number of different ways, as shown in Table 4-1.

TABLE 4-1	Client	Description
Sample Commands in /etc/hosts.allow and /etc/hosts.deny	.example.com	Domain name. Since this domain name begins with a dot, it specifies all clients on the example.com domain.
	172.16.	IP address. Since this address ends with a dot, it specifies all clients with an IP address of 172.16.x.y.
	172.16.72.0/255.255.254.0	IP network address with subnet mask. CIDR notation not recognized.
	ALL	Any client, any daemon.
	user@linux1.example.com	Applies to the specific user on the given computer.

As you can see in Table 4-1, there are two different types of wildcards. **ALL** can be used to represent any client or service, and the dot (**.**) specifies all hosts with the specified domain name or IP network address.

You can set up multiple services and addresses with commas. Exceptions are easy to make with the EXCEPT operator. Review the following sample excerpt from a /etc/hosts.allow file:

```
#hosts.allow
ALL : .example.com
telnetd : 192.168.25.0/255.255.255.0 EXCEPT 192.168.25.73
sshd, nfs : 192.168.1.10
```

The first line in this file is simply a comment. The next line opens **ALL** services to all computers in the example.com domain. The following line opens the Telnet service to any computer on the 192.168.25.0 network, except the one with an IP address of 192.168.25.73. Then the SSH and NFS services are opened to the computer with an IP address of 192.168.1.10.

The code that follows contains a hosts.deny file to see how lists can be built to control access:

```
#hosts.deny
ALL EXCEPT nfs : .example.org
telnetd : ALL EXCEPT 192.168.1.10
ALL:ALL
```

The first line in the hosts.deny file is a comment. The second line denies all services except NFS to computers in the example.org domain. The third line states that the only computer allowed to access our Telnet server has an IP address of 192.168.1.10. Finally, the last line is a blanket denial; all other computers are denied access to all services controlled by tcp_wrappers.

You can also use the **twist** or **spawn** command in /etc/hosts.allow or /etc/hosts. deny to access shell commands; they're primarily intended to send messages, track access, and log problems. For example, take the following line in a /etc/hosts.deny file:

```
telnetd : .crack.org : twist /bin/echo Sorry %c, access denied
```

This sends a customized error message for Telnet users on the crack.org domain. Different operators such as %c are described in Table 4-2. Some of these operators may be able to help you track the intruder.

TABLE 4-2	Field	Description	Field	Description
tcp_wrappers Operators	%a	Client address	%h	Client hostname
	%A	Host address	%H	Server hostname
	%c	Client information	%p	Process ID
	%d	Process name	%s	Server information

The Linux Terminal Server Project (LTSP)

Assuming you've run the command described earlier to install the LTSP server, run the following command:

```
$ sudo ltsp-build-client
```

If you're building clients for different architectures, the **--arch** switch can help. For example, when I built i386 LTSP clients on my AMD 64-bit desktop system, I ran the following command:

```
$ sudo ltsp-build-client --arch i386
```

This command takes a few minutes or more (depending on hardware capabilities) to build a client system, based on the configuration in the /etc/ltsp/ltsp-build-client. conf configuration file. If this file does not exist, the default is to create a client system in the /opt/ltsp/*arch* directory, where *arch* represents the architecture in work. If you want to create the client in the /var/lib/tftpboot directory, you'll need to add the **--base /var/lib/tftpboot** option:

```
$ sudo ltsp-build-client --base /var/lib/tftpboot --arch i386
```

Unless you've configured a local repository, as described in Chapter 6, this relies on network connections to repositories configured in /etc/apt/sources.list. As with all network downloads, any problems could mean that key files for the LTSP server client are not downloaded.

on the
()ob

Starting with Ubuntu Gutsy Gibbon, after the first reboot of each terminal server, you may need to run the ltsp-update-image and ltsp-update-sshkeys commands.

Configuring Services for LTSP

Pointing PXE clients to the proper LTSP files depends on whether you already have an existing DHCP server for the local network. If you do, you'll need to add the following to the DHCP server configuration file. Don't forget to substitute the actual IP address of the LTSP DHCP server for *ipaddress*:

```
next-server ipaddress;
```

Now for the DHCP server on the LTSP system, open up the DHCP configuration file, /etc/ltsp/dhcpd.conf. While this file is part of the ltsp-server-standalone package, strictly speaking, it's beyond the scope of the UCP exam.

First, the default version of the configuration file is authoritative, as suggested by the directive of the same name. The following directives are associated with a specific subnet; if you want to configure a different subnet, substitute appropriately:

```
subnet 192.168.0.0 netmask 255.255.255.0 {
    range 192.168.0.20 192.168.0.250;
```

On my own home local network, I use the same subnet, so I limit the **range** of available network addresses to those not assigned to other local systems. The **broadcast-address** directive, as suggested by its name, assigns a broadcast address. If you configure a different network address, remember to substitute an appropriate broadcast address for that network.

```
option broadcast-address 192.168.0.255
```

The directives that follow actually point the PXE network boot systems to the appropriate files and directories. The default is associated with the **--base** directory configured with the **ltsp-build-client** command.

```
        option root-path "/opt/ltsp/i386";
```

But for the client configuration described earlier, you'd need to change the path to

```
        option root-path "/var/lib/tftpboot/ltsp/i386";
```

The following directive receives the string sent by a PXE client system, *PXEClient*. It also connects the PXE client to an initial image (nbi.img).

```
if substring( option vendor-class-identifier, 0, 9 ) = "PXEClient" {
    filename "/ltsp/i386/pxelinux.0";
} else {
    filename "/ltsp/i386/nbi.img";
}
}
```

Other directives in the default version of the /etc/ltsp/dhcpd.conf configuration file are shown earlier in this chapter in the "Configure Servers for the Diskless Client" section. Don't forget to activate this service with the following command:

```
$ sudo /etc/init.d/dhcp3-server start
```

To confirm that it's reading the correct configuration file, I run the **ps aux | grep dhcp** command, which lists the following command line in the output:

```
/usr/sbin/dhcpd3 -q -pf /var/run/dhcp3-server/dhcpd.pid -cf \
/etc/ltsp/dhcpd.conf
```

on the **job**

To configure Internet access for LTSP clients, see https://wiki.ubuntu.com/ ThinClientHowtoNAT.

Booting the LTSP Client

Use the PXE boot techniques described earlier, the client network card should boot the LTSP system automatically, assuming the DHCP and TFTP servers are running, and are not blocked by any sort of firewall. When successful, you'll see a screen similar to that shown in Figure 4-3.

FIGURE 4-3

An LTSP client

If there are problems booting the LTSP client, open the default file in the /var/lib/tftpboot/ltsp/i386/boot directory. Delete the **quiet** and **splash** directives. The next time you boot the LTSP client, you'll see log messages associated with the boot process. In other words, it can help you identify where the LTSP client encounters a problem.

One common solution is to rebuild the client on the LTSP server, using the **ltsp-build-client** command described earlier in the section "The Linux Terminal Server Project (LTSP)." While this is an inelegant solution, user reports suggest that it works for many users.

CERTIFICATION SUMMARY

This chapter examines fundamental skills associated with configuring automated installations as well as creating a diskless client. Both skills require the configuration of the same network services.

Automated installations of Ubuntu Linux require the configuration of a file to answer the questions from the Ubuntu installer. There are two basic systems available to create an automated installation file. Ubuntu uses the Preseed system associated with Debian distributions. Ubuntu has also adapted the Kickstart system commonly associated with Red Hat distributions, including the GUI Kickstart Configurator. Ubuntu's modifications to both systems have been incorporated under the Kickseed project. Automated installations can be started from the installation CD/DVD, with reference to the installation file from the desired source.

Diskless clients require the configuration of the same services, including DHCP, NFS, and TFTP. The Ubuntu implementation of diskless clients is related to the work of the Linux Terminal Server Project. Diskless clients and automated network installations both require an available PXE boot environment on the client.

✓ TWO-MINUTE DRILL

Here are some of the key points from the certification objectives in Chapter 4.

Review Automated Installation Files

❏ Kickstart installation files can be created with the GUI Kickstart Configurator.

❏ Preseed files can be more versatile; for example, preseed can automate the installation of LVM partitions.

❏ Kickstart and preseed configuration files can be saved on removable (floppy, USB) or network media to help automate the installation of Ubuntu Linux on multiple systems.

❏ Ubuntu is consolidating the advantages of Kickstart and Preseed in the Kickseed project.

Configure Services for the Diskless Client

❏ DHCP services support automatic configuration of IP address information and more for the clients on a network.

❏ TFTP services allow configuration of diskless clients.

❏ NFS services support sharing of key directories and entire client systems.

❏ PXE services are required for booting diskless clients and automated installations.

Create the Diskless Client

❏ Ubuntu Linux configures diskless clients with an implementation of the Linux Terminal Server Project.

❏ Diskless client files can be bootstrapped on an LTSP server with the **ltsp-build-client** command.

❏ Security can be regulated with tcp_wrappers, using the /etc/hosts.allow and /etc/hosts.deny configuration files.

❏ Access to LTSP diskless clients can be configured through a custom DHCP server in the /etc/ltsp/dhcpd.conf configuration file.

SELF TEST

The following questions will help you measure your understanding of the material presented in this chapter. Read all the questions carefully, as there may be more than one correct answer. Some questions are "fill in the blank" and normally require an exact answer. Choose all correct answers for each question.

Review Automated Installation Files

1. Which of the following packages includes a tool that can help configure Kickstart files?
   A. kickstart-configurator
   B. system-config-kickstart
   C. ksconfig
   D. kickseed-configurator

2. What is the filename extension associated with a Kickstart configuration file?
   A. .config
   B. .seed
   C. .cfg
   D. .kick

3. What directive is most commonly shown at the start of a Preseed configuration command line?

   _____

4. What can you tell about a Kickstart installation from the following directive?

   ```
   install ks=http://192.168.0.50/ks.cfg
   ```

   A. The installation files are located on the boot CD.
   B. The installation files are located on an HTTP server.
   C. The installation files are located as specified in the Kickstart configuration file.
   D. The installation files are located on the boot floppy.

5. What can you tell about a Preseed installation from the following directive?

   ```
   d-i netcfg/choose_interface select auto
   ```

   A. Network cards are automatically configured.
   B. Ubuntu Linux prompts for network interface information after installation is complete.
   C. Network interface information is statically configured with other directives.
   D. Network interface information is dynamically configured from a DHCP server.

Configure Servers for the Diskless Client

6. What does the following directive mean in a DHCP server configuration file?

```
option routers 192.168.0.1;
```

- A. It depends on the type of DHCP server that was installed.
- B. It specifies a gateway IP address.
- C. It specifies a DNS server address.
- D. It specifies a router for a remote network served by this DHCP server.

7. What does the following directive mean in a DHCP server configuration file?

```
option root-path "/some/root/directory";
```

- A. The directory with the LTSP client files is /some/root/directory.
- B. The directory with the Kickstart configuration files is /some/root/directory.
- C. The directory with other shared files is /some/root/directory.
- D. The directory with root user configuration files is /some/root/directory.

8. Which of the following command options for the in.tftpd daemon specifies the /var/lib/tftpboot directory as the main TFTP server directory?

- A. -s /var/lib/tftpboot
- B. -d /var/lib/tftpboot
- C. -t /var/lib/tftpboot
- D. -f /var/lib/tftpboot

9. Which of the following files contain DHCP client configuration information?

- A. /etc/default/dhcpd
- B. /etc/default/dhcpcd
- C. /etc/default/bootp
- D. /etc/default/resolv.conf

10. Which of the following packages is associated with a shared NFS server?

- A. nfs-server
- B. nfs-kernel-server
- C. nfs-common-server
- D. nfsd

11. If there is no PXE option in the local computer's boot menu, which of the following options can help enable a diskless client?

    A. Update the BIOS menu

    B. Create a boot CD

    C. Install a different network card

    D. Boot through www.rom-o-matic.com

Create the Diskless Client

12. Name the full path to the file to be configured for an LTSP-based DHCP server. The filename is not required.

_____

13. Name the full path to the default LTSP client, as configured by the **ltsp-build-client** command. The architecture is not required.

_____

14. What switch would you include with the **ltsp-build-client** command to specify a different directory?

_____

15. What kind of hardware is required on the diskless client? (Two answers are correct.)

    A. A hard drive

    B. A CD-ROM

    C. A PXE-capable BIOS

    D. A network card

LAB QUESTIONS

These two labs are designed to help you configure key Ubuntu Linux services.

Lab 1

In this lab, you'll configure a regular DHCP server, based on the dhcp3-server package. In this lab and chapter, we assume the use of IP version 4 addresses.

   1. Make sure to disable any current DHCP server on the local network.

   2. Install the dhcp3-server package. Assuming an active network connection, one method uses the following command:

```
$ sudo apt-get install dhcp3-server
```

3. Open the appropriate configuration file, /etc/dhcp3/dhcpd.conf.

4. Configure the file for a **subnet**, **netmask**, and a range appropriate for your local network. These terms are all directives in the dhcpd.conf configuration file, which can help you identify the IP addresses to be changed.

5. Save the changes. Start the DHCP server with the **/etc/init.d/dhcp3-server start** command.

6. Go to another client on the same network and try accessing the DHCP server with an appropriate client. For example, on Ubuntu Linux systems, the **dhclient eth0** command should work. If the network card connected to the DHCP server has a device name other than *eth0*, substitute accordingly.

7. Test the result. If a client has a new IP address, it should show up in the output to the **ifconfig eth0** command. That IP address should be within the **range** of IP addresses as described in step 4.

8. Unless you want to enable this DHCP server permanently, go to that system and deactivate it with the **/etc/init.d/dhcp3-server stop** command.

9. Reactivate any standard DHCP services on the local network.

Lab 2

In this lab, you'll create and analyze LTSP client files in the default location. Depending on the system, you may need as much as 1GB (or perhaps more) of free space. This assumes that standard LTSP packages have already been installed, including ltsp-client, ltsp-client-core, ltsp-server, and ltsp-server-standalone.

1. Run the following command; I specify the i386 architecture, assuming a server configured on a different architecture:

```
$ sudo ltsp-build-client --arch i386 > ltspmessages
```

2. Watch as the installation progresses. Unless you've configured a local repository, the command retrieves and validates packages. Since step 1 saves the messages to the ltspmessages file, you can review the additions to this file (in a different console) with the following command:

```
$ tail -f ltspmessages
```

3. When you're done reviewing these messages, press CTRL-C.

4. As the installation progresses, you may observe as package information is added to the debpaths file in the /opt/ltsp/i386/debootstrap directory. You may also notice the actual packages as they're loaded and stored in the /opt/ltsp/i386/var/cache/apt/archives directory.

5. The installation takes some time, especially if you're using remote Internet repositories. This may be a good chance for a break.

6. When you get a chance, look at the original console. Even though messages are sent to the ltspmessages file, errors are still displayed in the original console.

7. Once the installation is complete, take another look at the ltspmessages file. Review the variety of packages installed, as well as the repositories cited. Does the file look familiar?

8. If you have a variety of errors, and want to collect them in a file, repeat the process with the following command:

```
$ sudo ltsp-build-client --arch i386 2> ltsperrors
```

SELF TEST ANSWERS

Review Automated Installation Files

1. ☑ **B.** system-config-kickstart includes a GUI tool that can help configure a Kickstart installation file.
   ☒ Answers **A** and **D** are packages that do not currently exist. Any resemblance to existing packages is purely accidental. While the ksconfig package does not exist, it is a command that is incidentally linked to the system-config-kickstart command. Still, answer **C** is also incorrect.

2. ☑ **C.** The standard extension associated with a Kickstart configuration file is .cfg.
   ☒ The .config and .kick extensions are not used for Ubuntu automated installation systems. While the .seed extension is used for Preseed automated installation files, that is different from Kickstart, so answers **A, B,** and **D** are all wrong.

3. The **d-i** directive, short for Debian Installer, is the most common directive in front of configuration lines in Preseed installation files.

4. ☑ **C.** The directive gives no direct hint on the location of the installation files. It's listed in a directive in the Kickstart configuration file, in this case, ks.cfg. The fact that it's located on an HTTP server is not relevant.
   ☒ As the directive gives no hint on the location of the installation files, answers **A, B,** and **D** are all incorrect.

5. ☑ **D.** The key directives in this command are netcfg and auto, which automatically configure the network connection; the standard for automatic configuration uses a DHCP server.
   ☒ Detection and configuration of network cards are closely related, but **D** is a better answer. Ubuntu Linux does not normally prompt for network interface information after installation is complete. And the auto directive is not compatible with static configuration. Therefore, answers **A, B,** and **C** are all incorrect.

   ```
   option routers 192.168.0.1;
   ```

Configure Servers for the Diskless Client

6. ☑ **B.** The **routers** directive specifies the gateway IP address.
   ☒ As the **routers** directive is not related to the type of DHCP server, and does not necessarily specify a remote network specified by this DHCP server, answers **A** and **D** are both wrong. As a DNS server address is associated with the **domain-name-servers** directive, answer **C** is also wrong.

7. ☑ **A.** The root-path directive specifies the directory with the LTSP client files.

   ☒ The directive for specifying Kickstart configuration files in a DHCP server configuration file has not been described in this chapter. There is no DHCP server directive that specifies the location of shared files or root user configuration files. Therefore, answers **B**, **C**, and **D** are all wrong.

8. ☑ **A.** The **-s** switch specifies the root directory associated with the TFTP daemon, in.tftpd.

   ☒ As there is no **-d** or **-f** option for **in.tftpd**, answers **B** and **D** are both incorrect. As the **-t** option is related to timeouts, answer **C** is also wrong.

9. ☑ **B.** Client configuration for DHCP is often associated with the dhcpcd file, and that is also true here.

   ☒ As the /etc/default/dhcpd file is associated with DHCP servers, answer **A** is wrong. As neither /etc/default/bootp or /etc/default/resolv.conf, if they even exist on an Ubuntu system, aren't directly related to a client, answers **C** and **D** are both incorrect.

10. ☑ **B.** The nfs-kernel-server package is associated with a standard NFS server.

    ☒ As there are no nfs-server, nfs-common-server, or nfsd packages, answers **A, C,** and **D** are incorrect.

11. ☑ **B.** Boot CDs are available from www.rom-o-matic.com that can simulate a PXE boot process from a network card.

    ☒ As it's unlikely (though possible) that a manufacturer has a BIOS update for PXE booting, answer **A** is incorrect. While it's possible to install a PXE-capable network card, it doesn't necessarily support PXE booting when starting a system, so answer **C** is wrong. While www.rom-o-matic.com is the source for PXE boot media, you can't boot a system from that web site, so answer **D** is also incorrect.

Create the Diskless Client

12. ☑ **/etc/ltsp** The dhcpd.conf configuration file for LTSP is included in the /etc/ltsp directory, courtesy of the ltsp-server-standalone package.

13. ☑ **/opt/ltsp** The default location for LTSP clients is /opt/ltsp. It's not used in this chapter, as it doesn't conform to the standard for the TFTP server.

14. ☑ **--base.** A different directory can be specified with the **ltsp-build-client** command, using the **--base** switch.

15. ☑ **C and D.** A PXE-capable BIOS and of course, a network card, are required for an LTSP-capable client.

    ☒ As no CD or hard drive is required, answers **A** and **B** are both incorrect.

LAB ANSWERS

These labs should help you improve your skills. It's not necessary to actually create a DHCP server during the exam. And the actual creation of an LTSP server or client is beyond the scope of the exam. However, the skills learned in these labs can help you as an Ubuntu administrator.

Lab 1

The intent of this lab is to practice the configuration of a DHCP server on Ubuntu Linux. It can be run on a system where Ubuntu Linux has been installed as a server or client.

Lab 2

The intent of this lab is to see what can happen when creating an LTSP client. The actual booting of an LTSP client depends on matching what you create here (or elsewhere in the chapter) with the settings in the /etc/ltsp/dhcpd.conf configuration file. Once the dhcp3-server and tftpd-hpa scripts in the /etc/init.d directory are active, you'll be able to test access with a PXE-capable client.

5

Basic Commands
and Filesystems

T he UCP exams assume that candidates have at least a couple of years of experience with Linux. At that level, candidates should know at least the fundamentals of the command-line. However, these are basic skills that serve as building blocks for more advanced topics. Home users, especially those who learned Linux from the GUI, may not be aware of all the commands and configuration files described in this chapter.

A related skill is knowing how to set up the shell. Once the shell is configured, commands become powerful. They can be even more powerful when combined. In addition, Ubuntu administrators need to know how to configure user startup scripts. Be aware that Ubuntu developers appear to be working toward converting from the long-time Linux standard bash shell to the lighter-weight Debian-based dash shell. But as the default is still the bash shell, the focus of the exam and therefore of this chapter is on bash.

Of course, any Linux administrator needs to know what happens at the command line. Despite the variety of Linux distributions, they share the vast majority of regular commands at the command line. These skills include directory navigation and file management/manipulation.

In addition, the Filesystem Hierarchy Standard (FHS) is standardizing the location of many key configuration files. In many cases, if you know where a configuration file, script, or set of defaults is located in one distribution, you already know where it's located in another distribution.

on the
()ob

If you've read my RHCE Red Hat Certified Engineer Study Guide, **you'll recognize a good part of this chapter from that book. In many ways, Linux is Linux, and what you learn on one distribution can apply to running and administering others.**

CERTIFICATION OBJECTIVE 5.01

Customize the Shell

As of this writing, Ubuntu developers still configure users to the traditional bash shell. But they are currently working on the lighter-weight dash shell. In fact, they implemented dash as the default shell for Edgy Eft (6.10), but went back in part to the bash shell for Feisty Fawn (7.04). As dash has fewer features, the dash shell has

INSIDE THE EXAM

Work with the Linux Command Line

While there are a lot of detailed commands in the UCP curriculum, the summary curriculum states: "Work with the Linux command line." Many of you may already know the command line. If so, consider this chapter to be a review, and skim it for the information that you need. Commands listed in the detailed UCP curriculum are covered in several other chapters.

But for the first time, many users are actually learning about Linux starting with the GUI. In that case, the fundamentals described in this chapter are important, perhaps even critical, toward building the skills required to become a competent Ubuntu Linux systems or network administrator.

broken some existing bash shell scripts. In this section, we test configuration files and commands primarily with the bash shell. All system-wide shell configuration files are kept in the /etc directory; a couple of examples include the bash.bashrc, bash_completion, profile, and the scripts in the /etc/bash_completion.d directory.

These files and scripts are supplemented and may be overridden by hidden files in each user's home directory. We'll look at these files in a moment.

Yes, the **useradd** command does configure the dash shell for new users on current distributions. However, the **users-admin** utility, which is specifically cited in the UCP curriculum, configures the bash shell for new users. That is why I focus on the bash shell.

on the !
①o b

Linux is filled with iterative acronyms. For example, bash is short for the Bourne-again shell. But bash itself is a shell. So one might believe that the full name for the default Linux shell is the Bourne again shell shell. The tradition continues with the dash shell, as dash is short for the Debian Almquist shell.

Configure the bash Shell

All system-wide shell configuration files are kept in the /etc directory. These files are bash.bashrc and profile; the bash_completion file promotes command completion and more. These files and scripts are supplemented and may be overridden by hidden files in each user's home directory. Let's take a look at these files.

on the **job**

Until the Gutsy Gibbon (7.10) release, terminal consoles were configured through the SystemVinit /etc/inittab configuration file. As SystemVinit has been replaced by Upstart, /etc/inittab no longer is used. Terminal consoles are now configured in the /etc/event.d/ directory, in ttyx files, where x is between 1 and 6.

/etc/bash.bashrc

The /etc/bash.bashrc file is used for aliases and functions, on a system-wide basis. Open this file in the text editor of your choice. Read each line in this file. Even if you don't understand the programming commands, you can see that this file sets bash shell parameters for each user. For example:

- It assigns a prompt, which is what you see just before the cursor at the command prompt.
- It includes settings from /etc/bash_completion to enable command completion.
- It configures messages associated with **sudo** access; for more information, see Chapter 8.

The settings here are called by the .bashrc file in each user's home directory. The default Ubuntu version of this file adds information on aliases. The settings are supplemented by the .bash_history and .bash_logout files in each user's home directory.

/etc/profile

The /etc/profile file is used for system-wide environment and startup files. The following is the profile script from my copy of Ubuntu Linux. It's a straightforward file, setting what's shown at the bash command prompt, for regular and the root user, as well as a default value for umask. Note how it calls the /etc/bash.bashrc file for other parameters.

```
# /etc/profile: system-wide .profile file for the Bourne shell
(sh(1))
# and Bourne compatible shells (bash(1), ksh(1), ash(1), ...).
if [ "$PS1" ]; then
  if [ "$BASH" ]; then
    PS1='\u@\h:\w\$ '
    if [ -f /etc/bash.bashrc ]; then
        . /etc/bash.bashrc
    fi
```

```
    else
      if [ "`id -u`" -eq 0 ]; then
        PS1='# '
      else
        PS1='$ '
      fi
   fi
 fi
```

```
 umask 022
```

Later versions of the /etc/profile file call other files in the /etc/profile.d/ subdirectory. As of this writing, Ubuntu has yet to include files in /etc/profile.d/; however, this new subdirectory suggests future directions in shell configuration.

/etc/bash_completion

The /etc/bash_completion file provides more than just TAB-key–based command completion. Heck, on my system, it's over 9,000 lines long! For example, the following excerpt of directives associates files with certain extensions with specific applications:

```
complete -f -X '!*.@(avi|asf|wmv)' aviplay
complete -f -X '!*.@(rm?(j)|ra?(m)|smi?(l))' realplay
complete -f -X '!*.@(mpg|mpeg|avi|mov|qt)' xanim
complete -f -X '!*.@(ogg|OGG|m3u|flac|spx)' ogg123
complete -f -X '!*.@(mp3|MP3|ogg|OGG|pls|m3u)' gqmpeg freeamp
complete -f -X '!*.fig' xfig
complete -f -X '!*.@(mid?(i)|MID?(I))' playmidi
```

It specifies default actions for certain commands; for example, the following is set for the **bg** command, as suggested by the comment:

```
# bg completes with stopped jobs
complete -A stopped -P '%' bg
```

This file includes a number of completion functions associated with signals, network interfaces, pathnames, process identifiers, user and group IDs, services, modules, and more. It specifies some aliases, functions, and service scripts. It enables access from the **mount** and **umount** commands to the configuration in /etc/fstab. Of course, with over 9,000 lines, it goes on and on. Suffice to say that the configuration file sets up the bash shell, as well as how it reacts to actions such as pressing the TAB key once or twice.

on the
(i)ob

The /etc/fstab configuration file has changed as of Ubuntu Linux Edgy Eft (6.10). While partition device filenames such as /dev/hda1 still work, Ubuntu is encouraging the use of Universally Unique Identifiers (UUID), which can be created with the uuidgen command and verified with the vol_id command. However, the /etc/fstab configuration file is not listed in the UCP curriculum.

EXERCISE 5-1

Securing Your System

You do want to keep your system as secure as possible. One approach is to change the default permissions users have for new files and directories they make. In this exercise, you'll set all new files and directories to prevent access from other users or groups.

1. Back up your current /etc/profile file. If you want to cancel any changes that you make during this exercise, restore from the backup after the final step.

2. Edit the /etc/profile file. One line in the file sets the **umask**.

3. Change the **umask** statement to exclude all permissions for groups and others. Use **umask 077** to do the job.

4. Save and exit the file.

5. Log in as a nonprivileged user. Use the **touch** command to make a new empty file. Use **ls -l** to verify the permissions on that file.

You have just changed the default umask for all shell users. If you backed up your /etc/profile in step 1, you can now restore the original version of this file.

Wildcards, Datastreams, and More

Wildcards are how users and administrators can specify a variety of different filenames and directives. Datastreams take advantage of the flow between different files and scripts, using different operators. The way wildcards and datastreams work with a given command often depends on the variables and parameters set for the local shell and environment.

Wildcards

Sometimes you may not know the exact name of the file or the exact search term. In this situation, a wildcard can be useful, to narrow the list of possible files. The standard shell wildcards are shown in Table 5-1.

on the **job**

Use of wildcards are sometimes known as *globbing.*

Piping, Input/Output, Error, and Redirection

Linux uses three basic datastreams. Data goes in, data comes out, and errors are sent in a different direction. These streams are known as standard input (stdin), standard output (stdout), and standard error (stderr). Normally, input comes from the keyboard and goes out to the screen, while errors are sent to a buffer. Error messages are also sent to the display (as text stream 2). In the following example, *filename* is stdin to the **cat** command:

```
$ cat filename
```

When you run **cat** *filename*, the contents of that file are sent to the screen as standard output.

You can redirect each of these streams to or from a file. For example, if you have a program named *database* and a datafile with a lot of data, the contents of that datafile can be sent to the database program with a left redirection arrow (**<**). As shown here, datafile is taken as standard input:

```
$ database < datafile
```

TABLE 5-1	Wildcard	Description
Wildcards in the Shell	*	Any number of alphanumeric characters (or no characters at all). For example, the **ls ab*** command would return the following filenames, assuming they exist in the current directory: ab, abc, abcd.
	?	One single alphanumeric character. For example, the **ls ab?** command would return the following filenames, assuming they exist in the current directory: abc, abd, abe.
	[]	A range of options. For example, the **ls ab[123]** command would return the following filenames, assuming they exist in the current directory: ab1, ab2, ab3. Alternatively, the **ls ab[X-Z]** command would return the following filenames, assuming they exist in the current directory: abX, abY, abZ.

Standard input can come from the left side of a command as well. For example, if you need to scroll through the boot messages, you can combine the **dmesg** and **less** commands with a pipe:

```
$ dmesg | less
```

The output from **dmesg** is redirected as standard input to **less**, which then allows you to scroll through that output as if it were a separate file.

Standard output is just as easy to redirect. For example, the following command uses the right redirection arrow (**>**) to send the standard output of the **ls** command to the *filelist* file.

```
$ ls > filelist
```

But the single right redirection arrow (>) would overwrite any existing data. Alternatively, you can add standard output to the end of an existing file with a double redirection arrow with a command such as **ls >> filelist**.

If you believe that a particular program is generating errors, redirect the error stream from it with a command like the following:

```
$ program 2> err-list
```

Variables and Parameters

Variables can change. Parameters are set. The bash shell includes a number of standard environment variables. Their default values are shown in the output to the **env** command. One critical variable is the value of **PATH**, which you can check at the command line with the **echo $PATH** command. The directories listed in **PATH** are automatically searched when you try to run a command. For example, if you want to run the **fdisk** command from the /sbin directory, you could do it with the following command:

```
$ /sbin/fdisk
```

However, since the /sbin directory is in the default Ubuntu Linux **PATH**, you don't need the leading **/sbin** to call out the command; the following would work:

```
$ fdisk
```

You can easily change the **PATH** variable. For example, when I created scripts in my /home/michael directory, I added that directory to my **PATH**, with the following commands:

```
# PATH=$PATH:/home/michael/bin
# export PATH
```

As for parameters, they are most commonly associated with Linux configuration files, often located in the /etc directory. For example, the /etc/resolv.conf file uses the **nameserver** parameter to represent the DNS servers for your network. This is normally set to the IP address for that DNS server.

EXERCISE 5-2

Checking the PATH

In this exercise, you'll identify the different values of the **PATH** directive between a regular and the root user.

1. Log in to the Linux command-line interface as a regular user. If you're in the GUI, you can get to a command-line login by pressing ctrl-alt-f2. From the command prompt, run the following command and note the result:

   ```
   $ echo $PATH
   ```

2. From the regular user command-line interface, try to log in as the superuser.

   ```
   $ su
   Password:
   ```

3. But wait a second; that doesn't work, at least if you have a standard Ubuntu configuration. Ubuntu gurus should already know that there is no direct access to the root account.

4. So to access the root account, run the following command. It allows you to enter your regular account password to access the root account.

   ```
   $ sudo su
   Password:
   #
   ```

5. Run the following command again and note the result. Compare it to the result as a regular user. Unlike other Linux distributions, in this case, there is no difference.

   ```
   # echo $PATH
   ```

6. Log out of Linux. If you followed steps 1 through 4, you'll need to type the **exit** command twice to log out.

7. As there is no default difference in the **PATH** for the root and regular users, there's less motivation to access the root administrative account.

User-Specific bash Configuration Files

When configured with the Users Settings tool described in Chapter 8, each user gets a copy of the hidden files from the /etc/skel directory. As users start working with their accounts, more configuration files are added to their home directories. Some are based on shells such as bash (.bash*); others draw their settings from GUI desktops, typically GNOME and KDE. I'll describe the GUIs in more detail in Chapters 11 and 12.

The default Linux shell is bash; if you or your users work with other shells, configuration files associated with those shells are hidden in each user's home directory.

CERTIFICATION OBJECTIVE 5.02

Review Command-Line Fundamentals

Linux was developed as a clone of Unix, which means that Linux has the same functionality with different source code. The essence of both operating systems is at the command line. Basic commands for file manipulation and filters are available to help you do more with a file.

Basic File Operations

Two basic groups of commands are used to manage Linux files. One group helps you get around Linux files and directories. The other group actually does something creative with the files. Remember that in any Linux file operation, you can take advantage of the history of previous commands, as well as the characteristics of command completion, which allow you to use the TAB key almost as a wildcard to complete a command or a filename, or give you the options available in terms of the absolute path.

Almost all Linux commands include *switches*, options that allow you to do more. Few are covered in this chapter. If you're less familiar with any of these commands, use their man pages. Study the switches. Try them out! Only with practice, practice, and more practice can you really understand the power behind some of these commands.

on the job

At this level, you should already know man pages. Just in case, go to the command line and try commands like man ls *and* man man. *Use the arrow and* PAGEUP/PAGEDOWN *keys to scroll through these manual pages.*

Basic Navigation

Basic file operations are important, as everything in Linux can be reduced to a file. Directories are special types of files that serve as containers for other files. Drivers are files. As discussed earlier, devices are special types of files. The nodes associated with USB hardware are just files, and so on. To navigate around these files, you need some basic commands to tell you where you are, what is there with you, and how to move around.

The Tilde (~)   But first, every Linux user has a home directory. You can use the tilde (~) to represent the home directory of any currently active user. For example, if your username is tb, your home directory is /home/tb. If you've run the **sudo su** command to log in as the root user, your home directory is /root. Thus, the effect of the **cd ~** command depends on your username. For example, if you've logged in as user mj, the **cd ~** command brings you to the /home/mj directory. You can list the contents of your home directory from anywhere in the directory tree with the **ls ~** command.

Paths   There are two path concepts associated with Linux directories: absolute paths and relative paths. An absolute path describes the complete directory structure based on the top-level directory, root (/). A relative path is based on the current directory, but does not include the slash in front.

The difference between an absolute path and a relative one is important. Especially when you're creating a script, absolute paths are essential. Otherwise, scripts executed from other directories may lead to unintended consequences.

pwd   In many configurations, you may not know where you are relative to the root (/) directory. The **pwd** command, which is short for print working directory, can tell you, relative to root (/). Once you know where you are, you can determine whether you need to move to a different directory.

cd   It's easy to change directories in Linux. Just use **cd** and cite the absolute path of the desired directory. If you use the relative path, just remember that your final destination depends on the present working directory. If you use the **cd** command by itself, it moves to your home directory by default.

ls   The most basic of commands lists the files in the current directory. But the Linux **ls** command, with the right switches, can be quite powerful. The right kind of **ls** can tell you everything about a file, such as creation date, last access date, and size. It can help you organize the listing of files in just about any desired order. Important variations on this command include **ls -a** to reveal hidden files, **ls -l** for long listings, **ls -t** for a time-based list, and **ls -i** for inode numbers. You can combine switches; I often use the **ls -ltr** command to display the most recently changed files last.

Looking for Files

There are two basic commands used for file searches: **find** and **locate**.

find   The **find** command searches through directories and subdirectories for a desired file. For example, if you wanted to find the directory with the xorg.conf GUI configuration file, you could use the following command, which would start the search in the /root directory:

```
$ find / -name xorg.conf
```

But this search on my old laptop computer (on an older version of Linux) with a 200MHz CPU took several minutes. Alternatively, if you know that this file is located in the /etc subdirectory tree, you could start in that directory with the following command:

```
$ find /etc -name xorg.conf
```

locate   If this is all too time-consuming, Linux includes a default database of all files and directories. Searches with the **locate** command are almost instantaneous. And **locate** searches don't require the full filename. The drawback is that the **locate** command database is normally updated only once each day, as documented in the /etc/cron.daily/find script.

File Management and Manipulation

There are a number of commands associated with managing and manipulating files. Most Linux files are text files; commands like **cat**, **more**, **less**, **head**, and **tail** help review these files. Files can be created, moved, and even linked to others.

Getting into the Files

Now that you see how to find and get around different files, it's time to start reading, copying, and moving the files around. Most Linux configuration files are text files. Linux editors are text editors. Linux commands are designed to read text files. If in doubt, you can check the file types in the current directory with the **file *** command.

cat   The most basic command for reading files is **cat**. The **cat** *filename* command scrolls the text within the *filename* file. It also works with multiple filenames; it concatenates the filenames that you might list as one continuous output to your screen. You can redirect the output to the filename of your choice.

more and less   Larger files demand a command that can help you scroll though the file text at your leisure. Linux has two of these commands: **more** and **less**. With the **more** *filename* command, you can scroll through the text of a file, from start to finish, one screen at a time. With the **less** *filename* command, you can scroll in both directions through the same text with the PAGEUP and PAGEDOWN keys. Both commands support vi-style searches.

head and tail   The **head** and **tail** commands are separate commands that work in essentially the same way. By default, the **head** *filename* command looks at the first 10 lines of a file; the **tail** filename command looks at the last 10 lines of a file. You can specify the number of lines shown with the **-n***xy* switch. Just remember to avoid the space when specifying the number of lines; for example, the **tail -n15 /etc/passwd** command lists the last 15 lines of the /etc/passwd file.

Creating Files

A number of commands are used to create new files. Alternatively, you can let a text editor such as vi or nano create a new file for you.

cp   The **cp** (copy) command allows you to take the contents of one file and place a copy with the same or different name in the directory of your choice. For example, the **cp** *file1 file2* command takes the contents of *file1* and saves the contents in *file2*. One of the dangers of **cp** is that it can easily overwrite files in different directories, without prompting you to make sure that's what you really wanted to do. Safeguards are possible; for example, you could add the following directive to the .bashrc file in the home directories of selected users:

```
alias cp="cp -i"
```

This prompts the user if he or she tries to overwrite an existing file.

mv   While you can't rename a file in Linux, you can move it. The **mv** command essentially puts a different label on a file. For example, the **mv *file1* *file2*** command changes the name of *file1* to *file2*. Unless you're moving the file to a different partition, everything about the file, including the inode number, remains the same.

ln   You can create a linked file. But what are they? Assuming you have a CD/DVD drive installed, one example is shown in the output to the **ls -l /dev/cdrom** command:

```
lrwxrwxrwx 1 root root 4 2007-02-18 08:41 /dev/cdrom -> scd0
```

The first letter on the left side of the output stands for link—specifically, a soft link. In other words, the /dev/cdrom device file is linked to the actual device, in this case, /dev/scd0. Links are also useful for making sure that multiple users have a copy of the same file in their directories. Hard links are file names from different directories which point to the same file. As long as the hard link is made within the same partition, the inode numbers are identical. You could delete a hard-linked file in one directory, and it would still exist in the other directory. For example, the following command creates a hard link from the actual Samba configuration file to smb.conf in the local directory:

```
$ ln /etc/samba/smb.conf smb.conf
```

To verify the hard link, check the inode number of each filename, which specifies the location on the hard drive partition. In this case, inode numbers of these two filenames can be checked with the following commands. The output should verify that each filename has the same inode number (as long as the files are on the same volume or partition). In other words, as they both point to the same location on the partition or volume, they are two names for the same file.

```
$ ls -i /etc/samba/smb.conf
$ ls -i smb.conf
```

On the other hand, a soft link serves as a redirect; when a file created with a soft link is opened, it directs you to the original file. If you delete the original file, the file is lost. While the soft link is still there, it has nowhere to go. The following command is an example of how to create a soft link:

```
# ln -s /etc/samba/smb.conf smb.conf
```

File Filters

Linux is rich in commands that can help you filter the contents of a file. Simple commands can help you search, check, or sort the contents of a file. And there are special types of files that contain others, colloquially known as a "tarball."

Tarballs are a common way to distribute Linux packages. They are normally distributed in a compressed format, with a .tar.gz or .tar.bz2 file extension, consolidated as a package in a single file. In this respect, they are similar to Microsoft-style compressed zip files.

sort

You can sort the contents of a file in a number of ways. By default, the **sort** command sorts the contents in alphabetical order depending on the first letter in each line. For example, the **sort /etc/passwd** command would sort all users (including those associated with specific services and such) alphabetically, by username.

grep and egrep

The **grep** command uses a search term to look through a file. It returns the full line that contains the search term. For example, **grep 'Michael Jang' /etc/passwd** looks for my name in the /etc/passwd file.

The **egrep** command is more forgiving; it allows you to use some unusual characters in your search, including +, ?, |, (, and). While it's possible to set up **grep** to search for these characters with the help of the backslash, the command can be awkard to use.

The locate *command is essentially a specialized version of the* grep *command, which uses the* updatedb *command–based database of files on the local Linux computer. It's updated on a daily basis with the job specified in the /etc/cron .daily/slocate script.*

wc

The **wc** command, short for word count, can return the number of lines, words, and characters in a file. The **wc** options are straightforward: For example, **wc -w** *filename* returns the number of words in that file. Furthermore, **wc -l** *filename* returns the number of lines in that file, and **wc -c** *filename* returns the number of characters in that file.

sed

The **sed** command, short for stream editor, allows you to search for and change specified words or even text streams in a file. For example, the following command changes the *first* instance of the word *Windows* to the word *Linux* in each line of the file opsys, and writes the result to the file newopsys:

```
# sed 's/Windows/Linux/' opsys > newopsys
```

However, this may not be enough. If a line contains more than one instance of *Windows*, the **sed** command just described does not change the second instance of that word. But you can make it change every appearance of *Windows* by adding a "global" suffix:

```
# sed 's/Windows/Linux/g' opsys > newopsys
```

awk

The **awk** command, named for its developers (Aho, Weinberger, and Kernighan), is more of a database manipulation utility. It can identify lines with a keyword and read out the text from a specified column in that line. Again, using the /etc/passwd file, for example, the following command will read out the username of every user with a *Mike* in the comment column:

```
# awk '/Mike/ {print $1}' /etc/passwd
```

Administrative Commands

You'll work with a number of administrative commands in this book. Most are covered in several other chapters. But every budding Linux administrator should be familiar with at least two basic administrative commands: **ps** and **who**.

ps

It's important to know what's running on your Linux computer. That's where the **ps** command can help. The **ps** command has a number of useful switches. When you diagnose a problem, use **ps** to get the fullest possible list of processes, and then identify the problem program. For example, if the Firefox web browser were to suddenly crash, you'd want to kill any associated processes. The **ps aux | grep firefox** command could then help identify the process(es) to kill.

who and w

If you want to know what users are currently logged into your system, use the **who** command or the **w** command. This can help you identify the usernames of those who are logged in, their terminal connections, their times of login, and the processes that they are running.

on the
job

If you suspect that a username has been compromised, use the w command to check currently logged-on users. Look at the terminal. If the user is in the office but the terminal indicates a remote shell connection, be concerned. The w command can also identify the current process being run by that user.

Service Management Commands

If you need to configure services to start in certain runlevels, the **update-rc.d** command is designed to help. Scripts in the /etc/rcx.d directory (where x corresponds to the runlevel) are started and stopped based on a couple of simple rules. But first, run the following command:

```
$ ls -l /etc/rc2.d
```

Note the links to scripts in the /etc/init.d directory. These scripts start, stop, and restart major services; for example, the following command restarts the Samba server:

```
$ sudo /etc/init.d/samba restart
```

You should also note that scripts in the /etc/rc2.d directory start either with a capital S or K. Scripts with an S in front are started in the given runlevel, in this case, runlevel 2. Conversely, scripts with a K in front are stopped in the noted runlevel. By default, when Ubuntu Linux is booted, all scripts in the /etc/rcS.d directory are started.

But what are runlevels? Standard runlevels include 0, 1, 2, 3, 4, 5, and 6. The default runlevel for Ubuntu Linux is 2. In other words, all scripts in the /etc/rcS.d directory, and all scripts that start with an S in the /etc/rc2.d directory start when Ubuntu Linux is started. The current runlevel can be verified with the **runlevel** command.

Now back to the **update-rc.d** command, and how it can change the defaults for specific runlevels. In this example, the update-rc.d command is used to remove the hypothetical *foo* service from all /etc/rcx.d directories:

```
$ sudo update-rc.d -f foo remove
```

To reverse the process, the following command adds the *foo* service as K and S scripts in appropriate /etc/rcx.d directories:

```
$ sudo update-rc.d -f foo defaults
```

Here's a second example, which configures start scripts for the *foo* service in runlevels S and 2, while stopping them in runlevels 0, 1, 3, 4, 5, and 6. Don't forget the space between runlevels, as well as the dots:

```
$ sudo update-rc.d -f start 17 S 2 . stop 81 0 1 3 4 5 6 .
```

Alternatively, you could just use the Services Settings tool, which can be started in a GUI with the **sudo service-admin** command. However, you should check the appropriate /etc/rcx.d directories to make sure the desired service starts (and stops) in appropriate runlevels.

CERTIFICATION OBJECTIVE 5.03

Work the Filesystem

Linux files and directories are organized to the Filesystem Hierarchy Standard (FHS). While not all distributions fully comply with FHS specifications, Ubuntu Linux comes as close as any major distribution. Within the FHS, administrators such as yourself can create and manage partitions with several different tools.

The Filesystem Hierarchy Standard (FHS)

The FHS is the official way to organize files in Unix and Linux directories. As with the other sections, this introduction provides only the most basic overview of the FHS. More information is available from the official FHS homepage at www.pathname .com/fhs.

Several major directories are associated with all modern Unix/Linux operating systems. These directories organize user files, drivers, kernels, logs, programs, utilities, and more into different categories. The standardization of the FHS makes it easier for users of other Unix-based operating systems to understand the basics of Linux.

Every FHS starts with the root directory, also known by its symbol, the single forward slash (/). All of the other directories shown in Table 5-2 are subdirectories of the root directory. Unless mounted separately, you can also find their files on the same partition or volume as the root directory. You may not see some of the directories shown in the table if you have not installed associated packages. Not all directories shown are officially part of the FHS.

Directories can be mounted on a single partition, or on parts of multiple partitions known as *volumes*. However, while the root directory (/) is the top-level directory in the FHS, the root user's home directory (/root) is just a subdirectory.

on the
ᵗob

In Linux, the word filesystem *has several different meanings. For example, a filesystem can refer to the FHS, an individual partition, or a format such as ext3. A filesystem device node such as /dev/sda1 represents the partition on which you can mount a directory. It's sometimes also written as two words: file system.*

| TABLE 5-2 | Basic Filesystem Hierarchy Standard Directories |

Directory	Description
/	The root directory, the top-level directory in the FHS. All other directories are subdirectories of root, which is always mounted on some partition.
/bin	Essential command-line utilities. Should not be mounted separately; otherwise, it could be difficult to get to these utilities when using a rescue disk.
/boot	Includes Linux startup files, including the Linux kernel. When configured as a separate partition, 100MB, is usually sufficient for a typical modular kernel and additional kernels that you might install.
/dev	Hardware and software device drivers for everything from CD/DVD drives to terminal consoles. Do not mount this directory on a separate partition.
/etc	Most basic configuration files.
/home	Home directories for almost every user.
/lib	Program libraries for the kernel and various command-line utilities. Do not mount this directory on a separate partition.
/media	The mount point for removable media, including USB keys, DVD/CD drives, and Zip disks.
/misc	Not strictly part of the FHS; if the autofs package is installed, this is the standard mount point for local directories mounted via the automounter.
/mnt	A legacy mount point; formerly used for removable media.
/net	Not strictly part of the FHS; if the autofs package is installed, this is the standard mount point for NFS directories mounted via the automounter.
/opt	Common location for third-party application files.
/proc	Not strictly part of the FHS; currently running kernel-related processes, including device assignments such as IRQ ports, I/O addresses, and DMA channels, as well as kernel configuration settings such as IP forwarding.
/root	The home directory of the root user; while activation of the root account is discouraged in Ubuntu Linux, the associated /root home directory is still there.
/sbin	System administration commands. Don't mount this directory separately.
/smb	Not strictly part of the FHS; the standard mount point for remote shared Microsoft network directories mounted via the automounter.
/srv	Commonly used as a top-level directory for various network servers.
/sys	Similar to /proc; for plug-and-play configuration. The FHS has not been updated for this directory.
/tftpboot	Not strictly part of the FHS; included if the TFTP server is installed.
/tmp	Temporary files.
/usr	Small programs accessible to all users. Includes many system administration commands and utilities. Source code is commonly stored in /usr/src.
/var	Variable data, including log files and printer spools.

To see how these directories might be mounted, run the **mount** command by itself. For example, here's the output from my Ubuntu Server system:

```
/dev/sda2 on / type ext3 (rw,errors=remount-ro)
proc on /proc type proc (rw,noexec,nosuid,nodev)
/sys on /sys type sysfs (rw,noexec,nosuid,nodev)
varrun on /var/run type tmpfs (rw,noexec,nosuid,nodev,mode=0755)
varlock on /var/lock type tmpfs (rw,noexec,nosuid,nodev,mode=1777)
udev on /dev type tmpfs (rw,mode=0755)
devshm on /dev/shm type tmpfs (rw)
devpts on /dev/pts type devpts (rw,gid=5,mode=620)
/dev/sda1 on /boot type ext3 (rw)
securityfs on /sys/kernel/security type securityfs (rw)
```

Note there are only two partitions mounted on specific directories, /dev/sda1 and /dev/sda2. The other mounts, such as those on the /proc, /sys, and /var/run directories, are virtual.

Partition Management Tools

Two of the basic partition management tools available for Linux are **fdisk** and **parted**.

This section includes a number of suggested actions that you can take with each of these tools. If you choose to take some of these actions, I urge you to have a test system such as a virtual machine ready for this purpose.

on the **Job**

There are important alternatives to fdisk *and* parted. *Well, strictly speaking, some like GParted and QTparted are not alternatives, but are front ends to* parted, *which can be controlled in the GUI. Third-party alternatives are also available; for example, Partition Magic can now be used to create and manage ext3 partitions.*

The fdisk Utility

The **fdisk** utility is a universally available tool that you should know well. There are many commands within **fdisk**, more in expert mode; I limit the discussion to those most commonly used to create and modify partitions on a regular Linux system.

Though there are many programs available that can modify the physical disk partition layout, this section explores the Linux implementation of **fdisk**. The FDISK.EXE command found on Microsoft systems has the same name and is also used for creating partitions, but it doesn't incorporate any Linux-compatible features. It also uses a different set of menus.

Using fdisk: Starting, Getting Help, and Quitting   The following screen
output lists commands that show how to start the **fdisk** program, how to get help,
and how to quit the program. The /dev/sdc drive is associated with the third SATA
drive on a regular PC, or could be associated with an external drive such as a USB
key. (The first two SATA drives would be /dev/sda and /dev/sdb, respectively.) Your
computer may have a different hard drive; for clues, check the output from the **df**
and **mount** commands.

As you can see, once you start **fdisk**, it opens its own command-line prompt:

```
$ sudo fdisk /dev/sdc
Command (m for help): m
Command action
   a   toggle a bootable flag
   b   edit bsd disklabel
   c   toggle the dos compatibility flag
   d   delete a partition
   l   list known partition types
   m   print this menu
   n   add a new partition
   o   create a new empty DOS partition table
   p   print the partition table
   q   quit without saving changes
   s   create a new empty Sun disklabel
   t   change a partition's system id
   u   change display/entry units
   v   verify the partition table
   w   write table to disk and exit
   x   extra functionality (experts only)

Command (m for help): q
```

There are a wide variety of commands associated with **fdisk**—and more when you
run the **x** command to access **fdisk**'s extra functionality.

Using fdisk: In a Nutshell

At the **fdisk** command-line prompt, start with the print command (**p**) to print
the partition table. This allows you to review the current entries in the partition
table. Assuming you have free space, you then create a new (**n**) partition, either
primary (**p**) or logical (**l**). If it doesn't already exist, you can also create an extended
partition (**e**) to contain your logical partitions. Remember that you can have up to
four primary partitions, which would correspond to numbers 1 through 4. One of
the primary partitions can be redesignated as an extended partition. The remaining
partitions are logical partitions, numbered 5 and above.

When you assign space to a partition, you're assigning a block of cylinders on that hard disk. If you have free space, the **fdisk** default starts the new partition at the first available cylinder. The actual size of the partition depends on disk geometry; do not worry about exact size here.

Using fdisk: Deleting Partitions   The following example removes the only configured partition. The sample output screen first starts **fdisk**. Then you print (**p**) the current partition table, delete (**d**) the partition by number (**1** in this case), write (**w**) the changes to the disk, and quit (**q**) from the program. Needless to say, *do not change any partition from which you need the data*.

```
$ sudo fdisk /dev/sdc
Command (m for help): p
Disk /dev/sdc: 255 heads, 63 sectors, 525 cylinders
Units = cylinders of 16065 * 512 bytes

Device    Boot    Start      End    Blocks   Id  System
/dev/sdc1   *          1     525   4217031    6  Linux
Command (m for help): d
Partition number (1-1): 1
```

This is the last chance to change your mind before deleting the current partition. If you want to change your mind, exit from **fdisk** with the **q** command. If you're pleased with the changes and want to make them permanent, proceed with the **w** command:

```
Command (m for help): w
```

You did it! Now you have an empty hard disk or hard disk area to create the needed partitions. You no longer have to reboot to get Linux to read the new partition table. Now, the **partprobe** command rereads the partition table without a reboot.

Using fdisk: Creating Partitions

The following screen output sample shows the steps used to create (**n**) the first (/boot) partition, make it bootable (**a**), and then finally write (**w**) the partition information to the disk. Don't expect precision with respect to numbers of megabytes; the geometry of the disk may not allow that precise size, as shown in the example.

```
# fdisk /dev/sdd

Command (m for help): n
Command action
   e   extended
   p   primary partition (1-4)
```

```
p
Partition number (1-4):
First cylinder (1-130, default 1): 1
Last cylinder or +size or +sizeM or +sizeK (1-130,def 130): +100M

Command (m for help): n
Partition number (1-4): 1

Command (m for help): p
Disk /dev/sdd: 255 heads, 63 sectors, 256 cylinders
Units = cylinders of 16065 * 512 bytes
   Device Boot     Start      End      Blocks   Id  System
/dev/sdd1                 1       13      104391   83  Linux

Command (m for help):
```

Repeat the commands to create any other partitions that you might need. One possible group of partitions is illustrated here:

```
Command (m for help): p

Disk /dev/sdb: 255 heads, 63 sectors, 256 cylinders
Units = cylinders of 16065 * 512 bytes
   Device Boot  Start  End    Blocks   Id  System
/dev/sdb1               1     13     104391   83  Linux
/dev/sdb2              14     19      48195   82  Linux swap / Solaris
/dev/sdb3              20     50     249007+  83  Linux
/dev/sdb4              51    130     642600    5  Extended
/dev/sdb5              51     80     240943+  83  Linux
/dev/sdb6              81    130     401593+  83  Linux

Command (m for help): w
```

While you could create more than 5 SATA/SCSI partitions using **fdisk**, they would not be recognized by Linux.

on the *job*

The number of blocks that you see may vary slightly depending on the size of the hard disk; the number of heads, sectors, and cylinders on that disk; and the version of fdisk being used.

Using fdisk: A New PC with No Partitions

After installing Linux on a new PC, you'll want to use **fdisk** to configure additional physical disks attached to the system. For example, if the additional disk is the first disk attached to the secondary IDE controller, run the **fdisk /dev/hdc** command.

Remember the limitations on partitions. If you need more than four partitions on the new physical disk, configure type Primary for the first three partitions, and then Extended for the rest of the disk as partition 4. You can then create logical partitions 5–16 within the extended partition.

Using fdisk: Creating a Swap Partition

You need to create a partition before you can reassign it as a swap partition. At the **fdisk** prompt, run the l command. You'll see a large number of file types, listed as hex codes. When you create a partition, **fdisk** creates a Linux Native type partition by default. As you can see from the output of the l command, the associated hex code is (83).

It's easy to reassign a partition as a swap partition. Run the **p** command. Remember the number of the partition you want to change. Make sure that partition doesn't contain data that you want to save.

Now run the **t** command. Type in the number associated with the partition that you want to change. Type in the hex code for the type you want—in this case, **82** for a Linux swap partition. For example, I could run the following sequence of commands to set up a new swap partition on the second IDE hard drive. The commands that I type are shown in boldface. The details of what you see depend on the partitions that you have created. This example illustrates a 1GB swap space on the first primary partition on that drive (/dev/hdb1).

```
# fdisk /dev/hdb
Command (m for help): n
Command action
     e   extended
     p   primary partition (1-4)
p
Partition number (1-4): 1
First cylinder (1-10402, default 1):
Using default value 1
Last cylinder or +size or +sizeM or +sizeK (1-10402, default
10402): +1000M

Command (m for help): p

Disk /dev/hdb: 5368 MB, 5368709120 bytes
16 heads, 63 sectors/track, 10402 cylinders
Units = cylinders of 1008 * 512 = 516096 bytes

    Device Boot     Start       End     Blocks   Id  System
/dev/hdb1               1      1939    977224+   83  Linux
```

```
Command (m for help): t
Selected partition 1
Hex code (type L to list codes): 82
Changed system type of partition 1 to 82 (Linux swap / Solaris)

Command (m for help): w
The partition table has been altered!

Calling ioctl() to re-read partition table.
Syncing disks.
#
```

The **fdisk** utility doesn't actually write the changes to your hard disk until you run the write (**w**) command. You have a chance to cancel your changes with the quit (**q**) command. To make sure Linux rereads the partition table after **fdisk** writes it, run the **partprobe** command.

The parted Utility

The **parted** utility is becoming increasingly popular. It's an excellent tool developed by the GNU foundation. As with **fdisk**, you can use it to create, check, and destroy partitions, but it can do more. You can also use it to resize and copy partitions, as well as the filesystems contained therein. For the latest information, see www.gnu .org/software/parted.

on the **job**

It's much easier to make a mistake with parted*. For example, I accidentally ran the* mklabel *command from the (*parted*) prompt on an existing Linux system. It deleted all existing partitions. Fortunately, I had a snapshot of this system on a VMware server and was able to recover quickly with little trouble.*

During our discussion of **parted**, we'll proceed from section to section, assuming that **parted** is still open with the following prompt:

```
(parted)
```

If you use **parted** and then check your partitions with **fdisk**, you might get errors such as

```
Partition 1 does not end on cylinder boundary.
```

Don't worry about it. While **fdisk** partitions are associated with hard drive cylinders, **parted** is not so limited.

Using parted: Starting, Getting Help, and Quitting

The next screen output lists commands that show how to start the **parted** utility, how to get help, and how to quit the program. In this case, the /dev/sdb drive is associated with the second SATA drive on a regular PC. Your computer may have a different hard drive; you can check the output from the **df** and **mount** commands for clues.

As you can see in Figure 5-1, once you start **parted**, it opens its own command-line prompt. It includes a wide variety of commands.

If you're familiar with **fdisk**, you can see that **parted** can do more: You can even format and resize partitions from **parted**. Unfortunately, the format functionality is limited and does not allow you to create or resize ext3 partitions, at least as of this writing.

Using parted: In a Nutshell

At the **parted** command-line prompt, start with the **print** command, which lists the contents of the partition table. Assuming you have free space, you then make a new (**mkpart**) partition or even make and format the filesystem (**mkpartfs**). If you need

FIGURE 5-1   parted command options

```
michael@ubuntuserver:~$ sudo parted /dev/sdb
GNU Parted 1.7.1
Using /dev/sdb
Welcome to GNU Parted! Type 'help' to view a list of commands.
(parted) help
  check NUMBER                            do a simple check on the file system
  cp [FROM-DEVICE] FROM-NUMBER TO-NUMBER  copy file system to another partition
  help [COMMAND]                          prints general help, or help on COMMAND
  mklabel LABEL-TYPE                      create a new disklabel (partition table)
  mkfs NUMBER FS-TYPE                     make a FS-TYPE file system on partititon NUMBER
  mkpart PART-TYPE [FS-TYPE] START END    make a partition
  mkpartfs PART-TYPE FS-TYPE START END    make a partition with a file system
  move NUMBER START END                   move partition NUMBER
  name NUMBER NAME                        name partition NUMBER as NAME
  print [free|NUMBER|all]                 display the partition table, a partition, or all devices
  quit                                    exit program
  rescue START END                        rescue a lost partition near START and END
  resize NUMBER START END                 resize partition NUMBER and its file system
  rm NUMBER                               delete partition NUMBER
  select DEVICE                           choose the device to edit
  set NUMBER FLAG STATE                   change the FLAG on partition NUMBER
  toggle [NUMBER [FLAG]]                  toggle the state of FLAG on partition NUMBER
  unit UNIT                               set the default unit to UNIT
  version                                 displays the current version of GNU Parted and copyright
        information
(parted)
```

more information about command options, use the **help** command with it; here's an example with the **mkpart** command:

```
(parted) help mkpart
  mkpart PART-TYPE [FS-TYPE] START END      make a partition

        PART-TYPE is one of: primary, logical, extended
        FS-TYPE is one of: ext3, ext2, fat32, fat16, hfsx,
        hfs+, hfs, jfs, linux-swap,ntfs, reiserfs, hp-ufs,
        sun-ufs, xfs, apfs2, apfs1, asfs, amufs5, amufs4,
        amufs3, amufs2, amufs1, amufs0, amufs, affs7, affs6,
        affs5, affs4, affs3, affs2, affs1, affs0
        START and END are disk locations, such as 4GB or 10%.
        Negative values count from the end of the disk.
        For example, -1s specifies exactly the last sector.

        mkpart makes a partition without creating a new
        file system on the partition.
        FS-TYPE may be specified to set an appropriate
        partition ID.
```

If that's too much for you, just run the command. The **parted** utility prompts you for the required information. Remember that standard disks can have up to four primary partitions, corresponding to numbers 1 through 4. One of the primary partitions can be redesignated as an extended partition. The remaining partitions are logical partitions, numbered 5 and above. While the Linux **parted** utility allows you to create more than 15 partitions on a drive, in this case, anything beyond /dev/sdb15 is not recognized by Linux.

Using parted: Deleting Partitions

Deleting partitions is easy. All you need to do from the **(parted)** prompt is use the **rm** command to delete the partition that you no longer need. Of course, before deleting any partition, you should do the following:

- Save any data you need from that partition.
- Unmount the partition.
- Make sure the partition isn't already configured in /etc/fstab, so Linux doesn't try to mount it the next time you boot.
- After starting **parted**, run the **print** command to identify the partition you want to delete, as well as its ID number.

For example, if you want to delete partition /dev/sdb10 from the **(parted)** prompt, run the following command:

```
(parted) rm 10
```

Using parted: A New PC (or Hard Drive) with No Partitions

Whenever a new hard drive is installed, you should create a new partition table. But before creating a partition table, you need to create a label for that drive. From the list of available commands, one method to create a new label is with the **mklabel** command. As strange as it sounds, the default label for a Linux hard disk is **msdos**. When I install a new hard drive, I create a new label with the following commands:

```
(parted) mklabel
New disk label type? msdos
```

on the job

Be careful! Never run mklabel from the (parted) prompt on a hard drive that stores data that you need.

Now you can create a new partition. Let me show you how **mkpart** works on the new hard drive. Naturally, if an extended partition already exists, you'll be able to create a logical partition.

```
(parted) mkpart
Partition type? primary/extended? primary
File system type? [ext2]? ext3
Start? 0
End? 100MB
```

Now review the results:

```
(parted) print

Disk /dev/sdb: 10.7GB
Sector size (logical/physical): 512B/512B
Partition Table: msdos

Number  Start    End     Size    Type      File system  Flags
 1      0.51kB   100MB   100MB   primary   ext2
```

The filesystem type is empty, unless you've accepted the suggestion for ext2. Unfortunately, **parted** does not work perfectly, and it does not always create ext3 filesystems from the command-line interface.

on the job

Smaller partitions, such as those commonly used for the /boot directory, are less likely to become corrupt. Some administrators format them with ext2 and not a journaling filesystem such as ext3.

After exiting from **parted**, reboot or run the **partprobe** command to make Linux read the new partition table. Now the new ext2 partition can also be formatted to the default ext3 filesystem. For the purpose of this chapter, don't exit from **parted** just yet.

on the job

The GUI parted **tools (GParted, QTParted) do support formatting to a wider variety of filesystem formats, even though they're just "front ends" to** parted.

Using parted: Creating a Swap Partition

Now repeat the process to create a swap partition. I'll leave that process to you. But after creating a partition, you can change the filesystem type with the **mkfs** command. Be aware that this **mkfs** command within **parted** is different from the **mkfs** command at the shell. If you don't remember the partition number, run the **print** command first.

```
(parted) mkfs
Partition number? 2
File system? [ext2]? linux-swap
```

Now review the result:

```
(parted) print

Disk /dev/sdb: 10.7GB
Sector size (logical/physical): 512B/512B
Partition Table: msdos

Number  Start    End     Size    Type     File system  Flags
  1     0.51kB   100MB   100MB   primary  ext2
  2     101MB    1100MB  1000MB  primary  linux-swap
```

Let's repeat the process, creating a regular partition after the swap partition:

```
(parted) mkpart
Partition type? primary/extended? primary
File system type? [ext2]? ext2
Start? 1101MB
End? 2100MB
```

After exiting from **parted**, reboot, or run the **partprobe** command to make sure Linux reads the new partition table. Now go ahead and exit from **parted**. After exiting, implement the changes. Format and then activate the swap partition on /dev/sdb2 using the following commands:

```
(parted) quit
$ sudo partprobe
$ sudo mkswap /dev/sdb2
$ sudo swapon /dev/sdb2
```

Don't forget to format and activate the partition created in the previous section to the third extended filesystem with a command like **sudo mkfs.ext2 /dev/sdb1**. If you prefer the Ubuntu default journaling filesystem, substitute **mkfs.ext3** for **mkfs.ext2**.

on the
ob

Sometimes there will be errors when running the partprobe command, even on a properly configured system. For example, if you haven't put a disk in a floppy drive, there will be errors related to the associated device (usually fd0). If the disk in your CD/DVD drive are read-only (as are most CD/DVD disks), there will be an error message to that effect.

Filesystem Formatting and Checking

Two basic tools are available to manage the filesystem on various partitions: **mkfs** and **fsck**. They can help you create, check, and repair different filesystems.

mkfs

To format a Linux partition, apply the **mkfs** command. It allows you to format a partition to a number of different filesystems. To format a typical partition such as /dev/hda2 to the current Ubuntu Linux standard, the third extended filesystem, run the following command:

```
# mkfs -t ext3 /dev/hda2
```

The **mkfs** command also serves as a "front end," depending on the filesystem format. For example, if you're formatting a Ubuntu Linux standard ext3 filesystem, **mkfs** automatically calls the **mkfs.ext3** command. Therefore, if you're reformatting an ext3 filesystem, the following command is sufficient:

```
# mkfs /dev/hda2
```

on the job *Be careful with the mkfs command. First, back up any data on the subject partition and computer. This command erases all data on the specified partition.*

fsck

The **fsck** command is functionally similar to the Microsoft **chkdsk** command. It analyzes the specified filesystem and performs repairs as required. Assume, for example, you're having problems with files in the /var directory, which happens to be mounted on /dev/hda7. If you want to run **fsck**, unmount that filesystem first. In some cases, you may need to go into single-user mode with the **init 1** command before you can unmount a filesystem. To unmount, analyze, and then remount the filesystem noted in this section, run the following commands:

```
# umount /var
# fsck -t ext3 /dev/hda7
# mount /dev/hda7 /var
```

The **fsck** command also serves as a "front end," depending on the filesystem format. For example, if you're formatting an ext2 or ext3 filesystem, **fsck** by itself automatically calls the **e2fsck** command (which works for both filesystems). Therefore, if you're checking an ext3 filesystem, once you unmount it with the **umount** command, the following command is sufficient:

```
# fsck /dev/hda7
```

CERTIFICATION SUMMARY

This chapter provides an overview of many Linux fundamentals. While the UCP curriculum may not explicitly cite the skills described in this chapter, you need to know many of these fundamentals to solve the problems presented on those exams.

Ubuntu Linux still configures the bash shell by default, and that's assumed for the UCP exam. However, the default may change to dash in the near future. In any case, configuration files such as /etc/bash.bashrc are supplemented by hidden configuration files in user home directories.

Basic command-line skills are a must for any serious Linux administrator. You need to know how to navigate around the Linux directory tree, find desired files, and read text files in different ways. You also need to know how to use file filters, administrative commands, and much more, as discussed in a number of other chapters.

You also need to understand the FHS, and how to make it work with different partitions with **fdisk** and **parted** utilities. New partitions can be formatted and checked with the **mkfs** and **fsck** commands.

✓ TWO-MINUTE DRILL

Here are some of the key points from the certification objectives in Chapter 5.

Customize the Shell

❑ The default shell is bash, but may be dash in the future.

❑ The /etc/bash.bashrc file is used for aliases and functions, on a system-wide basis.

❑ The /etc/profile file is used for system-wide environment and startup files.

❑ The /etc/bash_completion file configures behavior for certain keyboard actions.

❑ Wildcards, piping, and redirection symbols help customize how commands work with each other.

❑ Default configuration files for new users are stored in the /etc/skel directory.

Review Command-Line Fundamentals

❑ Linux administrators need to know how to use the command-line interface.

❑ Basic commands allow you to navigate, find the files that you need, read file contents, create new files, and more.

❑ File filters allow you to search through the files themselves for specific citations or other file characteristics.

❑ Administrative commands allow you to manage Linux in a number of ways, including running processes and managing logged-in users.

Work the Filesystem

❑ Linux directories are organized to the Filesystem Hierarchy Standard (FHS).

❑ FHS partitions can be managed and formatted with the **fdisk**, **parted**, **fsck**, and **mkfs** commands.

SELF TEST

The following questions will help you measure your understanding of the material presented in this chapter. Read all the questions carefully, as there may be more than one correct answer. Some questions are "fill in the blank" and normally require an exact answer. Choose all correct answers for each question.

Customize the Shell

1. Name the directory where system-wide user configuration files are stored.

_____

2. Where can you find user-specific shell configuration files for user labrador?
   A. /etc
   B. /tmp
   C. /
   D. /home/labrador

3. What single command would you run to list files f0401.tif, f0402.tif, f0403.tif, f0404.tif, and f0405.tif? The command can include as many switches or wildcards as you need.

_____

4. Which of the following operators can redirect output from the first command to the second command on a line? (Two answers are correct.)
   A. >
   B. <
   C. =
   D. |

5. If you want to add the /tmp/bin directory to your local **PATH**, and don't want the change to be active the next time you log in to your account, what command can you run?

_____

Review Command-Line Fundamentals

6. If you're currently in your home directory, and run the following command, where will you navigate to?

```
$ cd tmp
```

   A. /tmp
   B. /home/tmp
   C. /home/michael/tmp
   D. There's no way to know from the given data.

7. Which of the following commands searches for the location of the menu.lst file?

    A. **sudo find menu.lst**

    B. **sudo find -name / menu.lst**

    C. **sudo find / -name menu.lst**

    D. Any competent Linux administrator already knows the location of this file.

8. How would you know if one file has a hard link to another?

    A. Run the **ls -l** command on both files. You should see an l in the first column in the output to one of the files.

    B. Run the **ls -i** command on both files. You should see an l in the first column in the output to one of the files.

    C. Run the **ls -l** command on both files. You'll be able to identify a hard link when both files have the same inode number.

    D. Run the **ls -i** command on both files. You'll be able to identify a hard link when both files have the same inode number.

9. Write out the command that determines the number of lines in /etc/passwd.

    _____

10. Which of the following commands identify currently open terminals?

    A. **ps aux**

    B. **ps aux | grep term**

    C. **ps aux | grep tty**

    D. **ps aux | grep X**

Work the Filesystem

11. Name two directories that are based on virtual information, such as kernel settings.

    _____

    _____

12. What command at the **fdisk** prompt lists currently configured partitions?

    A. p

    B. m

    C. print

    D. part

13. What command at the **parted** prompt lists currently configured partitions?

    A. p

    B. m

    C. print

    D. part

14. After creating partitions in **fdisk**, you want to make sure Linux rereads the partition table. How can you do this? (Two answers are correct.)

    A. Run the **fdisk reread** command.

    B. Run the **partprobe** command.

    C. Call ioctl.

    D. Reboot the system.

15. Which of the following commands formats the second partition on the second SATA drive to the third extended filesystem?

    A. **mkfs.ext2 /dev/hdb2**

    B. **mkfs.ext2 /dev/sdb1**

    C. **mkfs.ext3 /dev/sdb2**

    D. **mkfs.ext3 /dev/sdb1**

LAB QUESTIONS

These labs may be run consecutively. As Ubuntu Linux is constantly changing, what you see may vary.

Lab 1

This lab assumes you have a new hard disk (or at least empty space on a current hard drive where you can add a new partition). You can simulate a new hard disk by adding appropriate settings to a VM-ware or Xen virtual machine. In this lab, you'll create a new partition using **parted**, format it, transfer the files currently on the /home (or if you don't have a lot of space, /tmp) directory to that partition, and revise /etc/fstab so the new partition is properly mounted the next time you boot Linux.

    If you're running Ubuntu Linux Edgy Eft or later, UUID numbers may be used in the /etc/fstab configuration file. If you're familiar with Red Hat distributions, it's functionally similar to the **LABEL** directive, which makes the filesystem independent of the partition.

    If you have a limited amount of available space, dedicate only half of it to this lab and leave the other half empty for Lab 2.

Lab 2

In this lab, you'll add a new swap partition using the **fdisk** utility. Remember to make the partition work with the appropriate file type, and then format and activate it. Make sure it's properly included in /etc/fstab so this partition is used the next time you boot Linux.

SELF TEST ANSWERS

Customize the Shell

1. ☑ **/etc.** System-wide user configuration files, as well as most other Linux configuration files, are stored in the /etc directory.

2. ☑ **D.** Shell configuration files specific for any user are stored in that user's home directory, in this case, /home/labrador.
   ☒ System-wide and not user-specific configuration files are stored in /etc; therefore, answer **A** is wrong. Few if any standard configuration files are stored in /tmp or /; therefore, answers **B** and **C** are both incorrect.

3. ☑ **ls f040[1-5].tif**
   ☒ The **ls f040*.tif** command would include any number of letters or numbers. The **ls f040?. tif** command would include f040a.tif through f040z.tif as well as f0400.tif through f0409.tif, and more.

4. ☑ **A and D.** The forward arrow (>) and the pipe (|) both redirect output from the first command as input to the second command.
   ☒ As the left-facing arrow is normally used for data input from a file on the right side, answer **B** is wrong. As the equals operator is associated with directives, answer **C** is also wrong.

5. ☑ **PATH=$PATH:/tmp/bin**

Review Command-Line Fundamentals

6. ☑ **D.** As there's no way to know the current directory, and the path redirection is relative, there is no way to know what the **cd tmp** command would do.
   ☒ While answers **A, B,** or **C** could be right if you're currently in the /, /home, or /home/ michael directories, there's no way to know what directory you're in. Therefore, answers **A, B,** and **C** are all incorrect.

7. ☑ **C.** The **find** command starts with the highest directory being searched followed by the **-name** of the file to search for.
   ☒ Answer **A** would work only if you're already in a directory with the menu.lst file; it wouldn't find other locations with menu.lst. Answer **B** is incorrectly formatted. Even though the standard location of menu.lst is known (the /boot/grub directory), it doesn't reveal other locations that might include documentation, examples, and more. Therefore, answers **A, B,** and **D** are all incorrect.

8. ☑ **D.** Hard links can be deciphered by common inode numbers. And inode numbers are revealed with the ls -i *filename* command.

☒ As the **ls -l** command reveals soft links, answers **A** and **C** are both wrong. Since the **ls -i** command does not reveal soft links, answer **B** is also wrong.

9. ☑ The simplest command that accomplishes the task is **wc -l /etc/passwd**. Another possible command is **cat /etc/passwd | wc -l**.

10. ☑ **C.** Piping the list of all processes to the grep tty command identifies all processes with terminals. The definition of terminals has not changed, despite the configuration file change from /etc/inittab to /etc/default/console-setup.

☒ While answer **A,** the generic **ps aux** command, would list terminals among the probably hundreds of running processes, it's less precise than answer **C**. Answers **B** and **D** do not use terminal-related search terms, so those answers are also wrong.

Work the Filesystems

11. ☑ **/proc, /sys**. The two most common virtual directories are /proc and /sys; strictly speaking, any directory output to the **mount** command, not associated with a physical partition, could be included in this list.

12. ☑ **A.** The **p** command at the **fdisk** prompt lists the current partition configuration.

☒ Answer **B** lists available commands at the **fdisk** prompt. Answer **C** works at the parted interface. Answer **D** does not work in either **fdisk** or **parted**. Therefore, answers **B, C,** and **D** are all incorrect.

13. ☑ **C.** The **print** command at the **parted** prompt lists the current partition configuration.

☒ Answer **A** works at the **fdisk** interface. Answer **B** lists available commands at the **fdisk** prompt. Answer **D** does not work in either **fdisk** or **parted**. Therefore, answers **A, B,** and **D** are all incorrect.

14. ☑ **B** and **D.** The **partprobe** command allows Linux to reread the partition table without rebooting. Of course, rebooting also works.

☒ Answer **A** is wrong, as there is no **fdisk reread** command. Answer **C** is wrong, as ioctl is unrelated to partition tables. But that may be confusing, as that is the directive called independently by **fdisk** when it rereads the partition table.

15. ☑ **C.** The **mkfs.ext3 /dev/sdb2** formats the second partition of the second SATA drive (/dev/sdb2) to the third extended filesystem (ext3).

☒ As the mkfs.ext2 command formats to the second extended filesystem (ext2), answers **A** and **B** are both incorrect. As /dev/sdb1 is the first partition of the second SATA drive, answer **D** is also wrong.

LAB ANSWERS

Remember, these labs can be run in sequence.

Lab I

1. If you've been able to add a new hard drive, you should be able to review it from the **(parted)** prompt. But make sure to open the appropriate drive. For example, if it's the second SATA drive, do so with the **parted /dev/sdb** command.

2. Run the **print** command from the **(parted)** prompt. If it's a new drive, you'll see an "unrecognized disk label" message and can run **mklabel** to add an **msdos** label as described in the chapter. Otherwise, don't run **mklabel!**

3. Make a note of available space in your partitions.

4. Create the new partition. The **mkpart** command provides prompts that help you define the new partition. If the partition is on a new hard drive, create a primary partition. Otherwise, you may only be able to create a logical partition.

5. Use the prompts to define the size of the partition from the start and ending MB location on the drive. As noted in the lab, make sure the size of the partition is half the available free space.

6. Run **print** again to confirm your changes. Make a note of the partition number. For example, if you've created partition 1 on /dev/sdb, the partition device file is /dev/sdb1.

7. Run **quit** to exit from **parted**. Run the **partprobe** command to make Linux reread the partition table (without rebooting).

8. Format the partition. Assuming you're using the default Ubuntu Linux filesystem format, use the **mkfs.ext3** *partitionname* command; substitute the device file for *partitionname*.

9. Mount the new partition on a temporary directory; I often create a /test directory for this purpose. For the aforementioned partition, the command would be **mount /dev/sdb1 /test**.

10. Copy all of the files recursively from the directory that you're going to mount on the new partition. For example, if you're moving the files from the /home directory using the noted partitions, the command would be **cp -ar /home/* /test**.

11. Unmount **/test** from the new partition with a command like **umount /test**.

12. Mount the new partition such as /dev/sdb1 on the /home directory.

13. Review the results. Are the files you transferred on the new partition?

14. When you're confident of your new configuration, unmount /home from the new partition. You can then delete the files from the /home directory mounted on the old partition, allowing you to use the space for other directories.

Lab 2

In this lab, you'll add a new swap partition using the **fdisk** utility. Remember to make the partition work with the appropriate file type, format, and activate it. Make sure it's properly included in /etc/fstab so this partition is used the next time you boot Linux.

1. If you've completed Lab 1, you presumably have half the free space—from either an existing or a newly installed drive—still available.

2. Use **fdisk** to open the drive with free space. You may need to be specific. The **fdisk -l** command can help you define the drive with free space, such as /dev/hdc. In that case, run the **fdisk /dev/hdc** command to edit the partition table of that drive.

3. Add a new partition using existing free space. From the **fdisk** prompt, the **p** command prints defined partitions, including the one you just created. Make sure to change the partition type; the **t** command from the **fdisk** prompt allows you to change the partition number you just created to the Linux swap system ID (82).

4. Write your changes from **fdisk**; if you want to reread the partition table without rebooting, use the **partprobe** command.

5. Format the new partition to the Linux swap filesystem: for example, if the new partition is on /dev/hdc3, you'd run the **mkswap /dev/hdc3** command.

6. Once the format process is complete, you can immediately activate this partition with the **swapon /dev/hdc3** command.

7. But that's not it. You need to make sure that swap partition is activated the next time you boot. To do so, you need to add information associated with that partition to /etc/fstab. One line that would work in this case is

```
/dev/hdc3   none   swap   sw   0 0
```

In many cases, this may look different from the first swap partition, probably created when you first installed Ubuntu Linux. If the swap filesystem is on a logical volume, it might look like this:

```
/dev/VolGroup00/LogVol01   none   swap   sw   0 0
```

Alternatively, a swap partition on a different location such as /dev/hda3 might have a directive such as

```
/dev/hda3   none   swap   sw   0 0
```

Or if you're using UUIDs, it might have a directive such as the following, where the UUID was created with the **uuidgen /dev/hda3** command:

```
UUID=febd39b9-fdb0-40d8-8dec-83f1810ffb50   none   swap   sw   0 0
```

6
Manage Updates
and Repositories

The management of updates and repositories is a key skill for the administrator, especially when that administrator is responsible for a group of Ubuntu Linux systems. As Ubuntu Linux is built on Debian Linux, many of the skills and key commands are the same. Both distributions configure packages in a variety of repositories. Client updates are configured in the local /etc/apt/sources.list configuration file. Administrators responsible for a substantial number of Ubuntu Linux systems may want to mirror one or more key repositories on the local network.

on the job

For more information on updates, repositories, and general Linux package management, see this author's Linux Patch Management, *published by Prentice Hall.*

CERTIFICATION OBJECTIVE 6.01

Manage Individual Packages and More

As Ubuntu Linux is based on and still uses packages developed for Debian Linux, both distributions use the Debian packaging system. So it should be no surprise that the Ubuntu Linux package-naming conventions are closely related to those for Debian Linux, and it uses the **dpkg** command with related tools to manage packages.

The related tools include **apt-*** commands, which can install packages with dependencies from remote repositories. The Synaptic and Update Manager tools are in essence front ends to the **apt-*** commands. If the "universe" and "multiverse" of packages available for Ubuntu Linux are not enough, it is possible that packages built for Debian Linux can work on Ubuntu Linux. And if that's not enough, the **alien** command can convert packages built for other systems, such as the Red Hat Package Manager (RPM), for possible use on Ubuntu Linux.

exam
watch

Practice with the dpkg, apt-get, apt-file, apt-cdrom, apt-cache, *and* alien *commands. The more you know about each* *of these commands, the more you can do as an Ubuntu Linux administrator (and the more you'll be ready for on the UCP exam).*

INSIDE THE EXAM

Managing Packages and Repositories (123.1)

The UCP curriculum suggests that you need to know how to "Perform Ubuntu Package Management And Manage Repositories." This item is addressed in some detail. You should be able to compare Ubuntu and Debian packages, and convert to and from packages associated with other Linux distributions. You also need to know how to manage Ubuntu packages from the command line, for installation, removal, and upgrades, as well as for security.

As Ubuntu updates (as well as installations) are highly dependent on package repositories, you need to understand the variety of available repositories, as well as how to mirror those repositories to a local network.

These skills require knowledge of both command-line and GUI tools.

Ubuntu Package-Naming Conventions

If you're one of the many Ubuntu Linux users who've never seen an Ubuntu Linux package file before, navigate to the /var/cache/apt/archives directory. Unless the system is booted directly from a Live CD, you'll see a variety of recently installed packages. The package format is straightforward:

```
packagename_version_architecture.deb
```

The *packagename* is straightforward. The version number often indicates the formal status of the package; production-ready packages normally are of version 1.0 or higher. For Ubuntu Linux, the version number often includes the *ubuntu* tag prior to the deb extension. This goes beyond what's listed in a standard Debian Linux package. The architecture is associated with the CPU of the system; if the package is architecture-independent, the architecture is listed as *all*. The .deb extension is associated with the Debian Package format.

The dpkg Command

The **dpkg** command is the first in a rich variety of commands associated with the Debian packaging system used on Ubuntu Linux. The command and options are rich and varied, and I believe could themselves be collected into a book-length work. This section examines only those command switches that I use most frequently.

First, select one of the packages already available in the /var/cache/apt/archives directory. It should be one with few if any dependencies. If the package is already installed, back up any existing associated configuration file and apply the **dpkg -P** command to that package. One suggestion for this purpose is listed in Exercise 6-1. For this section, let's say the package name is *test_1.2.3ubuntu2_i386*.deb.

When administrative privileges are required, you need to preface the command with the **sudo** command. Now install the package. The following command should work on any available Ubuntu Linux package, assuming there are no uninstalled dependent packages:

```
$ sudo dpkg -i  test_1.2.3ubuntu2_i386.deb
```

If there's a message associated with "dependency problems," there are other packages that also need to be installed. While that process is simplified with the **apt-get** commands described shortly in the section of the same name, the focus of this section is on the **dpkg** command.

To verify that a desired package is installed, the **dpkg -l** command can help. Be aware that it works only with the name of the package, in this case:

```
$ dpkg -l  test
```

If you've spelled the name of the *test* package correctly, the status of the package is shown in the output. One example is shown in Figure 6-1.

The first two or three letters on the left of the package name, in this case, the *pn* to the left of *hwdata*, indicate the status of the package. Hints are shown in Figure 6-1; for example, the first letter is the "Desired" status, where *i* is short for install and *p* is short for purge. The second letter is the actual status; in this case, *n* is short for not installed; *i* is short for installed. Try the **dpkg -l** command by itself; you'll see the full list of currently installed packages. For those of you more familiar with RPM-based distributions, note the similarity to the **rpm -qa** command.

For any installed package, it's easy to identify the list of files installed with that package. Just apply the **dpkg -L** command to it, and you should see the full list of files and directories installed through that package:

```
$ dpkg -L test
```

<table>
<tr>
<td>

FIGURE 6-1

Package status

</td>
<td>

```
michael@UbuntuGG:~$ dpkg -l hwdata
Desired=Unknown/Install/Remove/Purge/Hold
| Status=Not/Installed/Config-f/Unpacked/Failed-cfg/Half-inst/t-aWait/T-pend
|/ Err?=(none)/Hold/Reinst-required/X=both-problems (Status,Err: uppercase=bad)
||/ Name           Version        Description
+++-=============================-=======================================================
pn  hwdata         <none>         (no description available)
michael@UbuntuGG:~$ []
```

</td>
</tr>
</table>

If you're not sure about the source of a particular file, apply the **dpkg -S** command to the full path to that file. For example, when I run the following command, I see that it's based on the passwd package:

```
$ dpkg -S /etc/default/useradd
passwd: /etc/default/useradd
```

Just be aware that the **dpkg -S** command doesn't work on every file; some files are composite configuration files created from two or more packages.

Finally, there are a couple of options for uninstalling the package. The **dpkg -r** command removes a package, without removing associated configuration files. The **dpkg -P** command purges the configuration files along with the package.

EXERCISE 6-1

Testing dpkg Commands

The first step in learning about the Ubuntu Linux packaging system is running the **dpkg** command. To that end, you need to download an actual package—or use one that may already be downloaded in the /var/cache/apt/archives directory. This exercise assumes you haven't already downloaded or installed the hwdata package, have an active Internet connection and can access standard Ubuntu Linux software repositories described later in the "Update and Manage Clients" section. You may be able to substitute a different package, as long as that package doesn't have uninstalled dependencies.

1. Open a command-line interface.
2. Run the **sudo apt-get -d install hwdata** command.
3. Make sure the hwdata_*.deb package is now included in the /var/cache/apt/ archives directory.
4. Run the commands described in this section, including **dpkg -i**, **dpkg -l**, **dpkg -L**, **dpkg -S**, and **dpkg -P**. Apply these commands to the package just installed.
5. Restore the original configuration. As this exercise assumes the hwdata package was not originally installed, make sure it's purged with the dpkg -P command.

The apt-get Commands

In the previous section, I described one of the problems with the **dpkg** command, associated with dependencies. While there are ways to force installations despite existing dependencies, that can be risky. Installed packages without access to dependencies can lead to problems in associated commands and applications.

That's where the **apt-*** commands can help. Specifically, the **apt-get install** *package* and **apt-get remove** *package* commands install and remove the package of your choice, with all dependencies. Of course, as package installation using the **dpkg** command requires administrative privileges, so does the **apt-get** command.

The **apt-get** commands are nearly as rich and versatile as the **dpkg** command; some would say they're more versatile. Without the tools described in the "Update and Manage Clients" section, you should run the following command on a regular basis:

```
$ sudo apt-get update
```

This command updates the local package database, so your system knows what packages are available for updates. In addition, there's an upgrade option; the following command takes a look at all current packages and compares them against available upgrades:

```
$ sudo apt-get upgrade
```

Based on the current state of packages, there may be a few that should have been installed or removed, but may have been missed. Those packages can be caught with the following command:

```
$ sudo apt-get -u dselect-upgrade
```

The /var/cache/apt/archives directory can easily become filled with gigabytes of package files. You could clean out all packages from this directory with the following command

```
$ sudo apt-get clean
```

Alternatively, you could just clear out those packages which have become obsolete (and in most cases are superseded by more recent packages) with the following command:

```
$ sudo apt-get autoclean
```

on the **Ｊob** *Many Ubuntu and Debian gurus prefer the* aptitude **command in place of** apt-get. *In many cases, it does lead to "cleaner" output. However,* aptitude **is not listed in the UCP curriculum.**

Other apt-Based Commands

The **apt-get** command is just one of the many available **apt**-based commands. Others that I cover include **apt-cdrom**, **apt-file**, and **apt-ftparchive**. The **apt-ftparchive** command will be used to help create a local repository database later in the second Lab.

For a more complete list of **apt-** commands and options, see the Debian Linux apt HOWTO, available online from www.debian.org/doc/manuals/apt-howto/.

apt-cache

The simplest way to review available repositories for package information is with the **apt-cache** command. Assuming the local repository databases are up to date, the following command searches for all packages related to MythTV, a popular Linux-based personal video recorder package:

```
$ apt-cache search mythtv
```

If you want a preview of the dependencies associated with a package, the **depends** and **rdepends** switches can help. For example, the following command provides a list of dependencies, or packages that should be installed before The GIMP image manager can be installed. If you read the list carefully, you'll see suggested packages associated with some features of The GIMP, as well as recommended packages, conflicts, and updates of currently installed packages associated with dependencies.

```
$ apt-cache depends gimp
```

If you're interested in reverse dependencies, the **rdepends** switch can help. For example, to find packages that require The GIMP to be installed first, run the following command:

```
$ apt-cache rdepends gimp
```

But the information provided by **apt-cache** may not be up to date. To make sure the local system has the latest repository updates, run the following command before rerunning the **apt-cache** command of your choice.

```
$ sudo apt-get update
```

apt-cdrom

When installing Ubuntu Linux from a CD/DVD drive, the system automatically adds that media as an update repository. But if Ubuntu was installed from another source, it's possible to add the CD/DVD drive as an option. For example, if you've mounted the CD/DVD drive (or associated ISO file) on the /repo directory, the following command adds it as a repository option for the local system:

```
$ sudo apt-cdrom -d /repo add
```

on the job

The capabilities of the apt-cdrom *command may be limited; see bug 179322 at https://bugs.launchpad.net for more information.*

apt-file

The **apt-file** command uses the repository databases to help search for files within uninstalled packages. For example, starting with the Hardy Heron release, the /etc/inittab file is no longer installed by default. If you prefer a boot process with /etc/inittab, you could search for it from configured repositories with the following command:

```
$ apt-file search /etc/inittab
```

Of course, this assumes the local repository database is up to date. If unsure, run the **apt-get update** command. And if you need to install the **apt-file** command, run the **sudo apt-get install apt-file** command.

apt-ftparchive

The **apt-ftparchive** can be used to configure a repository for client access. Specifically, the following version of this command, when run in a directory with a bunch of Ubuntu Linux packages, creates an appropriate Packages.gz file database:

```
$ apt-ftparchive packages . | gzip -9c > Packages.gz
```

The dot (.) in the command refers to all files in the current directory. Of course, you could substitute the name of the directory with the packages to be configured into a repository, and send the output to the appropriate directory searched by clients.

For example, on the main Ubuntu Gutsy Gibbon archive in the United States of America, assuming a standard i386 repository, the directory with the Packages.gz file is

```
/ubuntu/dists/gutsy/main/binary-i386
```

More information on Ubuntu Linux repositories is described shortly in the next certification objective.

Use alien to Convert from Other Package Types

There are several different package types available for various Linux distributions. Debian-based distributions such as Ubuntu Linux typically end with the .deb extension. RPM-based packages, such as those for Red Hat and SUSE Linux, typically end with the .rpm extension. Stampede Linux packages typically end with the .slp extension. Slackware Linux packages typically end with the .tgz extension. The **alien** command can be used to convert between each of these package types.

For example, if a friend created a special RPM package for Fedora Linux that does not have any dependencies, I could try to install it on my Ubuntu Linux system. But first, I have to convert the RPM package with the following command:

```
$ sudo alien --to-deb package.rpm
```

I specified a package without dependencies to simplify the process. If the package you want to convert has dependencies, you might choose to convert those packages as well, but that could lead to conflicts with other packages native to Ubuntu Linux.

Compatibility with Debian Packages

As noted in Chapter 1, Ubuntu Linux is based on the developmental packages of Debian Linux. So yes, at some point in the Ubuntu development cycle, Debian Linux packages were used. However, Ubuntu developers do make changes. They may build a package to a different compiler. They may create different levels of functionality.

If you can satisfy the concerns about builds and functionality, you *might* be able to install a Debian Linux package on an Ubuntu Linux system.

CERTIFICATION OBJECTIVE 6.02

Review a Variety of Repositories

Ubuntu Linux has in many ways inherited the thousands of packages originally developed for Debian Linux. As Ubuntu's popularity has grown, it has also benefited from packages developed by the community and even those corporations who in some way support Linux.

As discussed in Chapter 1, Ubuntu updates are based on a series of regular repositories. These repositories can be downloaded and or mirrored on a local network. Some repositories are restricted due to their lack of compliance with open source licensing. Some third parties

Watch *Understand the difference between Ubuntu Linux, local, restricted, third- party, and Debian package repositories. Recognize repositories by Ubuntu Linux release.*

organize their contributions into their own repositories. If you're an Ubuntu developer, it may be appropriate to learn about and even connect to Debian Linux repositories. Of course, if you're a developer, you're probably also interested in the source code associated with each package and repository.

Distribution-Specific Ubuntu Repositories

Ubuntu Linux repositories are organized by distribution release. For example, Hardy Heron repositories are stored in hardy* subdirectories; Gutsy Gibbon repositories are stored in gutsy* subdirectories.

Ubuntu Linux also includes source code in its repositories, when available. There are separate repositories for security fixes, software updates, and backports. A backport is a feature adapted from a later version of Ubuntu Linux. It's most commonly found for the Ubuntu Long Term Support (LTS) releases.

To summarize, the standard repositories for each distribution release are as follows:

- *distro*   Standard Ubuntu Linux packages, supported by Canonical, available with source code under an open source license.
- *distro*-**security**   Security fixes for packages in standard repositories.
- *distro*-**updates**   Feature updates for packages in standard repositories.
- *distro*-**backports**   Feature updates for packages in standard repositories, from newer releases of Ubuntu Linux.
- *distro*-**proposed**   Proposed updates for packages in standard repositories; stored here for testing by the Ubuntu community. Packages in this repository are not for use on production systems.

    When available, source code packages are included in each of these repositories. To decipher this system, substitute the name of the Ubuntu Linux release for *distro*; for example, the Hardy Heron security repository is shown in the configuration file as hardy-security. To review the names of each available repository, refer to the basic URL listed in the /etc/apt/sources.list file. The basic URL listed in my version of this file is http://us.archive.ubuntu.com/ ubuntu/. Available repositories are listed in the dists/ subdirectory.

Standard Repository Categories

Every distribution release–specific repository is divided into four different categories. Standard Linux packages are associated with the Ubuntu main repository. It includes packages officially supported by Canonical. As Ubuntu Linux is freely available, users can't get professional support for installing that package (at least without a Canonical service subscription). However, if there is a security issue, or in many cases a functional issue with software in the Ubuntu main repository, the Ubuntu Linux organization will focus on creating a fix for that package.

As suggested in Chapter 1, software in any restricted repository is there because of some license that does not conform to open source principles. It may not comply with any standard open source licenses. Source code for packages in this repository may not be available, which means that packages in this repository might only be available for a certain architecture or even limited to a specific kernel version release.

Packages not officially supported by Canonical, but which conform to one or more open source licenses, and are supported by the Ubuntu community, are included in the Universe repository. Packages that might be considered for the Universe repository, but do not confirm to open source licenses, are included in the Multiverse repository.

To summarize, the standard repositories in this category are as follows:

- **Ubuntu main** Open source packages supported by Canonical
- **Ubuntu restricted** Packages supported by Canonical that are not open source
- **Universe** Open source packages not supported by Canonical but supported by the Ubuntu community
- **Multiverse** Packages not supported by Canonical and not open source

As an example, the list of standard Multiverse packages for Gutsy Gibbon is available from http://us.archive.ubuntu.com/ubuntu/, in the dists/gutsy/multiverse subdirectory. You might note that the packages are also segregated by architecture, such as 32-bit CPU-based packages in the binary-i386/ subdirectory, or source code in the source/ subdirectory.

There is also a Partner repository available for some releases of Ubuntu Linux. Examples of packages in this category include VMware server and the Opera web browser. Unlike other repositories, Partner repository packages may not be available on mirrors.

Local Repositories

Repositories can be created or copied to a local directory. Local repository directories can be shared using HTTP, FTP, or NFS servers. As the HTTP service is not currently included in the UCP curriculum, it is beyond the scope of this book. For more information on creating an FTP and NFS server, see Chapter 10.

Once the directory is shared, be sure that there is no firewall such as that associated with the **iptables** command or TCP Wrappers system. For more information on mirroring a repository, and pointing clients to that repository, see the "Create a Local Mirror" objective later in this chapter.

When configuring a local repository, keep in mind the basic structure just described in the section on "Distribution-specific Ubuntu Repositories."

Third-Party Repositories

Third-party repositories are not supported by Canonical or the Ubuntu community. Many third parties specify their own repositories; however, they may not be stable. For example, the Automatix project ceased development work in the spring of 2008, after it was recommended by the *New York Times*, in the fall of 2007. Other examples which may still be working are listed at www.linux-mag.com/id/5006.

 on the **Job**

The community Ubuntu documentation suggests that third-party repositories can cause problems, especially with upgrades. Yet some third-party repositories can be a terrific convenience. In other words, there is no right answer with respect to the use of third-party repositories.

Debian Repositories

If you are a developer of Ubuntu Linux software, you may need access to Debian Linux software. Prior to the Debian Import Freeze, Ubuntu Linux developers work from Debian packages in their "unstable" repository. If you're participating in that part of the Ubuntu development process, you'll need access to appropriate Debian Linux repositories. They're available from http://http.us.debian.org/debian/dists/unstable/, in the contrib/, main/, and non-free/ subdirectories.

In case you're wondering, Debian Linux packages generally should not be used on a production Ubuntu Linux system.

CERTIFICATION OBJECTIVE 6.03

Update and Manage Clients

Now that you know more about Ubuntu Linux repositories, you're ready to manage and update clients. Local repositories are stored in the /etc/apt/sources.list configuration file. You may not want to accept all security updates; some study of the Ubuntu Security Notices (USN) are in order for the informed Linux administrator.

e**x**a m

ⓦa t c h

Know how to update and manage the repository list using the /etc/apt/sources.list file, as well as the Software Sources tool. Understand update

management from the command line, as well as with the Update Manager and the Synaptic Package Manager.

Graphical management tools can help with the process; two important tools cited in the UCP include Synaptic and the Update Manager. Updates can be automated locally or remotely. Sometimes, you'll need to reconfigure packages with the **update-alternatives** tool.

on the

❶o b

One special update issue relates to the Linux kernel. Most Linux distributions, including Ubuntu Linux, automatically select kernels for upgrade when available. But kernel upgrades can affect currently running systems. For example, some databases are supported only to certain kernel releases. Some drivers are built only to certain kernel releases; upgrades may even require recompiling the kernel to retain support for the associated hardware.

The Local Repository List

Local repositories are configured in the /etc/apt/sources.list file. It's a fairly straightforward file; the following is an analysis of a version of this file available just after Ubuntu Linux Gutsy Gibbon was installed on my older laptop system. While I cover only active commands, this file also contains several comments, which are suggestions for alternative commands:

The first two commands point to basic Ubuntu Linux archives for the Gutsy Gibbon distribution, focused on the Ubuntu main and Ubuntu restricted repositories. The first command starts with a **deb**, which is associated with standard binary packages. The second command, **deb-src**, looks for accompanying source code packages in the same repositories.

```
deb http://us.archive.ubuntu.com/ubuntu/ gutsy main restricted
deb-src http://us.archive.ubuntu.com/ubuntu/ gutsy main restricted
```

The following directives point to Gutsy Gibbon updates, upgrades to what may have been included during the original installation process.

```
deb http://us.archive.ubuntu.com/ubuntu/ gutsy-updates main restricted
deb-src http://us.archive.ubuntu.com/ubuntu/ gutsy-updates main restricted
```

The next set of directives point to the Gutsy Gibbon universe repository. The associated comment notes that the Ubuntu team will not support any packages contained therein, and won't get any security updates. There are four directives in this group, as they point to the binary and source code in both the **gutsy** and **gutsy-updates** categories.

```
deb http://us.archive.ubuntu.com/ubuntu/ gutsy universe
deb-src http://us.archive.ubuntu.com/ubuntu/ gutsy universe
deb http://us.archive.ubuntu.com/ubuntu/ gutsy-updates universe
deb-src http://us.archive.ubuntu.com/ubuntu/ gutsy-updates universe
```

There are four more directives, almost identical to those shown in the preceding example, except they substitute **multiverse** for **universe**. As described earlier, the Multiverse repository does not conform to open source licenses.

There are the security repositories—the following six directives are associated with the Gutsy Gibbon security categories. Note the references to Ubuntu main, Ubuntu restricted, Universe, and Multiverse packages. You may have noted the Ubuntu warnings on how they don't provide support for packages in the Universe or Multiverse repositories. But when security updates are made available to Ubuntu, the responsible developers include them in the appropriate repositories.

```
deb http://security.ubuntu.com/ubuntu gutsy-security main restricted
deb-src http://security.ubuntu.com/ubuntu gutsy-security main restricted
deb http://security.ubuntu.com/ubuntu gutsy-security universe
deb-src http://security.ubuntu.com/ubuntu gutsy-security universe
deb http://security.ubuntu.com/ubuntu gutsy-security multiverse
deb-src http://security.ubuntu.com/ubuntu gutsy-security multiverse
```

There are several other suggested directives in comments. One group includes backports, which may be of special interest if you've installed one of the Ubuntu Linux Long Term Support (LTS) releases. As LTS releases are supported for three years on the desktop and five years on the server, backports may update such releases with the latest features. If you're interested in backports, activate the following directives (despite the format limits in this series, **main restricted universe multiverse** are all on the same line):

```
# deb http://us.archive.ubuntu.com/ubuntu/ gutsy-backports main
restricted universe multiverse
# deb-src http://us.archive.ubuntu.com/ubuntu/ gutsy-backports main
restricted universe multiverse
```

One other commented repository of interest is the Partner repository. Unlike the other repositories, this one may not be available on the mirror of your choice.

If you're interested in partner packages such as VMware Server and the Opera web browser, activate these directives:

```
# deb http://archive.canonical.com/ubuntu gutsy partner
# deb-src http://archive.canonical.com/ubuntu gutsy partner
```

Just be aware that not all software from Ubuntu partners is available from this repository. For a list of current Ubuntu partners, navigate to http://webapps.ubuntu .com/partners/software/. In fact, the only partner package available for the Hardy Heron release as of this writing is Opera.

Find the Right Mirror

During the installation process, you may have configured a connection to an appropriate national mirror. But it may not be the best mirror for you. For example, when I trace the route to the us.archive.ubuntu.com mirror from the west coast of the United States of America, it actually connects to a server in the United Kingdom.

on the
()ob

One way to trace the route to a remote server is with the traceroute *command. IP address locators available online can help identify the geographic position of a remote server.*

So for the best connection to a mirror, it is in my interest to find a mirror close to me. A current list of Ubuntu mirrors is available online from https://launchpad .net/ubuntu/+archivemirrors. When selecting a mirror, consider the following factors:

- ■ **Geographic distance**   A mirror physically close to you is less likely to be subject to Internet traffic problems.
- ■ **Desired protocol**   Not all mirrors support access through HTTP, FTP, and rsync servers.
- ■ **Speed**   Depending on the number of users who connect to a mirror, faster mirrors usually lead to faster downloads.

The process can be somewhat automated. Open the Software Sources application: in the GNOME desktop, click System | Administration | Software Sources, or run the **sudo software-properties-gtk** command. In the Ubuntu Software tab shown in Figure 6-2, click the Download From drop-down text box. Click Other to open the Choose A Download Server window shown in Figure 6-3.

Use the tool to evaluate the configured list of download servers. Try it out for yourself; click Select Best Server. Just remember to make your own judgment on the results, and evaluate it against the aforementioned list of Ubuntu mirrors.

FIGURE 6-2

The Software
Sources tool

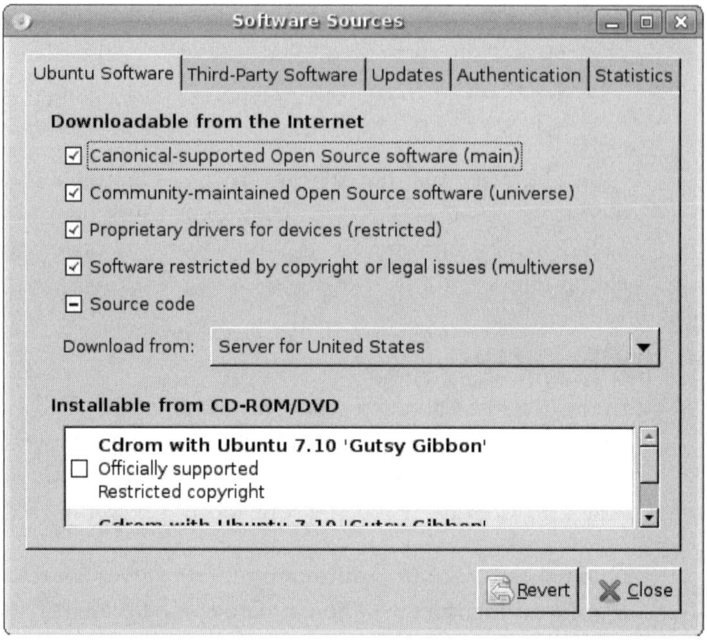

FIGURE 6-3

Choosing a
download server

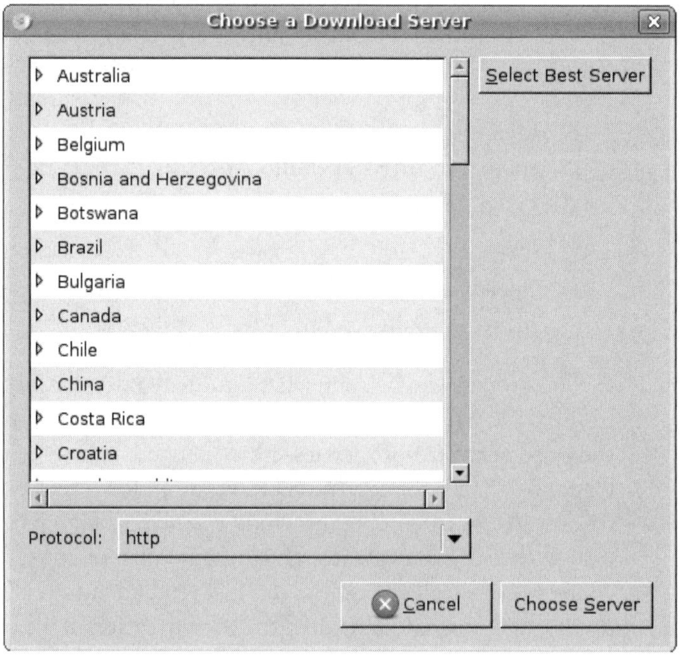

Finding the Right Mirror

To keep a system up to date, it's helpful to choose the best mirror for you. That mirror should respond quickly when updates are needed. Generally, that means a mirror physically close to you, up to date relative to the main Ubuntu repositories, and with a fast connection to the Internet. That's a fast connection between the mirror and the Internet, which is not related to the speed of your home or business connection. In this exercise, you'll use the Software Sources tool and the Ubuntu mirror list at https://launchpad.net/ubuntu/+archivemirrors to help.

1. Open the Ubuntu mirror list at https://launchpad.net/ubuntu/+archivemirrors. Based on the physical proximity and access speed from each mirror site, make your best guess on the optimal mirror.

2. Back up the current /etc/apt/sources.list file. Take a quick look at the file and make a note of the current repository mirror URL being used.

3. Open the Software Sources tool. In the GNOME desktop environment, open a terminal window. Run the **sudo software-properties-gtk** command.

4. When the Software Sources tool appears, click the drop-down text box adjacent to the Download From label, and click Other.

5. When the Choose A Download Server window appears, click Select Best Server. The Testing Download Servers window should appear, testing connections to available Ubuntu mirror sites.

6. Note the site that appears back in the Choose A Download Server window. Does it match your evaluation of the Ubuntu mirror list?

7. Don't close the window yet. Look at the command-line interface. Review the list of mirrors shown. Are all of the mirrors even geographically close to you?

8. Based on the information given, make a choice for a mirror, and then click Choose Server. Back in the Software Sources window, click Close.

9. When you see "The Information About Available Software Is Out Of Date," click Reload.

10. When the system is updated, and the Software Sources window closes, check the /etc/apt/sources.list file again. Has the repository URL changed?

When I first ran this exercise, it suggested that the best mirror for me is one in Canada. When I cross-checked with the aforementioned list of Ubuntu mirrors, I saw that the suggested mirror has a 10Mbps connection to the Internet. While a slow connection is not necessarily bad if few people connect to it, a slow distant connection is doubly troublesome.

Therefore, I overrode the suggestion made by the Software Sources tool with my best judgment. I selected a mirror physically close to me, with a fast connection, based on the aforementioned Ubuntu mirror list.

Studying Security Updates

As strange as it may sound, some administrators don't install all security updates. For example, if you're not using the Samba file server, and don't plan to install Samba in the near future, there's no reason to update a system for a Samba security update. So the security updates you install depend on the services you need.

New kernels can be especially difficult for some. Kernel updates may plug security holes. Certain databases may be certified to a certain kernel version. Upgrades would then invalidate support for that database. Specialized drivers may be available only for certain kernels; if source code is not available for that driver, it's not possible to recompile that driver to the new kernel.

Ubuntu Security Notices (USN) are designed to help the administrator understand if a security update is needed. The latest USN are available from www.ubuntu.com/usn. If you have a browser that supports RSS (Really Simple Syndication) feeds, it's possible to subscribe to these notices. One alternative is a subscription to the Ubuntu Security Announcements mailing list; the Ubuntu mailing lists are shown at https://lists.ubuntu.com/.

Graphical Management Tools

While you've already seen the Software Sources tool earlier in the section "Find the Right Mirror," there are other graphical management tools available. Two of the more common tools are Synaptic and Update Manager. These tools can be started from a GUI-based command line with the **sudo synaptic** and **update-manager** commands, respectively. They are also available from the System | Administration menu.

As with other graphical management tools, they do not provide all of the capabilities of the command-line tools. However, they also automatically upgrade the kernel, which is not always desirable.

This is another place where a Live CD/DVD can be useful. Starting an Ubuntu Linux installation from a Live CD/DVD provides a consistent starting point for updates. If you're testing the update process using different tools, starting from a Live CD/DVD supports a consistent comparison between different update tools.

Synaptic Package Manager

The Synaptic Package Manager is a front end to several of the **apt-*** commands, including **apt-get**, **apt-cdrom**, **apt-cache**, and more. It provides a visual overview of available packages. This section provides the briefest of overviews to Synaptic, shown in Figure 6-4. I only cover the most basic of Synaptic's capabilities. A full description of the Synaptic Package Manager could easily fill a chapter or more. The descriptions in this section are intended to be more than sufficient for the UCP exam.

FIGURE 6-4   The Synaptic Package Manager

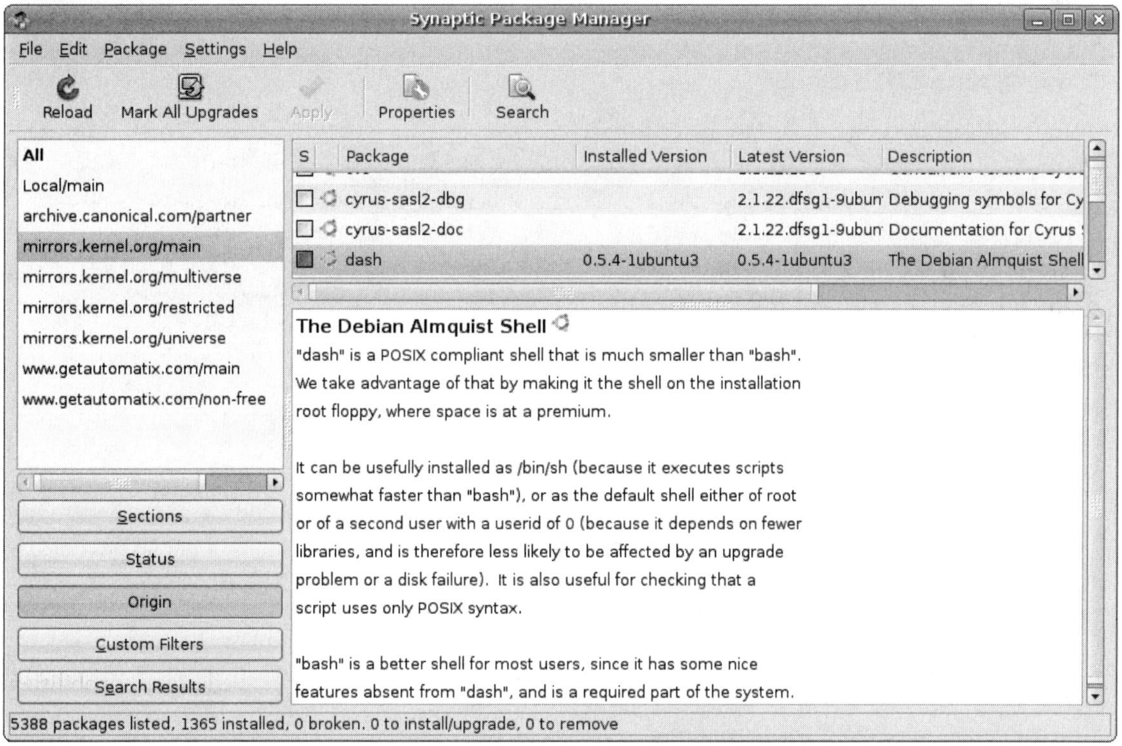

First, there are the buttons in the top toolbar. The Reload option is a front end to the **apt-get update** command, which updates databases to the latest information available from the repositories cited in the /etc/apt/sources.list file. The Mark All Upgrades button checks the local repository database against currently installed packages, and marks all packages with available upgrades. If you click this button, the Apply button becomes active, which prompts you to start the download and installation of all marked upgrades (as well as any other packages that you may have marked for installation or removal).

If you haven't marked any other packages for installation or removal, click the Status button in the lower-left area, and then click the Installed (upgradeable) option that appears in the upper left. You'll see a group of packages to be upgraded in the upper-right pane, as shown in Figure 6-5. If for some reason you don't want to upgrade a kernel, make sure the updates for the linux-headers and linux-image packages are disabled.

FIGURE 6-5   Upgrades in the Synaptic Package Manager

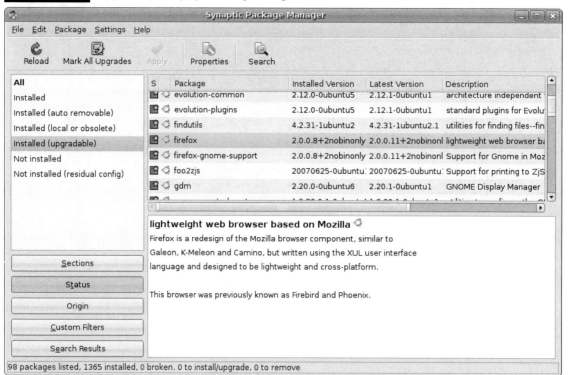

It's a fairly common practice to avoid kernel upgrades in certain circumstances. Software such as database managers may be certified only to a specific kernel version. Special drivers may be built to a specific kernel version. In either case, a kernel upgrade would mean trouble.

The Properties button opens an untitled window that provides detailed information about the highlighted package, including dependencies and installed files. The Search button supports a search through the database; it's a front end to the **apt-cache** command.

Note the organization of the Synaptic window. Categories are listed in the upper left. Packages in the highlighted category are shown in the upper right. A description of the highlighted package is shown in the lower right.

In the lower-left part of the screen, there are five options for sorting packages as listed in the upper left. Try them out for yourself. Briefly, the Sections button provides a functional grouping of packages; the Status button divides packages by installation status; the Origin button classifies packages by their original repository; the Custom Filters button divides packages by those which are marked for changes, those which are upgradeable, custom searches, and more; finally, the Search Results button lists the output of custom searches.

In Synaptic, click Settings | Repositories. The window that appears should be familiar—it's the Software Sources window described earlier.

There are a substantial number of other options available. Click Settings | Preferences. Explore the tabs that appear in the Preferences window. The options you see should be instructive in how you can customize updates on any Ubuntu Linux system.

One option that provides a list of dependencies and more is associated with the properties of a specific package. Select the package of your choice and click the Properties button. Under the Dependencies tab shown in Figure 6-6, note the list of dependencies for the gnome-control-center package.

Note that the Dependencies button is actually a drop-down menu box. The Dependent Packages option actually lists reverse dependencies, which correspond to the **apt-cache rdepends** command described earlier in this chapter. The Dependencies Of The Latest Version option lists dependencies of any upgrade that could be installed.

Update Manager

One other important GUI tool for package management is the Update Manager. It's easy to open; click System | Administration | Update Manager or type in the **update-manager** command from a command line in the GUI. It takes the current list of packages, and compares it against the local database, which lists available updates.

FIGURE 6-6

Dependencies of
a package

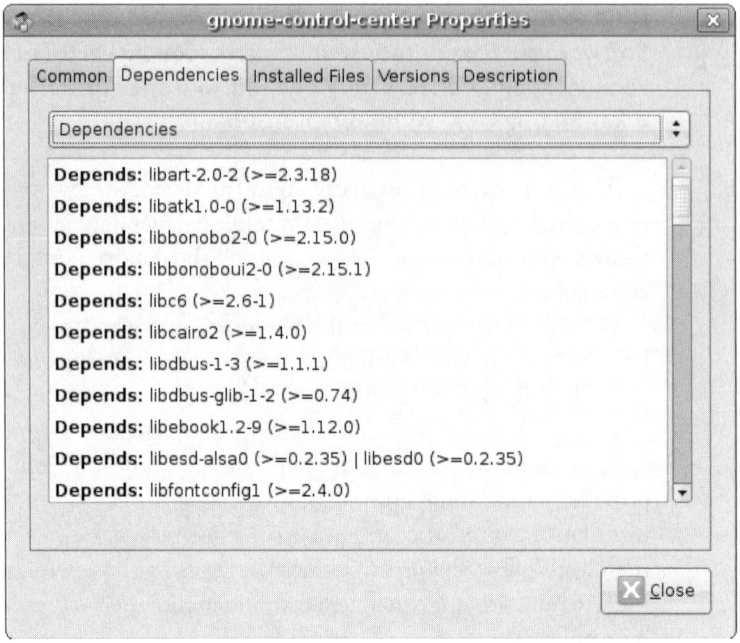

The Update Manager is straightforward. As shown in Figure 6-7, packages for
which updates are available are listed, and are selected by default. Administrative
password confirmation is not required until you click the Install Updates button.
As the comparison is against a local database, you may want to run the **sudo apt-get
update** command first to make sure that local databases are up to date. Alternatively,
just click the Check button, which performs the same function.

Note that I've also clicked the Description Of Update option, which supports
browsing of the change log and description for each selected package. If for some
reason you don't want to update a kernel, disable the updates for the linux-headers
and linux-image packages.

Remote Package Management

Systems can be managed remotely. The process is straightforward; any network
system such as virtual private networks (VPN) or the Secure Shell (SSH), which
supports remote logins allows remote package management.

When I need access to remote GUI applications, I prefer Secure Shell access to
my remote systems. When I log in with the **ssh -X** or **ssh -Y** commands, it supports

FIGURE 6-7

The Update
Manager

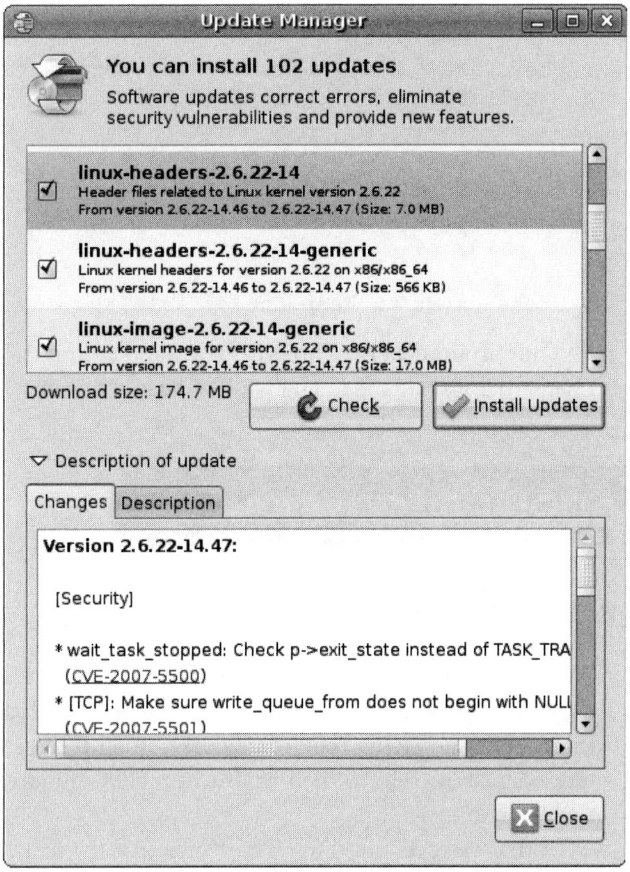

remote access to remote package management applications such as Synaptic or the Update Manager, assuming it's supported by the remote SSH server.

The Alternatives System

Sometimes there's more than one alternative package for an option. For example, I could configure vi, ed, or nano as the default editor for my system. If you've just added emacs, and want it configured as the default editor, the **update-alternatives** command can help.

The alternatives system depends on configuration files in the /etc/alternatives directory. To configure the default editor on my system, I run the following command:

```
$ sudo update-alternatives --config editor
```

which leads to the following output:

```
There are 4 alternatives which provide `editor'.
  Selection    Alternative
-----------------------------------------------
            1    /usr/bin/vim.tiny
            2    /bin/ed
*+          3    /bin/nano
            4    /usr/bin/emacs22

Press enter to keep the default[*], or type selection number:
```

The current default is noted as the nano editor. As suggested by the text menu, all I need to do is enter **4** to change the default to emacs.

CERTIFICATION OBJECTIVE 6.04

Create a Local Mirror

When there are a significant number of Ubuntu Linux systems on a network, large updates, if run simultaneously, can easily overload even business-level Internet connections. Seems like every time I turn around, there's an update to the OpenOffice.org suite, which leads to a several-hundred-megabyte update—for each system.

In that case, it's often more cost-effective to create a local mirror of at least certain repositories, such as those associated with updates. For that purpose, Ubuntu Linux includes tools that can copy and synchronize from a remote mirror. If you also want to keep systems up to date with custom packages, there are tools available that can help configure the repository database. But the related commands are beyond the scope of the UCP exam.

Of course, once a local mirror is created, it won't help unless local clients are configured to use that local mirror. And local mirrors need to be kept up to date, so you should set up a regular job such as an automated **cron** job to keep that mirror up to date.

exam

Watch *Understand the basic process and associated commands for creating a local repository.*

Synchronize from a Remote Repository

There are two basic options to synchronize a local client to a remote repository. The **rsync** command is the traditional method associated with synchronizing local and remote groups of files. The **apt-mirror** command is more focused, and in my opinion, a better choice at least for the initial mirroring of the remote repository. The focus of this section is on **apt-mirror**; you could subsequently use the **rsync** command if desired to keep the repository so created up to date.

As of this writing, the **apt-mirror** command is rarely installed with Ubuntu Linux. To install it, or to update it to the latest available version, run the following command:

```
$ sudo apt-get install apt-mirror
```

You could use the **sudo apt-mirror** command right away; but when I tried it on my home Gutsy Gibbon system, it warned me that it needed to download 40GB of files. Gosh, that was more than I was prepared to download at the time. And that would have overloaded the partition that I was using.

So I then reconfigured several files installed with the apt-mirror package. The key files are the /etc/apt/mirror.list configuration file and the /usr/bin/apt-mirror script. The default version of the /etc/apt/mirror.list configuration file lists default paths in comments, as well as configured repositories. You may also note a new apt-mirror user and group in the /etc/passwd and /etc/group files, respectively. I'll come back to that in a moment.

Now let's return to the /etc/apt/mirror.list configuration file. The first directive in the file sets the directory where files are copied. The default is /var/spool/apt-mirror; you could create a partition with sufficient space for the /var/ directory.

```
# set base_path    /var/spool/apt-mirror
```

Because of the demands of an Ubuntu Linux mirror, I set up a separate partition on a new hard drive, /media/sdb3, and documented it with the following directive:

```
set base_path /media/sdb3/apt-mirror/
```

The following directives (and associated comment—yes, "privlages" is misspelled) list the directories that need to be created, with privileges.

```
# if you change the base path you must create the directories
# below with write privlages
# set mirror_path  $base_path/mirror
# set skel_path    $base_path/skel
# set var_path     $base_path/var
# set cleanscript $var_path/clean.sh
```

So I ran the following commands to create the appropriate directories, as subdirectories of the value of the **base_path** directive:

```
$ sudo mkdir /media/sdb3/apt-mirror
$ sudo mkdir /media/sdb3/apt-mirror/mirror
$ sudo mkdir /media/sdb3/apt-mirror/skel
$ sudo mkdir /media/sdb3/apt-mirror/var
$
```

These commands create the noted directories with write privileges for the owner. But to make this work, you also need to set the owner for all these directories (and subdirectories) as the apt-mirror user and group. One way to do so is with the following command. The **chown -R** command changes ownership on the /media/sdb3/apt-mirror directory, and subdirectories, recursively.

```
$ sudo chown -R apt-mirror.apt-mirror /media/sdb3/apt-mirror
```

Now return to the /etc/apt/mirror.list configuration file. The default uses the running host architecture. As I'm creating a mirror on a 64-bit system, the following suggests that the default would be to copy from 64-bit repositories.

```
# set defaultarch  <running host architecture>
```

However, as my clients are 32-bit systems, I need to make a change here as well:

```
set defaultarch i386
```

After these directives, you'll see a series of URLs. They specify the repositories to be mirrored. You should change these URLs to list only those repositories that you feel the need to mirror. For example, I limit what is mirrored by activating only the following URLs.

```
deb http://us.archive.ubuntu.com/ubuntu gutsy-updates main restricted
```

Note that I limit the copying to the Ubuntu main and Ubuntu restricted repositories. I could add the Universe and Multiverse repositories if desired to this directive. The repositories you choose to copy depend on available disk space and your willingness to download tens of gigabytes of data.

Yes, the http://us.archive.ubuntu.com/ubuntu repository is the most up to date. However, based on the Software Sources tool described earlier, I've selected the http://mirrors.kernel.org/ubuntu repositories for my own system. So there's a choice—do I copy the mirror, or the more up-to-date but distant repository? There are arguments for both, which in part depend on how frequently the selected mirror site is kept up to date. I choose to copy from the mirror, but you may make a different choice. So I substitute this directive in /etc/apt/mirror.list:

```
deb http://mirrors.kernel.org/ubuntu gutsy-updates main restricted
```

Any other URL shown in this file is deactivated by adding a comment character (#) in front. As discussed earlier, there is also a change required to the /usr/bin/apt-mirror script. A change is required here only if you changed the default **base_path** defined earlier for the /etc/apt/mirror.list configuration file. Since I changed it to /media/sdb3/ apt-mirror, I change it in the /usr/bin/apt-mirror script as well:

```
"base_path"   => '/media/sdb3/apt-mirror',
```

Now I can run the **apt-mirror** command, which executes the /usr/bin/apt-mirror script. Instead of the 40GB of files that would have been downloaded earlier, the **apt-mirror** command in my configuration downloaded just over 1GB of files. This works if I've checked that there's sufficient free space available in the partition mounted on the /media/sdb3 directory.

Once the process is complete, examine the structure of the /media/sdb3/apt-mirror directory (or whatever directory you use). As I've copied the updates from the http:// mirrors.kernel.org/ubuntu site, the **apt-mirror** command as configured copies the repository to the /media/sdb3/apt-mirror/mirror/mirrors.kernel.org/ubuntu directory.

Pointing Clients to a Local Mirror

Once a repository is copied to a local source, it is a local mirror. Based on the **apt-mirror** command used in the previous section, that's a mirror of the Ubuntu Linux Gutsy Gibbon update files for the Ubuntu main and Ubuntu restricted repositories.

To prepare the local mirror for use by clients, you need to configure the appropriate directory for sharing using a server associated with the HTTP, FTP, or NFS services. For more information on configuring a share with an FTP or NFS server, see Chapter 10. HTTP services are not mentioned in the UCP curriculum and are therefore not covered in this book.

Based on an NFS share, and the repository created in the previous section, I've installed the nfs-kernel-server package and added the following directive to the /etc/exports file:

```
/media/sdb3/apt-mirror/mirror/mirrors.kernel.org/   *(rw,sync)
```

To help secure the repository, I could substitute the address for the local network for the asterisk (*). For example, 192.168.0.0/24 would limit access to the IP version 4 192.168.0.0 Class C network. IP addressing is a basic skill; the UCP exam and curriculum assume that you already understand the basics of IP addressing. If you need more information, there are many excellent sources online. Once the NFS server is started and the directory is shared as discussed in Chapter 10, remote clients can connect to that share. For example, if that NFS share is served from a system with an IP address of 192.168.0.50, I can mount it on the /repo directory with a command like this:

```
$ sudo mount -t nfs \
192.168.0.50:/media/sdb3/apt-mirror/mirror/mirrors.kernel.org /repo
```

I can then replace the standard reference in the /etc/apt/sources-list file to the gutsy-updates repository with the following:

```
deb file:/repo/ubuntu gutsy-updates main restricted
```

CERTIFICATION SUMMARY

One of the key administrative skills associated with Linux administration is the use and management of updates and their associated repositories. The fundamentals are based on the **dpkg** command, the Debian package manager. As many packages are dependent on others, the **apt-*** commands can help automatically resolve most dependencies. While Ubuntu Linux is built on Debian Linux, packages built for Debian Linux may not work on Ubuntu. As distributions such as Red Hat and Ubuntu Linux are both derivatives of the same operating system, the **alien** command can be used to convert from the Red Hat to the Ubuntu/Debian package format. Whether those converted packages are actually installable is another question.

Ubuntu package installations and updates are based on a variety of repositories. Different repositories are available for standard packages, updates, security, backports, and even proposed packages. Packages in each of these repositories can fall into four major repository categories: Ubuntu main, Ubuntu restricted, Universe, and Multiverse. Repositories can be local; some organizations configure their own repositories. If you're a developer, you may even want to enable Debian repositories for Ubuntu Linux.

Client updates are configured in the /etc/apt/sources.list configuration file. The Software Sources tool might be able to help find a more appropriate repository.

Administrators can use the USN to help decide whether to install security updates. The Synaptic Package Manager and Update Manager are two GUI update tools that can help with the update task. System updates can be managed remotely with the help of tools like **ssh**. Updates may require reconfiguration using the **update-alternatives** tool.

Administrators responsible for networks with many Ubuntu Linux systems may find it cost-effective to create their own local mirrors of Ubuntu Linux repositories. The **apt-mirror** command is optimized for this purpose. Once the gigabytes of data are copied from a remote mirror, and the associated directory is shared, the administrator can configure clients to connect to that local mirror.

✔ TWO-MINUTE DRILL

Here are some of the key points from the certification objectives in Chapter 6.

Manage Individual Packages and More

- ❑ Ubuntu Linux packages follow the *packagename_version_architecture*.deb naming convention.
- ❑ The **dpkg** command can help install, confirm package status, list files associated with a package, identify a package associated with a file, and much more.
- ❑ The **apt-get** commands can install and update the packages of your choice, with dependencies.
- ❑ Other **apt-*** based commands can identify dependencies, add CD/DVDs to the repository list, search within uninstalled packages, and more.
- ❑ Ubuntu Linux packages are built from developmental packages for Debian Linux.
- ❑ The **alien** command can convert from other Linux package types for Ubuntu Linux.

Review a Variety of Repositories

- ❑ Ubuntu Linux repositories are organized by distribution release.
- ❑ Standard repository categories include Ubuntu main, Ubuntu restricted, Universe, and Multiverse.
- ❑ Repositories can be copied to a local directory, and shared through an HTTP, NFS, or FTP server.
- ❑ There are a number of third-party repositories available designed for use by Ubuntu Linux.
- ❑ Ubuntu developers may choose to use Debian Linux repositories.

Update and Manage Clients

- ❑ Client repositories are configured in the /etc/apt/sources.list configuration file.
- ❑ While the Software Sources tool may help find a suitable mirror, judgment is also important.

❑ USN can help the administrator evaluate available security updates.

❑ The Synaptic Package Manager and Update Manager are two capable GUI update tools.

❑ Updated packages may need to be further configured using the **update-alternatives** command.

Create a Local Mirror

❑ Local mirrors can be copied and synchronized with remote repositories.

❑ Once a local mirror is created, it should be shared before use with an HTTP, FTP, or NFS server.

SELF-TEST

The following questions will help you measure your understanding of the material presented in this chapter. Read all the questions carefully, as there may be more than one correct answer. Some questions are "fill in the blank" and normally require an exact answer. Choose all correct answers for each question.

Manage Individual Packages and More

1. Which of the following commands identify the package associated with the **system-config-printer** command in the **/usr/bin/system-config-printer** command?
   A. sudo apt-get search system-config-printer
   B. sudo apt-get install system-config-printer
   C. dpkg -S /usr/bin/system-config-printer
   D. dpkg -L system-config-printer

2. Which of the following commands adds a DVD mounted on the /mnt directory? Assume it's properly configured in /etc/fstab.
   A. sudo apt-cache -d /mnt add
   B. sudo apt-cdrom -d /mnt add
   C. sudo apt-get -d /mnt add
   D. sudo apt-dvdrom -d /mnt add

3. What command lists dependencies associated with the hypothetical rdepends package? Assume the package isn't already installed, but you have a working connection to appropriate repositories.

   _____

4. What command and switch would you use to convert a package from a Red Hat–based distribution for use on an Ubuntu Linux system?

   _____

5. Which of the following commands updates and or installs the latest version of the package associated with The GIMP?
   A. sudo apt-get update gimp
   B. sudo apt-get upgrade gimp
   C. sudo apt-get install gimp
   D. sudo apt-get -U gimp

Review a Variety of Repositories

6. Name the repository used for supported packages where the developers don't make the source code available.

_____

7. Which of the following distribution names would not be seen in a list of Ubuntu repositories?
- **A.** Hardy
- **B.** Gutsy
- **C.** Feisty
- **D.** Etch

8. Which of the following is a reason for a Backports repository?
- **A.** To bring features available in older versions of Ubuntu Linux to the latest releases
- **B.** To bring features available in later versions of Ubuntu Linux to older releases
- **C.** To add features to the latest versions of Ubuntu Linux
- **D.** To update the latest releases

Update and Manage Clients

9. Name the full path to the file that configures access to local and remote repositories.

_____

10. Which of the following refers to the latest security announcements?
- **A.** Ubuntu Bugzilla
- **B.** Ubuntu Security Advisories
- **C.** USN
- **D.** The Fridge

11. Which of the following tools is dedicated to those packages with available upgrades?
- **A.** Synaptic
- **B.** Update Manager
- **C.** apt-cache
- **D.** sudo apt-get update

12. Name the command that reconfigures defaults in the /etc/alternatives directory. No switches are required.

_____

Create a Local Mirror

13. What command is commonly used to synchronize the files from a local and remote repository?

_____

14. What directive configures the mirrored repositories in the **apt-mirror** configuration file?

_____

15. Which of the following network services isn't normally used for client connections to download and install packages from local mirrors or repositories?

A. FTP

B. HTTP

C. Telnet

D. NFS

LAB QUESTIONS

Ideally, these labs should be run consecutively, as the content of Lab 2 depends on the output from Lab 1. However, if you've ever run an update before on the local system, it's possible to run Lab 2 first.

Lab 1

In this lab, you'll start with an Ubuntu Linux system booted from a Live CD. If you don't already have one available, read Chapter 2 for tips. In this lab, you'll compare the updates on your system using the **apt-get update**, Update Manager, and Synaptic Package Manager tools, and finally create an update. The system should have access to the Internet. If a DHCP server is not available, you'll have to assign an appropriate IP address to the system.

This lab assumes you have a high-speed Internet connection. If you connect with a telephone modem, the demands of this lab may exceed the capabilities of your connection.

1. Boot from the Live CD, and accept the option to Start or Install Ubuntu to boot the live Ubuntu desktop environment.

2. Move to the command-line interface. One method is to press CTRL-ALT-F1. Run the **sudo apt-get update** command. Do you know why this is done first?

3. Run the **sudo apt-get upgrade** command. Make a note of packages to be upgraded. If you want to save this output to a file, direct the output to a file with a command such as **sudo apt-get upgrade upgrades**.

4. Don't accept the request to continue. Make a note of the number of packages to be updated.

5. Move back to the GUI. Press CTRL-ALT-F7. Click System | Administration | Update Manager. Make a note of the number of packages to be updated.

6. Highlight a package to be updated. Click the Description Of Update arrow, and review more about the update. Repeat with another package.

7. Click Close to exit from the Update Manager.

8. Open a command line in the GUI; one way is to click Applications | Accessories | Terminal, and enter the **sudo synaptic** command.

9. Assuming this is the first time you've opened the Synaptic Package Manager, read the Quick Introduction that appears, and click Close.

10. In the Synaptic Package Manager window, click the Mark All Upgrades button.

11. In the Mark Additional Required Changes window that appears, click Mark to return to the Synaptic Package Manager window.

12. Click Status in the lower-left pane, and click Installed (Upgradeable) in the upper-left pane. Review the list of packages in the upper-right region. How many packages are set to install/ upgrade?

13. Select a package. Review the information that appears in the lower-right pane.

14. Click Properties and review the information in the tabs that appear.

15. Click Close to return to the Synaptic Package Manager window.

16. Click Apply. When the Summary window appears, review the information shown. How many packages will be upgraded? Click Apply in the Summary window.

17. The Synaptic Package Manager takes some time to download the noted packages. Once installed, it begins the installation and upgrade process. If you want to watch the details of the process, click the Show Process Of Single Files arrow.

18. Once the download process is complete, an Applying Changes window should appear. Click the Details arrow to review the changes as they're being made.

19. Once the update is complete, don't close this system. You'll need this configuration for the second lab.

Lab 2

In this lab, you'll take the packages downloaded in Lab 1 and create a compressed Packages.gz information file.

1. Navigate to the /var/cache/apt/archives directory; one method is with the **cd /var/cache/apt/archives** command.

2. Log in as the root user. Yes, it is possible in Ubuntu Linux, even though there is no root password assigned; just run the following command:

   ```
   $ sudo su
   ```

3. Use the archival command **apt-ftparchive**. It can be applied to the packages in the current directory with the help of the dot (.) in the following command:

   ```
   # apt-ftparchive packages . > Packages
   ```

4. Review the Packages file. It should look familiar based on what you did to review available package updates in Lab 1.

SELF-TEST ANSWERS

Manage Individual Packages and More

1. ☑ **C.** The **dpkg -S** command, when coupled with the full path to the file in question, leads to the package from which the subject file is installed.
    ☒ As the **apt-get** command does not identify a package associated with a full path to a file, answers **A** and **B** are both wrong. Since the **dpkg -L** command lists all files associated with a package name, answer **D** would work, but it would be less efficient than the **dpkg -S** command.

2. ☑ **B.** The **apt-cdrom** command focuses on repositories on CD/DVD drives.
    ☒ As the other answers don't associate the local repository list with any local optical drive, answers **A**, **C**, and **D** are all wrong.

3. ☑ The **apt-cache depends rdepends** command lists dependencies associated with the package named rdepends.

4. ☑ The **alien --to-deb** command converts packages from a Red Hat–based distribution (as well as other formats) for use on an Ubuntu Linux system.

5. ☑ **C.** The **sudo apt-get install gimp** command installs the gimp package if it isn't already installed, and upgrades it if a later version is available.
    ☒ As the **sudo apt-get update** command updates package lists and does nothing with individual packages, answer **A** is wrong. As the **sudo apt-get upgrade** command installs all available upgrades and does nothing with individual packages, answer **B** is wrong. As there is no **-U** switch to the **apt-get** command, answer **D** is also wrong.

Review a Variety of Repositories

6. ☑ The Ubuntu restricted repository includes packages that are supported by the Ubuntu team, but may not include source code. While the Multiverse repository may also include packages for which the source code is not available, packages in this repository are not officially supported.

7. ☑ **D.** Etch is a Debian Linux release code name.
    ☒ As Hardy Heron, Gutsy Gibbon, and Feisty Fawn are all Ubuntu Linux release code names, answers **A**, **B**, and **C** are all wrong.

8. ☑ **B.** A Backports repository provides features available in later releases to older versions of Ubuntu Linux.
    ☒ As answers **A**, **C**, and **D** all relate to the latest Ubuntu Linux release, they are all incorrect.

Update and Manage Clients

9. ☑ **/etc/apt/sources.list**. Access to local and remote repositories is configured through this file.

10. ☑ **C.** The Ubuntu Security Notice, USN for short, lists the latest security announcements. It's available online and can be easily monitored with an RSS format.
☒ While a few security advisories may be available in Bugzilla lists or the Fridge, it's not the primary venue, so answers **A** and **D** are both wrong. As there are no formal USN notices known as "Ubuntu Security Advisories," answer **B** is also wrong.

11. ☑ **B.** The Update Manager is dedicated to those packages with available upgrades.
☒ Synaptic has many functions. While it can also isolate updates, it is not so dedicated, so answer **A** is wrong. As the **apt-cache** command searches through remote repositories, answer **C** is wrong. As the **apt-get update** command updates local repository database lists, answer **D** is also wrong.

12. ☑ **update-alternatives**. This command with the **--config** switch reconfigures defaults in the /etc/alternatives directory.

Create a Local Mirror

13. ☑ **apt-mirror.** This command mirrors a remote repository locally.

14. ☑ **base_path.** This directive, in /etc/apt/mirror.list and /usr/bin/apt-mirror, specifies the top-level directory used to contain the local mirror files.

15. ☑ **C.** The Telnet service is not commonly used for client connections to download and install connections from local or remote mirrors.
☒ As client connections to repositories commonly use the FTP, HTTP, and NFS services, answers **A**, **B**, and **D** are all incorrect.

LAB ANSWERS

Remember, these labs should be run in sequence.

Lab 1

This lab is designed to show you that at least three tools are available for Ubuntu Linux that can provide the same updates. If you've accidentally tried to run more than one tool at a time, you'll note the error messages that appear. The questions on the number of packages to be updated should have the same answer for all three tools.

Lab 2

You can create a package list for any Ubuntu Linux package that may have been downloaded. By default, package downloads are stored in the /var/cache/apt/archives directory.

7

Printer
Configuration

T he focus of this chapter is CUPS, or more formally, the Common Unix Printing System. It's evolved into the Linux standard for managing local and remote printers, and is associated with the same Internet Print Protocol (IPP) used by other operating systems. It supports access to and configuration of groups of printers. Most key CUPS configuration files are located in the /etc/cups directory.

Several tools are available to manage and configure CUPS printers and associated print jobs. They work from the command line; they work using GUI tools; they even work with web-based interfaces. Trusted users can be configured as CUPS administrators without the risks associated with configuring general administrative access to regular users.

CERTIFICATION OBJECTIVE 7.01

Work the CUPS Packages

CUPS is a comprehensive print system. It includes a server, client commands, hardware detection drivers, and more. It includes a variety of print drivers, image libraries, and even a web-based management tool. CUPS is the successor to the Line Print Daemon (LPD) and Line Printer, Next Generation (LPRng) services, also known as the Berkeley printing system.

In this section, you'll examine and install applicable CUPS packages, take a brief look at the CUPS configuration files, and look at the variety of PostScript printer drivers. If you want to follow along, install the Ubuntu Server from the associated CD described in Chapter 2. As the GNOME desktop environment is part of the UCP exam, I've also installed the GNOME desktop environment on my Ubuntu Server system.

One key advantage of CUPS is the ability to configure print classes. A print class normally includes a group of printers, which may be collected together in a print room or print center, and can be shared like any single printer. Jobs sent to a print class are processed by the first available printer in that class. If none of the printers in a class are being used, the selection is made at random.

---

e x a m

🐦 a t c h *Understand the basic functionality of the CUPS server, including the variety of available packages, configuration files, and printer drivers.*

INSIDE THE EXAM

Install and Configure Local and Remote Printers (123.3)

The UCP curriculum suggests that certification candidates need to know how to install the printer daemon and print filters. It specifies the configuration of PostScript and non-PostScript printers. It also suggests that candidates should understand how to make local and remote printers accessible to a network, using CUPS protocols, or sharing via Samba.

Manage Printers and Print Queues (123.2)

Ubuntu Linux administrators also need to know how to manage print queues as well as specific print jobs associated with CUPS. This category encompasses general print problems, including ports, log files, and more.

The CUPS Packages

While the standard CUPS server packages are included in the Ubuntu desktop, the standard Ubuntu server installation that I tested does not include the CUPS packages. So it's appropriate to see what CUPS packages are available, and choose what should be installed.

Per the discussion of the **apt-cache** command in Chapter 6, the following command lists all available packages associated with the CUPS service:

```
$ apt-cache search cups
```

on the
Job

Another useful front end to the apt-* commands described in Chapter 6 is aptitude. It works from the command line and can help with systems where the GUI is not installed.

When I ran this command, there were 58 packages associated with CUPS. Such detail is well beyond the scope of the UCP curriculum. But a similar search, with the help of the **aptitude** tool, helps me identify that not all of these packages are actually related to printing. My output is shown in Figure 7-1.

```
$ aptitude search cups | less
```

Yes, the output looks almost identical to the output from the **apt-cache search cups** command, but there are subtle differences. The output is more organized;

FIGURE 7-1

Search output
from aptitude

```
p   apcupsd                       - APC UPS Power Management (daemon)
p   apcupsd-cgi                   - APC UPS Power Management (web interface)
p   apcupsd-doc                   - APC UPS Power Management (documentation/ex
p   bluez-cups                    - Bluetooth printer driver for CUPS
p   cups-pdf                      - PDF printer for CUPS
p   cupsddk                       - CUPS Driver Development Kit
p   cupsddk-drivers               - CUPS Driver Development Kit - Driver files
p   cupsys                        - Common UNIX Printing System(tm) - server
p   cupsys-bsd                    - Common UNIX Printing System(tm) - BSD comm
p   cupsys-client                 - Common UNIX Printing System(tm) - client p
p   cupsys-common                 - Common UNIX Printing System(tm) - common f
p   cupsys-driver-gimpprint       - printer drivers for CUPS
p   cupsys-driver-gutenprint      - printer drivers for CUPS
p   cupsys-pt                     - Tool for viewing/managing print jobs under
p   eggcups                       - notification area icon for printing jobs
p   gkrellmapcupsd                - gkrellm plugin displaying the current proc
p   gnome-cups-manager            - CUPS printer admin tool for GNOME
p   hal-cups-utils                - CUPS integration with HAL
v   libcupsimage-dev              -
p   libcupsimage2                 - Common UNIX Printing System(tm) - image li
p   libcupsimage2-dev             - Common UNIX Printing System(tm) - image de
v   libcupsys-dev                 -
i A libcupsys2                    - Common UNIX Printing System(tm) - libs
p   libcupsys2-dev                - Common UNIX Printing System(tm) - developm
p   libgnomecups1.0-1             - GNOME library for CUPS interaction
p   libgnomecups1.0-dev           - GNOME library for CUPS interaction (header
p   libgnomecupsui1.0-1c2a        - UI extensions to libgnomecups
p   libgnomecupsui1.0-dev         - UI extensions to libgnomecups (headers)
p   python-cups                   - Python bindings for CUPS
v   python2.4-cups                -
:
```

when I ran this command, I only had to sort through 31 packages. It's easier to read. Packages are organized in alphabetical order. The letter in the left column helps identify the current status of the package; *i* means the package is installed, and *p* or *c* suggests that the package is not currently installed.

The first packages I see, as shown in Figure 7-1, tell me that some of the packages aren't even related to printing. Generally, packages that start with a "lib" are package libraries, which should be automatically included as dependencies when major CUPS-related packages are installed. The packages associated with the Python programming language should also be automatically included when needed.

To find out more about an individual package, the **apt-cache show** *packagename* or **aptitude show** *packagename* command should help. For example, the output to the **aptitude show cupsys** command identifies that package as the CUPS server, and therefore something definitely to be installed to configure a Linux print server.

The other packages you choose from the list depend on your needs. For example, from the description, most administrators won't need the bluez-cups package, unless they have a printer connected using a Bluetooth network. Several packages that I consider important for a print server are listed in Table 7-1.

TABLE 7-1	Package	Description
Important CUPS Packages	cupsys	Adds the CUPS server
	cupsys-bsd	Includes commands familiar to LPD/LPRng administrators, such as **lpq**, **lpr**, and so on
	cupsys-client	Incorporates client commands based on LPD/LPRng
	cupsys-common	Supports both CUPS client and server packages
	cupsys-driver-gutenprint	Adds drivers for The GIMP; successor to cupsys-driver-gimpprint
	cupsys-pt	Provides a GUI print job management tool, accessible with the **pt** command
	gnome-cups-manager	Incorporates a tool for adding and managing CUPS printers and queues; the **gnome-cups-manager** and **gnome-cups-add** commands are key
	hal-cups-utils	Includes plug-and-play support for CUPS based on the hardware abstraction layer (HAL)

To install the packages I desire, I run the **apt-get install** or **aptitude install** commands followed by the names of desired packages shown in Table 7-1. Read carefully; you may not even want to install all of the packages shown in the table.

For the purpose of this chapter, I ran the following command on my Ubuntu Server Gutsy Gibbon system:

```
$ sudo apt-get install cupsys cupsys-bsd cupsys-client \
cupsys-common cupsys-pt hal-cups-utils gnome-cups-manager
```

This command included a substantial number of dependent packages in the installation. One thing you should be aware of is the CUPS daemon, which is started by the /etc/init.d/cupsys script: **/usr/sbin/cupsd**.

The CUPS Configuration Files

The CUPS packages install several configuration files in the /etc/cups directory. Most of the detail in these files is beyond the scope of the UCP exam. But first, standard options are configured in the /etc/default/cupsys configuration file. The default version of this file adds the parallel port print driver module. And yes, some computers (including two of mine) still have parallel ports.

A summary of each of the other CUPS files in the /etc/cups directory is listed in Table 7-2. This reflects what I see on my Ubuntu Linux Gutsy Gibbon system; as

TABLE 7-2	/etc/cups File	Description
	/etc/cups/classes.conf	Lists print classes, which consist of one or more printers
CUPS Configuration Files	/etc/cups/cupsd.conf	Adds the main CUPS configuration file
	/etc/cups/cups-pdf.conf	Configures a virtual printer that creates PDF files
	/etc/cups/lpoptions	Specifies a default printer; supersedes /etc/cups/printers.conf
	/etc/cups/mime.convs	Adds file format filters
	/etc/cups/mime.types	Specifies allowable file types
	/etc/printcap	Sets a share list used by Samba; configured via /etc/cups/cupsd.conf
	/etc/cups/ppd/	Inserts configured PPD print drivers
	/etc/cups/printers.conf	Documents configured printers
	/etc/cups/raw.convs	Adds file format filter for raw input
	/etc/cups/raw.types	Specifies allowable file type for raw input
	/etc/cups/ssl/	Sets a directory with SSL certificates
	/etc/cups/snmp.conf	Configures automated network printer discovery

CUPS changes, what you see in the /etc/cups directory may vary. In addition, you won't see an /etc/cups/printers.conf or /etc/cups/classes.conf file until a printer or print class is configured, respectively.

Generally, it's best to edit configuration files from the command line. However, in my opinion, CUPS directives are more cryptic than others for the average Linux service. I've found that the comments in /etc/cups files aren't as descriptive as seen for other services. Available GUI tools are an excellent option. But access is limited to the local system until a few minor changes are made to the main CUPS configuration file, /etc/cups/cupsd.conf.

While not even the RHCE exam requires detailed knowledge of CUPS configuration files, it can be helpful to understand a few key directives. The default Ubuntu Linux version of this file is excellent; it focuses on a few key directives. However, there are some additional defaults that you should be aware of. For example, there is a default **ServerRoot** directive, which sets the default top-level directory for CUPS configuration files:

```
ServerRoot /etc/cups
```

In addition, log files are normally stored in the /var/log/cups directory, and these directives specify their types and locations:

```
ErrorLog /var/log/cups/error_log
AccessLog /var/log/cups/access_log
PageLog /var/log/cups/page_log
```

There's a lot more available in directives, which can be examined in the CUPS documentation. When CUPS is installed, the documentation is available from the web-based tool, which I'll describe shortly.

Now to the configuration file. The default Ubuntu Linux configuration is much simpler than what you might see on other Linux distributions. Specifically, it makes it easy to configure dedicated print administrators. The following directive limits administrative access to members of the lpadmin group, as defined in /etc/group. Of course, you can change this definition, or add selected printer administrators to the lpadmin group in /etc/group.

```
SystemGroup lpadmin
```

Let's jump away from the cupsd.conf file for a moment. The following line in /etc/group gives users katie and dickens administrative privileges to CUPS on the local system.

```
lpadmin:x:108:katie,dickens
```

Now return to the cupsd.conf configuration file. The following directives specify where connections can be made. The default settings limit access to the localhost system, and only when CUPS is running:

```
Listen localhost:631
Listen /var/run/cups/cups.sock
```

Of course, you may want to allow access to all systems at least on the local network. Port 631, as shown in /etc/services, is associated with the Internet Print Protocol (IPP), the standard associated with CUPS (as well as the latest print systems associated with Microsoft and Apple operating systems). But the **Listen** directive is a bit more tricky. It should also be set to the IP address of the applicable network card. For example, as my print server connects to my LAN via a network card configured to IP address 192.168.0.50, I want to change the first **Listen** directive to

```
Listen 192.168.0.50:631
```

Generally, most print administrators will want to search configured printers on the LAN. If that applies to you, change the default value of the **Browsing** directive shown here from **Off** to **On**.

```
Browsing Off
```

The default **Browsing** directives that follow are optimized for sharing. If you want to make sure to limit browsing directives to the local network, change the value associated with the **BrowseAllow** directive from **all** to a network address such as 192.168.0.0/24. The **BrowseAddress** directive, as configured, allows broadcast access to allowed clients on the local network.

```
BrowseOrder allow,deny
BrowseAllow all
BrowseAddress @LOCAL
```

The **DefaultAuthType Basic** directive uses the /etc/passwd and /etc/group configuration files to search for allowed users. It works with the **SystemGroup** directive described earlier. Other authentication options are available.

```
DefaultAuthType Basic
```

The following stanza need not be changed, as the **Allow @LOCAL** directive supports access to the other systems on the local network:

```
<Location />
  Order allow,deny
  Allow localhost
  Allow @LOCAL
</Location>
```

However, the default version of the following stanza (not bolded), which regulates access to the administrative commands in the web-based CUPS configuration tool, must be modified slightly. It only allows administrative access from the local system. To allow administrative access from other systems on the network, you could add the aforementioned **Allow @LOCAL** directive shown in the previous stanza. I personally prefer to specify the IP addresses by adding the directive shown in bold in the following example.

```
<Location /admin>
  Order allow,deny
  Allow localhost
  Allow 192.168.0.0/24
</Location>
```

Similar action is required with the next directive, which regulates network access to the CUPS configuration files using the CUPS web-based tool:

```
<Location /admin>
  AuthType Default
  Require user @SYSTEM
  Order allow,deny
  Allow localhost
  Allow 192.168.0.0/24
</Location>
```

The remaining directives in the default version of the CUPS configuration file are beyond the scope even of several more advanced Linux certification exams. Once changes are made, they can be activated by starting or restarting the CUPS initialization script with the following command:

```
$ sudo /etc/init.d/cupsys restart
```

/etc/cups/printers.conf

Once a CUPS printer is configured, key settings are written to the /etc/cups/printers .conf configuration file. Once you've configured some printers as discussed later in this chapter, examine this file on your own system. While a full analysis of this file is beyond the scope of this book, some examples of how key directives can be used are shown in this section. For example, the following directive specifies a stanza associated with the default printer:

```
<DefaultPrinter LaserJet_4L>
```

Of course, without the **Default**, this directive just becomes a stanza container for a regular configured printer.

The **DeviceURI** specifies the URI, or Universal Resource Identifier location of the printer. For more information, see the section "The Universal Resource Identifier (URI)" later in this chapter. The URI can specify local printers; the following URI specifies a parallel port device:

```
DeviceURI hp:/par/LaserJet_4L?device=/dev/parport0
```

The **DeviceURI** can also specify a network port. The following examples specify a connection via a Samba server, a connection to a dedicated print server, and a direct IPP connection. Naturally, you should see only one **DeviceURI** for any configured printer.

```
DeviceURI smb://user:passwd@MSHOME/UBUNTUSERVER/LaserJet-4L
DeviceURI http://192.168.0.5/lp1
DeviceURI ipp://192.168.0.50/printer/UbuntuPrinter
```

The file may be updated dynamically. For example, the **State** directive can be set to **Idle** or **Stopped**; this indicates whether the printer queue is active. The **State** can also be changed with the **cupsaccept** or **cupsreject** commands. Similarly, the **Accepting** directive can be set to **Yes** or **No**, which indicates whether the printer is active and accepting jobs, or is disabled. The value of the directive can be changed with the **cupsenable** and **cupsdisable** commands. These commands are described in the last section of this chapter.

PostScript Printer Definitions (PPD) Files

The PostScript Printer Definition (PPD) language was developed for graphics, and adapted for the first Apple LaserWriter printers. Many developers give this hardware/software combination credit for starting the desktop publishing revolution in the 1980s. Without getting into the details of PPD, such drivers are available for many printers, and can be installed on Linux and Microsoft Windows operating systems.

There are a variety of packages of PPD print drivers available. The following command is one way to list current packages for the Ubuntu Linux release that you're using:

```
$ apt-cache search print | grep ppd
```

For example, as I personally own some HP LaserJet printers, I see the hp-ppd package available, so I install it to give me additional choices in print drivers. If there are *.ppd files available from your Microsoft Windows systems, you probably can use them as print driver files in CUPS. But that command doesn't reveal all available PPD print drivers; the standard database is associated with the Foomatic system. It's developed by the OpenPrinting workgroup, which is now part of the Linux Foundation. For more information, see www.linux-foundation.org/en/OpenPrinting/Database/Foomatic. To install the associated drivers, run the following command:

```
$ sudo apt-get install foomatic-filters
```

To make sure the PPD driver is formatted appropriately, the **cupstestppd** command is available. Just apply the command to the PPD driver file; for example, I ran the following command to test one of the PPD drivers on my Microsoft Windows XP partition (yes, I do dual-boot Microsoft Windows):

```
$ cupstestppd /media/sda2/WINDOWS/system32/spool/XPSEP/msxpsinc.ppd
```

Configure Printers

This section first describes how printers can be configured using three of the available GUI tools for Ubuntu Linux. While only the **gnome-cups-manager** command is listed in the current UCP curriculum, I believe that the UCP exam will be updated with information on the latest Ubuntu printer tool, developed after the current UCP curriculum was released, as well as the more common web-based tool.

CUPS printer configuration is a straightforward process. Printers are either connected to a local system on existing physical ports, or are connected over a network. The latest CUPS packages also support automatic detection of local and network printers, assuming the hal-cups-utils package is installed. However, automatic detection doesn't always work. Whatever tool is used, further action is required to install the associated print driver.

There are several tools available for configuring CUPS printers. Yes, they can be configured from the command line by editing additional files in the /etc/cups directory. But there are three excellent graphical tools available: a web-based tool, a GNOME-based tool, and an Ubuntu Linux tool originally developed by Red Hat under the GPL. Yes, there is also a KDE tool that can be used, but as GNOME is the desktop environment listed in the UCP curriculum, KDE tools are not addressed in this book.

Don't be concerned if you only have one printer. Ubuntu Linux allows you to configure the same printer several times under different names. Once printers are configured, they can be managed with commands like **cupsdisable**, **cupsaddsmb**, and **cupsenable**, as described toward the end of this chapter in the "Manage Printers" section.

Local and Network CUPS Printer Ports

CUPS printers can be configured on local and network CUPS printer ports. CUPS normally detects locally connected printers on standard parallel (LPT), serial, USB, IEEE1394, and SCSI ports.

One strength of CUPS is the support for a variety of network print protocols, including the IPP described earlier, associated with TCP/IP port 631. Several supported network print protocols are listed in Table 7-3. Note the bolded labels in the table, which indicate the output associated with the **lpinfo** command.

For a full list of local and network print protocols on a CUPS server, the **lpinfo** command can help. For example, the following output from the **lpinfo -v -h 192.168.0.70** command verifies available local (**direct**), print to **file**, and **network** printer options:

```
network socket
network beh
direct hal
direct hpfax
direct hp
network http
network ipp
network lpd
file cups-pdf:/
direct scsi
network smb
```

Some additional explanation is needed. The **network beh** output handles errors such as paper jams. The **direct hal** output uses HAL to detect local printers. The **direct hpfax** output can be associated with a fax machine. The **direct hp** output is associated with output direct to specialized printers from HP.

TABLE 7-3	Network Print Protocol	Description
CUPS Supported Network Print Protocols	IPP	(ipp) The Internet Print Protocol uses TCP/IP Port 631 for communication.
	LPD/LPRng	(lpd) The Line Print Daemon (and Line Printer Next Generation) protocols are based on older System V or Berkeley Standard print servers.
	SMB/CIFS	(smb) Configured CUPS printers can be shared on SMB/CIFS networks.
	Bluetooth	Bluetooth-enabled printers do exist.
	AppSocket/HP JetDirect	(socket) The AppSocket/HP JetDirect interface uses TCP/IP port 9100; may also connect to some dedicated print servers.
	PAP	The Printer Access Protocol is associated with printers connected to the AppleTalk network.

The CUPS Web-Based Configuration Tool

The CUPS web-based tool is an excellent print administration tool. Network access was configured in the previous section, and it does not require any GUI software on the print server system. Once configured as described earlier, the CUPS web-based tool is accessible by any standard browser—even text browsers on the configured network. Figure 7-2 illustrates access to a CUPS server on a remote system on my home network.

There are six virtual tabs atop the main page based on the current version of the CUPS web-based tool:

■ **Home** Accesses the introductory page shown in Figure 7-2, which introduces CUPS. Originally developed by Easy Software Products, it is now owned by Apple Inc.

FIGURE 7-2   The CUPS web-based configuration tool

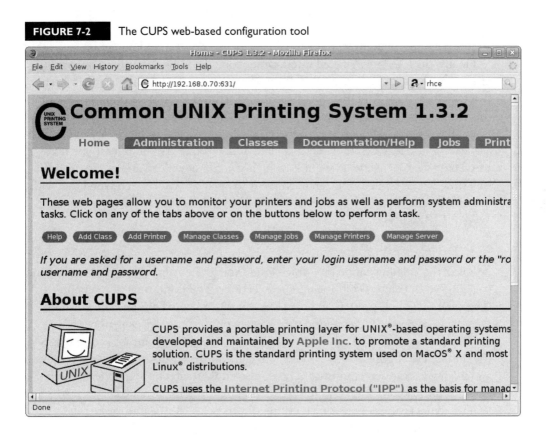

- ■ **Administration**   Opens a front-end interface that allows you to add or manage classes of printers, manage print jobs, and add or manage printers. You can also navigate directly to several of these administrative options from the Home page tab.
- ■ **Classes**   Supports viewing and management of installed printer classes.
- ■ **Documentation/Help**   Provides extensive documentation, including book-length works.
- ■ **Jobs**   Enables you to view and manage active print jobs.
- ■ **Printers**   Enables you to manage existing printers.

You can also manage Classes, Jobs, and Printers from the Administration tab. (I'll leave you to read the book-length Documentation/Help section on your own.) The heart of the CUPS Web-management tool is available through the Administration tab. At some point during administrative commands, the tool prompts for an appropriate administrative username and password. As described in the previous section, that print administrator should be a member of the lpadmin group.

Finally, the CUPS web-based interface supports the same extensive database of printers as is available via GNOME Print Manager and the Ubuntu Linux Printer Configuration tool. And the Ubuntu tool supports the creation of printer classes and the complete variety of print protocols supported by CUPS.

For those of you who are used to the GUI when browsing web pages, there are also excellent text-based browsers available. I urge you to try out at least one text-based browser. One example is elinks, which you can download and use to open the web sites of your choice. You can even use it to open the CUPS web-based tool with the following command (just substitute the IP address of the CUPS server for the 127.0.0.1 IP address):

```
$ elinks 127.0.0.1:631
```

Select the Administration tab, which brings you to the Administration management page, shown in Figure 7-3. It includes five sections: The Printers section supports configuration of new printers and management of configured printers. The Classes section also supports configuration of a group of printers or management of an existing printer class. The Jobs section helps you manage the print jobs currently in the print queue. In the Servers section, you can edit the configuration file, view logs, and modify various server settings. There's also an RSS subscription option, which allows you to monitor CUPS as new printers and print jobs are added.

The actual process of creating a printer or print class is straightforward, and should be elementary for the UCP candidate. Configuring a printer, if it isn't

FIGURE 7-3 CUPS Administration management page

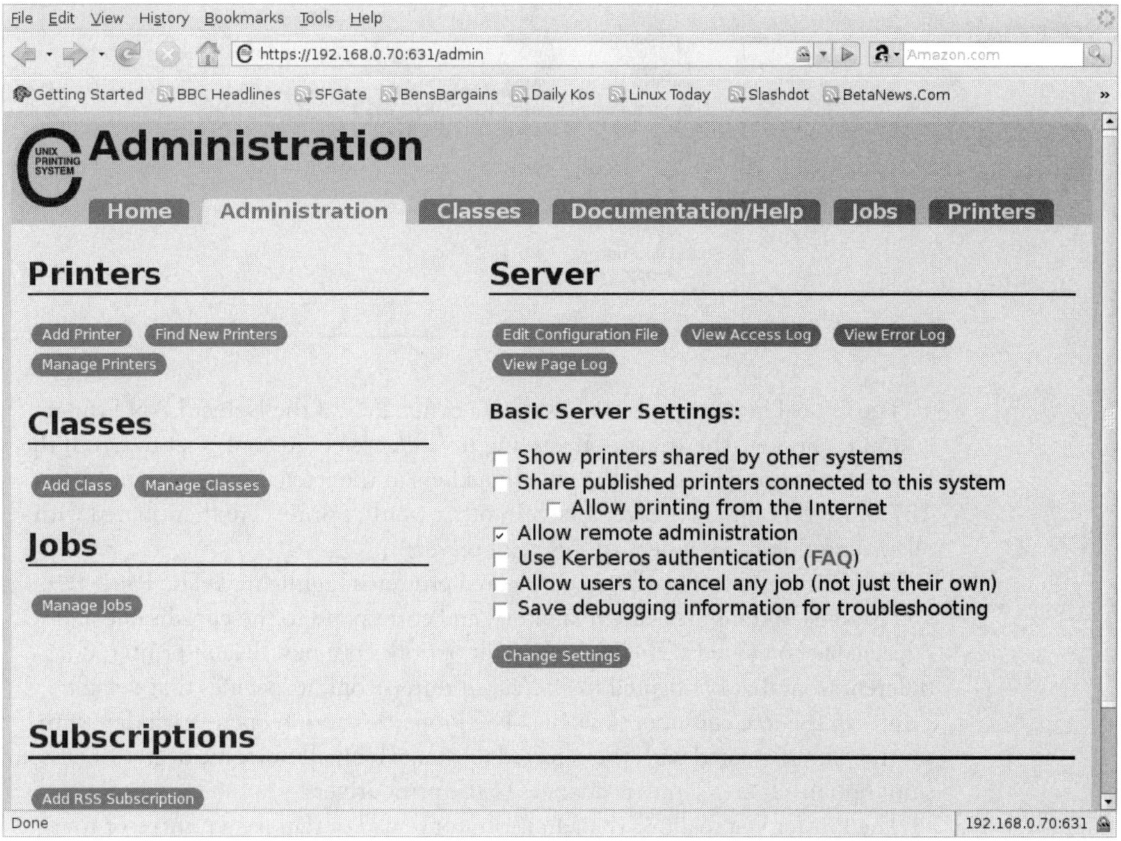

automatically detected, may require knowledge of the Universal Resource Identifier (URI). This is a superset of the URL (Universal Resource Locator).

For more information on the URI, see the section "Printers and The Universal Resource Identifier (URI)" later in this chapter.

The GNOME Print Manager

The GNOME Print Manager tool is started from a GUI-based command-line interface with the **gnome-cups-manager** command. It's a fairly simple tool; the options are available from the menus shown in Figure 7-4. Yes, the window is labeled "Printers," but it is the GNOME Printers tool. One weakness of this tool is that it does not support the configuration of a print class.

FIGURE 7-4

GNOME Printers tool

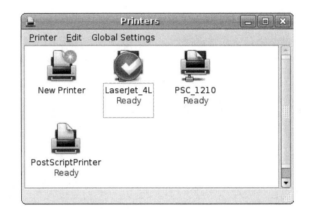

The Global Settings menu refers to two commands; if the Detect LAN Printers option is checked, the value of **Browsing** in /etc/cups/cupsd.conf is set to **On**. If the Share Printers option is checked, the IP address in the /etc/cups/cupsd.conf **Listen 127.0.0.1:631** directive is removed. In other words, printers are then shared with all systems that can connect to this print server.

The Edit menu works when a configured printer is highlighted. The Pause and Resume options are self-explanatory, and correspond to the **cupsdisable** and **cupsenable** commands. The Make Default option sets a new default printer; if it's different from that configured in /etc/cups/printers.conf, it specifies that default printer in the /etc/cups/lpoptions file. The Properties option opens a window with several tabs associated with the selected printer, which allows some degree of custom print options. It also supports changes to the print driver.

The Printer menu allows the administrator to add or remove a printer, or to examine the status of print jobs. The process of adding a printer is illustrated in the following exercise.

EXERCISE 7-1

Adding a Printer

In this exercise, you'll add a network printer to the local system. For the purpose of this exercise, the gnome-cups-manager package should be installed. This exercise also assumes that GNOME is installed, per the requirements of the UCP curriculum. It also assumes an available network printer. If you have only one system with a local printer, it's still possible to configure a network printer, using the information in the "Shared Samba Printers" section later in this chapter.

1. Start the GNOME Print Manager. Open a command line in a GUI desktop. In the GNOME desktop, click Applications | Accessories | Terminal.

2. If you're on a remote system, and the SSH server is active on the Print Server, connect with the **ssh -X *username*@remotepc**, where *username* is a valid username on the remote system.

3. Enter the **gnome-cups-manager** command. This should open the GNOME Print Manager tool shown in Figure 7-4.

4. Double-click New Printer, or click Printer | Add Printer. For a moment, you may see a message suggesting the tool is reading the current printer database, which includes available print drivers. It should automatically proceed to "Step 1 of 3" of the Add A Printer window.

5. The "Step 1 of 3" window allows you to choose between Local Or Detected Printer and Network Printer. Detected local printers are shown in a central window; detected printer ports are listed in the Printer Port drop-down text box. For the purpose of this exercise, select Network Printer.

6. When the Network Printer option is selected, there's an available drop-down text box with four options, described in the following table.

7. Enter information appropriate for the network printer, based on the Print Server's /etc/cups/printers.conf and /etc/printcap configuration files.

8. In the Printer Driver window that appears, labeled "Step 2 of 3," select a printer manufacturer from the Manufacturer drop-down text box. If your printer manufacturer isn't in the list, a Generic option is available.

GNOME Print Manager Network Print Option	Required Information
IPP Printer Or Printer On CUPS Server (IPP)	URI for the printer; for example, if it's named UbuntuPrinter on a system with an IP address of 192.168.0.70, the URI is ipp://192.168.0.70/printer/UbuntuPrinter
Windows Printer (SMB)	Hostname or IP address of print server, printer name, username, password
UNIX Printer (LPD)	Hostname or IP address of print server and queue name such as *lpt1*
TCP/Socket, HP JetDirect, Raw Connection	Hostname or IP address of print server; port 9100 is the default

9. Select the model number that most closely resembles the target printer. Alternatively, if a PPD file is available (possibly even from a Microsoft driver), click Install Driver and navigate to the location with the PPD file.

10. In the Driver drop-down text box, there may be multiple drivers available. Make a choice if available and click Forward to continue.

11. Type in a Name, Description, and Location for the printer. The printer name must be a single alphanumeric word. Click Apply.

12. Return to the Printers window, the main GNOME Print Manager screen. Confirm that the new printer is shown. Highlight the new printer, right-click it, and select Properties from the pop-up menu that appears.

13. Click the Print A Test Page button. Make sure the printer works. Explore the other tabs associated with the new printer to see if customization is appropriate. When any desired customization is complete, click Close.

When you've finished exploring the GNOME Print Manager tool, close the window to exit the tool.

The Ubuntu Linux GUI Tool

Starting with Ubuntu Linux Gutsy Gibbon, Ubuntu has incorporated one more GUI print management tool. Those of you familiar with Red Hat and Fedora Linux should recognize the new tool. Courtesy of the GPL, Ubuntu has adapted the same basic tool as a comprehensive alternative to the web-based tool for the distribution. It's available from the **system-config-printer** package. Once installed, it can be started from a GUI-based command line with the **system-config-printer** command.

Before running this tool, back up the files in the /etc/cups directory. The actions of this tool overwrite the comments in the default versions of the files in the /etc/cups directory. One way to copy these files to your home directory is with the following command:

```
$ sudo cp -ar /etc/cups ~
```

Now run the **system-config-printer** command in a GUI-based command line. When I start it from a local system, it brings me to the Printer Configuration tool shown in Figure 7-5.

Note that it's currently connected to the local system, as signified by the localhost label. If you'd rather connect to a CUPS server on another system, click File | Goto Server. When the Connect To CUPS Server window appears as shown in Figure 7-6,

FIGURE 7-5   Ubuntu Printer Configuration tool

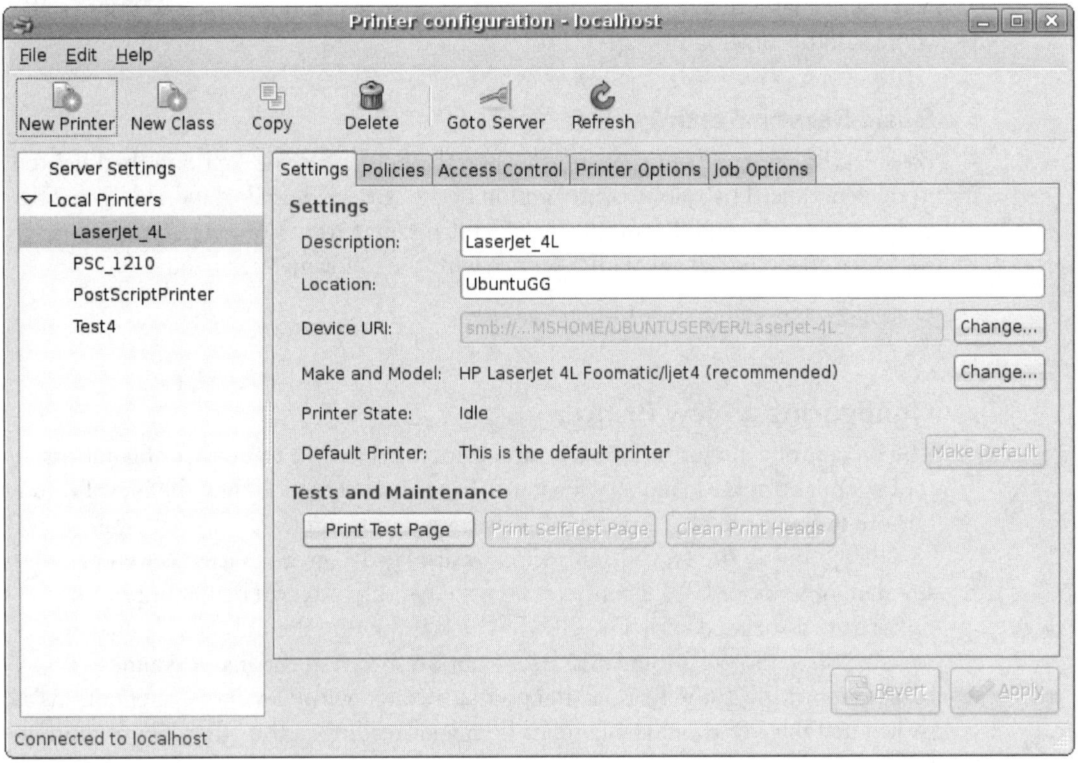

navigate to the hostname or IP address of the desired CUPS server, followed by the username. That username should be a member of the lpadmin group described earlier. Encryption is available for this connection, if desired. Enter the required information and click Connect. You'll be prompted for a password.

FIGURE 7-6

The Connect to CUPS Server window

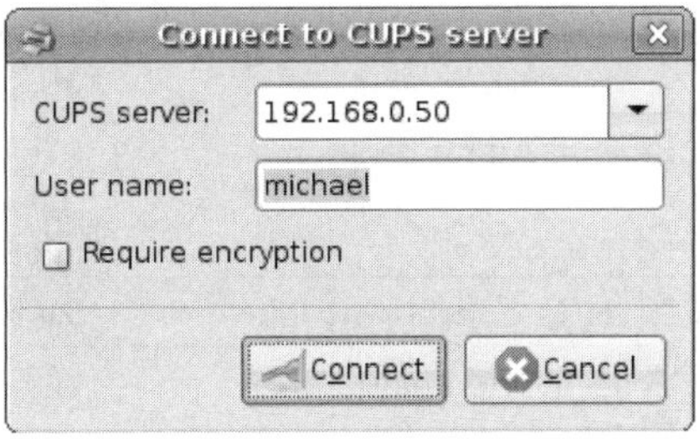

Once an appropriate password is entered, the title in the printer configuration tool window is changed. Specifically, "localhost" is changed to either the hostname or IP address of the target CUPS server.

Basic Server Settings

Basic CUPS server settings are shown when the Server Settings option is highlighted in the left pane. This allows configuration of the options described in Table 7-4. The changes affect the cupsd.conf file in the /etc/cups directory. However, to make sure they take effect, restart the CUPS service with the following command:

```
$ sudo /etc/init.d/cupsys restart
```

Configuring a New Printer

The process of configuring a new printer using the Ubuntu Printer Configuration tool is straightforward, and uses a wizard. To see how it works, click the New Printer button. It opens the New Printer window shown in Figure 7-7.

The options in the New Printer window display detected devices, as well as standard options for CUPS connections to network printers. The Gutenprint options are associated with The GIMP, which is the functional Linux equivalent to Paint Shop Pro. The standard LPT #1 option shown in the figure assumes a connection through the first parallel port, associated with /dev/lp0. Other options as shown in Table 7-5 should be familiar from your reading of the other Ubuntu Linux GUI print managers.

TABLE 7-4	Basic Server Setting	Description
Ubuntu Print Tool Basic Server Settings Options	Show Printers Shared By Other Systems	Configures **BrowseAllow All**
	Share Published Printers Connected To This System	Enables printer sharing with the **Browsing On** and **BrowseAddress @LOCAL** directives
	Allow Printing From The Internet	Changes **Allow @LOCAL** to **Allow All**, which disables the access limit to the local network
	Allow Remote Administration	Changes **Allow localhost** to **Allow @LOCAL** in the /admin and /admin/conf stanzas, which allows remote administration from the LAN
	Allow Users To Cancel Any Job	Removes the **Cancel-Job** limitations
	Save Debugging Information For Troubleshooting	**Changes LogLevel** warning to **LogLevel debug**

FIGURE 7-7

Ubuntu Printer
Configuration
tool

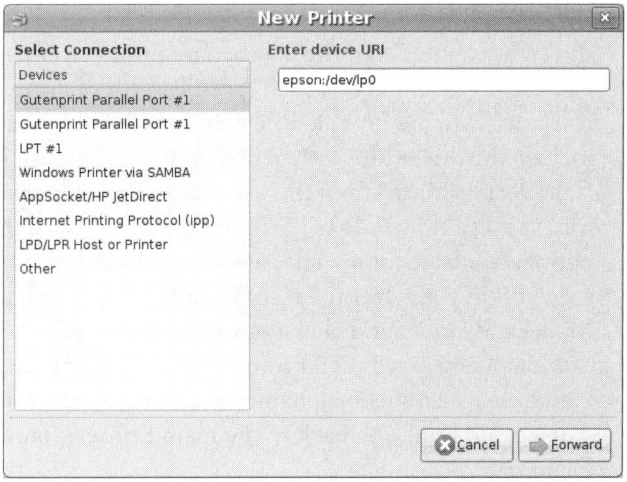

The list shown in Table 7-5 is not comprehensive, as I don't have specialty printers such as those associated with SCSI or Bluetooth devices, nor do I expect you to have to configure such printers during the UCP exam. But it does go beyond what's shown in Figure 7-7, as connections vary with connected hardware and installed packages.

TABLE 7-5

Ubuntu Print
Tool Printer
Connection
Configuration

Select Connection	Required Details
Gutenprint Parallel Port #*x*	Device URI, usually a device file associated with the brand, such as hp:/dev/lp0. Access limited to The GIMP.
LPT #*x*	No additional information is required; LPT #1 assumes device file /dev/lp0.
Print Into PDF File	Device URI; by default cups-pdf:/, which sends a print job to the ~/PDF directory.
Windows Printer via SAMBA	Device URI, starts with smb//. Requires the workgroup or domain name, print server hostname or IP address, and shared printer name.
AppSocket /HP JetDirect	Hostname of print server, and port number (9100 by default).
Internet Printing Protocol (ipp)	Hostname or IP address of print server; the Find Queue button lists available CUPS printers, which conform to IPP by default.
LPD/LPR Host or Printer	Hostname or IP address of LPD or LPRng print server, and printer name.
Other	Device URI.

Once a connection is configured, the tool proceeds to the New Printer window shown in Figure 7-8. If the appropriate print driver packages are installed, there will be a big list of "Makes," which specifies a list of printer manufacturers. Alternatively, if you activate the Provide PPD File radio button, the tool gives you the chance to include the driver file, with a .ppd or .ppd.gz extension.

I select a "Make" from the window and click Forward to continue. This changes the New Printer window shown in Figure 7-9. Note the variety of print driver options available for my HP LaserJet 4L. Unless you know what you're doing, I suggest that you select the recommended driver. Whatever the choice, select a Model and Driver and click Forward to continue.

Now you're asked for a Printer Name, Description, and Location. The Printer Name must be a single alphanumeric word. Type in your choices and click Apply. This should bring you back to the main Printer Configuration window shown in Figure 7-5.

Modify Settings for a Configured Printer

In the main Printer Configuration window, select a printer. Five tabs should appear on the right side of the tool, described in Table 7-6. Considerable customization is possible through these tabs.

FIGURE 7-8

Ubuntu Printer
Configuration
tool: the New
Printer window

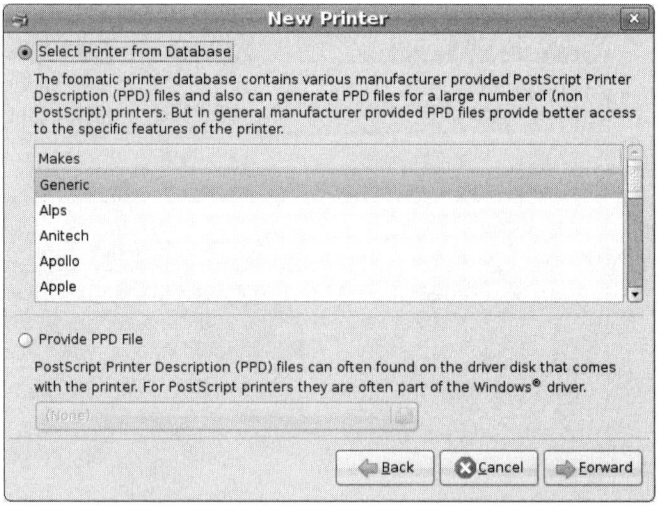

FIGURE 7-9

Many available
print drivers

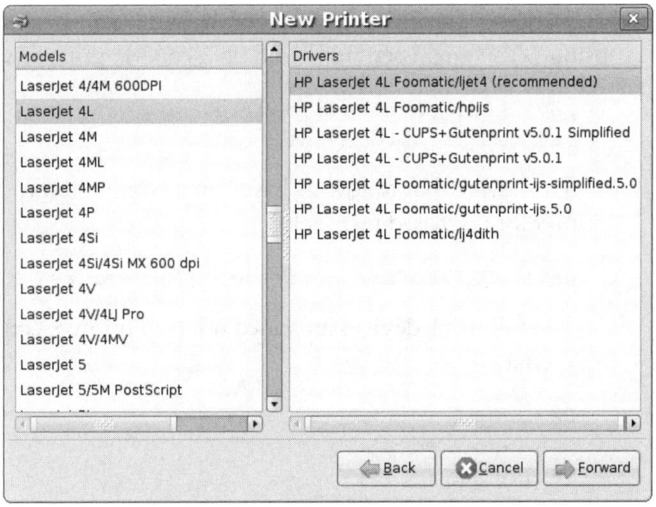

Models	Drivers
LaserJet 4/4M 600DPI	HP LaserJet 4L Foomatic/ljet4 (recommended)
LaserJet 4L	HP LaserJet 4L Foomatic/hpijs
LaserJet 4M	HP LaserJet 4L - CUPS+Gutenprint v5.0.1 Simplified
LaserJet 4ML	HP LaserJet 4L - CUPS+Gutenprint v5.0.1
LaserJet 4MP	HP LaserJet 4L Foomatic/gutenprint-ijs-simplified.5.0
LaserJet 4P	HP LaserJet 4L Foomatic/gutenprint-ijs.5.0
LaserJet 4Si	HP LaserJet 4L Foomatic/lj4dith
LaserJet 4Si/4Si MX 600 dpi	
LaserJet 4V	
LaserJet 4V/4LJ Pro	
LaserJet 4V/4MV	
LaserJet 5	
LaserJet 5/5M PostScript	

New Printer

Back   Cancel   Forward

Printers and the Universal Resource Identifier (URI)

Perhaps the most important piece of information in CUPS configuration is the URI, which is a superset of the more well-known URL. In other words, it includes regular HTTP URLs, as well as IPP interfaces, for example:

```
DeviceURI ipp://192.168.0.30/printer/LaserJonHP
```

There are local URIs, based on printers directly connected to the local system, and networked URIs, based on printers accessed over a network. First, I present several examples of local URIs, which are almost self-explanatory. The first URI is based on an HP LaserJet 4L printer connected via a parallel port:

```
DeviceURI hp:/par/LaserJet_4L?device=/dev/parport0
```

TABLE 7-6

Ubuntu Print
Tool Printer
Customization

Printer Configuration Tab	Description
Settings	Presents basic printer description, URI, driver, status, test and maintenance options
Policies	Includes print status, policies, and banner information
Access Control	Supports access limits by user
Printer Options	Allows custom options, such as resolution and page size, which vary by printer
Job Options	Configures options such as copies, scaling, and mirroring

The next two URIs suggests parallel and USB ports respectively, with no specified printer. You might see this based on a generic print driver.

```
DeviceURI parallel:/dev/lp0
DeviceURI usb:/dev/usb/lp0
```

The device that follows is based on a connection to a specific HP OfficeJet printer for fax-based print jobs:

```
DeviceURI hpfax:/officejet_7100_series?
```

The following devices are based on local printers connected to LPD/LPRng, SCSI, and serial ports:

```
DeviceURI lpd
DeviceURI scsi
DeviceURI serial
```

Examples of networked **DeviceURI**s include the following. The first option is one way to connect to a CUPS configured printer. While the connection uses HTTP, the IPP protocol is used courtesy of routing through TCP/IP port 631. For that reason, the port number is not required when the URI starts with an ipp://.

```
DeviceURI http://192.168.0.30:631/printer/LaserJonHP
DeviceURI ipp://192.168.0.30/printer/LaserJonHP
```

The socket:// is somewhat generic; port 9100 is commonly used for some HP and Apple printers.

```
DeviceURI socket://192.168.0.5:9100/
```

The following URI connects to a printer configured to an LPD or LPRng server.

```
DeviceURI lpd://192.168.0.10/LaserJonHP
```

Shared Samba Printers

Printers configured through CUPS can be shared over a Microsoft network. This is possible courtesy of the Samba server packages, which can share the /etc/printcap list of configured printers. Take a look at the /etc/printcap file. If CUPS is installed, there will be comments that associate it with the list of configured printers in the /etc/cups/printers.conf configuration file.

Note: *Starting with the Hardy Heron release, the use of /etc/printcap requires the Printcap /etc/printcap directive in the /etc/cups/cupsd.conf configuration file.*

The default Samba configuration file for Ubuntu Linux, /etc/samba/smb.conf, includes the following directives in comments, which you must activate before this system can share printers over the Microsoft-based network. The first refers to the aforementioned /etc/printcap file for a list of printers to share. The second looks to the CUPS service.

```
printcap name = /etc/printcap
printing = cups
```

These global directives work hand in hand with two stanzas near the bottom of the file. The first stanza, entitled **[printers]**, configures network access. The **browseable = no** directive may be confusing. First the word is misspelled; second, all it means is that the spool directory, /var/spool/samba, is not shared by the Samba service.

```
[printers]
   comment = All Printers
   browseable = no
   path = /var/spool/samba
   printable = yes
   public = no
   writable = no
   create mode = 0700
```

The next stanza sets the stage for the **cupsaddsmb** command, which copies Microsoft drivers from the /usr/share/cups/drivers directory. For the latest version of these drivers, the custom CUPS package can be downloaded from www.cups.org/windows/software.php. It's available in compressed format. For example, when I downloaded the version 6.0 drivers from the noted URL, I processed them with the following command:

```
$ tar xzvf cups-windows-6.0-source.tar.gz
```

And then I copied the files from the cups-windows-6.0/i386/ subdirectory to the /usr/share/cups/drivers directory:

```
$ sudo cp cups-windows-6.0/i386/*  /usr/share/cups/drivers
```

With the appropriate switches and options, the **cupsaddsmb** command then copies drivers to the /var/lib/samba/printers directory.

```
[print$]
   comment = Printer Drivers
   path = /var/lib/samba/printers
   browseable = yes
   read only = yes
   guest ok = no
```

But the command only works if the appropriate **write list** directive is activated for that stanza. To take advantage of the printer administration group of users described earlier, I've revised the default suggested **write list** to

```
write list = @lpadmin
```

Of course, any changes made to this configuration file must be saved. Changes are then reread by the Samba service with the following command:

```
$ sudo /etc/init.d/samba restart
```

Now the appropriate **cupsaddsmb** command can process those Windows drivers from the /usr/share/cups/drivers directory:

```
$ cupsaddsmb -U michael -a -h localhost -v
```

The switches for this command are straightforward, as described in Table 7-7.

In other words, the noted **cupsaddsmb** command cites Samba user michael (**-U michael**), adds all printers (**-a**), targets the local system (**-h localhost**), and adds verbose messages (**-v**) in case of problems.

on the *Job*   *Samba network commands store user/password information in a Microsoft-style authentication database. Older Samba systems stored that database in /etc/samba/smbpasswd. Newer systems store them in several .tdb files in the /var/lib/samba directory.*

Client Printer Access via IPP

The latest Microsoft operating systems can connect directly to printers using the IPP protocol. So if you understand the URI associated with IPP connections described earlier, you can use that URI directly to connect to the CUPS configured printer, bypassing the Microsoft network and Samba service.

TABLE 7-7	Switch	Description
cupsaddsmb Command Switches	-H *server*	Specifies the Samba *server* system; if not specified, assumes the Samba server is on the same system as the CUPS server.
	-h *server*	Specifies the CUPS server system; if not specified, assumes the local system.
	-U *user*	Assigns a *user*; that user should have a Samba password per Chapter 10.
	-a	Exports all available print drivers.
	-v	Uses verbose mode, useful in problem diagnosis.

Manage Print Queues

Print queue management from the GUI is an almost trivial subject, so toward the end of this section, I'll briefly describe how it's done from the GNOME print manager. Print queues can also be managed with the CUPS web-based tool described earlier in this chapter. But more importantly, you need to know how to manage print queues from the command line.

e x a m

w a t c h

Understand the command-line options for managing print queues; **know how to use commands like** *lpq, lprm,* **cupsdisable, and** *cupsenable.*

Print Queue Management at the Command Line

There are three major commands available for managing print queues: **lpr**, **lpq**, and **lprm**. They are used to add print requests, list queued print requests, and remove print requests, respectively. One more command can help administer print queues: **lpc**. While these commands were developed for the LPD/LPRng services, they've been adapted for and are commonly used on CUPS servers, and are installed from the cupsys-bsd package.

There are several more line print commands available, but these are the basic commands associated with command-line print queue management.

lpc: Line Print Control

To view all known queues, run the **lpc status** command; it implements the result shown in Figure 7-10. As you can see, the output helps you easily scan all configured print devices and queues.

on the

job

The lpc command that comes with CUPS does not support starting or stopping of print queues.

FIGURE 7-10

Review print
queues and more

```
michael@UbuntuGG:~$ lpc status
FirstClass:
        printer is on device 'ipp' speed -1
        queuing is enabled
        printing is enabled
        no entries
        daemon present
LaserJet_4L:
        printer is on device 'smb' speed -1
        queuing is enabled
        printing is enabled
        no entries
        daemon present
PDF_file_generator:
        printer is on device 'cups-pdf' speed -1
        queuing is enabled
        printing is enabled
        no entries
        daemon present
PSC_1210:
        printer is on device 'http' speed -1
        queuing is disabled
        printing is enabled
        no entries
        daemon present
Test4:
        printer is on device 'ipp' speed -1
        queuing is enabled
        printing is disabled
        1 entries
        daemon present
UbuntuPrinter:
        printer is on device 'ipp' speed -1
        queuing is enabled
        printing is enabled
        no entries
        daemon present
michael@UbuntuGG:~$ []
```

lpr: Line Print Request

Any user can use **lpr** to send print requests to any local print queue. You can **lpr** any files to a queue, or you can redirect any output via **lpr**. If you wanted to print to the queue named color, for example, you'd use a command like this: **lpr -Pcolor** *filename*. Note that there is no space between the **-P** switch and the name of the queue (though a space is allowed in more recent versions of this command).

lpq: Line Print Query

Now it's time to examine how the **lpq** command works. By itself, it displays the current queue on the default printer. The **-a** option displays the queue for all configured printers.

Similarly to the **lpr** command, the **-P***printer* option limits the command to a specific printer.

```
$  lpq -a
Rank     Owner    Job   File(s)         Total Size
1st      michael  118   passwd          2048 bytes
active   michael  119   fstab           2048 bytes
active   michael  120   smb.conf        11264 bytes
2nd      michael  121   wireless.sh     1024 bytes
```

lprm: Line Print Job Removal

Now you can delete the jobs of your choice. It's simple; just use the **lprm** command with the job number, as shown in the output to the **lpq** command.

```
$ lprm 121
```

GUI Print Queue Management

It's possible to manage print queues using the GNOME Print Manager or the web-based tool. If you prefer the GNOME Print Manager, open it in a GUI desktop with the **gnome-cups-manager** command. As shown in Figure 7-11, it displays all configured printers. Note how it shows jobs pending for each printer.

To cancel a job for a printer, right-click that printer and click Jobs in the pop-up menu that appears. A window that displays all jobs pending for that printer should appear. You can then right-click the job that should be canceled, and click Cancel in the pop-up menu that appears.

FIGURE 7-11

Review print jobs

FIGURE 7-12	Review print queues in the web-based interface

It's even easier to manage print jobs from the web-based interface. Figure 7-12 displays the same print jobs, and the options available for each job.

CERTIFICATION OBJECTIVE 7.04

Manage Printers

Print management is almost trivial using the GUI tools described in this chapter. However, the UCP curriculum suggests that you should know how to manage printers from the command line. This section is straightforward, as it's focused in two areas: accepting and rejecting print jobs, and enabling and disabling print queues.

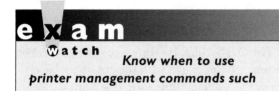

Print Queue Management

The queues on every configured printer can be managed with the **cupsaccept** and **cupsreject** commands. The commands are straightforward; the **cupsreject** *printer* command disables the queue on the noted printer. After the **cupsreject** command is run, any job that is sent to that printer leads to the following message:

```
lpr: Destination "printer" is not accepting jobs.
```

You can review the result in the output to the **lpc status** command; as you can see here, queuing is disabled for the *printer*. Similar information is also available in the /etc/cups/printers.conf configuration file described earlier.

```
PSC_1210:
    printer is on device 'http' speed -1
    queuing is disabled
    printing is enabled
    no entries
    daemon present
```

The status can be reversed with the **cupsaccept** *printer* command.

Printer Management

The status of a printer can be managed with the **cupsenable** and **cupsdisable** commands. The commands are straightforward; the **cupsdisable** *printer* command disables the queue on the noted printer. After the **cupsdisable** command is run, print jobs are still accepted by a printer, but you'll see the following message associated with *printer* in the output to the **lpc status** command:

```
printing is disabled
```

But the **cupsdisable** command isn't the only thing that can disable a printer. Ordinary problems such as a printer running out of paper and toner can lead to a disabled printer. Once the problem is fixed, the following command works as a reset to re-enable the printer:

```
$ cupsenable printer
```

CERTIFICATION SUMMARY

CUPS is short for the Common Unix Printing System. It's the successor to the LPD/LPRng service. The main CUPS server is associated with the cupsys package. CUPS configuration files are available in the /etc/cups directory. The main CUPS configuration file can be modified for remote administration and access.

CUPS supports access to a variety of print protocols, and can be managed with command-line and GUI tools. CUPS printers can be shared using IPP or Samba. Printers and print queues can be enabled and disabled, also with the same command-line and GUI tools.

While the UCP curriculum cites the **gnome-cups-manager** tool, there are also other GUI tools such as a web-based interface and the Ubuntu Linux print manager.

✓ TWO-MINUTE DRILL

Here are some of the key points from the certification objectives in Chapter 7.

Work the CUPS Packages

❑ CUPS is the successor to the LPD/LPRng service.

❑ CUPS packages to consider include cups-pdf, cupsys, cupsys-bsd, cupsys-client, cupsys-common, cupsys-driver-gutenprint, cupsys-pt, gnome-cups-manager, and hal-cups-utils.

❑ Most CUPS configuration files are stored in the /etc/cups directory.

❑ The main CUPS configuration file, /etc/cups/cupsd.conf, can be modified to support remote administration, using the lpadmin group.

❑ CUPS supports PPD driver files, even those created for Microsoft Windows. These drivers can be tested with the **cupstestppd** command.

Configure Printers

❑ CUPS supports access to a variety of network print protocols.

❑ CUPS includes a web-based configuration tool accessible via http://127.0.0.1:631.

❑ The GNOME Print Manager can help add, enable, or disable printers.

❑ The Ubuntu Linux printer tool, available with the **system-config-printer** command, can help configure the print server, set up a new printer, and modify settings for an existing printer.

❑ CUPS printers can be shared with Samba with selected directives in /etc/samba/smb.conf.

❑ Microsoft drivers can be processed with the **cupsaddsmb** command.

Manage Print Queues

❑ CUPS print queues can be managed at the command line, using commands originally developed for the LPD/LPRng system.

❑ Print queues can also be managed using GUI tools, including the GNOME Print Manager and the CUPS web-based tool.

Manage Printers

❑ CUPS print queues can be activated and deactivated with the **cupsaccept** and **cupsreject** commands.

❑ CUPS printers can be enabled and disabled with the **cupsenable** and **cupsdisable** commands.

SELF TEST

The following questions will help you measure your understanding of the material presented in this chapter. Read all the questions carefully, as there may be more than one correct answer. Some questions are "fill in the blank" and normally require an exact answer. Choose all correct answers for each question.

Work the CUPS Packages

1. If it is not already installed, type in the command that installs the main CUPS server. Do not include the full path to the command.

   _____

2. Which of the following configuration files can be used to share CUPS printers over a Microsoft network?
   A. /etc/cups/cupsd.conf
   B. /etc/cups/printers.conf
   C. /etc/samba/smb.conf
   D. /etc/printcap

3. What is the command that tests the conformance of a .ppd print driver file? No switches are required. Do not include the full directory path.

   _____

Configure Printers

4. To access the web-based CUPS print configuration tool on a local system, what is the appropriate URL?

   _____

5. Which of the following port numbers should be kept open through any firewall on a print server?
   A. 22
   B. 80
   C. 361
   D. 631

6. Name the command that starts the Ubuntu printer configuration tool in the GUI, starting with Gutsy Gibbon. No switches are required. Do not include the full directory path to the command.

   _____

7. Which of the following commands starts the web-based configuration tool at the command-line interface? Assume you're in the GUI, and all associated packages are installed.

   A. **gnome-cups-manager**

   B. **firefox 127.0.0.1:631**

   C. **system-config-printer**

   D. **elinks 127.0.0.1:631**

8. Which of the following files is cited in the Samba configuration file for shared printers?

   A. /etc/cups/cupsd.conf

   B. /etc/printcap

   C. /etc/cups/printers.conf

   D. /etc/samba/smb.conf

9. What is the name of the group of users who are allowed by default to configure CUPS printers?

   A. lpadmin

   B. lp

   C. cups

   D. cupsadmin

Manage Print Queues

10. Name the full command that lists print queues on all configured printers. Do not include the directory path to the command.

   _____

11. Name the command that removes the print job number 585. Do not include the directory path to the command.

   _____

12. Which of the following directives in the /etc/cups/printers.conf configuration file suggests that a printer is disabled?

   A. **Accepting No**

   B. **Shared No**

   C. **State Stopped**

   D. **Location No**

Manage Printers

13. Which of the following URIs can be used to support access from a Microsoft Windows XP client to a CUPS printer? The name of the printer is *printername*, and Samba is not enabled on the CUPS server.

    A. http://server/printer/*printername*

    B. ipp://server/printer/*printername*

    C. cups://server/printer/*printername*

    D. ftp://server/printer/*printername*

14. Which of the following tools does not configure local printers? Assume all associated packages are installed.

    A. **gnome-cups-manager**

    B. Open Firefox and navigate to http://127.0.0.1:631

    C. Open Firefox and navigate to ipp://127.0.0.1:631

    D. **system-config-printer**

15. Name the command that may be used to re-enable a paused printer named wasoutofpaper. Do not include the directory path to the command.

LAB QUESTIONS

These labs are to be run consecutively. Ideally, the first lab should be run on an Ubuntu Linux server with a physical printer; the second lab should be run on an Ubuntu Linux client. However, with the cups-pdf package, it's possible to perform these labs with a virtual printer associated with a print-to-file configuration.

Lab 1

In this lab, you'll work with the CUPS web-based configuration tool. It may be more convenient to log in to the Ubuntu Linux GUI for this purpose, but it's not necessary if you have a text browser such as elinks installed.

   1. If you need to connect to the web-based tool remotely, revise the /etc/cups/cupsd.conf configuration as described in the chapter to support remote access.

   2. Check the /etc/group configuration file for print administrator access. If the desired users are not part of the lpadmin group, use the information from Chapter 8 to include them in that group.

3. Open the browser of your choice, and navigate to port 631 of the IP address or hostname of the CUPS server. For example, if the print server name is ubuntucups, navigate to http://ubuntucups:631.

4. Click Add Printer, and follow the prompts to add the printer connected to the local system.

5. Once the new printer is configured, check the result. Review the contents of the /etc/cups/printers.conf configuration file. Check to see if the new printer is shown in the /etc/printcap file.

Lab 2

In this lab, you'll work with the GNOME Print Manager, with the printer created in Lab 1. If it's not available, make sure to install the gnome-cups-manager package. Remember, this lab should be run in sequence, after Lab 1.

1. Open the GNOME Print Manager. For this purpose, you'll need to be in the Ubuntu Linux GUI. Open a command-line interface; in the default GNOME desktop, click Applications | Accessories | Terminal.

2. In the command-line interface that appears, enter the **gnome-cups-manager** command.

3. When the GNOME Print Manager appears, you'll see a window of currently detected printers in the Printers window. Assuming it isn't already checked, click Global Settings | Detect LAN Printers. (If it's already checked, skip to step 5.)

4. Read the warning about Port 631 and click OK.

5. Assuming your network and the CUPS server on the local and remote systems are active, wait a few seconds. The printer configured in Lab 1 should appear in the Printers window.

6. Select the detected network printer. Right-click it and click Properties in the pop-up menu that appears.

7. In the Properties window named after the printer, click the Connection tab. What is the URI associated with the printer?

SELF TEST ANSWERS

Work the CUPS Packages

1. ☑ The simplest way to install the CUPS server package is with the **sudo apt-get install cupsys** command. Of course, there are other options; if the package is available locally, and other dependencies are satisfied, the **dpkg -i cupsys-*.deb** command would also work. Of course, there are GUI tools discussed in Chapter 6 that can also be used to install packages such as cupsys, with dependencies.

2 ☑ **C.** The /etc/samba/smb.conf file shares printers and directories on a Microsoft network. However, that file also cites information in /etc/printcap, so it could be argued that **D** is correct. But as Samba does the sharing, **C** is correct.
☒ While /etc/cups/cupsd.conf can share printers, even with IPP-capable Microsoft systems, it does not by itself share on a Microsoft network. While /etc/printcap is developed from /etc/cups/printers.conf on a CUPS system, that is even further removed from a Microsoft network. Therefore, answers **A** and **B** are both also wrong.

3. ☑ The **cupstestppd** command tests the conformance of a .ppd print driver file with PostScript Print file standards.

Configure Printers

4. ☑ The **http://127.0.0.1:631** or **http://localhost:631** URLs would work; 127.0.0.1 is a synonym to localhost.

5. ☑ **D.** CUPS print servers communicate using TCP/IP port 631.
☒ Based on the information in /etc/services, port 22 is associated with the Secure Shell, port 80 is associated with HTTP connections, and port 361 is unused. Therefore, answers **A**, **B**, and **C** are all incorrect.

6. ☑ The **system-config-printer** command starts the Ubuntu Linux print configuration tool, and has been the tool since Gutsy Gibbon was released.

7. ☑ **D.** This is a bit of a picky question; while answer **B** opens the GUI tool in a web browser, only **elinks** opens the web-based tool in the command-line interface.
☒ As the **gnome-cups-manager** and **system-config-printer** commands also open GUI tools— but they're not web-based tools, answers **A** and **C** are also wrong.

8. ☑ **B.** The /etc/printcap configuration file is explicitly cited in the Samba configuration file, /etc/samba/smb.conf.

⊠   Answers **A** and **C** are CUPS configuration files not cited in the Samba configuration file. Answer **D** is the Samba configuration file. Therefore, they are all incorrect.

9. ☑   **A.** The lpadmin group, as cited in /etc/cups/cupsd.conf and configured as a group in /etc/group, is the group of users allowed by default to configure CUPS printers on Ubuntu Linux systems. Be aware that they may not be so configured on other Linux distributions.
⊠   While the lp group actually exists in /etc/group, it is not so configured in /etc/cups/cupsd.conf, so answer **B** is wrong. As there is no cups or cupsadmin group in /etc/group, answers **C** and **D** are also wrong.

Manage Print Queues

10. ☑   **lpq -a.** The **lpq -a** command lists all queued print jobs on all configured printers.

11. ☑   **lprm 585.** This command removes print job number 585.

12. ☑   **A.** The **Accepting No** directive in /etc/cups/printers.conf suggests the printer is disabled.
⊠   The **Shared No** directive means sharing is disabled, and the **State Stopped** directive means queuing is disabled. The **Location No** directive is associated with the commented location of the printer. Therefore, answers **B**, **C**, and **D** are all wrong.

Manage Printers

13. ☑   **B.** CUPS is associated with the IPP protocol; the URI shown is the appropriate format.
⊠   The only other protocol that can be used for printer URIs uses HTTP, and is associated with HP and Apple print servers. Therefore answers **A**, **C**, and **D** are all wrong.

14. ☑   **C.** While IPP is the protocol associated with CUPS, this URI doesn't work in a web browser.
⊠   As answers **A**, **B**, and **D** all open GUI-based programs to configure local printers, they are all incorrect.

15. ☑   **cupsenable wasoutofpaper.** It's common to run a command such as **cupsenable** to re-enable a printer that was temporarily stopped due to a physical problem such as a lack of paper.

LAB ANSWERS

Remember, these labs are to be run in sequence.

Lab 1

The more practice you get using available CUPS configuration tools, the more you understand the process. But even if you use only GUI tools, examine their effects on critical configuration files. For CUPS, the configured printer configuration files are /etc/cups/printers.conf and /etc/printcap.

Lab 2

You should see that when printers are detected between CUPS servers, access to the printer is available using an IPP-based URI. The detection process illustrates the power of the SNMP (Simple Network Management Protocol), which is used by CUPS to automatically detect shared printers from other systems on a network.

8

Languages and Accounts

T he main topics in this chapter, languages and accounts, are loosely related. But if you work in a multilingual environment, you may need to consider both factors when creating new users. Languages are covered in the UCP curriculum as localization. The locale is associated with a set of environment variables, which range from language to time defaults to currency formats.

You'll also learn about Ubuntu filesystem security. As defined in the UCP curriculum, filesystem security is focused on users, administrators, and the Shadow Password Suite. Users can be created with the Users Settings tool, which can be started with the **users-admin** command. Administrators can be configured with varying levels of privilege in the /etc/sudoers configuration file. You'll even see how to configure these users by directly editing the files associated with the password authentication database.

CERTIFICATION OBJECTIVE 8.01

Configure Localization

Localization specifies how Linux systems are customized for language, dialect, custom, country-specific formats such as currencies, character sets, and more. The locale specifies the current localization settings for the system. More languages can be installed and configured with the Language Support tool.

Closely related to localization is Rosetta, the Launchpad system for automated language translations. As with other human-language translators, Rosetta is a work in progress. Any documentation translated with this application should be still be closely checked by a native speaker of the target language. For more information, see https://launchpad.net/rosetta. Rosetta is cited in the UCP curriculum, under item 121.1, related to Ubuntu's technical infrastructure.

Localization is a rich and complex topic. While this topic may have the least weight in the UCP curriculum, the subject is still fair game for the UCP exam. Incidentally, the UCP curriculum uses the British spelling for local language settings, *localisation*.

e x a m

ⓦ a t c h   *Recognize the function of Rosetta, understand how the* locale *command can read localization settings, and practice installing language packs with the* gnome-language-selector *command.*

INSIDE THE EXAM

Localize the Operating System (123.4)

Ubuntu Linux administrators need to know how to localize the operating system. In other words, you need to know how to set up the locale, as well as install and update from available language packs. The commands cited in the curriculum include **locale** and **gnome-language-selector**. Beyond localization, Ubuntu's technical infrastructure includes Rosetta to help assist with document translations.

Configure Ubuntu File System Security (123.5)

Ubuntu filesystem security relates primarily to user rights and permissions. Once configured,

allowed users have administrative rights with the **sudo** command. They can also edit administrative files with the **sudoedit** command. Administrative rights can be configured with the **visudo** command, which edits the /etc/sudoers configuration file.

Regular users and groups can be configured with the Users Settings tool, accessible with the **users-admin** command. They can also be configured from the command line using the vi editor with the **vipw** and **vigr** commands.

on the
job
While it is possible to open files like /etc/sudoers, /etc/shadow, and /etc/gshadow in regular text editors, they are read-only even for the root administrative user, unless opened with file-specific commands like visudo, vipw -s, and vigr -s.

The Current Language Configuration

The current language is set in /etc/default/locale; detailed configuration is set in a series of variables, shown with the **locale** command. My /etc/default/locale includes the following line:

```
LANG="en_US.UTF-8"
```

You might realize this is the same value as shown in the /etc/environment configuration file. In any case, **LANG** is an environment variable. The **en_US** specifies a language and national dialect, U.S. English in this case. The UTF-8 specifies a character map, associated with the Unicode Transformation Format, which includes standard US ASCII characters and much more.

To review available languages, look at the /usr/share/i18n/locales directory; to review available character maps, examine the /usr/share/i18n/charmaps directory. For more information on supported language and character map combinations, see the contents of the /usr/share/i18n/SUPPORTED file.

The language is just the foundation of how language is localized on your system. For more information, try the **locale** command. When run alone (no switches), it provides output, which I analyze line by line in Table 8-1. When I run **locale**, I see en_US.UTF-8 in the output.

Several more files provide additional information: the en_US file in the /usr/share/i18n/locales directory, the UTF-8 file in the /usr/share/i18n/charmap directory, and various files in the /usr/lib/locales/en_US.utf8 directory. For example, there's an extensive series of settings associated with number formats in the **LC_NUMERIC** stanza in the /usr/share/i18n/locales/en_US file.

The format of the locales can be confusing; for a more human-readable translation of some of the codes, review the /etc/locale.alias file. For example, it cites French as the language associated with fr_FR.ISO-8859-1.

TABLE 8-1	Output	Description
Output from the locale Command	LANG	The language environment variable, as configured in /etc/default/locale
	LC_CTYPE	Includes character classification, case conversions, and more
	LC_NUMERIC	Defines nonmonetary numeric information, such as the decimal point or comma
	LC_TIME	Sets date and time formats
	LC_COLLATE	Configures character collation sequence
	LC_MONETARY	Sets monetary formats
	LC_MESSAGES	Defines format of messages and responses
	LC_PAPER	Sets print output paper size; associated with /etc/papersize
	LC_NAME	Defines name format, such as last name first in East Asia
	LC_ADDRESS	Configures postal addressing
	LC_TELEPHONE	Configures telephone number format
	LC_MEASUREMENT	Sets measurement scales, such as imperial, nautical, and metric
	LC_IDENTIFICATION	Identifies the source of the code, the Free Software Foundation (FSF)

To translate these localization settings to a more understandable format, the **locale -ck *variable*** command can help. For example, the following output illustrates the available formats for the **LC_NAME** variable:

```
$ sudo locale -ck LC_NAME
LC_NAME
name_fmt="%d%t%g%t%m%t%f"
name_gen=""
name_mr="Mr."
name_mrs="Mrs."
name_miss="Miss."
name_ms="Ms."
name-codeset="UTF-8"
```

Yes, this particular localization may seem limited, as that does not include honorifics like Dr., but that reflects the information in the /usr/share/i18n/locales/en_US file.

Installing More Languages

To start the Ubuntu Linux Language Support tool, you could click System | Administration | Language support in the GNOME desktop. But the UCP curriculum explicitly cites the **gnome-language-selector** command. As language configuration requires administrative privileges, start the tool in a GUI command line with the following command:

```
$ sudo gnome-language-selector
```

The first time I ran the Language Support tool, I got a warning, suggesting that language support wasn't completely installed. In my case, the warning also displayed the packages to be installed, which I accepted for a complete system baseline.

Once the configuration is complete, the Language Support window opens as shown in Figure 8-1.

First, review the available default languages. Click the Default Language drop-down menu box. In Ubuntu Linux Gutsy Gibbon, I see 14 choices associated with the English language, such as English (Canada), English (Singapore), as well as English (United States of America). Any changes to the default language are reflected in the /etc/environment and /etc/default/locale configuration files.

To see what the Language Support tool can do, install at least one language based on something other than a Western European alphabet. For this purpose, I've activated the check boxes associated with the Chinese and Korean languages, and

FIGURE 8-1

The Language
Support tool

then clicked Apply. The Language Support tool proceeds to download, install, and configure several dozen packages.

When a special language is installed, the Input Method option to Enable Support To Enter Complex Characters option is available, and should be activated to help enter specialized characters, especially from nonstandard keyboards. Once the process is complete, click OK to exit from the tool, and run the following command to see all newly available languages and character sets:

```
$ sudo dpkg-reconfigure locales
```

Once a new language is installed, you may want to add the locale to the list. The **sudo locale-gen** command adds the new locales to the /var/lib/locales/supported.d/ directory. Special locale settings are configured in the /etc/belocs/locale-gen.conf configuration file.

Additional Localization Settings

Based on the installed languages, the **locale -a** command returns available default language options. For example, if I didn't add any more languages to my system, I'd see the standard variations on English in the output, such as en_GB.utf8 (British English) and en_AU.utf8 (Australian English). If you were paying attention in the previous section, you'll remember that the list matches the Default Language list in the Language Support tool.

In contrast, there is a huge variety of available character maps. Review the output of the **locale -m** command to see them for yourself.

CERTIFICATION OBJECTIVE 8.02

Create Regular Users

While I normally recommend that administrators learn the Linux command line, the UCP curriculum specifically cites the Users Settings GUI user and group management tool. So this section illustrates how you can create users and groups, as well as configure special groups with desired users. But do not worry; toward the end of this chapter, I'll show you how to add users by directly editing authentication databases files from the command-line interface.

But before adding or configuring users or groups, it's important to understand the basics of Linux authentication databases.

> **e x a m**
>
> **ⓦ a t c h** *Learn how to use the Users Settings GUI tool, which can be started with the *users-admin* command, to create and configure regular users and special groups.*

Users and Authentication in Ubuntu Linux

There are three basic types of Linux user accounts: administrative (root), regular, and service. The administrative root account is automatically created when you install Linux, and it has administrative privileges for all services on your Linux computer. A cracker who has a chance to take control of this account can take full control of your system.

Ubuntu Linux normally disables the administrative root account. By default, "no password" is set for the root user, so there's no login available. Be aware that "no password" is different from a blank password; Linux does not allow logins to an account with no password. In contrast, a blank password would automatically allow logins without a password. Normally, administrative access in Ubuntu Linux is available only with commands like **su** and **sudo**, which I'll explain shortly.

Regular users have the necessary privileges to perform standard tasks on a Linux computer. They can access programs such as word processors, databases, and web browsers. They can store files in their own home directories. Since regular users do not normally have administrative privileges, they cannot accidentally delete critical operating system configuration files. You can assign a regular account to most users, safe in the knowledge that they can't disrupt your system with the privileges they have on that account. But regular users who are members of the adm group are configured with administrative access. Users in the adm group can access administrative commands with the **sudo** command. Users in the adm group can confirm their use of administrative commands with their regular password.

Services such as Apache, Squid, mail, games, and printing have their own individual service accounts. These accounts exist to allow each of these services to interact with your computer. Normally, you won't need to do anything to a service account, but if you see that someone has logged in through one of these accounts, be concerned. It's a sign that someone may have broken into your system.

The standard local authentication database in Linux includes four files: /etc/passwd, /etc/group, /etc/shadow, and /etc/gshadow. The last two of these files are available only when the Shadow Password Suite is active.

In the default /etc/passwd file, you should see an "x" in the second column. Older versions of Linux (and those where the Shadow Password Suite is not active) had an encrypted version of user passwords in this column. As /etc/passwd is accessible to all users, a cracker could copy this file and decrypt everyone's password on a Linux computer. This problem led to the development of the Shadow Password Suite.

The Shadow Password Suite was created to provide an additional layer of protection. It is used to encrypt user and group passwords in shadow files (/etc/shadow and /etc/gshadow) that are readable only by users with root privileges. The Shadow Password Suite is now enabled by default. Standard commands for creating new users and groups automatically set up encrypted passwords in the noted shadow files, as you'll see toward the end of this chapter.

The default group IDs shown in the table are relatively new; older versions of Ubuntu Linux configured users together in a single group. Current versions of Ubuntu Linux follow the "User Private Group" scheme, where every user is an exclusive member of his or her own group, which secures each user's files from access by other users.

In the following subsections, you'll examine the authentication database files associated with the Shadow Password Suite.

/etc/passwd

Read the /etc/passwd file; one method that allows you to browse this file with arrow and PAGEUP/PAGEDOWN keys is with the **less /etc/passwd** command. If you've added regular users to your system, you'll normally see them listed near the bottom of this file. Scroll around this file, and you should see a series of lines like the following:

```
michael:x:1000:1000:Michael Jang,,,:/home/michael:/bin/bash
```

Each column in /etc/passwd, delineated by a colon, has a purpose, which is described in Table 8-2.

/etc/group

Every Linux user is assigned to a group. By default in Ubuntu Linux, every user gets his own private group. By default, the user is the only member of that group, as defined in the /etc/group configuration file. Read the /etc/group file; one method that allows you to browse this file with arrow and PAGEUP/PAGEDOWN keys is the **less /etc/group** command. You should see lines similar to the following:

```
michael:x:1000:
donna:x:1001:
scanner:x:104:hplip,michael,donna
```

TABLE 8-2	Field	Example	Purpose
Columns in /etc/passwd	Username	michael	The user login name; should not start with a number or uppercase letters.
	Password	x	The password. May be an *x*, an asterisk (*), or a random-looking group of letters and numbers. An *x* points to /etc/shadow for the actual password. An asterisk means the account is disabled. A group of letters and numbers represents the encrypted password.
	User ID	1000	The unique numeric user ID (UID) for that user. By default, Ubuntu starts user IDs at 1000.
	Group ID	1000	The numeric group ID (GID) associated with that user. By default, Ubuntu Linux creates a new group for every new user, and the number matches the UID. Some other Linux and Unix systems assign all users to the default Users group (GID=100).
	User info	Michael Jang	Intended for comments about the user, such as a full name, phone number, e-mail address, or physical location. May be blank.
	Home Directory	/home/ michael	By default, Ubuntu Linux places new home directories in /home/*username*.
	Login Shell	/bin/bash	By default, Ubuntu Linux assigns users to the bash shell. May be changed to any legal installed shell.

The contents are straightforward. The users michael and donna are members of their own groups as well as the scanner group. The four columns in each /etc/group line are described in Table 8-3.

/etc/shadow

Read the /etc/shadow file; one method that allows you to browse this file with arrow and PAGEUP/PAGEDOWN keys is the **sudo less /etc/shadow** command. If you've added regular users to your system, you'll normally see them listed near the bottom of this file. Scroll around this file, and you should see a series of lines like the following:

```
michael:$1oXeB6$EVUxsMDWaeGLYx4UJr1:14022:0:99999:7:::
```

While similar to /etc/passwd, /etc/shadow can includes additional information such as password life and account expiration. The details are beyond the scope of the current UCP curriculum; for more information, run the **man chage** command. Each column in /etc/shadow, delineated by a colon, has a purpose, which is described in Table 8-4. The command switches listed therein are associated with and can be modified by the **chage** command.

One key difference is with the root account. It's atop the /etc/shadow file. Note the exclamation point in the second column of this line, which disables direct logins into this account.

/etc/gshadow

Every Linux user is assigned to a group. By default in Ubuntu Linux, every user gets his own private group. By default, the user is the only member of that group, as defined

TABLE 8-3	Field	Example	Purpose
Columns in /etc/group	Groupname	michael	Each user gets his own group, with the same name as his username. You can also create unique groupnames.
	Password	x	The password. You should see either an x or a seemingly random group of letters and numbers. An x points to /etc/gshadow for the actual password. A random group of letters and numbers represents the encrypted password. Groups may not have a password.
	Group ID	1000	The numeric group ID (GID) associated with that user. By default, Ubuntu Linux creates a new group for every new user.
	Group members	michael, donna	Lists the usernames that are members of the group. If it's blank, and there is a username that is identical to the groupname, that user is the only member of that group.

TABLE 8-4	Column	Field	Description
Columns in /etc/shadow	1	Username	Username
	2	Password	Encrypted password; requires an *x* in the second column of /etc/passwd. If there's an ! in this column, the account is disabled
	3	Password history	Date of the last password change, in number of days after January 1, 1970
	4	mindays	Minimum number of days that you must keep a password (**-m**)
	5	maxdays	Maximum number of days after which a password must be changed (**-M**)
	6	warndays	Number of days before password expiration when a warning is given (**-W**)
	7	inactive	Number of days after password expiration when an account is made inactive (**-I**)
	8	disabled	Number of days after password expiration when an account is disabled (**-E**)

in the /etc/group configuration file. Review the contents of the /etc/gshadow file; one method that allows you to browse this file with arrow and PAGEUP/PAGEDOWN keys is the **sudo less /etc/gshadow** command. You should see lines similar to the following:

```
michael:!::
donna:!::
scanner:!::hplip,michael,donna
```

The contents are straightforward. The users michael and donna are members of their own groups as well as the scanner group. The four columns in each /etc/gshadow line are described in Table 8-5.

Creating Users and Groups

Ubuntu Linux supports configuration of users and groups with the Users Settings GUI tool. It supports fairly fine-grained customization of user and group settings. To open it from a command-line interface in the GUI, run the following command:

```
$ sudo users-admin
```

TABLE 8-5	Field	Example	Purpose
Columns in /etc/gshadow	Groupname	donna	Each user gets his own group, with the same name as his username. You can also create unique groupnames.
	Password	!	Encrypted password; requires an x in the second column of /etc/group; ! if there's no group password
	Group administrators	michael	The numeric group ID (GID) associated with that user. By default, Ubuntu Linux creates a new group for every new user.
	Group members	michael, donna	Lists the usernames that are members of the group. May be blank if the user is the only member of the group

This opens the Users Settings tool shown in Figure 8-2. It displays currently configured users with standard accounts. In this case, there are two regular users on the local system, and the root user.

Now you'll see how to create a user and a group using this tool.

If you're not already familiar with the Users Settings tool, review the password authentication database files before and after making changes with the tool.

Creating a User

To create a user in the Users Settings tool, click Add User. This opens the New User Account window shown in Figure 8-3. This window includes three tabs: Account, User Privileges, and Advanced. Standard user information can be configured under

FIGURE 8-2

The Users Settings tool

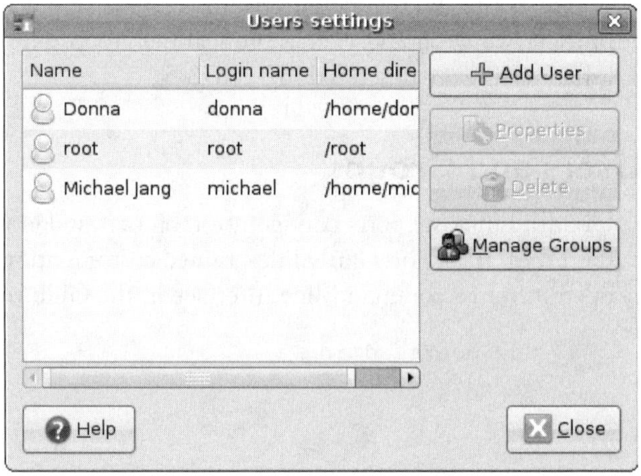

FIGURE 8-3

FIGURE 8-3

Options for
basic account
information

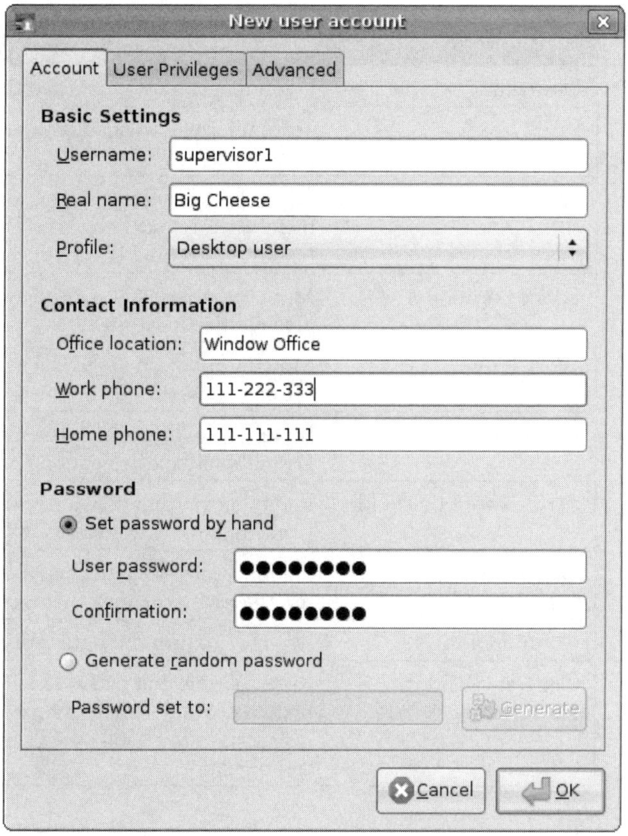

the Account tab, as described in Table 8-6. When you add a user, the changes may affect the four files in the standard authentication database: /etc/passwd, /etc/group, /etc/shadow, and /etc/gshadow.

For the purpose of this section, I've selected Desktop User under the Account tab. When I click the User Privileges tab, I see a series of options shown in Figure 8-4. What you see is probably different, depending in part on installed hardware.

Each of the checkbox options is associated with a specific group, as defined in /etc/group, and described in Table 8-7. In other words, if you activate a specific group under the User Privileges tab, that user is made a member of that group.

When I select the Advanced tab, I see four options as shown in Figure 8-5.

■ The Home Directory is set to /home/*username*, matching the *username* set under the Account tab.

TABLE 8-6	Option	Description
Basic Options for New Users	Username	Login name; must be one word, starting with a lowercase letter
	Real Name	More information about the user; you don't have to include the real name
	Profile	Supports three options, which determine default group memberships under the User Privileges tab: Administrator, Desktop User, and Unprivileged
	Office Location	More information about the user; you don't have to include the actual office location
	Work Phone	More information about the user; you don't have to include the actual telephone number
	Home Phone	More information about the user; you don't have to include the actual home telephone number
	Set Password By Hand	Radio button that activates the User Password and Confirmation text boxes
	User Password	Administrator-specified password; administrators should then tell the user to change their password
	Confirmation	Used to confirm the right Administrator-specified password
	Generate Random Password	Radio button that activates the Generate Random Password text box, which should then be given to the user, with instructions to change the password to something that the user can remember

- The Shell is set to /bin/bash, the bash shell. Ubuntu developers are working towards changing this to the dash shell, the Debian-Almquist shell; the default is actually set to dash if a new user is created with the **useradd** command.

- The Main Group is blank by default; it's a drop-down menu box. If you select a Main Group, the new user is added as a member of that group in the /etc/group and /etc/gshadow configuration files.

- The User ID (UID) is a number. Traditionally, regular users in Linux must have a UID of 100 or higher. By default, Ubuntu Linux systems assign UIDs of 1000 or higher, leaving lower UIDs for special and system users. Before kernel 2.6 was released, the maximum UID number was 65536. It's now about 4 billion (2^{32}).

FIGURE 8-4

Configuring user
privileges

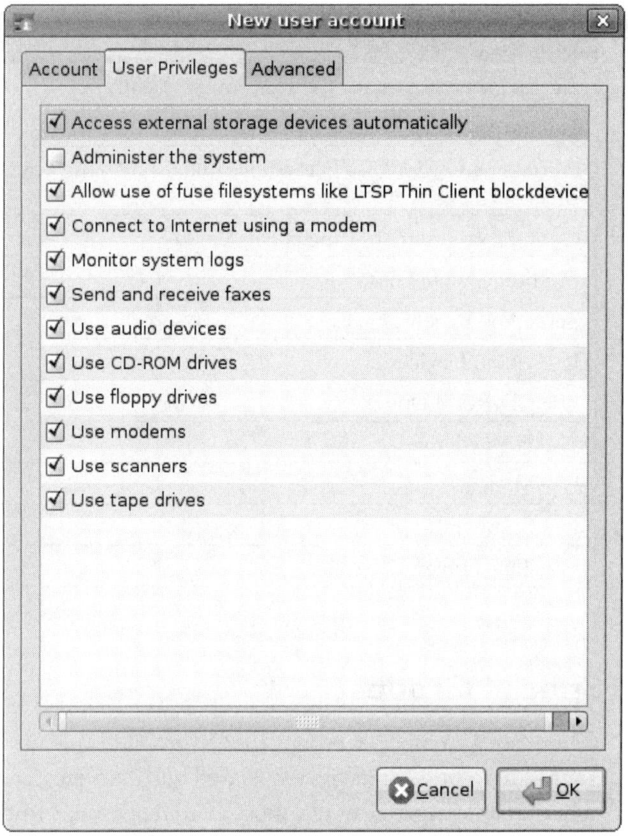

Creating a Group

Now create a new group using the Users Settings tool. Remember, it can be opened
from the GUI command line with the **users-admin** command. From the Users
Settings window, click Manage Groups. This opens the Groups Settings window.
Click Add Group to open the New Group window shown in Figure 8-6.

The options are straightforward. The group name is limited in the same way as
the user name; it must start with a lowercase letter. The Group Members window
lists eligible users, which you can select to make a part of the new group. The only
slightly tricky bit is the Group ID (GID); it can't be the same as any existing GID
in /etc/group, and should be different from any standard range of UID numbers.

TABLE 8-7

User Privileges
Group Options

Option	Name in /etc/group
Access External Storage Devices Automatically	plugdev
Administer The System	admin
Allow The Use Of Fuse Filesystems Like LTSP Thin Client Blockdevice	fuse
Connect To Internet Using A Modem	dip
Monitor System Logs	adm
Send And Receive Faxes	fax
Use Audio Devices	audio
Use CD-ROM Drives	cdrom
Use Floppy Drives	floppy
Use Modems	dialout
Use Scanners	scanner
Use Tape Drives	tape

Users and Special Groups

There are a number of groups in /etc/group. Some are associated with real users, including root. Others are associated with services, such as dovecot, postfix, mysql, ssh, and apt-mirror. Review most available groups in the Users Settings tool. If it isn't already open, run the **sudo users-admin** command in a GUI. Click Manage Groups to open the Group Settings window. Review the available groups on your system; some are described back in Table 8-7.

To add a user to a group, select it and click Properties. In the window that appears, you can select or deselect desired users as group members. Some of the other special groups are listed in Table 8-8.

There are a number of other groups available, but that level of detail is beyond the scope of the UCP curriculum.

FIGURE 8-5

Advanced user privileges

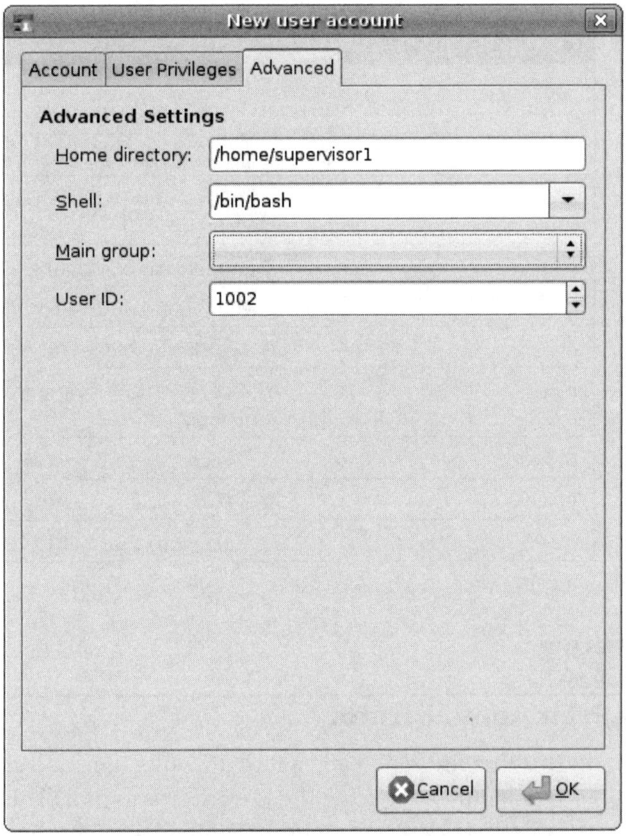

FIGURE 8-6

Creating a new group

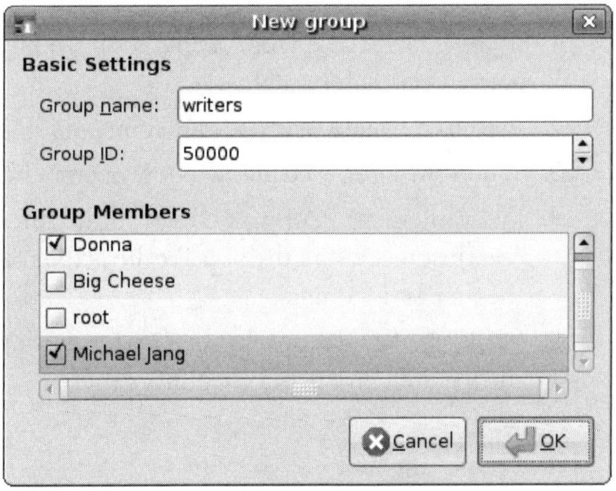

TABLE 8-8	Group (per /etc/group)	Function
Some privileged groups	daemon	For services without other user or group accounts to write to the system
	tty	For command-line text consoles; group owner of /dev/ttyx
	lp	Members allowed direct access to parallel ports; group owner of /dev/lp0
	mail	Mailboxes in /var/mail are owned by group mail
	news	Available for news servers and spools
	uucp	Based on the older Unix to Unix Copy system
	man	Supports writing by the man program to the /var/cache/man directory
	proxy	For access by proxy server services
	voice	Supports local answering machine access
	irc	Available to Internet Relay Chat (IRC) daemons

EXERCISE 8-1

Add a New Print Administrator

In this exercise, you'll add another regular user, and give that user privileges as a print administrator using the Users Settings tool. This exercise assumes a login to the GNOME desktop environment, and assumes the gnome-system-tools package is installed, which includes the noted tool.

1. In the GNOME desktop, open a command-line interface. Click Applications | Accessories | Terminal.

2. Type in the **sudo users-admin** command.

3. When the Users Settings window opens, click Add User.

4. Enter information of your choice in the three tabs associated with the new user. Just make sure the user Profile is that of a Desktop User. Click OK when the process is complete.

5. Click Manage Groups. In the Groups Settings window that appears, scroll to the lpadmin group and click Properties.

6. In the Properties window that opens, select the print administrator user just created, to make that user a part of the lpadmin group.

7. Click OK to exit the Properties window. Click Close to close the Groups Settings window. Click Close to close the Users Settings tool.

8. Confirm the result with the **less /etc/group** command. Scroll to the lpadmin group, and confirm that the new user is a member of that group.

9. Confirm the result again with the **sudo less /etc/gshadow** command. If the new user is a member of the lpadmin group in this file as well, the changes are complete.

Some of you may wonder why in step 4, I didn't take advantage of the Advanced tab in the New User Account window and suggest assigning lpadmin as this print administrative user's main group. When I did this in Ubuntu Gutsy Gibbon, it only changed the default group in the /etc/passwd configuration file. It did not assign the new user to the lpadmin group in /etc/group. Of course, a careful system administrator like yourself will be careful to check such details—and of course know how to edit such files at the command-line interface, as discussed in this part of the chapter.

Creating Users at the Command Line

Alternatively, you can automate this process with the **useradd** command. If you wanted to add a new user named pm, you could just type **sudo useradd pm** to add this user to the /etc/passwd file. It creates a private group in the /etc/group file. If the Shadow Password Suite is active, it also creates parallel entries in the /etc/shadow and /etc/gshadow files.

The **useradd** command also assumes that the default shell is /bin/sh, which is actually linked to the dash shell. As suggested earlier, the default shell may vary depending on the Ubuntu Linux release.

By default, it assumes the home directory is /home/pm. You'll need to create the directory and add the standard files from the /etc/skel directory. This process is described in the last certification objective in this chapter.

The **useradd** command is versatile. It includes a number of command options shown in Table 8-9.

TABLE 8-9

User Privileges
Group Options

Option	Purpose
-u *UID*	Overrides the default assigned *UID*. By default, in Ubuntu Linux this starts at 1000 and can continue sequentially the maximum number of users supported by kernel 2.6, which is 2^{32}.
-g *GID*	Overrides the default assigned *GID*. By default, Ubuntu Linux assigns the same *GID* and *UID* numbers to each user. If you assign a *GID*, it must be either 100 (users) or otherwise already exist.
-c *info*	Enters the comment of your choice about the user, such as his or her name.
-d *dir*	Overrides the default home directory for the user, /home/*username*.
-s *shell*	Overrides the default shell for the user, /bin/bash.

Modifying or Deleting a User Account

Removing user accounts is a pretty straightforward process. The easiest way to delete a user account is with the **userdel** command. By default, this command does not delete that user's home directory. However, it does delete that user's account information from /etc/passwd and /etc/shadow, as well as that user's private group from /etc/group and /etc/gshadow. Alternatively, the **userdel -r *username*** command deletes that user's home directory along with all of the files stored in that home directory.

If you just want to make a few changes, the **chage** command described earlier can help. The information described in Table 8-4 lists much of the information that can be modified with that command.

Creating Groups at the Command Line

Sometimes, administrators need to configure special groups of users, such as supervisors, engineers, drafters, and mechanics. While the **useradd** and **userdel** commands can create and remove groups, the **groupadd** and **groupdel** commands work just with group information in the /etc/group and /etc/gshadow configuration files.

Once such groups are created, the administrator can add appropriate users to those groups with the tools described throughout this chapter.

Assigning a Password

If you've created a username from the command line, use the **sudo passwd *username*** command to assign a new password to that user. For example, the **sudo passwd pm** command lets you assign a new password to user pm. You're prompted to enter a password twice. Relatively insecure passwords such as dictionary words and sequential numbers are allowed, but are something I strongly discourage.

on the Job

Good passwords are important. Any cracker who may have tapped into your network can try to match the password of any of your users. A password-cracking program may be able to find dictionary-word passwords in a matter of minutes. In contrast, it may take quite a bit longer to crack a more complex password such as Ie20cbeS (which could stand for "I eat 20 candy bars every Sunday").

CERTIFICATION OBJECTIVE 8.03

Set Up More Administrators

Ubuntu Linux disables the root account by default. While it's possible to set up a password for the root user, it's discouraged, to limit the risks to the system. Ubuntu Linux includes a very specific configuration in the authentication database and more, which allows access by at least the first regular user to administrative commands. By editing the /etc/sudoers configuration file, you can customize these privileges by administrative command and user.

exam
watch

Understand the commands and configuration files that allow regular users to run administrative commands. The commands are su, sudo, and sudoedit. The
visudo command supports modification of the /etc/sudoers configuration file, where administrative access for regular users is configured.

Super User Concepts

Based on the standard password authentication database, passwords for standard users are stored in the /etc/shadow configuration file. As explained earlier in the description of this file, it includes an encrypted password in the second column for regular users—and an exclamation point, which disables the password for the root (and other system) users.

on the job

Super user and superuser are interchangeable terms.

Now review the /etc/group configuration file. As implied back in Table 8-7, the admin group is available for administrative purposes. The first regular user created on an Ubuntu Linux system should be a member of this group. But that works only with the following directive in the /etc/sudoers configuration file, which allows password-protected access—to members of the admin group—for all administrative commands.

```
%admin ALL=(ALL) ALL
```

Years ago, when I first examined the /etc/sudoers configuration file, I thought the required password for users and groups configured in this file was the administrative password. I was wrong. It actually allows administrative access based on the password of the regular user. Yes, that means if someone were to crack my account password, that user would have administrative access to my system.

But at least it makes me think a bit before running an administrative command. For example, if I accidentally tried to run the sudo **mkfs** command on an unmounted partition, I get the following message, which serves as an "Are You Sure?" message:

```
[sudo] password for michael:
```

One variation on sudo is the **sudoedit** command, which automatically opens the text file that follows in the default text editor. For example, the following command automatically opens the /etc/shadow file:

```
$ sudoedit /etc/shadow
```

The **sudoedit** command is equivalent to the **sudo -e** command. Just be aware that as the default editor in Ubuntu Linux is nano, the above command opens /etc/sudoers in the nano editor.

Ubuntu, nano, and Changing the Default Editor

The default text editor for Ubuntu is nano. It's fairly easy to use, and the commands are listed in the lower pane. The carat (^) indicates that you should use the CTRL key; so the CTRL-X command exits from the nano editor. But I prefer the vi editor, so I run the following command, which allows me to choose between nano, vi, ed, emacs, and other editors if installed. The default editor is then stored in a binary file, /etc/alternatives/editor. As a binary file, it can't be edited directly, at least not easily. So the command shown here is the easiest way to configure a default editor:

```
$ sudo update-alternatives --config editor
```

More on Super User Privileges

Now that I've changed the default editor, I'm ready to open a file such as /etc/shadow in the vi editor with the following command:

```
$ sudoedit /etc/shadow
```

One more tip: as there is no root password configured on normal Ubuntu Linux systems, the **su** command does not normally work. The command requires the password of the root user. But there is no default root password in Ubuntu Linux. So here's a small trick—if you're used to administering Linux from the root account. The following command logs in to the root account from a regular account, using that regular user's password:

```
$ sudo su
```

If you absolutely want to create a password for the root user, run the **passwd** command now. Furthermore, if you really want the full environment of the root account, run the following command:

```
# su -
```

One of the weaknesses of the **sudo** command is that once a correct password is given and accepted, further **sudo** commands are accepted without a password for the next 15 minutes. In the /etc/sudoers configuration file, this is known as a ticket. In the sections that follow, I'll analyze the default /etc/sudoers configuration file, and show you how to edit it to add another level of administrative users. A few of the important sudo switches are described in Table 8-10.

TABLE 8-10	sudo Command Switch	Description
Important sudo Command Switches	-e	Runs the **sudoedit** command; should be applied to an administrative file
	-K, -k	Eliminates the **sudo** 15-minute timestamp; the next time **sudo** is used, the password is required
	-l	Specifies the commands that can be run with administrative privileges for the subject user
	-V	Prints out the version number

The Super User Configuration File

The super user configuration file is /etc/sudoers. This file regulates access to the **sudo** command. Don't open it in a text editor just yet; one way to review this file from the command-line console is with the following command:

```
$ sudo less /etc/sudoers
```

The first active line in this file sets **Defaults**. The exclamation point, known in Linux lingo as the "Bang," negates the effect of a directive. Let's break down this line. The **!lecture** negates the "lecture" given to users who run the **sudo** command. The **tty_tickets** requires users to confirm with their password when running **sudo** in different consoles, also known as ttys. The **!fqdn** directive disables the use of fully qualified domain names (FQDNs) in this file. I like this last setting, as it avoids problems with access to DNS servers. (This line has changed for the Hardy Heron release.)

```
Defaults        !lecture,tty_tickets,!fqdn
```

The next active line provides sudo privileges to the root user.

```
root    ALL=(ALL) ALL
```

The format is as follows:

```
user  system=run_as_username  command
```

This helps explains the last standard active directive. When the percent sign (%) precedes a name associated with users, it specifies a group. So this line specifies permissions for users in the admin group. The first **ALL** specifies all systems; one alternative is to substitute **localhost to** limit access to the local system. The **(ALL)** allows access to all usernames. That's not a problem, as the line still limits access to users in the admin group. Finally, the last **ALL** supports administrative access to all commands.

```
%admin    ALL=(ALL) ALL
```

If you're confident enough to disable the password requirement, the following would enable password-free access from users in the admin group to all administrative commands:

```
%admin    ALL=(ALL) NOPASSWD: ALL
```

Now you're ready to make changes to this file.

Modifying /etc/sudoers

The /etc/sudoers file can be edited with the **visudo** command. As might be expected, access to this command requires administrative privileges. Therefore in Ubuntu Linux, you'd run the following command to open /etc/sudoers in a text editor:

```
$ sudo visudo
```

Now you're ready to make changes. As an example, if you've created a power group in /etc/group, and want to allow that group the ability to reboot the local system, you could add the following line. The localhost means that members of the power group can only reboot when on the local system. In other words, they can't log in remotely and reboot that system.

```
%power    localhost=(ALL)   /sbin/reboot
```

This is just the briefest of introductions to the /etc/sudoers configuration file. The **man sudoers** command provides an extensive manual to this configuration file.

CERTIFICATION OBJECTIVE 8.04

Work the Shadow Password Suite

As described earlier, older versions of Linux had an encrypted version of user passwords in the second column of /etc/pas file. As /etc/passwd is accessible to all users, a cracker could copy this file and decrypt everyone's password on a Linux computer. This problem led to the development of the Shadow Password Suite.

In this section, you'll create a new user directly from the command-line interface by editing the text files associated with the password authentication database. These files are /etc/passwd, /etc/shadow, /etc/group, and /etc/gshadow.

e x a m

ⓦ a t c h   *Understand how to edit the files associated with the Shadow Password Suite, along with the functionality of the vipw and vigr commands.*

Shadow Password Files

Historically, all that was needed to manage Linux users and groups was the information included in the /etc/passwd and /etc/group files. These files included passwords and are, by default, readable by all users.

The Shadow Password Suite was created to provide an additional layer of protection. It is used to encrypt user and group passwords in shadow files (/etc/shadow and /etc/gshadow) that are readable only by users with administrative privileges.

The Shadow Password Suite is now enabled by default in Ubuntu Linux. Standard commands for creating new users and groups automatically set up encrypted passwords in the Shadow Password Suite files, as described in the sections that follow.

If for some reason, such as backward compatibility, you prefer a system where the Shadow Password Suite is disabled, the **shadowconfig** command can help. It's a simple command: while **sudo shadowconfig off** disables the Shadow Password Suite, **sudo shadowconfig on** enables it. Older releases used commands like **pwconv** and **grpconv** to activate this suite. In contrast, take a look at the script in the /sbin/shadowconfig file. You'll see those commands appropriately configured within the script.

Create a New User via Configuration File

There are a couple of special commands specifically designed to edit the user configuration files. The **vipw** command automatically opens the /etc/passwd configuration file. The **vipw -s** command automatically opens the /etc/shadow configuration file. Even if the default editor is nano, these files are automatically opened in the vi editor. However, I wouldn't be surprised to see this changed in future releases of Ubuntu Linux. For example, for the Hardy Heron release, the visudo command used the nano editor by default.

Of course, each of these commands requires administrative access. Open the /etc/passwd configuration file with the **sudo vipw** command. Entries for regular users will be found near the bottom of this file. Scroll around this file, and you should see a series of lines like the following:

```
michael:x:1000:1000:Michael Jang,,,:/home/michael:/bin/bash
```

The columns are each as depicted back in Table 8-2. You can create a new user in /etc/passwd by copying and then editing a line associated with an existing user. Just substitute the information of your choice to create the new user. Make sure that you at least assign a new username and user ID. For example, the following depicts the entry for a new user ez:

```
ez:x:1010:1010:elizabeth,,,:/home/ez:/bin/bash
```

After changes are saved and written, and the editor is closed, you may see a message that prompts you to open and edit /etc/shadow with the **vipw -s** command. Don't forget the **sudo**:

```
$ sudo vipw -s
```

Make changes that parallel those made in /etc/passwd. If you copy a line entry associated with an existing user, the only thing that must be changed is the username in the first column. For more information on each column in /etc/shadow, see Table 8-4.

Now you can assign a password to the new user ez with the following command:

```
$ sudo passwd ez
```

Before creating and populating the new user's home directory, you'll need to configure group information for the new user.

Create a New Group via Configuration File

Every Linux user is assigned to a group. By default, starting with Ubuntu Linux Gutsy Gibbon, every user gets his own private group. The user is the only member of that group, as defined in the /etc/group configuration file. Open that file in the editor of your choice. If want to use the vi editor, use the **sudo vigr** command. You should see lines similar to the following:

```
michael:x:1000:
donna:x:1001:
lpadmin:x:108:michael,donna
```

The contents are straightforward. The users michael and donna are members of their own groups as well as the lpadmin group. The four columns in each /etc/group line are described back in Table 8-3.

You can create a new group in /etc/group by copying and then editing a line associated with an existing group. Just substitute the information of your choice to create the new user. Make sure that you at least assign a new group name and group ID. For example, the following depicts the entry for a new user ez:

```
ez:x:1010:
```

After changes are saved and written, and the editor is closed, you may see a message that prompts you to open and edit /etc/gshadow with the **vigr -s** command. Don't forget the **sudo**.

```
$ sudo vigr -s
```

Make parallel changes to those made in /etc/group. If you copy a line entry associated with an existing group, the only thing that must be changed is the group name in the first column. For more information on each column in /etc/gshadow, see Table 8-5.

Now you're ready to create and populate the new user's home directory, as follows.

Creating a New User Home Directory

The new home directory for ez is as defined in the /etc/passwd configuration file. I've used the default format, which means I need to create the /home/ez directory. I can create that directory with the following command:

```
$ sudo mkdir /home/ez
```

I can then populate that new user's home directory. A default environment is available in the /etc/skel directory. I copy the contents of that directory to the new user's home directory with the following command:

```
$ sudo cp -ar /etc/skel/. /home/ez/
```

Next, I want to make sure that ez has ownership permissions on that directory and all the files and subdirectories. One way to do so is with the following command. The **-R** changes permissions recursively:

```
$ sudo chown -R ez.ez /home/ez
```

One way to test the result is to log in to the new ez user account. You could open a command-line console by pressing CTRL-ALT-F1, or you could do so directly from the current account with the following command.

```
$ su - ez
```

The output prompts for the password created earlier for user ez. The exit command returns to the regular account.

CERTIFICATION SUMMARY

Localization is more than just language. It includes the environment variables, which configure the dialect, labels, and time associated with a specific language and country. It can be listed with the **locale** command. New languages can be added with the Language Support tool, which can be started with the **gnome-language-selector** command.

There are three types of Linux users: regular, administrative, and service users. They're configured through the Shadow Password Suite, associated with the /etc/passwd, /etc/shadow, /etc/group, and /etc/gshadow files. New users and groups can be created and configured with the Users Settings tool. When configuring new users, you may want to add them to one or more special groups that give privileges to audio devices, faxes, modems, and more.

Super user privileges are available to authorized users with the **sudo** and **sudoedit** commands. Super user privileges are configured in /etc/sudoers, which can be edited by users with administrative privileges with the **visudo** command.

Linux authentication databases are associated with the Shadow Password Suite; with the **vipw** and **vigr** commands, any administrator can create a new user by directly editing the files in the suite.

✓ TWO-MINUTE DRILL

Here are some of the key points from the certification objectives in Chapter 8.

Configure Localization

❑ Rosetta is an Ubuntu project for document translations, available at https://launchpad.net/rosetta.

❑ The **locale** command can identify specific information about the local environment, related to the configured language and dialect.

❑ Additional languages can be configured with the Language Support tool, which can be started with the **gnome-language-selector** command.

Create Regular Users

❑ Regular users are configured with privileges needed for standard tasks.

❑ In the Shadow Password Suite, encrypted passwords are stored in /etc/shadow.

❑ Users and groups can be added and modified with the Users Settings tool, which can be started with the **users-admin** command.

❑ Users and groups can be added from the console with commands like **useradd** and **groupadd**.

Set Up More Administrators

❑ Ubuntu Linux configures members of the admin group with administrative privileges. Users in that group can run administrative commands by prefacing them with the **sudo** command.

❑ The **sudoedit** command is like **sudo**, but opens configuration files, which require administrative privileges in the vi editor.

❑ Additional administrative users can be configured with varying privileges in /etc/sudoers. That file can be changed in the default editor with the **visudo** command.

Work the Shadow Password Suite

❑ The Shadow Password Suite provides an additional layer of protection for user passwords.

❑ The Shadow Password Suite can be disabled and enabled with the **shadowconfig** command.

❑ The **vipw** and **vigr** commands can be used to directly edit the files in the Shadow Password Suite.

❑ If users are created directly, their home directories must be created, ownership modified, and their contents populated with appropriate files.

SELF TEST

The following questions will help you measure your understanding of the material presented in this chapter. Read all the questions carefully, as there may be more than one correct answer. Some questions are "fill in the blank" and normally require an exact answer. Choose all correct answers for each question.

Configure Localization

1. What configuration file includes localization settings for the system? Specify the full directory path to the file.

_____

2. Which of the following commands supports adding and configuring more languages?

    A. **sudo gnome-language**

    B. **sudo gnome-language-selector**

    C. **sudo gnome-language-add**

    D. **sudo gnome-language-config**

3. What is the command that lists current language settings? Do not include switches. Do not include the directory path to the command.

_____

Create Regular Users

4. Which of the following commands deletes user traitor while leaving that user's home directory intact?

    A. **useradd -d traitor**

    B. **userdel -d traitor**

    C. **userdel traitor**

    D. **userdel -r traitor**

5. If you want to allow user katie dial-up access to the Internet, which of the following groups should she be a member of?

    A. *dip*

    B. *sound*

    C. *cable*

    D. *admin*

6. Name the group that a user needs to join to mount a data DVD.

_____

7. Name the default group configured for users to access system logs.

_____

8. Say you've opened the Users Settings tool and are creating a regular user. Which of the following groups is not enabled by default?

A. _audio_

B. _floppy_

C. _admin_

D. _fuse_

Set Up More Administrators

9. When you have privileges in /etc/sudoers, what command would you run to preface an administrative command such as users-admin? Do not include the directory path to the command.

_____

10. Which of the following commands allow you to change the contents of /etc/shadow? Assume you're logged in as a regular user, with an account that's a member of the admin group.

A. **vi /etc/shadow**

B. **visudo /etc/shadow**

C. **sudonano /etc/shadow**

D. **sudo -e /etc/shadow**

11. Which of the following entries in /etc/sudoers allows user katie to run the /bin/chasecats script only from the local system?

A. **katie   ALL=(ALL)   /bin/chasecats**

B. **katie   localhost=(ALL)   /sbin/chasecats**

C. **katie   ALL=(ALL)   chasecats**

D. **katie   ALL=localhost /bin/chasecats**

12. What command logs in as the root user from a regular shell prompt? Assume there is no password configured for the root user, and you have administrative privileges in /etc/sudoers. Do not include the directory path to the command.

_____

Work the Shadow Password Suite

13. If the Shadow Password Suite is not active, which of the following files contain user passwords?

    A. /etc/passwd

    B. /etc/group

    C. /etc/shadow

    D. /etc/gshadow

14. Which of the following commands allows a regular user to edit the standard password configuration file, without naming the file?

    A. sudo vi /etc/passwd

    B. sudo -e /etc/passwd

    C. sudoedit /etc/passwd

    D. sudo vipw

15. If you've created a new user dickens, know her password, and want to log in directly as user dickens without a login prompt, what command would work? Do not include the directory path to the command.

    _____

LAB QUESTIONS

Lab 1

In this lab, you'll use the Users Settings tool to add group memberships for a new user, one at a time. After every change, you'll review the result in the /etc/groups configuration file.

  1. Open the Users Settings tool. It's available from a GUI command line with the **sudo users-admin** command.

  2. Create a new user for the purpose of the lab. Click Add User in the Users Settings tool.

  3. Add desired information under the Account tab. Accept the default as a Desktop User.

  4. Open the User Privileges tab. Deselect all checked options. Click OK.

  5. Open a second command line, and review the contents of the /etc/group configuration file. Review the information associated with the new user, and confirm that user is not a member of any group other than his own. Close the /etc/group configuration file.

  6. Return to the Users Settings tool. Click Properties. In the Account window that appears, click the User Privileges tab. Select one option, and click OK.

7. In the second command line, open /etc/group again, and review the changes associated with the new user. What's the name of the group to which the new user has been added?

8. Repeat steps 6 and 7 for another option except Administer The System. Repeat again as needed until you have a better understanding of available privileged groups.

9. When you're finished, click Close to exit from the Users Settings tool.

Lab 2

In this lab, you'll create a new user by directly editing the configuration files of the Shadow Password Suite. You'll also need to give that new user privileges to mount CD/DVDs. This lab requires some knowledge of the vi editor, which I recommend. However, if you prefer another editor such as nano, substitute **nano** followed by the name of the file to be edited (/etc/passwd, /etc/shadow, /etc/group, and /etc/gshadow) for **vipw**, **vipw -s**, **vigr**, and **vigr -s** in the following steps.

Do not give that user privileges to mount external devices. Without such privileges, it's more difficult for a malicious user to copy sensitive data to a portable device such as a USB key.

1. Open the /etc/passwd configuration file; the standard method to do so is by running the **sudo vipw** command. Create a new user; it can be modeled on the line for an existing user. Just make sure the UID and GIDs for the new user (in the third and fourth columns) are unique for the local system. Make sure the home directory is /home/*username*. Save your changes.

2. Now open /etc/shadow; the standard method to do so is by running the **sudo vipw -s** command. Create a new user based on similar information as configured in /etc/passwd. Don't be concerned about the password in the second column at this time. Save your changes.

3. Now open /etc/group; the standard method to do so is by running the **sudo vigr** command. Create a new group, with the same name as the user and GID created in steps 1 and 2. Make sure the new user is a member of the cdrom group. Don't add that user to the plugdev group.

4. Now open /etc/gshadow; the standard method to do so is by running the **sudo vigr -s** command. Create a new group, with the same name as the user and GID created in steps 1 and 2. Make sure the new user is a member of the cdrom group. Don't add that user to the plugdev group.

5. Create an appropriate home directory for the new user, matching that created in /etc/passwd.

6. Copy the hidden files from /etc/skel to the home directory for the new user.

7. Change ownership of the files and directories in the new user's home directory.

8. Create a new password for the new user.

9. Open a new login console. If you're in the GUI, press CTRL-ALT-F1. Try logging in as the new user. Review the active directory with the **pwd** command. Review files in this directory with the **ls -a** command.

10. Exit from the new login console.

Lab 3

In this lab, you'll configure limited administrative privileges for a new user. Allow that user to run the **ifconfig** command. As this command changes network settings, it has to be run from a local system. It is acceptable if you need to create a new user for this purpose; just make sure that user is not included in the admin group in /etc/group or /etc/gshadow. Alternatively, use the new user created in Labs 1 or 2.

1. First, back up the current version of the /etc/sudoers configuration file; one method is to copy it to your home directory. If changes are made incorrectly, you may be denied access to administrative commands, even if you're logged in as a user that's also a member of the admin group.

2. If there are problems with changes, reboot the system, and open the GRUB menu. When open, select the option associated with Recovery Mode. You should then be able to restore the /etc/sudoers file from the saved location. If you're running Hardy Heron (8.04) or later, you'll see a Recovery Menu, and have to select the Drop To Root Shell Prompt option. You'll then be able to restore the /etc/sudoers file.

3. Open the /etc/sudoers configuration file. The standard method to do so from the command-line interface is to run the **sudo visudo** command.

4. In the /etc/sudoers configuration file, add an appropriate configuration line. Remember, the first column specifies the configured user, and the last column specifies the full path to the command in question.

5. Save the changes.

6. Log in as the new user. Can that user run the **ifconfig eth0 192.168.0.100** command? If so, you'll see that IP address in the output to the **ifconfig eth0** command.

7. Log out from the new account. Log in as a user with administrative privileges. Restore the original network settings with the **sudo /etc/init.d/networking restart** command.

SELF TEST ANSWERS

Localize the Operating System

I. ☑   The standard file for localization settings is **/etc/default/locale**. One might argue that the settings are actually stored in files such as /usr/share/i18n/locales/en_US, but that would not apply if there is more than one locale available.

2. ☑   **B.** The **gnome-language-selector** command allows users with administrative privileges to add languages and configure a default language dialect with the Language Support tool.
☒   The other noted commands do not exist in Ubuntu Linux; therefore, answers **A, C,** and **D** are all wrong.

3. ☑   The **locale** command displays all character settings.

Create Regular Users

4. ☑   **C.** The **userdel** command does not touch a user's home directory, unless you use the **-r** switch.
☒   There is no **-d** switch for the **userdel** command. The **useradd** command only adds users. The **userdel -r** switch deletes the subject user's home directory. Therefore, answers **A, B,** and **D** are all incorrect.

5. ☑   **A.** The *dip* group is associated with dial-up access.
☒   There is no standard *sound* or *cable* group, so answers **B** and **C** are wrong. Sure, a user who is part of the *admin* group could access the modem for dial-up access, but that would be insecure, and therefore answer **D** is inferior.

6. ☑   Members of the **cdrom** group can mount DVDs.

7. ☑   Members of the **adm** group can access system logs.

8. ☑   **C.** By default, regular users should not be configured as administrators.
☒   As regular users should have access to the *audio* system, any available *floppy* drives, and the *fuse* system for thin clients, answers **A, B,** and **D** are all wrong.

Set Up More Administrators

9. ☑   **sudo users-admin**. This is the simplest way to run an administrative command if you have privileges in /etc/sudoers.

10. ☑   **D. sudo -e** command opens the contents of the text file that follows for editing, with administrative privileges.
☒   As editing the /etc/shadow file requires administrative privileges, answer **A** is not sufficient. As **visudo** is intended only for the /etc/sudoers file, answer **B** is wrong. As there is no sudonano command, answer **C** is also wrong.

11.   ☑   **B.** The localhost must be specified first to limit access to the local system; the full path to the script or any administrative command (/bin/chasecats) is also required.
        ☒   As answers **A** and **D** do not limit access to the local system, they are incorrect. As answer **C** does not cite the full path to the script, it is also incorrect.

12.   ☑   **sudo su.** This command, when run by a regular user with administrative privileges, logs in as the root user. No root password is required.

Work the Shadow Password Suite

13.   ☑   **A.** If the Shadow Password Suite is not active, passwords are stored in /etc/passwd.
        ☒   As /etc/group and /etc/gshadow cannot contain user passwords, answers **B** and **D** are incorrect. As /etc/shadow contains passwords (and exists only) when the Shadow Password Suite is active, answer **C** is also incorrect.

14.   ☑   **D.** This is the only command choice that does not name the file to be edited.

15.   ☑   **su - dickens.** This command logs in as user dickens without having to find a login prompt. It does prompt for the password for dickens' account.

LAB ANSWERS

While these labs do not need to be run in sequence, it may be helpful to run at least Lab 1 or Lab 2, both of which create a new user, before running Lab 3, which requires a new user.

Lab 1

This lab is intended to familiarize you with the different groups in /etc/group, and the associated functionality as described in (relatively) plain English in the Users Settings GUI tool. As you add the new user to another group in the Users Settings tool, this lab should help you recognize the actual group being configured in /etc/group.

Lab 2

This lab should help demonstrate that everything can be done at the command-line interface, at least with respect to adding and configuring new users and groups. Once the configuration is complete, the new user should not be a member of the plugdev group, as defined in /etc/group. Otherwise, that user will be able to plug in an external device such as a USB key, which would help that user copy files off the system, potentially compromising security.

Lab 3

This lab demonstrates how privileges can be granted to regular users. While the focus is on a single user, the chapter also demonstrates how privileges can be granted to a group of users as defined in /etc/group.

9

Configuring Network Interfaces and Profiles

There are two basic topics in this chapter, network interfaces and network profiles. In this chapter, you'll learn how networks are started during the boot process. Defaults are configured in files; current settings can be reviewed with the right commands. The GUI tool started with the **network-admin** command is especially important. And as suggested by the UCP curriculum, you need an understanding of how both command-line and GUI tools can be used to configure network interfaces.

Network profiles support different network configurations on the same system. For example, laptop systems might require different network interfaces in an office connected to a wired network, and a home connected via a wireless network. The variety of tools available for wireless configuration is especially broad.

CERTIFICATION OBJECTIVE 9.01

Configure Network Interfaces

In this section, I'll go through how the boot process starts the network, using key configuration files and scripts. You'll learn how directives work in files like /etc/network/interfaces, and the sequence of scripts in the /etc/network directory. I'll even show you how to set up Ubuntu Linux as a router by setting up IP forwarding. The Network Settings tool can be a great help in the configuration of wired and wireless network cards—and even telephone modems.

The Network Boot Process

Ubuntu Linux has a well-deserved reputation as an operating system that "just works." To that end, let's analyze what normally happens to networking during the boot process, after the kernel and appropriate network modules are loaded.

INSIDE THE EXAM

Configure Network Interfaces

As with other systems, the UCP curriculum suggests that exam candidates should be able to configure network interfaces using command-line and graphical tools. The categories include static and dynamic configuration, as well as wired and wireless interfaces. The UCP curriculum also suggests a need to know how to configure telephone modems from the GUI, as command-line configuration is covered on the complementary LPI exams.

Set Up Network Profiles

The UCP curriculum suggests that candidates know how to configure profiles for mobile devices such as laptop systems. That requires some understanding of command-line and graphical tools for wireless and wired configurations.

1. Services in the /etc/rcS.d directory are started at all runlevels. This includes the S40networking link, which starts the /etc/init.d/networking script.

2. All configured network interfaces are activated, courtesy of the **ifup -a** command.

3. Activation is based on files in the /etc/network/ directory. This includes the *interfaces* configuration file, as well as the files in the if-pre-up.d/ and if-up.d/ subdirectories.

That's the big picture. Now to see how this starts the loopback interface on the local system, run the following **ifup** and **ifdown** commands, which deactivate and reactivate all (**-a**) local network interfaces, in verbose (**-v**) mode. Figure 9-1 illustrates the messages associated with activating network interfaces.

on the
🖐 o b   *The loopback interface is associated with the lo device. The existence of the loopback interface, as shown in the output to the ifconfig command, confirms proper installation of networking software.*

```
$ sudo ifdown -av
$ sudo ifup -av
```

FIGURE 9-1

Activating
network
interfaces

```
michael@UbuntuGG:~$ sudo ifup -av
Configuring interface lo=lo (inet)
run-parts --verbose /etc/network/if-pre-up.d
run-parts: executing /etc/network/if-pre-up.d/wireless-tools
run-parts: executing /etc/network/if-pre-up.d/wpasupplicant
ifconfig lo 127.0.0.1 up
run-parts --verbose /etc/network/if-up.d
run-parts: executing /etc/network/if-up.d/avahi-autoipd
run-parts: executing /etc/network/if-up.d/avahi-daemon
run-parts: executing /etc/network/if-up.d/clamav-freshclam-ifupdown
run-parts: executing /etc/network/if-up.d/mountnfs
run-parts: executing /etc/network/if-up.d/ntpdate
run-parts: executing /etc/network/if-up.d/wpasupplicant
Configuring interface eth1=eth1 (inet)
run-parts --verbose /etc/network/if-pre-up.d
run-parts: executing /etc/network/if-pre-up.d/wireless-tools
run-parts: executing /etc/network/if-pre-up.d/wpasupplicant

ifconfig eth1 192.168.0.6 netmask 255.255.255.0              up
 route add default gw 192.168.0.1 metric 100 eth1
run-parts --verbose /etc/network/if-up.d
run-parts: executing /etc/network/if-up.d/avahi-autoipd
run-parts: executing /etc/network/if-up.d/avahi-daemon
run-parts: executing /etc/network/if-up.d/clamav-freshclam-ifupdown
run-parts: executing /etc/network/if-up.d/mountnfs
run-parts: executing /etc/network/if-up.d/ntpdate
run-parts: executing /etc/network/if-up.d/wpasupplicant
michael@UbuntuGG:~$
```

To limit the action to a specific network device, just include the device without the **-a**. For example, the following command deactivates the second Ethernet device on the local system:

```
$ sudo ifdown -v eth1
```

Courtesy of the NetworkManager script in the /etc/NetworkManager/dispatcher.d/ directory, other scripts are called with the **run-parts** command shown in Figure 9-1. These scripts are all listed in subdirectories of /etc/network, and are described in Table 9-1. Scripts in the if-up.d/ or if-pre-up.d/ subdirectories are activated by the **ifup** command. Scripts in the if-down.d/ or if-post-down.d/ subdirectories are deactivated by the **ifdown** command.

Several other services may be configured in the directories listed in Table 9-1. For example, I've configured the SSH and Postfix servers on another Ubuntu Linux system; associated scripts are shown in the /etc/network/if-up.d/ directory. On that system, I did not install the avahi-daemon package, so the associated Zeroconf scripts are not installed.

TABLE 9-1	Script	Subdirectory of /etc/network	Purpose
Typical /etc/ network Scripts	wireless-tools	if-pre-up.d/, if-post-down.d	Activates and deactivates wireless interfaces.
	wpasupplicant	all	Reads and uses WPA keys for a wireless network, as available. Identical in all four directories.
	avahi-autoipd	if-up.d/, if-down.d/	Associated with Zeroconf (see the following On the Job).
	avahi-daemon	if-up.d/	Associated with Zeroconf (see the following On the Job).
	clamav-freshclam-ifupdown	if-up.d/, if-down.d/	Starts and stops the Clam AntiVirus daemon.
	mountnfs	if-up.d/	Mounts NFS filesystems configured in /etc/fstab.
	ntpdate	if-up.d/	Starts the NTP service, if configured to start on boot.

on the **❶ ob**

The avahi service in several /etc/network subdirectories is associated with Zero Configuration Networking (Zeroconf) on IP network 169.254.0.0/16. It's designed to work where static networking is not configured and a DHCP server is not available. It's also known in the Microsoft world as Automatic Private IP Addressing and in the Apple world as Bonjour.

As shown in the output from the **ifup -av** command, interfaces are processed in a specific order. First, the following message tells me that the loopback interface, signified by the *lo* label, is being configured on an IP version 4 (IPv4) network, as signified by the *inet* message. If it were an IP version 6 network, there would be an *inet6* message.

```
Configuring interface lo=lo (inet)
```

Note the **run-parts** commands that follow, as they run the scripts in the /etc/network/if-pre-up.d directory—before a network interface is activated. The scripts in this directory activate wireless interfaces (**wireless-tools**) and look for a configured WPA (Wi-Fi Protected Access) key (**wpasupplicant**). As there are no wireless characteristics to a loopback adapter, these scripts have no effect.

Then the following **ifconfig** command assigns the loopback IP address, 127.0.0.1, to the loopback adapter, **lo**, and then activates the adapter (**up**).

```
ifconfig lo 127.0.0.1 up
```

There are references to several more scripts in the /etc/network/if-up.d/ directory. The process then is repeated with regular configured network adapters. The following messages provide clues to how the second Ethernet adapter (eth1) has been configured. I'll describe these commands in more detail shortly.

```
ifconfig eth1 192.168.0.6 netmask 255.255.255.0 up
route add default gw 192.168.0.1 metric 100 eth1
```

Now you're ready to review the default network settings configured in the /etc/network/interfaces configuration file

Default Network Settings

The default network settings for an Ubuntu Linux system are stored in the /etc/network/interfaces configuration file. This file may seem cryptic to newer Linux users, so let's analyze one version from my system, line by line. First, the **auto** directive identifies the network interface to be configured, in this case, the loopback adapter, as noted by the *lo* label:

```
auto lo
```

Without the **auto** directive, the specified interface is not activated the next time you run the **/etc/init.d/networking restart** script or the **ifup -a** command.

But that directive does not actually configure a loopback adapter. The interface also needs to be configured, and that's the purpose of the **iface** directive. It applies IPv4 networking, as defined by the **inet** directive, along with the **loopback** address, to the loopback adapter, **lo**:

```
iface lo inet loopback
```

The next set of directives illustrates that their order is not critical. The directive that follows, as suggested by the **static** directive, specifies a static configuration, using IPv4 addressing, for interface eth1:

```
iface eth1 inet static
```

As befits a static configuration, the IP **address** is specified as shown:

```
address 192.168.0.6
```

The noted **address** and **netmask** are configured with the noted network card using the **ifconfig** command, as described in the next two sections. As a candidate for the UCP, you should already be familiar with IPv4 addressing in detail. So the network mask (netmask) and gateway directives should be self-explanatory:

```
netmask 255.255.255.0
gateway 192.168.0.1
```

But the gateway directive actually does more; it's related to the **route** command described in the previous section, which adds the noted IP address (192.168.0.1) as the default gateway for the network, using the configured network adapter (eth1). The **route** command is described in more detail in the next two upcoming sections.

Finally, the following configures a specific wireless network ID, the ESSID (Extended Service Set ID). The **wireless-essid** directive shown here names my home wireless network ID, **nancyrandy**:

```
wireless-essid nancyrandy
```

It's followed by the **auto eth1** directive, which identifies the previous lines as configuring the second Ethernet adapter on this system. The first Ethernet adapter is not active, as that is a wired adapter, and I use my wireless network. But if I activated that first Ethernet adapter, using my home DHCP server, I'd see the following directives added to this same /etc/network/interfaces file:

```
iface eth0 inet dhcp
auto eth0
```

Remember, you also need to know how to configure access to a DHCP server on a remote network. Assuming routing is properly configured (which is a separate issue), configuring access to a remote DHCP server would make the preceding directives look just a bit different:

```
iface eth0 inet bootp
auto eth0
```

There are more directives available for the /etc/network/interfaces file. Commonly used directives, including those already described, are listed in Table 9-2. This does not include directives associated with Novell's older Internetwork Packet Exchange (IPX) networks.

TABLE 9-2	Directive	Purpose
Common /etc/network/ interfaces Directives	auto	Identifies a device file associated with the network interface, such as lo and eth0
	allow-hotplug	Supports hot plug-and-play access to network interfaces, such as those connected to PC Card and USB ports
	iface	Identifies the network address system and type associated with a device
	lo	Associated with the loopback adapter
	eth0	Associated with the first Ethernet card; uses the same name as network device files, such as eth1, ath0, ppp0, and so on
	static	Specifies a static IP address; requires additional directives for IP address information
	dhcp	Specifies that the associated device look to a DHCP server for IP address information
	bootp	Specifies that the associated device look to a remote network for a DHCP server for IP address information
	ppp	Specifies that the associated device look to modem configuration information in the /etc/ppp/peers directory
	inet	Configures IPv4 networking
	inet6	Configures IPv6 networking
	address	Precedes a static IP address
	netmask	Precedes a static IP address network mask
	gateway	Precedes a default gateway IP address for the network
	hwaddress	Precedes a hardware address
	hostname	Specifies the hostname to be used; overrides any hostname assigned by a DHCP server
	network	Specifies the network address
	dns-nameservers	Assigns a DNS server

Current Network Settings

After Ubuntu Linux has booted, it's easy to find the current network settings. That information is available with the **ifconfig** and **route** commands. They're also set up in configuration files, as described later in the "Key Configuration Files" section.

ifconfig

The **ifconfig** command is used to configure and display network devices. Here is some sample output from this command, focused on one specific network adapter. In this case, the adapters are eth0, the first Ethernet adapter on this system, and lo, the loopback adapter.

```
$ ifconfig
eth0  Link encap:Ethernet  HWaddr 00:0C:29:30:4E:EA
      inet addr:192.168.0.70  Bcast:192.168.0.255
Mask:255.255.255.0
      inet6 addr: fe80::20c:29ff:fe30:4eea/64 Scope:Link
      UP BROADCAST RUNNING MULTICAST  MTU:1500  Metric:1
      RX packets:94619 errors:0 dropped:0 overruns:0 frame:0
      TX packets:6950 errors:0 dropped:0 overruns:0 carrier:0
      collisions:0 txqueuelen:1000
      RX bytes:17349628 (16.5 MB)  TX bytes:1293983 (1.2 MB)
      Interrupt:18 Base address:0x1400

lo    Link encap:Local Loopback
      inet addr:127.0.0.1  Mask:255.0.0.0
      inet6 addr: ::1/128 Scope:Host
      UP LOOPBACK RUNNING  MTU:16436  Metric:1
      RX packets:47 errors:0 dropped:0 overruns:0 frame:0
      TX packets:47 errors:0 dropped:0 overruns:0 carrier:0
      collisions:0 txqueuelen:0
      RX bytes:8479 (8.2 KB)  TX bytes:8479 (8.2 KB)
```

The preceding command specifies configuration data for the first Ethernet device on the system, eth0. If you just specify **ifconfig eth0**, information is displayed only about the specified interface. If you don't specify a device, **ifconfig** shows all network adapters, including the loopback adapter. Now, break down the information a bit. From the first line, the hardware address is associated with the *HWaddr* label:

```
eth0  Link encap:Ethernet  HWaddr 00:0C:29:30:4E:EA
```

The second line is associated with IPv4 addresses, as noted by the *inet addr* label. It specifies the IP address, the broadcast address (*Bcast*), and network mask (*Mask*).

```
inet addr:192.168.0.70  Bcast:192.168.0.255  Mask:255.255.255.0
```

The third line is associated with the IPv6 address, as noted by the *inet6 addr* label:

```
inet6 addr: fe80::20c:29ff:fe30:4eea/64 Scope:Link
```

The line that follows describes the status of the adapter; it's running (*up*), in broadcast mode, supports multicast messages, and supports a maximum transmission unit (*MTU*) of 1500 bytes per packet.

```
UP BROADCAST RUNNING MULTICAST  MTU:1500  Metric:1
```

The next two lines are associated with received (*RX*) and transmitted (*TX*) packets. If there are errors in either direction, they'll show up in these lines. Errors in wireless network adapters are more common. The final line specifies hardware channels, specifically the Interrupt, also known as the IRQ (interrupt request port), and the base address, also known as the I/O (input/output) address.

```
Interrupt:18 Base address:0x1400
```

As you can see from the output to the **ifconfig** command, similar information is available for the loopback adapter (*lo*). As there is no physical network card for the loopback adapter, there is no IRQ or I/O address assigned to that adapter.

route

The **route** command, not surprisingly, is associated with routing tables. The command is most commonly used without an option, and is equivalent to **netstat -r**. The following is a sample of the output:

```
$ route
Kernel routing table
Destination    Gateway        Genmask         Flags Metric  Ref   Iface
localnet       *              255.255.255.0   U     0       0     eth0
default        192.168.0.1    0.0.0.0         UG    100     0     eth0
```

The Destination column lists networks by their IP addresses. Under this column, the *localnet* label is associated with the local network; the *default* label specifies all other IP addresses. The Gateway column indicates gateway addresses. If the destination is on the LAN, no gateway is required, so an asterisk (or *0.0.0.0*) is shown in this column. The Genmask column lists the network mask. Networks look

TABLE 9-3

The netstat Flag
Indicates the
Route

Flag	Description
G	The route uses a gateway.
U	The network adapter (Iface) is up.
H	Only a single host can be reached via this route.
D	This entry was created by an ICMP redirect message.
M	This entry was modified by an ICMP redirect message.

for a route appropriate to the destination IP address. The IP address is compared against the destination networks, in order. When the IP address is found to be part of one of these networks, it's sent in that direction. If there is a gateway address, it's sent to the computer with that gateway. The Flags column describes how this is done. Flag descriptions are listed in Table 9-3. The last key column is Iface, which stands for the interface device in question.

Administrators commonly add the **-n** flag, which tells **route** to display addresses as IP addresses, instead of as hostnames. This avoids delays associated with DNS servers, and provides a slightly different view of the routing table, as numeric destination addresses are substituted in the first two columns.

```
$ route -n
Kernel routing table
Destination    Gateway       Genmask          Flags Metric Ref   Iface
192.168.0.0    0.0.0.0       255.255.255.0    U     0      0     eth0
0.0.0.0        192.168.0.1   0.0.0.0          UG    100    0     eth0
```

Configuring from the Command Line

Just as network settings can be reviewed with the **ifconfig** and **route** commands, they can also be modified with the same commands. But to make sure such commands survive a reboot, they should be added to the /etc/network/interfaces file described earlier.

Network Configuration with ifconfig

The **ifconfig** command can also be used to configure network interfaces. For example, you can assign a new IP address for eth0 with the following command:

```
$ sudo ifconfig eth0 10.11.12.13
```

The first parameter, **eth0**, tells you which interface is being configured. The next argument, **10.11.12.13**, indicates the new IP address being assigned to this interface. To make sure your change worked, issue the **ifconfig** command again (with the name of the adapter device) to view its current settings:

```
$ ifconfig eth0
eth0      Link encap:Ethernet  HWaddr 00:50:56:40:1E:6A
          inet addr: 10.11.12.13  Bcast:10.255.255.255  Mask:255.0.0.0
          inet6 addr: fe80::2e0:4cff:fee3:d106/64 Scope:Link
          UP BROADCAST RUNNING MULTICAST  MTU:1500  Metric:1
          RX packets:11253 errors:0 dropped:0 overruns:0 frame:0
          TX packets:1304 errors:0 dropped:0 overruns:0 carrier:0
          collisions:0 txqueuelen:1000
          RX bytes:2092656 (1.9 Mb)  TX bytes:161329 (157.5 Kb)
          Interrupt:10 Base address:0x10a0
```

The output of this command shows that you've successfully changed the IP address on the eth0 interface. But this may not be enough, as you should realize that the broadcast address may not work with this IP address. For example, you may have configured a private network with the 10.11.12.0 network address.

With the right switch, the **ifconfig** command can modify a number of other settings for your network adapter. Return to the **ifconfig** command described earlier in the /etc/network/interfaces file. This specifies an IP address of 192.168.0.6 and a network mask of 255.255.255.0 before activating the adapter.

```
ifconfig eth1 192.168.0.6 netmask 255.255.255.0 up
```

Several other switches for **ifconfig** are shown in Table 9-4.

Network Configuration with route

In Linux network configuration, the **route** command can be used to set up a default gateway for the network. A default gateway is the route used if the desired destination address does not exist elsewhere in the routing table. If the default gateway does not exist in the output to the **route** command, as shown here:

```
default         192.168.0.1   0.0.0.0           UG    100    0    eth0
```

it can be added to the routing table. The noted gateway can be added with the following command:

```
$ sudo route add default gw 192.168.0.1 dev eth0
```

If there's only one physical network device, the **dev eth0** is not required.

TABLE 9-4	Parameter	Description
ifconfig Switches	up	Activates the specified adapter.
	down	Deactivates the specified adapter.
	netmask *address*	Assigns the *address* subnet mask.
	broadcast *address*	Assigns the *address* as the broadcast address. May be required if a nonstandard network mask is used.
	metric N	Allows you to set a metric value of N for the routing table associated with the network adapter.
	mtu N	Sets the maximum transmission unit as N, in bytes.
	-arp	Deactivates the Address Resolution Protocol, which collects network adapter hardware addresses.
	promisc	Activates promiscuous mode; the network adapter reads all packets to all hosts. Can help analyze the network for problems or to try to decipher messages between other users.
	-promisc	Deactivates promiscuous mode.
	irq *port*	Assigns a specific IRQ *port*.
	io_addr *address*	Assigns a specific I/O *address*.

Routing Forward

A router is a key device in network communication. Linux systems are commonly configured as routers. While the public UCP curriculum does not specify anything about configuring Linux as a router, I believe it's a key skill for Ubuntu Linux administrators. And it's relatively easy to do.

To configure Ubuntu Linux as a router, all you need to do is configure a kernel variable. The following command confirms the default for IPv4 addressing, where Linux is *not* configured as a router:

```
$ cat /proc/sys/net/ipv4/conf/default/forwarding
0
```

If your computer has two or more network cards, you can configure the system as a router. To do so, enable IP forwarding in /etc/sysctl.conf by adding the following directive:

```
net.ipv4.conf.default.forwarding=1
```

on the
Job

Some versions of Ubuntu Linux suggest an incorrect directive for IPv4 forwarding. For more information, see bug 84537 at https://bugs.launchpad.net. There are some differences for the Hardy Heron release.

Of course, if you're working with IPv6 networking, you'll also want to activate the following directive:

```
net.ipv6.conf.default.forwarding=1
```

You don't need to reboot to activate these changes; the following command rereads the /etc/sysctl.conf configuration file:

```
$ sudo sysctl -p
```

Finally, to confirm the changes, run the following commands:

```
$ cat /proc/sys/net/ipv4/conf/default/forwarding
$ cat /proc/sys/net/ipv6/conf/default/forwarding
```

Key Configuration Files

There are several other important configuration files associated with network interfaces on an Ubuntu Linux system. Not all are required. For example, if the system is configured with static networking, there is no need for a DHCP client, as configured in the /etc/dhclient.conf configuration file.

Databases are also required to translate domain names such as www.mcgraw-hill.com to IP addresses such as 12.26.55.108. Two standard databases for this purpose are local /etc/hosts configuration files and DNS (Domain Name System) servers. When DNS servers are used, they are listed by their IP address in the /etc/resolv.conf configuration file. But such databases can conflict. The /etc/host.conf or /etc/nsswitch.conf configuration file is used to determine which database is searched first, also known in associated lingo as the search order.

Other key configuration files are listed in the /etc/network directory, but they were already addressed at the beginning of this chapter.

/etc/dhclient.conf

The /etc/dhclient.conf configuration file is associated with the Ubuntu Linux dhcp-client package. The default version of this file is functionally empty, as it just includes a bunch of comments. I'll examine just a couple of the more important suggested directives here.

Removing the comment character (#) from the front of each of these lines would activate these directives. If you activate the first directive, you should change the actual hostname from andare.fugue.com to that you want assigned to the local system.

```
#send host-name "andare.fugue.com";
```

The following directive, if active, would request the specified information from the DHCP server. Naturally, requesting a hostname from a DHCP server is incompatible with the previous **send host-name** directive. For more information, see Table 9-5.

```
#request subnet-mask, broadcast-address, time-offset, routers,
#        domain-name, domain-name-servers, host-name;
```

Be aware that Table 9-5 only describes directives discussed in this section. A more complete list is available in the man pages associated with dhcp-options and dhclient.conf.

on the **Job** *UTC is a non-English acronym based on a political compromise. It's functionally equivalent to Greenwich Mean Time.*

/etc/hosts

The first database of hostnames and IP addresses was set up in a static text file, /etc/hosts. When there were just a few nodes on the network that eventually turned into the Internet, it was possible to maintain identical /etc/hosts files on each computer.

TABLE 9-5	dhclient.conf Directive	Description
Description of Key Directives from dhclient.conf	send	Provides information for the directives that follow
	host-name	Associated with the hostname
	request	Asks for information related to the directives that follow
	subnet-mask	Specifies the subnet mask, also known as the network mask
	broadcast-address	Specifies the broadcast address
	time-offset	Specifies the time offset, in seconds, relative to UTC
	routers	Notes the IP address for connected routers
	domain-name	Notes the domain name for the local network
	domain-name-servers	Associated with the DNS server
	require	Requires the list of directives that follow

Here's a typical line in /etc/hosts, which lists the IP address, fully qualified domain name, and alias for one computer connection:

```
192.168.132.32    linux1.mommabears.com   laptop
```

/etc/resolv.conf

There are millions of hosts on the Internet. Even if it were possible to collect all domain names and IP addresses into a /etc/hosts file, the file would overwhelm every computer. And it would overwhelm every network administrator who would have to make sure that all the /etc/hosts files on the Internet match—and get updated every time a new web site appears. That's why the Domain Name System (DNS) was developed, based on the Berkeley Internet Name Domain (BIND). In /etc/resolv.conf, the IP address of each DNS server is listed with a simple line similar to this:

```
nameserver 192.168.0.1
```

/etc/host.conf

Many networks configure an /etc/hosts file for the local network and a DNS server for other networks and/or the Internet. When your computer looks for an IP address, this file determines whether it searches though /etc/hosts or DNS first. This is usually a one-line file:

```
order hosts,bind
```

A computer with this line looks through /etc/hosts first. If it can't find the computer name that you want in that file, it next looks to the DNS server (bind) for the computer name.

/etc/nsswitch.conf

The /etc/nsswitch.conf file relates to the configuration on a network of Linux- and Unix-type computers, which are configured to communicate using the NFS (Network File System). When this file is used in concert with the Network Information Service (NIS), networks can maintain a single database of usernames and passwords for all NFS-enabled computers on that network.

For the purpose of network configuration, one line in /etc/nsswitch.conf is important. The order means that the local database (/etc/hosts) is searched before DNS servers.

```
hosts: files dns
```

Other databases can be part of the process, and that is one reason why /etc/nsswitch.conf supersedes /etc/host.conf for most services. For example, if there's an NIS server, a Samba database of hostnames, and an LDAP server, you might see the following line in /etc/nsswitch.conf; the order may vary.

```
hosts: files dns nis ldap winbind
```

The Network Settings Tool

This section describes the use of the Network Settings tool, described in the UCP curriculum by the name of the command that starts the tool, **network-admin**. Like other administrative tools, it requires administrative privileges. It can be started with the following command:

```
$ sudo network-admin
```

The focus of this section is the configuration of a wired and wireless network card. The configuration of a telephone modem with this tool is covered in the next section.

In most cases, network adapters are automatically detected during the installation process. If you find that one or more network adapters aren't displayed in the Network Settings window shown in Figure 9-2, review Chapter 3 for tips. If the missing adapter is shown in the output to the **lspci**, **lsusb**, or **lspcmcia** commands, you may just need to find, install, and load the associated network driver.

FIGURE 9-2

Network Settings window

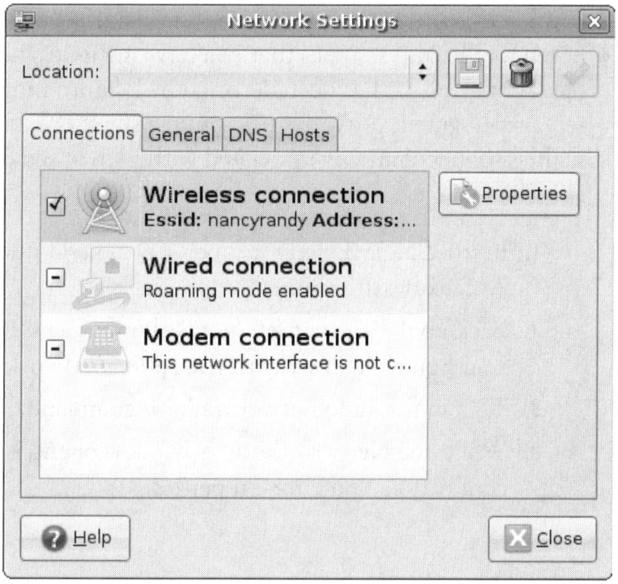

There are four tabs available for the Network Settings tool: Connections, General, DNS, and Hosts.

Network Settings Connections

The Connections tab of the Network Settings window displays detected network adapters. There are three adapters shown in Figure 9-2, one wireless, one wired, and one telephone modem connection. To configure any detected connection, highlight it and click Properties. The next exercise will configure a detected wireless connection; the parallel process for a wired connection is simpler. A telephone modem will be configured in the next major subsection.

on the
O o b

Linux drivers are available for most wireless network adapters. Those adapters with the Atheros chipset can be configured with so-called "MadWifi" software. If only Microsoft Windows drivers are available, the NDISwrapper packages support their use on Linux. For related Ubuntu Linux packages, run the apt-cache search madwifi or apt-cache search ndiswrapper commands.

EXERCISE 9-1

Configure a Wireless Network Connection

In this exercise, you'll configure a wireless network connection with the Network Settings tool. This exercise assumes a login to the GNOME desktop environment, and assumes the gnome-system-tools package is installed, which includes the noted tool. It also assumes that you have a wireless network adapter installed and operational, and it has been detected by Ubuntu Linux. If you don't have a DHCP server configured, you'll have to set up a static IP address. However, a DHCP server such as those commonly associated with high-speed home routers is adequate for this exercise.

1. In the GNOME desktop, open a command-line interface. Click Applications | Accessories | Terminal.

2. Back up the current /etc/network/interfaces file. One option is to copy it to your home directory with the **cp /etc/network/interfaces ~** command.

3. Type in the **sudo network-admin** command.

4. When the Network Settings window opens, highlight the available wireless connection, and click Properties.

5. In the Properties window named after the network device, as shown in the following illustration, note the Enable Roaming Mode option. This would be simplest, as it would automatically search for and connect to an available wireless network. But that's too simple for our purposes, so make sure this box is not checked.

6. Under Wireless Settings, click the drop-down text box next to Network Name (ESSID). If there are any wireless networks in range, they will be shown in a list. Select an appropriate wireless network.

7. Cross-check this list. Open up a second GUI command-line interface, and run an **iwlist dev scan** command. Substitute the device file name such as wlan0, eth1, or ath0 for *dev*. The list shown here should match that shown in the Network Name (ESSID) drop-down text box.

8. If the wireless network is password protected in some way, select the type in the Password Type drop-down text box.

9. If the wireless network is password protected, enter that password in the Network Password text box.

10. Under Connection Settings, click the drop-down text box adjacent to Configuration. Select an appropriate option; if you have a DHCP server

available for this system, select Automatic Configuration (DHCP), and skip to step 10. If you don't have a DHCP server available, select Static IP Address.

11. If you've selected Static IP Address, enter that information in the IP Address and Subnet Mask text boxes. If you want to configure access outside the local network, such as to the Internet, also type in the Gateway Address.

12. Click OK to exit the Properties window. Click Close to exit the Network Settings window. Open the /etc/network/interfaces file. Can you see what changed? If needed, compare this file to the backup of this file created in your home directory in step 2.

13. If you want to restore the original configuration, copy the backup of the *interfaces* file from your home directory with the **sudo cp ~/interfaces /etc/network** command. Restore the original configuration with the **/etc/init.d/networking restart** command.

Network Settings General Tab

There are two settings available under the General tab: the Host Name and Domain Name. The Host Name corresponds to the name of the system, also known as the hostname. Changes made to this setting are reflected in the /etc/hostname and /etc/hosts configuration files.

The Domain Name should be set to the domain name for the local network. If it's a private network and you don't have a domain name, the example.com, example.net, and example.org domain names, which are reserved for documentation, can be used. Changes made to this setting are reflected in the /etc/resolv.conf configuration file. For example, when I set up the example.net domain on my home network, the Network Settings tool added the following line to my /etc/resolv.conf configuration file:

```
domain example.net
```

Network Settings DNS Tab

There are two options under this tab: DNS Servers and Search Domains. DNS Servers can be added and deleted, if you know their IP addresses. Depending on your ISP, IP address information for these servers may be available, or you can create your own DNS server.

The Search Domains option adds a domain name suffix to a hostname. For example, when I added google.com to the list, I could type *news* into the address text box in the browser. It adds google.com, and then my browser navigated to news.google.com. That action is courtesy of the following line that is added by the Network Settings tool to the /etc/resolv.conf configuration file:

```
search google.com
```

Network Settings Hosts Tab

The Network Settings Hosts tab provides a view of the local /etc/hosts configuration file. Of course, it supports deleting the entries of your choice from this file. If you want to add an entry to this file, you'll need the IP address and alias(es) such as the hostname or fully qualified domain name (FQDN).

Configuring a Modem

As noted in the UCP curriculum, telephone modems can be configured using GUI tools. While text commands are important, the UCP curriculum notes that text modem configuration is addressed in other certifications. First, to confirm that a modem is detected by Ubuntu Linux, run the **ls -l /dev/modem** command. If the /dev/modem file exists, it should be linked to a device file associated with a physical port. As an example, the following is the output from my laptop system:

```
lrwxrwxrwx 1 root root 8 2008-01-17 07:00 /dev/modem -> ttySHSF0
```

There are other excellent GUI modem configuration tools available. One is GNOME PPP, which is available from Ubuntu Linux repositories as the gnome-ppp package. I personally prefer the KPPP tool; but as the UCP exam is focused on the GNOME desktop environment, and specifically the Network Settings tool, I don't consider the other options in this book. So I cover the detection of a modem port and the configuration of a modem with the Network Settings tool described earlier.

Finding a Modem Port

One problem for Linux hardware detection is based on software telephone modems, specifically those which rely on Microsoft Windows driver libraries. As Linux developers don't have access to Microsoft source code, not all so-called "Winmodems" work on Linux. One source for Linux work on Winmodems is www.linmodems.org. Another source may be manufacturers; for example, I was able to get Linux drivers for my Dell laptop system from their web site.

One tool to detect configured modem ports is the **wvdialconf** command. The following command configures /etc/wvdial.conf with all needed settings except the telephone number, username, and password:

```
$ sudo wvdialconf /etc/wvdial.conf
```

If the **wvdialconf** command doesn't detect the modem, it asks if you've run the **setserial** command correctly. If these options don't work, one other possible alternative is available from www.linuxant.com. The people behind this web site sell a fully featured Linux-compatible driver for modems with the Conexant chipset "for a modest price."

Configuring a Modem with Network Settings

To configure a telephone modem with the Network Settings tool, first open it in the GUI. It should be done from the command-line interface, as described earlier. If the modem is detected as described earlier, it should show up as an option in the Network Settings window, in the Connections tab. Assuming it's shown, highlight it and click Properties. The ppp0 Properties window for a modem is shown in Figure 9-3. Note the three tabs in the ppp0 Properties window.

on the
job

The standard network device for the first telephone modem, ppp0, does not show up in the output to the ifconfig *command unless the modem is active.*

FIGURE 9-3

Network Settings
general modem
properties

The information required under the General tab is straightforward, and should be well-known to anyone with a regular dial-up Internet account. Specifically, you need to know the Phone Number, any Dial Prefix required to access the public telephone network, as well as a Username and Password for the dial-up account. This information is stored in the pap-secrets and chap-secrets files in the /etc/ppp directory.

The information under the Modem tab shown in Figure 9-4 is also straightforward.

The Modem Port should correspond to the device file, typically /dev/modem. The Dial Type allows you to select between touch-tone and pulse dialing. The Volume allows you to listen to the tones, if a speaker is available for the modem.

on the

Ø o b

Pulse dialing is associated with older rotary phones, without buttons. If you don't know what that means, don't worry about it!

The Options tab supports three connection settings:

- Set Modem As Default Route To Internet
- Use The Internet Service Provider Nameservers
- Retry If The Connection Breaks Or Fails To Start

FIGURE 9-4

Network
Settings modem
properties

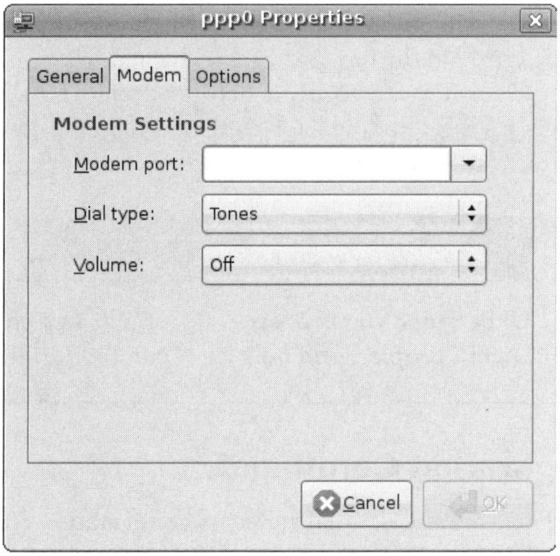

Changes based on the Network Settings tool are reflected in the /etc/chatscripts/ppp0 and /etc/network/interfaces files. Details of modem messages in the /etc/chatscripts/ppp0 file are beyond the scope of the UCP curriculum. A configured modem includes the following directives in the /etc/network/interfaces file:

```
iface ppp0 inet ppp
provider ppp0
```

To actually make a connection to the configured ISP, open the Network Settings tool again. Make sure the telephone modem is actually connected with an appropriate cable, and activate the check box next to the Modem Connection option shown back in Figure 9-2. Log messages related to success or failure should be written to the /var/log/messages file.

CERTIFICATION OBJECTIVE 9.02

Set Up Network Profiles

A network profile configures a group of network interfaces for a specific situation. Network profiles can be configured as needed with the Network Settings tool described in the first part of this chapter.

One other way to create network profiles for mobile systems is with the laptop-net package. But the UCP curriculum specifically cites the use of the graphical tool to create such profiles.

exam

ⓦatch

Understand the process for setting up network profiles, and how it *affects key configuration files. Know the commands described in this chapter.*

Basic Configuration Commands

There are a substantial variety of configuration commands covered in the UCP curriculum, under the Network Profiles section (124.3). Several are described in the first part of this chapter. Others include **iwconfig**, **wpa_action**, **wpa_passphrase**, and **wpa_supplicant**. As of this writing, there is no longer a **wpa_client** command available, despite its listing in the curriculum. However, there now exists a **wpa_action** script, which incorporates similar functionality.

iwconfig

The **iwconfig** command can help configure a wireless network interface. By itself, it lists the wireless extensions associated with existing network adapters. If the network adapter is a wired connection, the corresponding message looks like this:

```
eth0      no wireless extensions
```

If the network adapter is wireless, it provides a lot of information about the interface, in some ways similar to that shown earlier in this chapter in the output to the **ifconfig** command. When I run **iwconfig eth1** on my system, I get the following output:

```
eth1 IEEE 802.11g  ESSID:"nancyrandy"
     Mode:Managed Frequency:2.452 GHz Access Point: 00:14:D1:C0:36:44
     Bit Rate:54 Mb/s    Tx-Power:15 dBm
     Retry limit:15    RTS thr:off    Fragment thr:off
     Power Management:off
     Link Quality=84/100 Signal level=-50 dBm Noise level=-51 dBm
     Rx invalid nwid:0  Rx invalid crypt:0  Rx invalid frag:0
     Tx excessive retries:0  Invalid misc:3537   Missed beacon:0
```

This information is broken down in Table 9-6. Several of these parameters can be customized with the right **iwconfig** options.

While the protocol is usually fixed, the **iwconfig** command can be used to change other parameters. For example, the following command points the eth1 wireless adapter to a wireless network named *default*:

```
$ sudo iwconfig eth1 essid default
```

If the network in question is not open, this command isn't enough. You'll need the encryption key. The following command connects to the network named Friend with the noted encryption (*enc*) key. The *enc* and *key* options are synonymous.

```
$ sudo iwconfig eth1 essid Friend enc 2C0BB80617
```

On occasion, you might encounter two adjacent wireless networks with the same ESSID. In that case, you can specify the desired connection with the hardware address of the access point:

```
$ sudo iwconfig eth1 ap 00:14:D1:C0:36:45
```

TABLE 9-6

Output from
the iwconfig
Command

iwconfig Output	Description
IEEE 802.11g	Notes the connection protocol; others include 802.11a, 802.11b, and so on. If there's an *unassociated* in this position, there is no active connection.
ESSID	Points to the wireless network name.
Mode	Specifies the functionality of the device; Managed is associated with roaming mode.
Frequency	Notes the transmission frequency; should be in the range associated with the connection protocol.
Access Point	Lists the hardware address of the remote access point.
Bit Rate	Notes the current maximum transmission rate.
Tx-Power	Specifies current transmission power, in decibels.
Link Quality	Measures the quality of the connection.
Rx	Reads the number of problems in received packets.
Tx	Reads the number of problems in transmitted packets

The WPA Service

The WPA service is controlled by the /etc/init.d/wpa-ifupdown script. It serves as a front end to the aforementioned **wpa_supplicant** and **wpa_action** commands.

The **wpa_supplicant** command is designed as a background service that controls the wireless connection. It works only when the wireless network is connected, and an encryption key of some sort is enabled.

The **wpa_action** command is used by related scripts to stop and start an interface.

wpa_passphrase

The **wpa_passphrase** command is designed to create a preshared key (PSK), which enables the use of a shared passphrase on both the wireless client and access point. The format of the command specifies the ESSID and passphrase. For example, to create a WPA-PSK key on my personal network, I need to use the same passphrase on all clients and the access point.

For example, if my ESSID is nancyrandy and my passphrase is donnamike, the command I use on Ubuntu Linux clients would be

```
$ wpa_passphrase nancyrandy donnamike
```

The output includes a generated PSK. The equivalent is available with the Network Settings command. Once the properties window of the wireless card is open, you can enter the passphrase in the network password text box. The passphrase is generated in the /etc/network/interfaces configuration file:

```
wpa-psk 09caf1d1376d8f1a53f16cc7d3b965dceac1d321aa4ac05d23665ebc5ce6637a
wpa-driver wext
wpa-key-mgmt WPA-PSK
wpa-proto WPA
wpa-ssid nancyrandy
```

Switching Between Home and Office Networks

To switch between home and office networks assumes that you've created a network profile. Different profiles can be configured through the Network Settings tool. Start it in your system with the **sudo network-admin** command. It opens the Network Settings tool shown back in Figure 9-2. With the three network adapters available, I'll show you in Exercise 9-2 how I created three network profiles.

EXERCISE 9-2

Create Network Profiles

In this exercise, you'll use the Network Settings tool to create three different network profiles. This exercise assumes the availability of a wired Ethernet adapter, a wireless network adapter, and a telephone modem. If you have only two of these tools available (or only two have working drivers), your ability to work through this exercise will be limited.

1. In the GNOME desktop, open a command-line interface. Click Applications | Accessories | Terminal.
2. Back up the current /etc/network/interfaces file. One option is to copy it to your home directory with the **cp /etc/network/interfaces ~** command.
3. Type in the **sudo network-admin** command.
4. When the Network Settings window opens, review the detected network devices. I'm assuming you have a configuration similar to that shown in Figure 9-2.
5. Make sure the check box adjacent to the Wireless Connection is active. Deselect the check boxes adjacent to the other adapters.

6. Click the button of the disk shown in the upper-right section of the window. The Save Location window should appear. Type in a location name associated with a mobile office; I've used the label "Coffee Shop" for my first profile. Click Save.

7. Make sure the check box adjacent to the Wired Connection is active. Deselect the check boxes adjacent to the other adapters.

8. Click the button of the disk shown in the upper-right section of the window. The Save Location window should appear. Type in a location name associated with a fixed office; I've used the label "Wired At Work" for my second profile. Click Save.

9. Make sure the check box adjacent to the Modem Connection is active. Deselect the check boxes adjacent to the other adapters.

10. Click the button of the disk shown in the upper-right section of the window. The Save Location window should appear. Type in a location name associated with a telephone modem; I've used the label "Modem Connection" for my third profile. Click Save.

11. You should now have three configured network profiles. The Location drop-down box should now include three options, corresponding to the three network profiles created in earlier steps. Select one of the profiles. To activate it, click the green check mark button that appears in the upper-right corner.

12. Verify the activation of the desired profile. Are you connected with the desired network card?

CERTIFICATION SUMMARY

This chapter explained commands that can be used to activate and deactivate network interfaces, such as **ifup** and **ifdown**. These commands work with scripts and configuration files in the /etc/network directory. The **ifconfig** command can be used to review and reconfigure the network interfaces of your choice. The **route** command can be used to review and revise current routing tables. IPv4 and IPv6 forwarding can be configured by activating commented directives in the /etc/sysctl.conf configuration file. They can be activated without rebooting with the **sysctl -p** command.

Other key configuration files are associated with client configuration on a network. The /etc/dhclient.conf configuration file configures a client interface to a DHCP server. The /etc/hosts file provides a static database of hostnames and IP addresses. The /etc/resolv.conf configuration file lists search domains, and addresses of available DNS servers. The search order between DNS and /etc/hosts can be determined in the /etc/host.conf and /etc/nsswitch.conf configuration files.

The Network Settings tool, which can be started in the GUI with the **network-admin** command, can be used to configure various network interfaces and configuration files. It can even be used to configure different network profiles for different locations such as a home wired network and road wireless network.

You also learned about several wireless configuration commands, such as **iwconfig** for basic device configuration, **wpa_supplicant** to control the wireless connection, **wpa_action** to start and stop the interface, and **wpa_passphrase** for additional security.

✓ TWO-MINUTE DRILL

Here are some of the key points from the certification objectives in Chapter 9.

Configure Network Interfaces

❑ Network interfaces can be activated and deactivated with the **ifup -av** and **ifdown -av** commands.

❑ Default network settings are stored in the /etc/network/interfaces file.

❑ Current network settings can be reviewed and revised with the **ifconfig** and **route** commands.

❑ Forwarding can be set up in the /etc/sysctl.conf configuration file.

❑ Other key network configuration files include dhclient.conf, hosts, resolv.conf, host.conf, and nsswitch.conf, all in the /etc/directory.

❑ The Network Settings tool, which can be started with the **network-admin** command, can be used to configure wired, wireless, and telephone modem connections.

Set Up Network Profiles

❑ To configure wireless network profiles, you need to understand the **iwconfig**, **wpa_action**, **wpa_passphrase**, **wpa_supplicant**, and **wpa_action** commands.

❑ Different network profiles can be configured through the Network Settings tool.

SELF TEST

The following questions will help you measure your understanding of the material presented in this chapter. Read all the questions carefully, as there may be more than one correct answer. Some questions are "fill in the blank" and normally require an exact answer. Choose all correct answers for each question.

Configure Network Interfaces

1. What configuration file contains directives that specify how local interfaces are to be activated? Do not include the full path to the file.

   _____

2. Based on the following output to the **ls /etc/network** command, scripts in what subdirectory are run after a network is deactivated?

   ```
   if-down.d  if-post-down.d  if-pre-up.d  if-up.d  interfaces
   ```

   _____

3. Which of the following protocols supports access to a DHCP server from a remote network?
   A. TCP
   B. BOOTP
   C. DHCP
   D. PPP

4. What is the command that starts the Network Settings tool? No switches are required. Do not include the full path to the command.

   _____

5. Which of the following files contains the IPv4 setting that allows forwarding through the local system?
   A. /proc/net/ipv4/ip_forward
   B. /proc/sys/net/ipv4_forward
   C. /proc/ipv4/ip_forward
   D. /proc/sys/net/ipv4/conf/default/forwarding

6. What is the full path to the device file associated with a telephone modem? It doesn't matter if it's on the first serial or USB port.

   _____

7. Which of the following commands activates only the second Ethernet card, assuming it's not currently active?
   A. ifup -a eth1
   B. ifup -a eth2
   C. ifup -v eth1
   D. ifup -v eth2

8. Which of the following IP addresses is the default address?
   A. 127.0.0.1
   B. 192.168.0.1
   C. 0.0.0.0
   D. 255.255.255.255

9. Which of the following options configure a subnet mask for the **ifconfig** command?
   A. subnet
   B. netmask
   C. genmask
   D. subnetmask

10. If you've configured a default search domain of mcgraw-hill.com, what is the associated directive in the /etc/resolv.conf configuration file?

    _____

11. Which of the following device files represents a telephone modem in the output to the **ifconfig** command?
    A. eth0
    B. modem0
    C. ppp0
    D. wlan0

Set Up Network Profiles

12. Which of the following commands changes the default wireless network for the wireless adapter device ath0 to Restaurant?
    A. sudo iwconfig Restaurant
    B. sudo iwconfig essid Restaurant
    C. sudo iwconfig eth0 essid Restaurant
    D. sudo iwconfig ath0 essid Restaurant

13. Name the full path to the file that is changed when you select a network profile.

_____

14. What do you have to do to prepare a passphrase for entry in the Network Settings tool?
   A. Run the **wpa_passphrase** command.
   B. Run the **passphrase** command.
   C. Nothing
   D. Run the **iwconfig passphrase** command.

15. When activating a network profile with a telephone modem using the Network Settings tool, what else do you need to do? Assume the right physical wires are properly connected.
   A. Run the KPPP tool to dial into the desired ISP.
   B. Run the GNOME PPP tool to dial into the desired ISP.
   C. Nothing
   D. Make sure the check box next to the modem option is selected.

LAB QUESTIONS

Lab 1

In this lab, you'll experiment with the /etc/network/interfaces configuration file. So especially if you're running this lab on your main system (which is NOT recommended), back up that file first. This lab assumes you have a wired or wireless connection and access to a DHCP server. A DHCP server on a hardware router such as those commonly used on high-speed home connections is acceptable. As suggested in the exercises in this chapter, you could back it up to your home directory.

1. Review your current network settings with the **ifconfig** command. If you want to save current network settings, one method is with the following command, which saves the settings in the local directory in the netcfg file. Based on the IPv4 address, network mask, and broadcast address, you should be able to determine assignable IPv4 addresses on the local network.

```
$ ifconfig > netcfg
```

2. Back up the current version of the /etc/network/interfaces configuration file; to back it up to your home directory, run the following command:

```
$ cp /etc/network/interfaces ~
```

3. Open /etc/network/interfaces in the text editor of your choice. As the default permissions allow writing only by the administrative user, preface the editor with the **sudo** command. For example, the following command opens the file in the vi editor:

```
$ sudo vi /etc/network/interfaces
```

4. If it's set to a dynamic configuration, the following steps allow you to configure a static configuration. If you have a static configuration, skip to step 9, and then return to this step after completing step 12. One example of a dynamic configuration looks like the following code:

```
iface eth0 inet dhcp
auto eth0
```

5. Set up a static configuration. Change the *dhcp* (or possibly *bootp*) shown in step 4 to static.

6. Add an IP *address*, *netmask*, and *gateway* address to the configuration for the target network card. The process should be simple; just add the desired IP address after the **address**, **netmask**, and **gateway** directives. One example for my home network is as follows. The IP addresses you set should be appropriate for your home network.

```
address 192.168.0.2
netmask 255.255.255.0
gateway 192.168.0.1
```

7. Save the changes and restart the network with the following command:

```
$ sudo /etc/init.d/networking restart
```

8. Now rerun the **ifconfig** command. Are the changes what you expected? The IPv4 address in the output for the target network card should match that used in step 6.

9. Return to editing the /etc/network/interfaces configuration file. Delete or comment out the directives associated with **address**, **netmask**, and **gateway**. Commenting out a directive is easy; just add a hash mark (#) in front.

10. Change the **iface** directive associated with the target network card. It should match that shown in step 4.

11. Save the changes and restart the network with the following command:

```
$ sudo /etc/init.d/networking restart
```

12. Now rerun the **ifconfig** command. Are the changes what you expected? The IPv4 address in the output for the target network card should match that used in step 10.

13. Restore the original network configuration. As access to the /etc/network directory is limited to the administrative user, the **sudo** preface is required:

```
$ sudo cp ~/interfaces /etc/network/
```

14. Restart the network with the following command:

```
$ sudo /etc/init.d/networking restart
```

Lab 2

This lab is fairly simple. It illustrates the name service switch order, as configured in /etc/nsswitch. conf. You'll set up an IP address on the local network for a common web site. Before starting this lab, close and exit from the preferred web browser (or disable caching on that browser).

1. Back up the current version of the /etc/hosts and /etc/nsswitch.conf configuration files; to back them up to your home directory, run the following commands:

```
$ cp /etc/hosts ~
$ cp /etc/nsswitch.conf ~
```

2. Open /etc/hosts in the text editor of your choice. As the default permissions allow writing only by the administrative user, preface the editor with the **sudo** command. For example, the following command opens the file in the vi editor:

```
$ sudo vi /etc/hosts
```

3. Add an IP address on your local network for a popular web site. While not required, it helps for illustrative purposes if the Apache web server (or another web server) is active on the system with that IP address. On my personal network, I've added the following entry to my /etc/hosts configuration file:

```
192.168.0.50   www.google.com
```

4. Save the changes, and open a web browser. Navigate to the web site added to /etc/hosts. The result is as shown in Figure 9-5. Close the web browser.

5. Now open the /etc/nsswitch.conf configuration file. Look for the line associated with the **hosts** directive. In my case, it looks like this:

```
hosts:   files dns
```

6. Change this line to

```
hosts:   dns files
```

7. Open the web browser again and navigate to the same web site as added to /etc/hosts. What happened?

FIGURE 9-5

The /etc/hosts file is read first

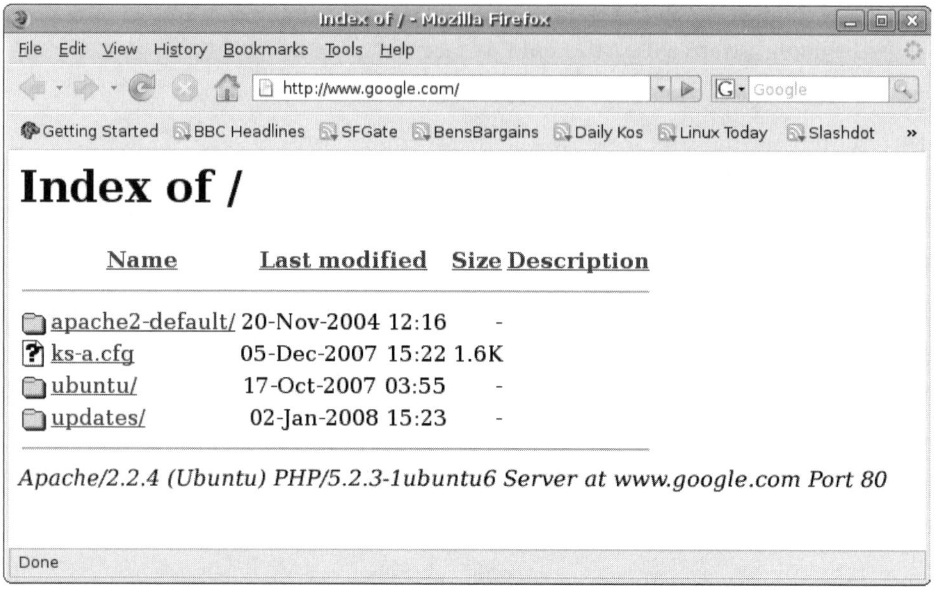

8. Now restore the original versions of /etc/hosts and /etc/nsswitch.conf. To do so from backups created in step 1, run the following commands:

```
$ sudo cp ~/hosts /etc
$ sudo cp ~/nsswitch.conf /etc
```

SELF TEST ANSWERS

Configure Network Interfaces

1. ☑ The standard file for network configuration is *interfaces*, in the /etc/network directory.

2. ☑ **if-post-down.d/**. The **ifup -a** command runs scripts in the if-pre-up.d/ and then the if-up.d/ directories. The **ifdown -a** command runs scripts in the if-down.d/ and then the if-post-down.d/ directories.

3. ☑ **B.** The BOOTP protocol is used to transmit messages from a DHCP server to and from remote networks. The DHCP protocol itself is limited to the local network. The other protocols are only tangentially related to the transmission of DHCP messages.

4. ☑ **sudo network-admin**. The **sudo** is required for all but the root user, and that user is disabled by default in Ubuntu Linux.

5. ☑ **D.** The /proc/sys/net/ipv4/conf/default/forwarding file contains the setting that determines whether IPv4 forwarding is active.
☒ Incidentally, the /proc/sys/net/ipv6/conf/default/forwarding file contains the setting that determines whether IPv6 forwarding is active. The other files do not exist. Therefore, answers **A**, **B**, and **C** are incorrect.

6. ☑ **/dev/modem**. This file is linked to the actual device associated with the modem; it doesn't matter whether the device is a serial or USB port.

7. ☑ **C.** The second Ethernet card is eth1. The **ifup -v** command just uses verbose mode to activate the noted card.
☒ Since the **ifup -a** command activates all cards, answer **A** is incorrect. Since eth2 refers to the third Ethernet card, answers **B** and **D** are also incorrect.

8. ☑ **C.** The default address is 0.0.0.0.
☒ The 127.0.0.1 is the loopback address. The 192.168.0.1 is just a common private IP address. The 255.255.255.255 is the universal broadcast address. Therefore, answers **A**, **B**, and **D** are all incorrect.

9. ☑ **B.** The netmask switch specifies the subnet mask, also known as the network mask.
☒ The only other option that actually refers to the subnet mask is genmask, but that's in the output to the **route** command, in a routing table. Therefore, answers **A**, **C**, and **D** are all incorrect.

10. ☑ **search mcgraw-hill.com**. This search term appends mcgraw-hill.com to hostnames not otherwise available in a /etc/hosts, DNS, or related database.

11. ☑ **C.** The ppp0 device represents the first telephone modem.

 ☒ The eth0 device is commonly associated with the first Ethernet network card. The wlan0 device is commonly associated with a generic wireless card. I've never seen a modem0 device used. Therefore, answers **A**, **B**, and **D** are all incorrect.

Set Up Network Profiles

12. ☑ **D.** To change the connected ESSID for the network card, you have to name the device (ath0) and the name of the desired network.

 ☒ As none of the other commands name the actual device, answers **A**, **B**, and **C** are all incorrect.

13. ☑ **/etc/network/interfaces**.

14. ☑ **C.** The Network Settings tool automatically creates an encryption key based on the network ESSID and passphrase, and enters it in /etc/network/interfaces.

 ☒ The **wpa_passphrase** command, when used with the ESSID and passphrase, does create an encryption key. But if you enter that key in the Network Settings tool, it takes that key as a passphrase. The other commands don't currently exist, at least not with the cited options. Therefore, answers **A**, **B**, and **D** are all incorrect.

15. ☑ **D.** Once a network profile is active in the Network Settings tool, and proper physical connections are made, all you need to do is make sure the check box next to the desired option is active.

 ☒ While you could use KPPP or GNOME PPP to connect a properly configured telephone modem, neither is required. Therefore, answers **A**, **B**, and **C** are all incorrect.

LAB ANSWERS

These labs are fairly straightforward. Do remember to make the backups of the configuration files as suggested in the steps.

Lab 1

This lab is designed to create a more in-depth understanding of configuration directives associated with networking in Ubuntu Linux. Once you understand the power of different directives in the /etc/network/interfaces configuration file, you might even discover things that can't be done with the Network Settings tool described in this chapter.

Lab 2

This lab is designed to demonstrate the power of the name server search order. An understanding of this lab demonstrates one area where problems might arise based on simple errors.

10

Network
Authentication
and File Systems

There are two basic topics in this chapter, network authentication for clients and the configuration of network file systems. Clients can connect to a number of different authentication services, including the Network Information Service (NIS), Samba, and the Lightweight Directory Access Protocol. While not strictly part of network authentication, a similar service involves Pluggable Authentication Modules (PAM).

Three filesystem services are specified in the UCP curriculum: the File Transfer Protocol (FTP), the Network File System (NFS), and the Samba services. You'll learn to configure an Ubuntu Linux system to connect to each of these services. You'll also learn to configure the noted servers to share files over a network.

CERTIFICATION OBJECTIVE 10.01

Configure Network Authentication for Clients

If you use a variety of network authentication systems, it's important to get the order right for your clients, as configured in /etc/nsswitch.conf. Regular authentication is configured as discussed in Chapter 8. You need to know the basics (not the details) of sharing these files over a network using NIS. Similarly, you need to know the basics of LDAP authentication. You need to know how to take advantage of shared folders on a Microsoft-style Samba network.

e x a m

watch

Understand the key files associated with network authentication. The search sequence is determined by nsswitch.conf. NIS is configured via yp.conf and ypserv.conf, and the mksmbpasswd command can prepare a Linux *authentication database for use by Samba. These configuration files are in the /etc/ directory. Don't forget the authentication controls provided by files in the /etc/pam.d directory.*

INSIDE THE EXAM

Configure Network Authentication for Clients (124.1)

Linux systems can use a variety of authentication databases. The standard local Shadow Password Suite authentication database files, /etc/passwd, /etc/shadow, /etc/group, and /etc/gshadow, can govern a network with the help of an NIS server. As LDAP (Lightweight Directory Access Protocol) can govern authentication for a number of different operating systems, many networks have replaced authentication using NIS with authentication using LDAP. For those who still prefer Microsoft NT4-style networks, Linux can also authenticate systems to those databases as well.

While not strictly a topic for network authentication, pluggable authentication modules (PAM) and how they regulate access to key administrative commands are also in this part of the UCP curriculum.

Manage Network File Systems (124.4)

There is a wide variety of ways to share files from a Linux system. Three that are covered in the curriculum are FTP, Samba, and NFS. Well, strictly speaking, FTP is not covered, but one version of FTP, TFTP, is used for terminal servers, as discussed in Chapter 4.

The focus from the UCP curriculum is on NFS, and to a lesser extent, on Samba services.

Network Information Service (NIS) Authentication

You've already seen a local authentication database in Chapter 8. That database can be made the primary database for the network, courtesy of an NIS server. That requires the installation of the nis package:

```
$ sudo apt-get install nis
```

The first time you install the nis package, you're prompted for the NIS domain name. If there's already an NIS server on the local network, you should enter that domain name. If necessary, go to that server and run the **nisdomainname** command to find that domain name. It does not have to correspond to any Internet domain name; I often use the name *nisdomain* when I test NIS services.

on the
ⓘob

For the purpose of this book, I do not detail the differences between NIS and NIS+, which relate to NIS domain hierarchies. For more information, see www.linux-nis.org.

The basic parameters can be set up in the /etc/default/nis configuration file; standard variables are explained in Table 10-1.

Further parameters are detailed in the /var/yp/Makefile configuration file. While details are beyond the scope of the UCP exam, they are commonly used when configuring NIS servers. So if you need more information about configuring NIS services on a local network, one place to start is the NIS HOWTO, available online from www.tldp.org, and my upcoming *Ubuntu Server Administration* book, to be released in late 2008, also published by McGraw-Hill.

There are some basics that you need to know about a couple of other NIS-related configuration files: /etc/ypserv.conf and /etc/yp.conf. In general, the /etc/ypserv.conf file has been supplanted in Ubuntu Linux by the aforementioned /etc/default/nis file. However, /etc/ypserv.conf includes some comments for special options for configuring NIS servers.

NIS Client Configuration in /etc/yp.conf

NIS clients are configured in the /etc/yp.conf configuration file. It's straightforward; there are typically up to three lines in this file. First, there's a line that specifies the name of the NIS domain, as well as the hostname of the NIS server. Just substitute the actual NIS domain for *NISDOMAIN* and hostname for *HOSTNAME*.

```
domain NISDOMAIN server HOSTNAME
```

TABLE 10-1	NIS Parameter	Purpose
Standard NIS Parameters per /etc/default/nis	NISSERVER	Specify type of NIS server; options are *false*, *slave*, *master*
	NISCLIENT	Identify NIS clients; options are *true*, *false*
	YPPWDDIR	Point to the directory with the password file, usually /etc
	YPCHANGEOK	Lists allowed commands for changing the shell, user information
	NISMASTER	Point to the name of the NIS master server
	YPSERVARGS	Allows default start options for the **ypserv** daemon
	YPBINDARGS	Allows default start options for the **ypbind** daemon
	YPPASSWDDARGS	Allows default start options for the **yppasswdd** daemon
	YPXFRDARGS	Allows default start options for the **ypxfrd** daemon

If you're unsure about the hostname of the NIS server, you could substitute **broadcast** for **server** *HOSTNAME*. If there's a slave NIS server on the system (as is common for redundancy), you could add a copy of the previous line with the *HOSTNAME* of the NIS slave server system. Finally, it's common to specify the hostname or IP address of the NIS server(s) with the **ypserver** directive:

```
ypserver 192.168.0.2
```

Changes to Shadow Password Suite Configuration Files

To make this work, you could add the following entries to the files of the Shadow Password Suite. Note how the colons correspond to the columns as shown in each configuration file:

- /etc/passwd   **+:::::::**
- /etc/group   **+:::**
- /etc/shadow   **+:::::::::**

There is no entry for /etc/gshadow, as it does not include authentication information. If the local system configures group passwords or administrators, you could of course add a corresponding entry to that file.

This entry works with the **compat** directive in the /etc/nsswitch.conf configuration file, as described later in this chapter.

Lightweight Directory Access Protocol (LDAP) Authentication

As Linux systems are configured for local authentication, LDAP packages are not included by default. Therefore, you'll need to install several packages to enable LDAP authentication:

```
$ sudo apt-get install libpam-ldap libnss-ldap
```

Administrators often also install the nss-updatedb package, which can cache authentication information locally. As there is an impact to security and performance, every administrator needs to make their own decision on the issue.

When you run the installation program, it brings up several low-resolution screens with several questions. As these are text screens, they're not "clickable" even if open in the GUI. To switch between options and text boxes in these screens, use the TAB key.

If after completing these steps you want to change the configuration, either edit the /etc/ldap.conf configuration file directly, or run the following command:

```
$ sudo dpkg-reconfigure ldap-auth-config
```

Just be aware that there are a number of other LDAP scripts available. For access, install the ldapscripts and smbldap-tools packages.

Should Debconf Manage LDAP Configuration?   Answer Yes to this question, as it allows you to return to these prompts when changes need to be made.

LDAP Server Uniform Resource Identifier   The URI (Universal Resource Identifier) is a superset of the well-known URL. In other words, it's like an address that you'd put in a browser, except it starts with one of three protocols:

- **ldap://**   A regular LDAP server
- **ldaps://**   A secure LDAP server, encrypted using the SSL (Secure Sockets Layer)
- **ldapi://**   For LDAP communication over a Unix domain socket

Typically, the URI would point to the hostname, fully qualified domain name (FQDN) or IP address of the system configured as the LDAP authentication server; for example, if it's a regular LDAP server on the local system, you could enter the following:

```
ldap://127.0.0.1
```

Distinguished Name of the Search Base   It's common to configure the components of a regular domain name as an LDAP distinguished name. For example, if you use the example.org domain on a local private network, one option is

```
dc=example,dc=org
```

However, this convention is just for convenience; there is no requirement that an LDAP distinguished name has to match a domain name.

LDAP Version to Use   There are two versions of LDAP available: 2 and 3. As LDAP details at this level are beyond the scope of the UCP curriculum, refer to www.openldap.org for more information. If unsure, select LDAP 3.

Make Local Root Database Admin   Unless you've configured NFS shared directories of active configuration files, such as those in the /etc directory, the standard administrative root user should also be given privileges as an LDAP root database administrator. If that is your choice, select Yes.

Does the LDAP Database Require Login?   Normally there is no need for a separate login for an LDAP database. Networks with multiple and large numbers of users may lead to a different decision. If you concur, select No.

LDAP Account for Root   LDAP databases can have an administrative account with a name other than root. That account name is the Common Name, or **cn** in an LDAP configuration file. The remainder of the account should match the previous choices for the Distinguished Name for the Search Base. So if you want the LDAP administrative account to be admin, based on the previous choices, you'd enter the following in the LDAP Account For Root text box:

```
cn=admin,dc=example,dc=org
```

LDAP Root Account Password   What you enter in the LDAP Root Account Password text box should correspond to the password you assign to the LDAP administrative account just created. Be warned—this password is stored in clear text in the /etc/ldap.secret configuration file.

Samba Authentication

Linux can be configured to use Microsoft authentication databases. It can use older Microsoft Windows NT4-style databases, Microsoft Windows 2000/2003 Security Accounts Manager (SAM) databases, or LDAP databases compatible with Linux authentication systems. Unless LDAP is used, the password encryption for a Microsoft authentication database is incompatible with Linux. In other words, while Microsoft NT4 databases use MD4 encryption, the Linux Shadow Password Suite uses MD5 encryption.

The authentication system used depends on the **passdb backend** directive in the main Samba configuration file, /etc/samba/smb.conf. There are three optional values for this directive: **smbpasswd**, **tdbsam**, and **ldapsam**. The **smbpasswd** option is the default; in other words, it's the active option if you don't see a **passdb backend** directive in the Samba configuration file.

The **smbpasswd** option implies a Samba-based NT4-style authentication database. The **tdbsam** option incorporates Microsoft Security Accounts Manager (SAM) information with the data. The **ldapsam** option incorporates LDAP-based authentication into Samba-based network shares.

Samba NT4 Authentication Database

When Microsoft ended official support for the NT4 servers, a number of groups were able to retain their Domain network structure by replacing Windows NT4 Servers with Linux servers configured with Samba. With the **passdb backend = smbpasswd** option, these groups found it fairly easy to configure Linux with the same Primary Domain Controller (PDC) functionality as was found on many NT4 servers.

There are two key commands associated with a Samba NT4 authentication database. The **smbpasswd** command can be used to create an MD4-encrypted password, and Samba users for a Microsoft network. It's a straightforward command; this option adds and configures a password for user michael on the local server. The Samba password can be different from the Linux password.

```
$ sudo smbpasswd -a michael
```

Similarly, users can be deleted from the databases with the **-x** switch:

```
$ sudo smbpasswd -x michael
```

But that can be a long process. The **mksmbpasswd** command can be used to set up users from /etc/passwd for a Samba password database. For example, the following command sequence sets up the same database of usernames in /etc/samba/smbpasswd:

```
$ sudo su
# cat /etc/passwd | mksmbpasswd > /etc/samba/smbpasswd
# exit
```

This is one of the few commands that has to be run as the administrative user. The **sudo su** command effectively logs into the root account—if your account has administrative permissions as configured in /etc/sudoers, as discussed in Chapter 8. But this is just the database. To populate it with passwords, you still have to enable each account with the aforementioned **smbpasswd** command.

Samba Windows 2000/2003 Authentication Database

The **passdb backend = smbpasswd** option in /etc/samba/smb.conf incorporates the SAM information associated with the Microsoft concepts of user and computer accounts. The account and connection databases are stored in the /var/lib/samba and /var/cache/samba directories. The authentication databases are encrypted. While Samba usernames and passwords can be created with the same **smbpasswd** command, the **pdbedit** command is required to read the databases.

The **pdbedit** command can also be used to add or delete users. The same **-a** and **-x** switches used for the **smbpasswd** command serve the same general purpose. But take a look at Figure 10-1, which illustrates the range of information available in a TDB database, when I added a user.

The **pdbedit -L** command can be used to list users. The **pdbedit -L -w** command lists users in a Samba password-style format; it includes MD4-encrypted passwords if they have been added for a specific user.

Actually, the **pdbedit** command can do much more. Run the **pdbedit** command by itself. It'll show you a whole range of options that correspond to the fine-grained authentication database control also available to Microsoft Windows 2000/2003 servers.

The **mksmbpasswd** command does not work for a TDB database. Incidentally, although TDB is short for a "trivial database," a password database certainly isn't trivial.

Samba LDAP Authentication Database

The **passdb backend = ldapsam** option in /etc/samba/smb.conf incorporates Samba with an LDAP server for authentication. However, this LDAP configuration can't by

FIGURE 10-1

Adding a user

```
michael@ubuntuserver1:~$ sudo pdbedit -a michael
[sudo] password for michael:
new password:
retype new password:
Unix username:        michael
NT username:
Account Flags:        [U        ]
User SID:             S-1-5-21-27439187-3755529620-2103156865-1005
Primary Group SID:    S-1-5-21-27439187-3755529620-2103156865-513
Full Name:            Michael Jang, bagt,,
Home Directory:       \\ubuntuserver1\michael
HomeDir Drive:
Logon Script:
Profile Path:         \\ubuntuserver1\michael\profile
Domain:               UBUNTUSERVER1
Account desc:
Workstations:
Munged dial:
Logon time:           0
Logoff time:          never
Kickoff time:         never
Password last set:    Wed, 23 Jan 2008 07:17:13 PST
Password can change:  Wed, 23 Jan 2008 07:17:13 PST
Password must change: never
Last bad password   : 0
Bad password count  : 0
Logon hours         : FFFFFFFFFFFFFFFFFFFFFFFFFFFFFFFFFFFFFFFFFFFF
michael@ubuntuserver1:~$ 
```

itself retrieve information from a Microsoft Active Directory server. For access to the associated tools, install the smbldap-tools package:

```
$ sudo apt-get install smbldap-tools
```

The details of configuring a Samba system with an LDAP database are beyond the scope of the UCP curriculum. One option for more information on creating that database is available from www.howtoforge.com.

on the job

The current version of Samba available for Ubuntu is 3.0.x. When Samba 4.0 is released, I anticipate that administrators will configure Linux as a replacement for Microsoft Active Directory Domain Controllers.

Automated Authentication Tools

Ubuntu developers are also actively working on a couple of utilities to ease the configuration process: **authtool** and **auth-client-config**. As of this writing, work is not complete on these packages, as their support does not go beyond NIS authentication.

The Authentication Sequence

Authentication can be configured through local files, NIS services, LDAP databases, and even Microsoft Windows domains. The /etc/nsswitch.conf determines the search order, as associated with three directives: **passwd**, **group**, and **shadow**. These directives correspond to the three files of the Shadow Password Suite described earlier in the /etc directory.

The default values for these directives, as shown here, take advantage of the lines added earlier in this chapter, such as **group +::::**.

```
passwd: compat
group:  compat
shadow: compat
```

In other words, compatibility (**compat**) mode uses these lines in the noted configuration files to bring authentication information from an NIS server. If you're using another service such as LDAP, the following directives first look to local files in the /etc/ directory, followed by a configured LDAP database:

```
passwd: files ldap
group:  files ldap
shadow: files ldap
```

For those systems that also use NIS authentication databases, you could include nis and nisplus in the list, depending on the versions available on the local network. If you're using a Microsoft authentication database prior to LDAP, you could configure lines like this:

```
passwd: files winbind
group:  files winbind
shadow: files
```

As the encryption scheme for Microsoft passwords is different, the **winbind** directive should not be applied to the **shadow** variable. Naturally, this means the winbind package should also be installed.

Authentication with PAM (Pluggable Authentication Modules)

Pluggable authentication modules (PAM) regulate access to specified administrative tools via various authentication databases. Relevant packages associated with LDAP, Samba, and even web services, can be installed with the following command:

```
$ sudo apt-get install libpam-ldap libpam-smbpass libpam-http
```

But there are a number of packages that are "PAM-aware"; in other words, they incorporate modules into the /etc/pam.d directory. Associated packages range from those which install the CUPS and SSH servers or the **sudo** and **passwd** commands, to common files associated with the Dovecot and Samba services.

PAM includes a group of dynamically loadable library modules that govern how individual applications verify their users. PAM configuration files can be modified to suit your needs.

PAM was developed to standardize the user authentication process. For example, the login program uses PAM to require usernames and passwords at login. Take a look at the first line in the /etc/pam.d/login file:

```
auth requisite pam_securetty.so
```

This line means that root users can log in only from secure terminals as defined in the /etc/securetty file.

on the
jo b

In older Linux distributions, the full path to the PAM module was required. It is now understood that these modules are stored in the /lib/security directory.

Many of the configuration files shown in the /etc/pam.d directory are named after applications which are known as "PAM-aware." In other words, you can change the way users are verified for applications such as the console login program. Just modify the appropriate configuration file in the /etc/pam.d directory.

The PAM system divides the process of verifying users into four separate tasks. These are the four different types of PAM modules:

- **Authentication management (auth)** Establishes the identity of a user. For example, a PAM **auth** command decides whether to prompt for a username and/or a password.

- **Account management (account)** Allows or denies access according to the account policies. For example, a PAM **account** command may deny access according to time, password expiration, or a specific list of restricted users.

- **Password management (password)** Manages other password policies. For example, a PAM **password** command may limit the number of times a user can try to log in before a console is reset.

- **Session management (session)** Applies settings for an application. For example, the PAM **session** command may set default settings for a login console.

The code shown in Figure 10-2 is an example of a PAM configuration file, /etc/pam.d/login. Every line in all PAM configuration files is written in the following format:

```
module_type  control_flag  module_path  [arguments]
```

The **module_type**, as described previously, can be **auth**, **account**, **password**, or **session**. The **control_flag** determines what PAM does if the module succeeds or fails. The **module_path** specifies the location of the actual PAM module file. Finally, as with regular shell commands, you can specify arguments for each module.

The **control_flag** field requires additional explanation. It determines how the configuration file reacts when a module flags success or failure. The five different control flags are described in Table 10-2.

To see how control flags work, take a look at the commands from the /etc/pam.d/su configuration file:

```
auth    sufficient    pam_rootok.so
```

The first **auth** command checks the pam_rootok.so module. In other words, if the root user runs the **su** command, the **control_flag** is **sufficient**, and the other **auth** commands in this file are ignored. Linux runs the **su** command. This is explained in the associated man page, available with the **man pam_rootok** command.

FIGURE 10-2

The PAM
/etc/pam.d/login
module

```
#
# The PAM configuration file for the Shadow `login' service
#

# Outputs an issue file prior to each login prompt (Replaces the
# ISSUE_FILE option from login.defs). Uncomment for use
# auth        required   pam_issue.so issue=/etc/issue

# Disallows root logins except on tty's listed in /etc/securetty
# (Replaces the `CONSOLE' setting from login.defs)
auth        requisite  pam_securetty.so

# Disallows other than root logins when /etc/nologin exists
# (Replaces the `NOLOGINS_FILE' option from login.defs)
auth        requisite  pam_nologin.so

# This module parses environment configuration file(s)
# and also allows you to use an extended config
# file /etc/security/pam_env.conf.
#
# parsing /etc/environment needs "readenv=1"
session     required   pam_env.so readenv=1
# locale variables are also kept into /etc/default/locale in etch
# reading this file *in addition to /etc/environment* does not hurt
session     required   pam_env.so readenv=1 envfile=/etc/default/locale

# Standard Un*x authentication.
@include common-auth
```

Besides the active session commands, the remaining active commands in this file refer to other files, also in the /etc/pam.d directory. As suggested by their filenames, the **auth**, **account**, and **session** directives from each of the noted files are included in this PAM file.

```
@include common-auth
@include common-account
@include common-session
```

TABLE 10-2

PAM Control
Flags

control_flag	Description
required	If the module works, the command proceeds. If it fails, PAM proceeds to the next command in the configuration file—but the command controlled by PAM will still fail.
requisite	Stop the process if the module fails.
sufficient	If the module works, the login or other authentication proceeds. No other commands need be processed.
optional	PAM ignores module success or failure.
include	Includes directives from the noted file; for example, the **@include** common-auth directive includes all directives from the common-auth file.

So next examine the /etc/pam.d/common-auth configuration file. Unless the appropriate LDAP module is installed, it has one active line:

```
auth    required        pam_unix.so nullok_secure
```

As noted on the pam_unix man page, the **nullok_secure** directive that follows prohibits null passwords. And that's especially necessary to minimize trouble from anyone who actually has broken into the root administrative account.

Now examine the /etc/pam.d/common-account configuration file. Unless the appropriate LDAP module is installed, it has one active line:

```
account    required        pam_unix.so
```

In this context, the **pam_unix.so** module brings up username information, assuming that the user's account is active based on settings in the /etc/shadow configuration file.

Lastly, examine the /etc/pam.d/common-session configuration file. Unless the appropriate LDAP module is installed, it has two active lines:

```
session required        pam_unix.so
session optional        pam_foreground.so
```

The first **session** command records logins and logouts. With the second command, as it's set as *optional*, PAM ignores the success or failure of the module.

CERTIFICATION OBJECTIVE 10.02

Set Up Network File Systems

In this section, you'll see how to configure NFS, CIFS, and FTP services for basic operation. NFS provides interoperability with other Linux and Unix systems. CIFS provides interoperability with Microsoft systems. FTP is one of the oldest file-sharing services, available to just about every commonly used operating system, and is still in common use today.

Understand the basics about configuring network file systems. While there are brief references to "Windows shares" and FTP, the UCP curriculum focuses mostly on NFS concepts, related to /etc/exports and the daemons related to the NFS kernel server.

The Network File System (NFS)

NFS is the standard for sharing files and printers on a directory with Linux and Unix computers. It was originally developed by Sun Microsystems in the mid-1980s. Linux has supported NFS (both as a client and a server) for years, and NFS continues to be popular in organizations with Unix- or Linux-based networks.

One weakness of NFS sharing is the lack of encryption. By default, NFS shares are not encrypted, and there is no way with current NFS sharing daemons to encrypt such data over a network.

You can create shared NFS directories directly by editing the /etc/exports configuration file, or with Ubuntu's Shared Folders tool, which can be started with the **sudo shares-admin** command, discussed towards the end of this chapter.

Required Packages

Three packages are closely associated with NFS: portmap, nfs-common, and nfs-kernel-server. As they're not installed by default, you may need to use a command like the following to integrate them into your system.

```
$ sudo apt-get install portmap nfs-common nfs-kernel-server
```

The portmap package must be running for NFS shares to work—on clients and servers. If you're having trouble connecting to an NFS server, make sure the portmap daemon is running with the following command:

```
$ sudo /etc/init.d/portmap restart
```

It's also a prerequisite for the smooth functioning of an NIS server, so it may already be installed and running on the local system. It is normally configured to start by default during the boot process.

Once the portmap service is started, you should be able to run the **rpcinfo -p** command to see the services that use portmap. The following excerpts from the output from my Ubuntu Server system tell me that the **/sbin/portmap**, **/usr/sbin/rpc.nfsd**, and the **/usr/sbin/rpc.mountd** daemons are running:

```
100000    2    udp     111   portmapper
100003    2    udp    2049   nfs
100005    1    udp   36883   mountd
100005    1    tcp   37988   mountd
```

Configuring NFS for Basic Operation

NFS is fairly simple. The only major NFS configuration file is /etc/exports. Each line in this file lists the directory to be exported, the hosts to which it will be exported, and the options that apply to this export. You can export a particular directory only once. Take the following examples from an /etc/exports file:

```
/pub           (ro,sync) one.example.net(rw,sync)
/home          *.example.net(rw,sync)
/tftpboot      nodisk.example.net(rw,no_root_squash,sync)
```

In this example, the /pub directory is exported to all users as read-only. It is also exported to one specific computer with read/write privileges. The /home directory is exported, with read/write privileges, to any computer on the .example.net network. Finally, the /tftpboot directory is exported with full read/write privileges (even for root users) on the nodisk.example.net computer.

All of these options include the **sync** flag. This requires all changes to be written to disk before a command such as a file copy is complete.

on the ❶ **o b** *Be very careful with /etc/exports; one common cause of problems is an extra space between (or at the end of) expressions. For example, if there is a space after the comma in (ro,sync), the directory won't get exported, and you'll get an error message.*

Wildcards and Globbing

In Linux network configuration files, you can specify a group of computers with the right wildcard, which in Linux is also known as *globbing*. What you do for a wildcard depends on the configuration file. The NFS /etc/exports file uses "conventional" wildcards: for example, *.example.net specifies all computers within the example.net domain. In contrast, /etc/hosts.deny is less conventional; .example.net, with the leading dot, specifies all computers in that same domain.

For IPv4 networks, wildcards often require some form of the subnet mask. For example, 192.168.0.0/255.255.255.0 specifies the 192.168.0.0 network of computers with IP addresses that range from 192.168.0.1 to 192.168.0.254. Some services support the use of CIDR (Classless InterDomain Routing) notation. In CIDR, since 255.255.255.0 masks 24 bits, CIDR represents this with the number 24. If you're configuring a network in CIDR notation, you can represent this network as 192.168.0.0/24.

Activating the List of Exports

Once you've modified /etc/exports, you need to do more. First, this file is simply the default set of exported directories. You need to activate them with the **exportfs -a** command. The next time you boot Ubuntu Linux, the NFS kernel server start script

(/etc/init.d/nfs-kernel-server) automatically runs the **exportfs -r** command, which synchronizes exported directories.

When you add a share to /etc/exports, the **exportfs -r** command adds the new directories. However, if you're modifying, moving, or deleting a share, it is safest to temporarily unexport all filesystems first with the **exportfs -ua** command before re-exporting the shares with the **exportfs -a** command.

Once exports are active, they're easy to check. Just run the **showmount -e localhost** command on the server. If you're looking for the export list for a remote NFS server, just add the name of the NFS server. For example, the **showmount -e enterprise5** command looks for the list of exported NFS directories from the enterprise5 computer.

Mounting an NFS Directory from the Command Line

Before doing anything elaborate, you should test the shared NFS directory from a Linux or Unix client computer. But first, you should check for the list of shared NFS directories. If you're on an NFS server and want to check the local list, the command is easy:

```
$ showmount -e localhost
```

If you don't see a list of shared directories, review the steps described earlier in this chapter. Make sure you've configured your /etc/exports file properly. Remember to export the shared directories. And your NFS server can't work if you haven't started the **nfs-kernel-server** and **portmap** daemons on the NFS server system.

If you're on a remote NFS client computer and want to see the list of shared directories from the ubuntuserver1 computer, run the following command:

```
$ showmount -e ubuntuserver1
```

If it doesn't work, there are a couple more things to check: firewalls and your /etc/hosts or DNS server. If there is a problem with the authoritative /etc/hosts or DNS server, substitute the IP address of the NFS server. You'll see output similar to the following:

```
Export list for ubuntuserver1
/home/michael *
```

Now to mount this directory locally, you'll need an empty local directory. Create a directory such as /mnt/remote if required. You can then mount the shared directory from the ubuntuserver1 computer with the following command:

```
$ sudo mount -t nfs ubuntuserver1:/home/michael /mnt/remote
```

This command mounts the /home/michael directory from the computer named ubuntuserver1. It also specifies the use of the NFS protocol (**-t nfs**), and mounts the share on the local /mnt/remote directory. Depending on traffic on your network, this command may take a few seconds, so be patient! When it works, you'll be able to access files on the remote /home/michael directory as if it were a local directory.

EXERCISE 10-1

NFS

This exercise requires two computers: one set up as an NFS server, the other as an NFS client. It also assumes that the portmap package is installed on both systems. It assumes the nfs-kernel-server package is installed on the server, and at least the nfs-common package is installed on the client. On the NFS server, take the following steps:

1. Set up a group named IT for the Information Technology group in /etc/group.
2. Create the /MIS directory. Assign ownership to the MIS group with the **chgrp** command.
3. Set the SGID bit on this directory to enforce group ownership.
4. Update the /etc/exports file to allow read and write for your local network. For example, if the local network is 192.168.0.0/24, the directive in this file would be

   ```
   /MIS    192.168.0.0/24(rw,sync)
   ```

5. Run the following command to set it up under NFS:

   ```
   $ sudo exportfs -a
   ```

6. Restart the NFS service; the simplest method is with the following command:

   ```
   $ sudo /etc/init.d/nfs-kernel-server restart
   ```

   Then, on an NFS client, take the following steps:

7. Create a directory for the server share called /mnt/MIS.
8. Mount the shared NFS directory on /mnt/MIS. One option would be with the following command (substitute the name or IP address of the NFS server for *ubuntuserver*).

   ```
   $ sudo mount ubuntuserver:/MIS /mnt/MIS
   ```

9. List all exported shares from the server and save this output as /mnt/MIS/
shares.list. The **showmount -e ubuntuserver > /mnt/MIS/shares.list** command
should work. Substitute the hostname or IP address of the NFS server. If the
command doesn't work, try starting the portmap daemon on the local system.

Samba and the Common Internet File System (CIFS)

SMB network communication over a Microsoft-based network is also known as
NetBIOS over TCP/IP (NBT). Through the collective works of Andrew Tridgell and
the Samba team, Linux systems provide transparent and reliable SMB support over
TCP/IP via a package known as Samba. You can do four basic things with Samba:

- Share a Linux directory tree with Windows and Linux/Unix computers
- Share a Windows directory with Linux/Unix computers
- Share a Linux printer with Windows and Linux/Unix computers
- Share a Windows printer with Linux/Unix computers

Some of the printer-sharing features associated with Samba were discussed throughout
Chapter 7. Overall, Samba emulates many of the advanced network features and
functions associated with the Win9x/ME and NT/2000/XP/2003/Vista/2008 operating
systems through the SMB protocol. Complete information can be found at the official
Samba web site at www.samba.org. It is easy to configure Samba to do a number of
things on a Microsoft-based network.

Some Samba Background

Samba services provide interoperability between Microsoft Windows and Linux/Unix
computers. Before you begin configuring Samba, you need a basic understanding of
how Microsoft Windows networking works with TCP/IP.

The original Microsoft Windows networks were configured with computer
hostnames, known as NetBIOS names, limited to 15 characters. These unique
hostnames provided a simple, flat hostname system for the computers on a LAN.
All computer identification requests were made through broadcasts. This overall
network transport system is known as NetBEUI, which is not "routable." In other
words, it does not allow communication between two different LANs. As a result,
the original Microsoft-based PC networks were limited in size to 255 nodes.

While Microsoft networks could use the Novell IPX/SPX protocol stack to route
messages between networks, that was not enough. As the Internet grew, so did

the dominance of TCP/IP. Microsoft adapted its NetBIOS system to TCP/IP with SMB. Since Microsoft published SMB as an industry-wide standard, anyone could set up their own service to work with SMB. As Microsoft has moved toward CIFS, Samba developers have adapted well. But some fairly recent changes have affected the configuration file as well as the main command-line client, the **mount.cifs** command, available from the smbfs package.

Now we'll examine the basic Samba configuration file, and mount a shared directory from a different client system. But first, let's take a look at Samba as a client.

Samba Client Commands

Samba shares can be browsed with the **smbclient** command. Specifically, the **smbclient -L //hostname** command reviews shared directories and printers from the Samba server on the computer named *hostname*. Furthermore, Samba shares accessible to a specific user can be viewed with the **-U username** option. For example, if the **[homes]** share is activated in the Samba server configuration file, the following command would reveal the home directory of the given user as a shared directory:

```
$ smbclient -L //hostname -U username
```

Once a Microsoft network shared directory is configured on a remote system (even from a Samba server), you can connect to it from a Linux client with the **mount.cifs** command. For example, if the share name from the computer named sambahost is **[backups]** as defined in the Samba configuration file, the directory can be mounted on the local /mnt directory with the following command:

```
$ mount.cifs //sambahost/backups /mnt
```

This command does not require administrative privileges courtesy of the SUID bit associated with the **mount.cifs** command, which can be confirmed with the **ls -l /sbin/mount.cifs** command.

Configuring a Samba Server

If you want to configure a Samba server, you'll need to edit the main Samba configuration file, /etc/samba/smb.conf. This file is long and includes a number of commands that require a good understanding of Microsoft Windows networking. Fortunately, the default version of this file also includes helpful documentation with suggestions and typical configurations that you can use.

To help you with this process, I've copied the Ubuntu Linux version of this file. The code shown in the following section is essentially a complete view of this file. I've replaced the comments in the file with my own explanations. You might want to browse your own /etc/samba/smb.conf file as well. With a couple of exceptions, I limit the analysis to the active directives in the default version of the file. In some cases, that means I leave out any description of several categories of directives.

The smb.conf file includes two types of comment lines. The hash symbol (**#**) is used for a general text comment. This is typically verbiage that describes a feature. The second comment symbol is the semicolon (**;**), used to comment out Samba directives (which you may later wish to uncomment to enable the disabled feature).

(Note that the physical dimensions of this book limit the lengths of lines of code. In a few cases, I've modified the code lines slightly to meet this limitation, without changing the intent of any command in this configuration file. In addition, I've left out several groups of default comments.)

Global Settings

Now examine the critical global settings. First, with respect to the **workgroup** variable, this Samba server will become a member of that Microsoft workgroup or domain. If a variable is not listed, the value reverts to the default. The default Samba **workgroup** is **WORKGROUP**, different from what's shown in the following example. Some of you may recognize WORKGROUP as the old name of the default Microsoft peer-to-peer workgroup, and MSHOME as the more current default. The same variable is used if you're joining this computer to a Microsoft-style domain.

```
# workgroup = NT-Domain-Name or Workgroup-Name, eg: MIDEARTH
    workgroup = MSHOME
```

The **server string** directive that follows is used in place of the current Microsoft Windows description field for a server. The **%h** is a variable that reads the local hostname; so for a Samba server named UbuSam,

```
# server string is the equivalent of the NT Description field
    server string = %h Server (Samba, Ubuntu)
```

the description field would read "UbuSam Server (Samba, Ubuntu)".

If you change this setting to **yes**, name searches can go through available DNS databases:

```
dns proxy = no
```

Debugging/Accounting   The next active command sets up separate log files for every computer that connects to this Samba server. For example, if a computer named allaccess connects to this Samba server, you can find a log of its access problems in /var/log/samba/allaccess.log. The **max log size** parameter limits log sizes to 1000Kb, with a minimum amount of information, as determined by the **syslog** directive. For more detailed log information, you could set **syslog** as high as 4.

```
log file = /var/log/samba/%m.log
max log size = 1000
syslog = 0
```

Authentication   The **security** directive may be a bit confusing. This command means that connections check the local password database. It is appropriate if you're configuring this computer as a Domain Controller (DC), specifically a PDC.

```
security = user
```

There are several options for this directive: **domain** is a member server on a Microsoft domain—but not a DC; **ads** is a member server on an Active Directory domain.

Now-obsolete versions of Microsoft operating systems did not encrypt passwords; this line is now the default, which means passwords are encrypted on all Samba systems unless this line is changed:

```
encrypt passwords = true
```

The following directive is critical, as it points to the password database. As discussed earlier in this chapter, the **smbpasswd**, **tdbsam**, and **ldapsam** correspond to Windows NT4, 2000/2003, and LDAP authentication databases, respectively.

```
passdb backend = tdbsam
```

The next active directive configures authentication support through the PAM modules described earlier, as applicable.

```
obey pam restrictions = yes
```

The directive that follows prohibits access by the root administrative user, promoting security.

```
invalid users = root
```

The following directives synchronize changes made on a Microsoft Windows client to a local Linux-based authentication database. Due to the limitations of formatting in this book, the **passwd chat** command is split into three lines. If you choose to copy this code, do not include a carriage return character between the lines.

```
passwd program = /usr/bin/passwd %u
passwd chat = *Enter\snew\sUNIX\spassword:* %n\n \ *Retype\
snew\sUNIX\spassword:* %n\n \
*passwd:*password\supdated\ssuccessfully* .
```

Share Definitions   Authenticated clients who connect to a local Samba server will want access to their home directories. It's available if you activate the following stanza of directives. In other words, home directories are limited and available to users who log in with an appropriate password.

```
; [homes]
;    comment = Home Directories
;    browseable = no
```

The following directive limits access to the username associated with the home directory:

```
;    valid users = %S
```

Most users will want writable access to their home directories, which is possible if you change **no** to **yes**. To help minimize errors due to spelling mistakes, **writeable** is a synonym for **writable** in the Samba configuration file.

```
;    writable = no
```

Finally, the following directives set permissions for files and directories created on the local directory through a Samba connection. This affects remote users who create files and directories remotely. Candidates for the UCP should already understand permissions in detail, and such topics are covered on the companion LPI exams.

```
;    create mask = 0700
;    directory mask = 0700
```

I often add stanzas similar to that shown here to share files. Be aware; it's the name in the square brackets that appears as the "shared directory." The name you include between those brackets does not have to match any existing directory.

```
[tmp]
   comment = Temporary file space
   path = /tmp
   read only = no
   public = yes
```

Testing Changes to /etc/samba/smb.conf

After making any changes to /etc/samba/smb.conf, you should always test your system before putting it into production. You can do a simple syntax check on the Samba configuration file with the **testparm** command. This does not actually check to determine whether the service is running or functioning correctly; it checks only basic text syntax and command stanzas.

Implementing Changes

Of course, changes must be implemented by the Samba script. In most cases, I restart the script with the following command:

```
$ sudo /etc/init.d/samba restart
```

I could reload the configuration file without restarting Samba, which means existing connections don't have to be broken:

```
$ sudo /etc/init.d/samba reload
```

Of course, this assumes you've addressed issues related to the password database described throughout this section—and unless you've implemented LDAP authentication, you won't be able to use the same database as that used for a Linux network.

An FTP Service

The FTP (File Transfer Protocol) is one of the original network applications developed with the TCP/IP protocol suite. It follows the standard model for network services, as FTP requires a client and a server. The FTP client is installed by default on most operating systems, including Ubuntu Linux. While there are several options available, the focus of this chapter will be on vsFTP, which is the default on a number of Linux distributions—and in fact is the only FTP server used on current Red Hat distributions. You can install it as needed with the following command:

```
$ sudo apt-get install vsftpd
```

Two key configuration files are /etc/vsftpd.conf and /etc/ftpusers. The vsftpd.conf configuration file is the standard configuration file. The /etc/ftpusers file is commonly used by other FTP servers to configure users who are not allowed access through the server.

The commands in this file are straightforward. I urge you to read the file for yourself; the comments make many of the commands self-explanatory. You can examine a few of these commands in Table 10-3. I focus here on those commands that you might change to enhance the security of your system. The commands in the default vsftpd.conf file are just a small fraction of the commands that you can use.

Once the configuration is complete, restart the server with the following command. You can connect from the local system, or from a remote system on the same network.

```
$ sudo /etc/init.d/vsftpd restart
```

	Command	Description
TABLE 10-3		
	listen=YES	Supports a control script in /etc/init.d.
Some	anonymous_enable=YES	If you don't want anonymous access, you'll have to set this to **NO**.
vsFTP Server	# local_enable=YES	If you want regular users to log in, activate this by removing the hash mark (**#**).
Configuration	# write_enable=YES	If you want regular users to write to accessible directories, activate this by removing the hash mark (**#**).
Commands	dirmessage_enable=YES	Allows directory messages; by default, located in .message file.
	xferlog_enable=YES	Activates logging of uploads and downloads.
	connect_from_port_20=YES	Supports data transfers through TCP/IP port 20.
	secure_chroot_dir=/var/run/vsftpd	Points to a directory that should be empty, and not writable by the ftp user.
	pam_service_name=vsftpd	Configures Pluggable Authentication Module (PAM) security.
	rsa_cert_file=/etc/ssl/certs/ssl-cert-snakeoil.pem	Points to a certificate for secure connections.
	rsa_private_key_file=/etc/ssl/private/ssl-cert-snakeoil.key	Notes a certificate key for secure connections.

As I've enabled anonymous access, I'd expect to be able to access this FTP server with the username *anonymous*. But I can't yet until I create the /home/ftp directory. Unless you've also enabled anonymous uploads, that directory must be owned by the ftp user and must not be writable. I've set this up with the following commands:

```
$ sudo mkdir /home/ftp
$ sudo chown ftp /home/ftp
$ sudo chmod 555 /home/ftp
```

I can now access the local vsFTP server anonymously.

Shared Folders GUI Tool

The Shared Folders GUI tool can be opened with the **sudo shares-admin** command. If the Samba and NFS servers are installed on the local system, this tool can be used to configure shared directories through either service.

FIGURE 10-3

Shared Folders
configuration tool

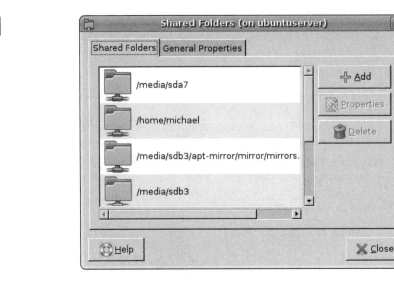

Before you begin, back up the current versions of the /etc/exports and /etc/samba/ smb.conf configuration files. The simplest option is to backup these files to your home directory with the following commands:

```
$ cp /etc/exports ~
$ cp /etc/samba/smb.conf ~
```

Now open the Shared Folders tool. The first time it's open, the window shown in Figure 10-3 will be blank.

The Shared Folders tab lists the shared directories configured on both Samba and NFS services. Directories are listed whether you've configured them through the Shared Folders tool or shared them by directly editing the associated configuration files. The General Properties tab configures some basic settings for a Samba server. In the following exercises, I'll describe how to share a directory via Samba, then another directory via NFS. Once configured, the settings can be reviewed and changed via the Properties button.

EXERCISE 10-2

Create a Samba Share with a GUI Tool

In this exercise, you'll see how to configure a directory for sharing via the Samba server. This does not address any firewalls that may exist, or network problems that may arise between server and client computers. This also assumes the gnome-system-tools, samba, and samba-common packages are installed, and your account has sudo administrative privileges.

1. In the GNOME desktop, open a command-line interface. Click Applications | Accessories | Terminal.

2. In the terminal window that appears, type the **sudo shares-admin** command. Once you've verified your password, the Shared Folders tool should appear.

3. Click Add in the Shared Folders tab.

4. In the Share Folder window that appears, as shown in the following illustration, the Share Through drop-down text box may have two options: Windows Networks (SMB) and Unix Networks (NFS). Since this exercise shares a directory via Samba, select the Windows Networks (SMB) option.

5. Use the Path drop-down text box to select the path to the directory you want to share. The default should be the directory from where you ran the **shares-admin** command. If the desired directory is not on the list, click Other from the Path drop-down text box, and navigate to the desired directory. For this exercise, select the /tmp directory.

6. Retain the default for the Name text box under Share Properties. This should match the last bit of the shared directory, and will be the name seen and used by clients for sharing.

7. Add a comment as desired; this comment will be visible on clients in the output to the **smbclient -L** *smbserver* command.

8. Deselect the Read Only option and click OK.

9. The directory that you just configured for sharing should appear in the main Shared Folders window, under the Shared Folders tab.

10. Click Properties. The settings just created should appear. Make any changes if desired and click OK.

11. Don't close this window; open a second terminal window as described in Step 1. In that terminal window, open the Samba configuration file, /etc/samba/ smb.conf. The share for the /tmp folder should appear at the bottom of the list.

12. Don't close the Shared Folders window, if you're ready to start the next exercise.

EXERCISE 10-3

Create an NFS Share with a GUI Tool

In this exercise, you'll see how to configure a directory for sharing via the NFS server. This does not address any firewalls that may exist, or network problems that may arise between server and client computers. This also assumes the portmap, nfs-common, and nfs-kernel-server packages are installed, and your account has sudo administrative privileges.

1. If the Shared Folders window isn't already open, in the GNOME desktop, open a command-line interface. Click Applications | Accessories | Terminal.

2. In the terminal window that appears, type the **sudo shares-admin** command. Once you've verified your password, the Shared Folders tool should appear.

3. Click Add in the Shared Folders tab.

4. In the Share Folder window that appears, as shown in the illustration in Exercise 10-2, the Share Through drop-down text box may have two options: Windows Networks (SMB) and Unix Networks (NFS). Since this exercise shares a directory via NFS, select the Unix Networks (NFS) option.

5. Use the Path drop-down text box to select the path to the directory you want to share. The default should be the directory from which you ran the **shares-admin** command. If the desired directory is not on the list, click Other from the Path drop-down text box, and navigate to the desired directory. For this exercise, select the /home directory.

6. Click Add. If you selected the right option in step 4, the Add Allowed Hosts window shown in the following illustration should appear.

```
┌────────────────────────────────────────────┐
│  📁        Add allowed hosts          [ ✕ ] │
├────────────────────────────────────────────┤
│  Allowed Hosts                              │
│  Allowed hosts:  [ 🖳 Specify hostname  ▲▼] │
│                                             │
│  Host name:      [                        ] │
│                                             │
│  Hosts Settings                             │
│     ☐ Read only                             │
│                                             │
│              [ ✖ Cancel ]    [ ⬅ OK ]       │
└────────────────────────────────────────────┘
```

7. Select the Allowed Hosts drop-down text box. Review the three available options.

- ■ If you select Specify Hostname, you can enter the hostname or FQDN in the Host Name text box. That FQDN can include wildcards, such as *.example.net to represent all systems on the example.net network.

- ■ If you select Specify IP Address, you can then enter a single allowed IP address in the IP Address text box.

- ■ If you select Specify Network, two text boxes appear for the Network IP address and associated network mask.

8. If you want the share to be writable, deselect the Read Only option near the bottom of the window. Click OK to continue.

9. Close the Shared Folders window.

10. Review the result in the /etc/exports configuration file.

11. Run the **sudo exportfs -r** and **showmount -e localhost** commands. You should see the /home directory share just configured.

CERTIFICATION SUMMARY

In this chapter, you learned about the variety of available network authentication services. NIS supports a single authentication database using the files of the Shadow Password Suite. LDAP supports a common authentication database also usable by Microsoft systems. Samba allows the use of a Microsoft-style authentication database using Windows NT4, 2000/XP/2003/Vista, and LDAP systems. The /etc/nsswitch.conf determines the search order if multiple databases are used. PAM provides a different level of authentication.

You also reviewed the basics of configuring NFS, Samba, and FTP servers. These servers can be set up through their configuration files. NFS is fairly simple to configure; each share takes a line in /etc/exports. Samba is more complex; you reviewed the default configuration file in this chapter. One option to configure NFS and Samba shared directories is based on the Shared Folders tool.

✓ TWO-MINUTE DRILL

Here are some of the key points from the certification objectives in Chapter 10.

Configure Network Authentication for Clients

❏ Default NIS settings are configured in /etc/default/nis. While the server is configured in /etc/ypserv.conf; the client is configured in /etc/yp.conf.

❏ LDAP services can be configured when the packages are installed, or reconfigured with the **sudo dpkg-reconfigure ldap-auth-config** command.

❏ Samba supports authentication to the variety of available Microsoft password databases; however, Microsoft MD4 password encryption is not compatible with Linux's MD5 encryption.

❏ The search order between authentication databases is configured in /etc/nsswitch.conf.

❏ PAM helps regulate access to administrative tools, with files configured in the /etc/pam.d directory and modules in the /lib/security directory.

Set Up Network File Systems

❏ NFS services can be configured in /etc/exports. NFS clients and servers require a running **portmap** daemon.

❏ Samba can be configured to share directories in /etc/samba/smb.conf, customizable with a wide variety of directives. The syntax of the Samba configuration file can be tested with the **testparm** command.

❏ With just a couple of changes, an anonymous vsFTP server can be configured in the /home/ftp directory.

❏ Shared directories can be configured to NFS or Samba requirements with the Shared Folders GUI tool.

SELF TEST

The following questions will help you measure your understanding of the material presented in this chapter. Read all the questions carefully, as there may be more than one correct answer. Some questions are "fill in the blank" and normally require an exact answer. Choose all correct answers for each question.

Configure Network Authentication for Clients

1. What authentication system is traditionally associated with Linux/Unix networks?
   A. NIS
   B. LDAP
   C. Samba
   D. Shadow Password Suite

2. What is the name of the configuration file associated with an NIS client? The full path to the file is not required.

   _____

3. What is the normal directory for the **YPPWDDIR** directive associated with an NIS domain?
   A. /home
   B. /etc
   C. /var
   D. /mnt

4. What is the command (without the directory path) that converts the username database associated with users configured to the Shadow Password Suite to a form usable by a Microsoft-based network?

   _____

5. Which of the following commands can be used to connect to a shared Samba directory to the latest Microsoft operating systems?
   A. **smbclient**
   B. **mount.smbfs**
   C. **mount.cifs**
   D. **smbmount**

6. What directive in the /etc/nsswitch.conf configuration file searches for group information first through the local password database followed by an LDAP database?

   _____

7. Which of the following PAM files would include information on encryption in authentication databases? These files are all in the /etc/pam.d directory.
   A. common-account
   B. common-auth
   C. common-password
   D. common-session

Set Up Network File Systems

8. Which of the following directives in /etc/exports includes reads and writes done at the same time?
   A. **atime**
   B. **async**
   C. **sync**
   D. **rw**

9. Which of the following options prevents administrative access to an NFS share?
   A. admin
   B. no_atime
   C. root_squash
   D. no_root_squash

10. What command shares the changes to the /etc/exports configuration file? Type in the command (without the directory path). Be aware, there are several options that can work.

    _____

11. How would you encrypt an NFS share?
    A. Share the directory over an RSH connection.
    B. Create an encryption key for shared NFS directories.
    C. Use the Shadow Password Suite.
    D. It can't be done with current versions of NFS.

12. Based on the following stanza, which of the following is shown as the shared "directory"?

```
[disk]
comment = Samba server's CD-ROM
writable = no
locking = no
path = /cdrom
public = yes
```

   A. disk

   B. path

   C. cdrom

   D. public

13. Which of the following commands browses the shared directories from the system named poohbear?

   A. smbclient -l //poohbear

   B. mount.cifs //poohbear

   C. smbclient -L //poohbear

   D. mount.smbfs //poohbear

14. Name the directory normally shared by a vsFTP server for anonymous users. The full path is required.

_____

15. What network file systems can be configured with shared directories with the Shared Folders tool?

_____

LAB QUESTIONS

Lab 1

This lab is designed to help you review basic LDAP settings. It assumes you have installed packages as described in this chapter, especially ldap-auth-config. Before starting this lab, be sure to back up key configuration files, in this case, /etc/ldap.conf and /etc/ldap.secret.

   1. Open a command-line interface. If you're in the Ubuntu Linux GNOME desktop, click Applications | Accessories | Terminal.

   2. In the command-line terminal, type in the following command:

```
$ sudo dpkg-reconfigure ldap-auth-config
```

3. Make sure to allow the debconf utility to manage LDAP configuration in the future.

4. Assume the LDAP server is available at the ldaps://127.0.0.1 URI.

5. If it's not already assigned for the local network, assume the LDAP distinguished name corresponds to a domain name of example.net.

6. Set LDAP to use version 3.

7. Allow the local root user administrative access to the database.

8. Do not require a login to the database.

9. Specify the canonical name of root for the LDAP privileged account.

10. Select an authentication format associated with Microsoft's Active Directory.

11. Review the /etc/ldap.secret file. Is there a surprise in there?

12. Review the /etc/ldap.conf file. Do you recognize the changes you've made in this lab?

13. Remember to restore the /etc/ldap.conf and /etc/ldap.secret files from their backups.

Lab 2

In this lab, you'll create a shared NFS directory in the /etc/exports configuration file, mount the directory from a remote client, and review the results in the Shared Folders GUI tool. This lab assumes the installation of basic NFS server packages, as well as the gnome-system-tools package for the **shares-admin** command.

1. Open the /etc/exports configuration file. Note the sample options in comments. Ubuntu Linux does include a /srv directory by default, and you'll configure sharing on that directory.

2. Copy several files of your choice to the /srv directory. If you're not sure what files to select, choose some of the configuration files in the /etc directory.

3. Configure read-only sharing of the /srv directory. The sample shown here and in the default version of /etc/exports should provide a model. The last expression provides read-only sharing.

   ```
   /srv/homes    hostname1(rw,sync) hostname2(ro,sync)
   ```

4. Substitute the IP address of a local network client or network with subnet. Two examples:

   ```
   /srv    192.168.0.50(ro,sync)
   /srv    192.168.0.0/255.255.255.0(ro,sync)
   ```

5. Save the changes to /etc/exports. Export the new configuration by restarting the NFS kernel server.

   ```
   $ sudo /etc/init.d/nfs-kernel-server restart
   ```

6. Review the output; it should include the settings created for the /srv directory.

7. Move to a remote client with the IP address configured for the /srv directory.

8. Mount the remote directory on the local /srv directory. For example, if the NFS server is on IP address 192.168.0.10, the appropriate command would be

```
$ sudo mount 192.168.0.10:/srv /srv
```

9. Review the results. Do you see the copied files on the client /srv directory?

10. Unmount the directory with the following command:

```
$ sudo umount /srv
```

11. Return to the NFS server. Open the Shared Folders tool with the **sudo shares-admin** command.

12. Highlight the setting for the /srv directory. Click the Properties button. In the Settings window that appears, review the Allowed Hosts window. Is the Read Only check box selected?

SELF TEST ANSWERS

Configure Network Authentication for Clients

1. ☑ **A.** The traditional authentication system for Linux/Unix networks is NIS.
   ☒ LDAP is fairly new. Samba uses Microsoft-style authentication databases, and the Shadow Password Suite is associated with local authentication. Therefore, answers **B**, **C**, and **D** are incorrect.

2. ☑ **yp.conf.** The /etc/yp.conf configuration file is for clients; incidentally, the /etc/ypserv.conf configuration file is for the server.

3. ☑ **B.** The standard directory for passwords (and other files in the Shadow Password Suite) is the /etc directory.
   ☒ As password files are not normally stored in the /home, /var, or /mnt directories, answers **A**, **C**, and **D** are incorrect.

4. ☑ **mksmbpasswd.** This command is designed to convert databases in the/etc/passwd format.

5. ☑ **C.** Shared directories on a Microsoft network can be mounted with the help of the **mount.cifs** command.
   ☒ The **smbclient** command only reads a list of shared directories. The **mount.smbfs** and **smbmount** commands are associated with older Samba servers. Therefore, answers **A**, **B**, and **D** are incorrect.

6. ☑ **group: files ldap.** This entry determines the search order, first searching local files before checking a configured LDAP authentication database for usernames and passwords.

7. ☑ **C.** Encryption is associated with passwords.
   ☒ The common-account file is associated with the status of the user account. The common-auth file is associated with authentication status. The common-session file relates to logins. Therefore, answers **A**, **B**, and **D** are incorrect.

Set Up Network Profiles

8. ☑ **C.** The *sync* option means reads and writes are done simultaneously, which incidentally minimizes the risk of lost data.
   ☒ The *atime* option updates the time stamp. The *async* option means reads and writes don't have to be done simultaneously. The *rw* option means that the share can be mounted in read/write mode. Therefore, answers **A**, **B**, and **D** are all incorrect.

9. ☑ **C.** The *root_squash* option prohibits root access to a shared directory.
☒ There is no *admin* option in NFS shares. The *no_atime* option means timestamps are not updated. The *no_root_squash* option means root access is allowed over a share. Therefore, answers **A**, **B**, and **D** are all incorrect.

10. ☑ Several options can work. The **sudo exportfs -r** is simplest and should work fine. The **sudo /etc/init.d/nfs-kernel-server restart** command would also work.

11. ☑ **D.** One weakness of NFS is the lack of encryption options.
☒ The RSH service does not support encryption. Encryption keys aren't available for NFS shares. The Shadow Password Suite encrypts passwords, not shared directories. Therefore, answers **A**, **B**, and **C** are all incorrect.

12. ☑ **A.** The share in a Samba stanza is contained in the square brackets.

13. ☑ **C.** The **smbclient -L //poohbear** command lists shares configured from the Samba server named *poohbear*.
☒ There is no -l switch for **smbclient**; the **mount.cifs** and **mount.smbfs** commands don't browse shared directories. Therefore, answers **A**, **B**, and **D** are all incorrect.

14. ☑ **/home/ftp.** This directory is what's configured in the Ubuntu implementation of the vsFTP server for sharing by anonymous users. Remember, proper ownership and permissions are also required on this directory.

15. ☑ **NFS, Samba.** Other acceptable answers are the other names for these shared network filesystems, such as CIFS and SMB.

LAB ANSWERS

These labs are fairly straightforward. Do remember to make the backups of the configuration files as suggested in the steps.

Lab 1

The steps in this lab include hints for what to enter when allowing the debconf tool to configure LDAP settings. The changes you make should be reflected in /etc/ldap.conf, and the password you set is shown in /etc/ldap.secret—in clear text! Yes, this file is accessible only to the root administrative user, but if you've backed up this file to your home directory, it's readable by all other users.

Lab 2

This lab is designed to demonstrate how the Shared Folders tool views configured shared directories. It's one way to confirm working—or at least proper syntax for—shared folders configured through the Samba or NFS configuration files.

11

Configure and Localize GNOME

T here are two basic topics in this chapter: how to configure the desktop environment, and how to manage screen features and fonts. Ubuntu Linux and the UCP curriculum are focused on the GNOME desktop environment, so you need to know how to configure the GNOME desktop on Ubuntu, using graphical and command-line tools. If you truly understand how to configure GNOME, you know at least the locations of associated configuration files. One key part of the GUI desktop is the overall look and feel, as depicted by the screen resolution and associated fonts.

on the
()ob

Be aware that there have been significant changes in the look and feel of some GUI tools between the Gutsy Gibbon and Hardy Heron releases. The focus of this chapter (and book) is on the Gutsy Gibbon release. What you see under the Hardy Heron, Intrepid Ibex, or later releases may vary.

CERTIFICATION OBJECTIVE 11.01

Configure the Desktop Environment

Ubuntu Linux includes the GNOME desktop environment. Per the GNOME project, "GConf simplifies the administration of preferences for GNOME Desktop users." With the GConf tools, you can customize GNOME in quite a bit of detail. While default settings are stored in the /etc/gconf directory, individual GConf settings are stored in users' home directories. Details of panels, menus, as well as the overall look and feel of a GNOME desktop can be changed to match user tastes or corporate policies. The GConf software associated with the latest versions of Ubuntu Linux is version 2. Installed packages have names like gconf2 and gconf2-common (the successors to the gconf package).

This section explores many of the GNOME customization tools available from the System | Preferences menu, with respect to how they affect the look, feel, panels, menus, and other elements of the GNOME desktop environment.

I'll explain how to open these tools using a GUI desktop menu, as well as the appropriate terminal command. Most of these tools are also available through the GNOME Control Center, which you can open with the **gnome-control-center** run in a GUI command line.

INSIDE THE EXAM

Configure GNOME (125.1)

As noted in the UCP curriculum, candidates need to know how "to configure the desktop environment using graphical tools and GConf. This objective includes the customization of panels, menus, look and feel (backgrounds and sounds), and addition of icon shortcuts to file systems on the desktop." There are a variety of graphical tools associated with GNOME, available in the System | Preferences menu. There are also a variety of ways to customize the GNOME desktop, through files in user and /etc/ directories, using the graphical and command-line GConf editors.

Display configuration, the display manager, and font management are separate issues covered in other parts of the UCP curriculum. While font management and the display

configuration are covered in this chapter, the display manager and Evolution e-mail manager are covered in Chapter 12.

Configure Screen Features and Fonts (125.3)

The UCP curriculum specifies the configuration of screen resolution and refresh rates. With the command-line and graphical tools available, you don't need detailed knowledge of the X Window configuration file, /etc/X11/xorg.conf. However, you do need to know how to manage fonts—and even incorporate Win32 fonts to maximize interoperability with Microsoft applications.

e x a m

ⓦatch

While GUI tools are useful, focus on command-line tools and file locations when learning to configure the

GNOME desktop environment on Ubuntu Linux.

The GConf Daemon

The GConf daemon governs the configuration settings associated with each user's GNOME desktop environment. It doesn't work like a standard service daemon such as Apache or Samba. It takes the mandatory, default, and custom settings associated with the GNOME desktop, and creates a look and feel for the GUI.

The daemon is **gconfd-2**, located in the /usr/lib/libgconf2-4/ directory. An additional instance of this daemon can be started and stopped with the following commands:

```
$ sudo gconftool-2 --spawn
$ sudo gconftool-2 --shutdown
```

e x a m

ⓦ a t c h   *While GConf version 1 is*   *for the purpose of the UCP exam, the*
also available through the Gutsy Gibbon   *differences are trivial.*
release, it's essentially obsolete. However,

GConf Settings

Per the GNOME documentation, GConf settings are expressed as "key-value" pairs. In other words, GConf settings are a bunch of variables with some value. Some variables are Boolean (true or false); for example, the buttons on a mouse can be reversed by setting the *left_handed* option as true. Others are more conventional; for example, the *cursor_blink_time* can be set in milliseconds.

GConf settings can be divided up into five categories:

- **apps**   Includes a variety of custom settings for GUI applications that can be opened in the GNOME desktop environment.
- **desktop**   Integrates options that affect the behavior, look, and feel of the GNOME desktop; options range from peripheral settings to fonts to actions associated with portable storage devices.
- **GNOME**   Notes language settings, and is *shown only if multiple languages are or have been included* on the local desktop.
- **schemas**   Sets up keys with documentation, which can modify variables in all other GConf categories.
- **system**   Includes defaults for mounting non-Linux partitions, Samba workgroups, proxy services, and so on.

GConf keys in each of these categories can be edited with the GUI GConf Configuration Editor or the **gconftool-2** command, described in the next section.

on the job

The authoritative source for GConf information is the GNOME Desktop System Administrative Guide, available at www.gnome.org/learn/admin-guide/ latest/.

The GConf Tools

There are several GConf tools available. The **gconf-editor** command opens the Configuration Editor GUI tool, which I find to be functionally similar to the Microsoft Registry Editor. But the effect is limited to the GNOME desktop environment, and GNOME-based tools available on the Xfce desktop environment. With the **gconftool-2** command, administrators can change the GConf settings of their choice. Of course, there are dozens, perhaps thousands of GConf settings, so you also need a bigger-picture understanding of how GNOME is configured in directories such as /etc/gconf, ~/.gconf, and more.

GConf Configuration Files

There are three categories of GConf configuration files. The standard configuration file is %gconf.xml; the same name is used for files in different directories. And yes, it's a file that starts with a %. What's seen on a user's GNOME desktop is an amalgamation of settings in these categories, collected by the GConf daemon in the following order:

- Mandatory settings are configured by the administrative user and are suitable for organizations that desire a consistent "look and feel" for their GNOME desktops. Configured in the /etc/gconf/gconf.xml.mandatory directory, mandatory settings supersede default and user settings.

- User settings are as customized by individuals, and are stored in each user's home directory, in the hidden .gconf/ subdirectory. If this directory were deleted by an administrator, that user's GNOME desktop would depend solely on mandatory and default settings.

- Default settings are also configured by the administrative user, but can be modified by individuals. Configured in the /etc/gconf/gconf.xml.defaults directory, default and mandatory settings, when taken together, create the standard GNOME desktop environment seen by users when they first log in to the Ubuntu Linux GUI desktop.

The GConf Configuration Editor

The GUI version of the GConf configuration editor can help illustrate the wide variety of available settings for the GNOME desktop environment. To start it in the GNOME desktop, open a command-line interface. Click Applications | Accessories | Terminal. In the command-line interface that appears, type in the **sudo gconf-editor** command, which opens the Configuration Editor shown in Figure 11-1.

The **gconf-editor** command, when run by itself from a regular account, edits the GNOME desktop environment for that user's account. Changes are recorded in the .gconf/ subdirectory of that user's home directory.

When the GConf Configuration window is opened with the **sudo gconf-editor** command, it configures settings for the root user, in the /root/.gconf directory. However, if you then click File | New Defaults Window, it also supports the configuration of GConf default settings. Changes made in this window affect settings in the /etc/gconf/gconf.xml.defaults directory. As of this writing, the GConf Configuration

FIGURE 11-1   The GConf Configuration Editor

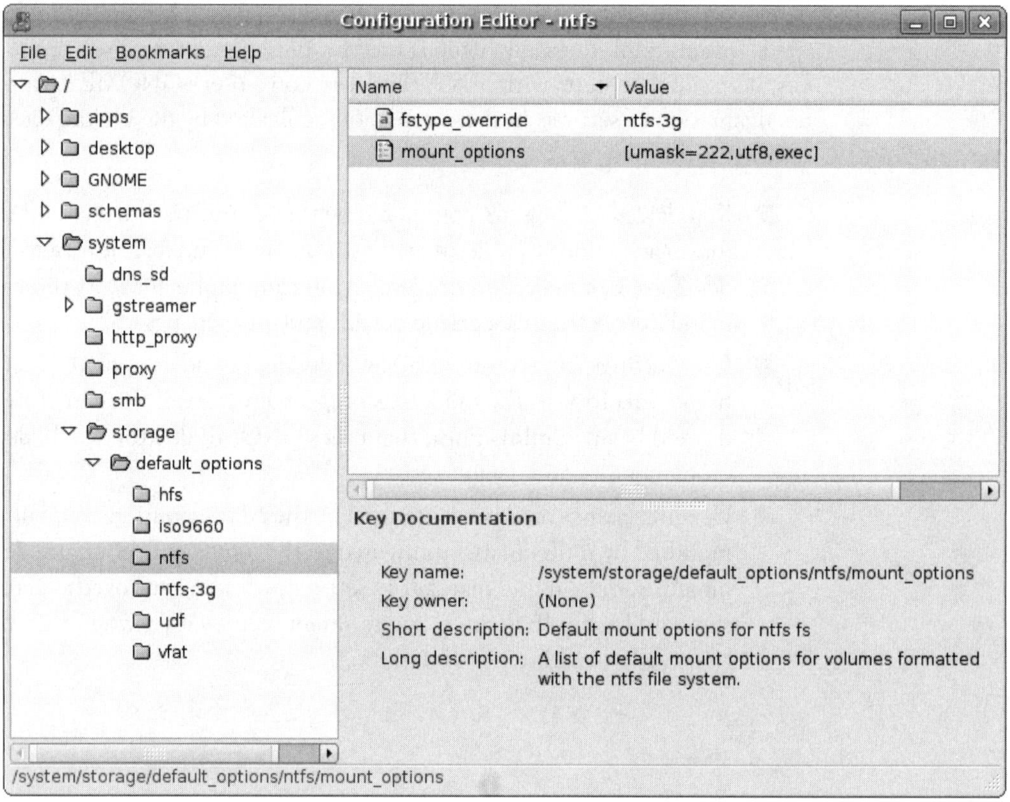

tool cannot be used to change mandatory settings in the /etc/gconf/gconf.xml. mandatory directory.

The options shown in Figure 11-1 show how the GNOME desktop automounts partitions formatted to the Microsoft NTFS file system. In many cases, when you want to change a key in the GConf Editor, just right-click on the name of the key. In the pop-up menu that appears, click Edit Key. That will open a window that allows you to change the value of keys such as the default **umask** for mounting detected NTFS partitions. In some cases, GConf keys are Boolean; in other words, either they're true or false (or in some cases, 1 or 0). For example, if you select System | Http_proxy in the GConf menu, the *use_http_proxy* option, if checked, configures the local system to connect to external web pages using an installed proxy server. When the GConf editor is closed, the changes are written to the appropriate file.

The gconftool Command

Any change made in the GUI GConf Configuration Editor can also be made with the **gconftool-2** command. As shown by its man page, it's a rich and complex tool, with complexities well beyond the scope of this book. By itself, it can change options associated with the current user. When run with the **sudo** command, it changes options associated with the root user.

However, there are some helpful basic options. For example, the following command lists all key-value pairs in the **apps** section.

```
$ gconftool-2 --recursive-list /apps
```

When run on a local system, the list of key-value pairs is long. The following command isolates this to a setting described earlier, associated with a left-handed mouse.

```
$ gconftool-2 --recursive-list /desktop/gnome/peripherals/mouse
 double_click = 400
 single_click = true
 drag_threshold = 8
 cursor_font = (no value set)
 tap_to_click = true
 pad_horiz_scroll = false
 left_handed = true
 locate_pointer = false
 pad_vert_scroll = true
 cursor_theme = Human
 motion_acceleration = -1
 motion_threshold = -1
 cursor_size = 18
```

The options shown here are associated with the touchpad on my laptop computer. For example, I could disable the *left_handed* option with the following command:

```
$ gconftool-2 --set /desktop/gnome/peripherals/mouse/left_handed \
--type bool "0"
```

I could set the size of the cursor with the following command:

```
$ gconftool-2 --set /desktop/gnome/peripherals/mouse/cursor_size \
--type integer "24"
```

Customize Panels and Menus

One part of the "look and feel" of any GUI desktop is the panels and the menus. The standard panels in the GNOME desktop environment are the strips at the top and bottom of the desktop. The menus are accessible in the upper-left corner of the desktop. Three menus are available by default; just click Applications, Places, or System as shown in Figure 11-2 to activate these menus.

To customize each panel, right-click on an empty area of the panel. In the pop-up menu that appears, you could click Add To Panel to add a menu item to the panel.

FIGURE 11-2

The GNOME desktop environment

Alternatively, click Properties. In the Panel Properties window that appears, you can change the color, font, and orientation, as well as whether the panels are hidden by default.

Perhaps more importantly, you can change what's shown in the drop-down menus from the upper left of the desktop. To open the Main Menu editing feature, click System | Preferences | Main Menu, or type **alacarte** in a GUI command line. The Main Menu window that appears as shown in Figure 11-3 supports detailed editing of the GNOME drop-down menus. The actual editing process is elementary, and not covered in this book.

Customize the Look and Feel

While there are many elements to the "look and feel" of a GUI desktop environment, several basic tools are available. The Appearance Preferences tool supports customization of the overall look and feel. With the new Compiz compositing window manager, users can manage and support detailed graphical effects. Also part of the "look and

FIGURE 11-3

The GNOME
Main Menu editor,
alacarte

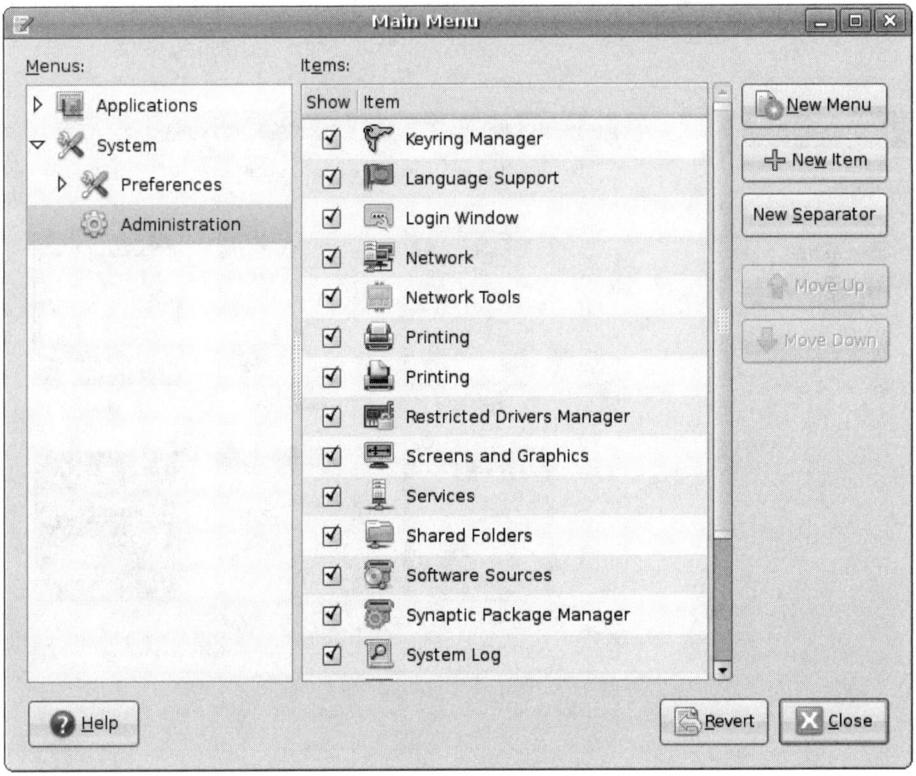

feel" of a GUI desktop is the management of a mouse or pointing device, as well as the icons shown on the desktop. Don't forget the sound preferences, as that's also part of the UCP curriculum.

Appearance Preferences

To open the Appearance Preferences window, click System | Preferences | Appearance Preferences, or run **gnome-appearance-properties** in a command-line window. As shown in Figure 11-4, a number of Appearance settings can be customized. The tabs are described in Table 11-1.

Compiz Customization

To open the Appearance Preferences window, click System | Preferences | Advanced Desktop Effects Settings Preferences, or run **ccsm** in a command-line window. If Compiz isn't already installed, you'll need to run a command similar to the following:

```
$ sudo apt-get install compiz compizconfig-settings-manager
```

As shown in Figure 11-5, a number of Compiz settings can be customized. The categories are described in Table 11-2.

FIGURE 11-4

GNOME
Appearance
Preferences
window

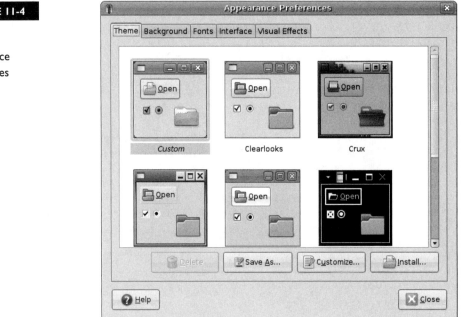

Tab	Description
Theme	Includes custom themes, which support configuration of the look of controls, colors, window borders, and pointers
Background	Supports custom wallpapers with different styles, colors, and color gradients
Fonts	Described later in this chapter
Interface	Allows customized menu displays, associated with icons and shortcuts
Visual Effects	Supports a variety of visual effects

TABLE 11-1

Tabs in the Appearance Preferences Window

Mouse Management

Perhaps the simplest of the custom tools in this chapter is related to mouse management—which also affects pointing devices such as trackballs and touchpads. To open the Mouse Management window, click System | Preferences | Mouse, or run **gnome-mouse-properties** in a command-line window. As shown in Figure 11-6,

FIGURE 11-5

Compiz options

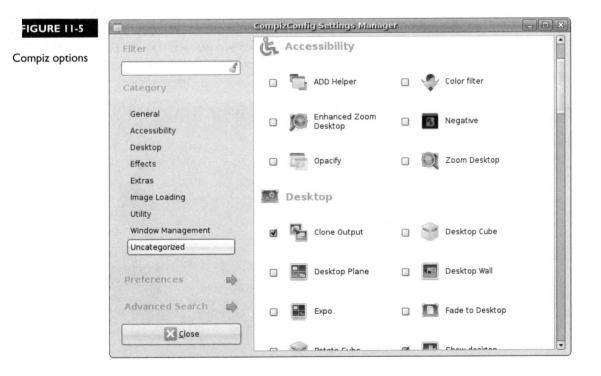

TABLE 11-2	Category	Description
CompizConfig Settings Manager Categories	General	Includes detailed options associated with taskbars, number of desktops, display filters, focus behavior, opacity, and linked commands
	Accessibility	Selects settings primarily for sight-impaired users
	Desktop	Lists a series of applets for GUI desktop behavior
	Effects	Supports the addition of whiz-bang effects
	Extras	Collects features such as screenshot takers, thumbnails, and previews
	Image Loading	Allows loading of several image types
	Utility	Includes a variety of utilities for crash handlers, video playback, resize information, and so on
	Window Management	Supports customization of window behavior within the desktop
	Uncategorized	Lists other applets

mouse settings are divided into three tabs. (As of the Hardy Heron release, these settings have been reorganized into two tabs.)

Under the Buttons tab, the Left-Handed Mouse option switches the functionality of left and right buttons. Under the Motion tab, the speed and the drag-and-drop

FIGURE 11-6

Mouse
Preferences
window

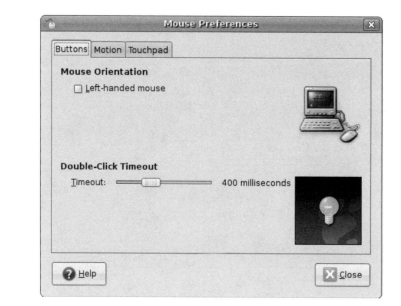

behavior of the mouse can be modified. The Touchpad tab (which exists only if you have a touchpad) supports standard features such as Tap To Click and scrolling.

Sound Preferences

To open the Sound Preferences window, click System | Preferences | Sound, or run **gnome-sound-properties** in a command-line window. As shown in Figure 11-7, the Devices tab supports the configuration of sound events for different hardware components. For example, when I select the associated drop-down selection box, the

FIGURE 11-7

Sound
Preferences
window

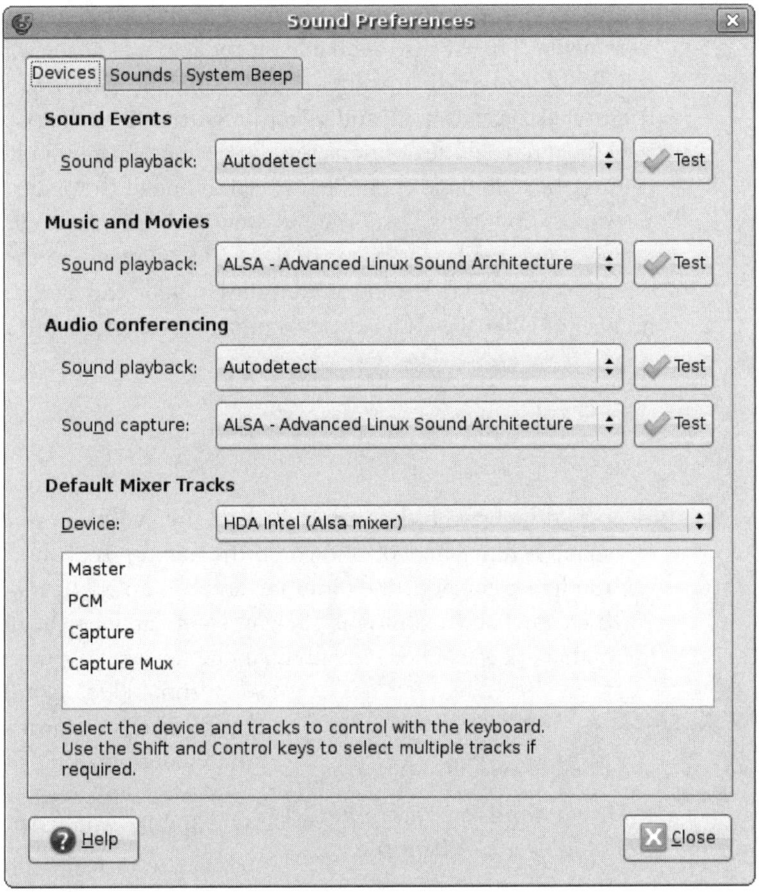

options support sound configuration for the modem (if a telephone modem is detected), and for digital and analog systems, as well as three different Linux sound servers.

The Sounds tab supports the configuration of different sounds with various system events, from logins to warnings to menu selections. The System Beep tab toggles between an audible and visual system beep, appropriate for hearing-impaired users (or users like myself who prefer a quiet computer).

Icons and .desktop Configuration Files

Icons can be found everywhere on the GUI desktop, and are shown with most standard items from the Applications and System menus. They are commonly included on the Desktop as a quick way to access frequently used applications or documents. They're also available on the left area of the top taskbar; for example, the default icon of an envelope is configured to open the Evolution e-mail manager. Right-click on that icon, and select Properties from the pop-up menu that appears. When open, you'll see options for Type, Name, Command, and Comment. The full path to the command should be shown in one of the associated text boxes.

Application icons are normally associated with .desktop configuration files. To review some standard versions of these files, navigate to the /usr/share/applications directory. Most of these and similar files include the name and a comment in a number of languages. The critical command directives are shown here:

```
Exec=evolution --component=mail
Icon=evolution
Terminal=false
Type=Application
```

To translate, when the icon is clicked, the **evolution --component=mail** command is run. The icon shown on the desktop is evolution.png. The program is not run in a command-line terminal, and it is an application.

To create a new icon, right-click an empty area on the desktop. In the pop-up menu that appears, select Create Launcher to open a window of the same name.

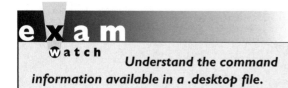

It should look familiar; the options should be the same as shown in the properties for the Evolution icon. The Name is the name associated with the application. The Command provides the full path to the application. The Comment provides more information to users who want help diagnosing a problem.

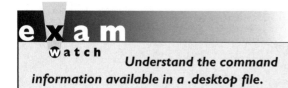
Understand the command information available in a .desktop file.

User-specific .desktop files are located in various .gnome/apps/ subdirectories. Generic .desktop files can be found in the /usr/share/applications directory.

Custom and Default Settings

Default settings can be customized. In this section, you'll review how default settings can be customized for a few basic items, specifically the keyboard, removable media, and window preferences, as well as the files that are changed when these options are customized.

Customize the Keyboard

To customize actions associated with the keyboard, select System | Preferences | Keyboard, or run the **gnome-keyboard-properties** command. This opens the Keyboard Preferences window, shown in Figure 11-8.

This window contains four tabs of keyboard preferences. (As of the Hardy Heron release, these settings have been reorganized into five tabs, incorporating the Accessibility Preferences described shortly.) The Keyboard tab customizes behavior when a key is pressed, and the blink behavior of the cursor. The Layouts tab supports a selection of different keyboard models. The Layout Options tab allows the configuration of special keys and key combinations. The Typing Break tab supports the temporary disabling of the keyboard to enforce typing breaks.

FIGURE 11-8

Keyboard
Preferences
window

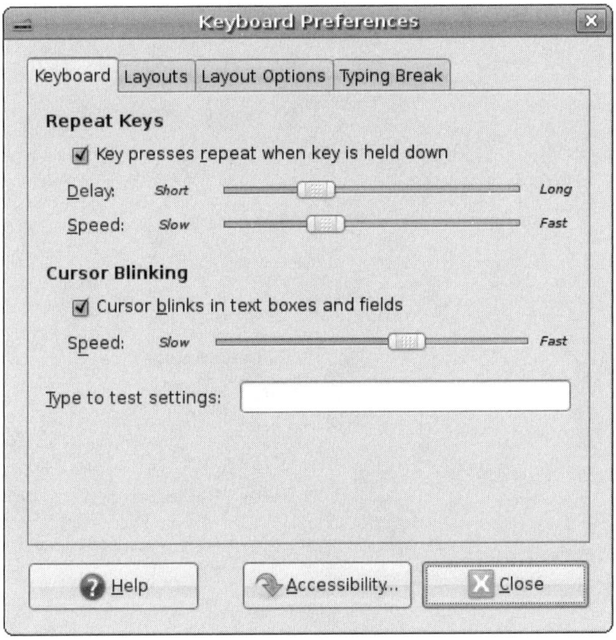

Additional preferences are available; just click the Accessibility button to open the Keyboard Accessibility Preferences window. To customize more features, activate the Enable Keyboard Accessibility Features option shown in Figure 11-9.

There are three tabs associated with this window. In the Basic tab, you can customize repeat and sticky key behavior. In the Filters tab, you can customize reactions to slow, bounce, and toggle keys. In the Mouse Keys tab, you can customize the behavior of the mouse pointer on the screen.

When I customized settings with this tool, it changed configuration files in my home directory, in .gconf/desktop/gnome/peripherals/keyboard/ subdirectories. You may recognize a related subdirectory, .gconf/desktop/gnome/peripherals/mouse from changes made earlier using the GConf Configuration Editor.

Customize Keyboard Shortcuts

To customize actions associated with keyboard shortcuts, select System | Preferences | Keyboard Shortcuts, or run the **gnome-keybinding-properties** command. This opens the

FIGURE 11-9

Keyboard
Accessibility
Preferences
window

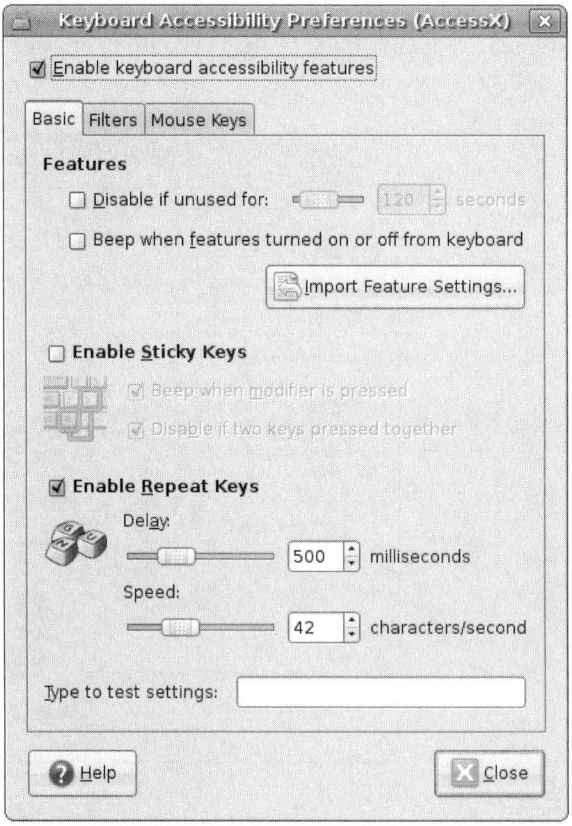

Keyboard Shortcuts window shown in Figure 11-10. As shown, this associates custom key combinations with actions such as the launching of specific applications or logouts.

To change a shortcut, highlight it and press the keys that you want used as a shortcut for the associated action. If the key combination is already assigned to another action, a warning is displayed.

When I customized settings with this tool, it changed a configuration file in my home directory, %gconf.xml, in the .gconf/apps/gnome_settings_daemon/ keybindings subdirectory. The following is the contents of the file; the code is shown in XML (eXtensible Markup Language) format:

```
<gconf>
   <entry name="power" mtime="1201725092" type="string">
      <stringvalue>&lt;Control&gt;&lt;Alt&gt;0</stringvalue>
   </entry>
</gconf>
```

Customize Actions with Removable Drives and Media

To customize actions associated with removable drives and media, select System | Preferences | Removable Drives and Media, or run the **gnome-volume-properties** command. This opens the Removable Drives and Media window shown in Figure 11-11.

FIGURE 11-10

Keyboard
Shortcuts
window

Removable
Drives and Media
window

There are six tabs shown in this window, supporting custom preferences for
different types of removable media and storage devices. Changes are reflected in the
%gconf.xml file, in the .gconf/desktop/gnome/volume_manager/ subdirectory of the
current home directory.

on the
Ò o b

*The look and feel of the Removable Drives and Media window is significantly
different in the Hardy Heron release. The information from the former Storage
and Multimedia tabs have been distributed to other tools.*

Storage   Under the Storage tab, administrators can configure actions when
"hot-pluggable" media such as USB keys are connected. Administrators can also
configure default actions associated with blank, audio, and data CD/DVD media.

Multimedia   Under the Multimedia tab, administrators can specify the default
applications automatically run when audio CDs, video DVDs, and portable music
players are inserted.

Cameras   Under the Cameras tab, administrators can specify the default applications
automatically started when digital cameras and digital video cameras are attached.

PDAs   Under the Cameras tab, administrators can specify the default applications automatically started when Palm Pilots and PocketPCs are attached.

Printers and Scanners   Under the Printers and Scanners tab, administrators can specify the default applications automatically started when Printers and Scanners are attached.

Input Devices   Under the Input Devices tab, administrators can specify the default applications automatically started when a USB mouse, a keyboard, and a graphics tablet are attached.

Customize Window Preferences

To customize the GUI behavior associated with windows, select System | Preferences | Windows, or run the **gnome-window-properties** command. This opens the Window Preferences window shown in Figure 11-12.

This window supports custom preferences for window behavior associated with the pointing device, including title bar reactions and window movement.

FIGURE 11-12

Window
Preferences
window

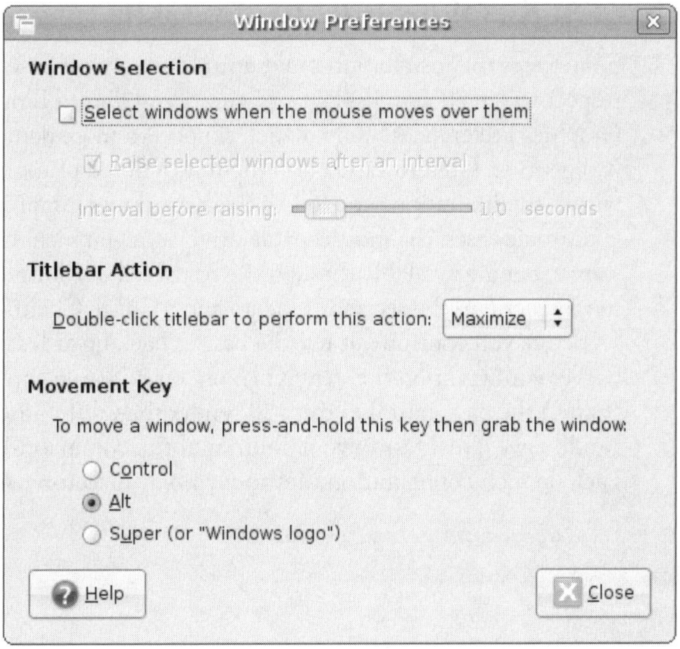

CERTIFICATION OBJECTIVE 11.02

Manage Screen Features and Fonts

Before any GNOME desktop can work, the X Window server must be configured. Like other current Linux distributions, Ubuntu Linux depends on the X.org server software. Administrators need to know how to configure the X.org server, as well as associated fonts. The UCP curriculum also specifies several font-related issues, which are evolving as Ubuntu becomes more user-friendly.

exam
watch

Understand the commands that can help manage screen resolution— first by detecting hardware, then by setting a custom resolution within the *capabilities of the hardware. Know how to include Microsoft fonts with appropriate commands.*

Manage Screen Resolution from the GUI

Sometimes the installation of Ubuntu Linux involves some compromises with respect to screen and display configuration. Ubuntu Linux includes a Screen and Graphics Preferences menu, which supports a more detailed configuration of the X.org server. Ubuntu Linux also includes a Screen Resolution tool, which works within the limitations created by the Screen and Graphics Preferences tool.

In some cases, the most capable drivers for graphical hardware may not be open source, but are available through the restricted or Multiverse repositories, as discussed in Chapter 6 in the section "Update and Manage Clients."

Before you continue, it may be best to back up at least the current X Window Server configuration file, /etc/X11/xorg.conf. While configuration is much easier than in the past, mistakes can still render the GUI unusable. At that point, you would have a real test to your abilities at the command-line interface. I normally back up such configuration files to my home directory with the following command:

```
$ cp /etc/X11/xorg.conf ~
```

Screen and Graphics Preferences

To open the Screen and Graphics Preferences tool, click System | Administration | Screens and Graphics, or in a GUI command line, enter the **sudo displayconfig-gtk** command. In the Screen And Graphics Preferences window shown in Figure 11-13, you can configure multiple monitors, if the hardware supports it. I see two screens in my version of this tool on my laptop, as it also includes an external video port.

As suggested by the Location drop-down box, this tool supports multiple X server configurations. Once you're satisfied with one configuration, click the disk icon, and save the configuration under a specific Location. Repeat the process with the second configuration.

There are two tabs associated with this tool. The Screen tab configures monitors, and the Graphics Card tab configures the driver and video memory associated with the graphics card, which should be configured first.

The Driver option under the Graphics Card tab opens a menu of available drivers, as shown in Figure 11-14. If you click the Choose Driver By Name drop-down box, it allows you to select from a list of available drivers. If in doubt, the VESA and VGA driver options are most likely to work. However, as they are generic drivers, they probably won't enable the features which make current video cards so desirable.

FIGURE 11-13

Screen and
Graphics
Preferences
window

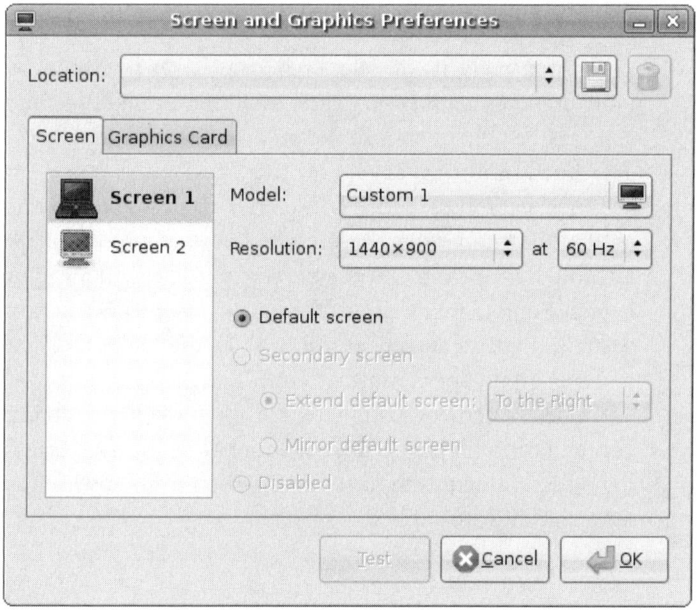

FIGURE 11-14

Choose a
graphics card
driver.

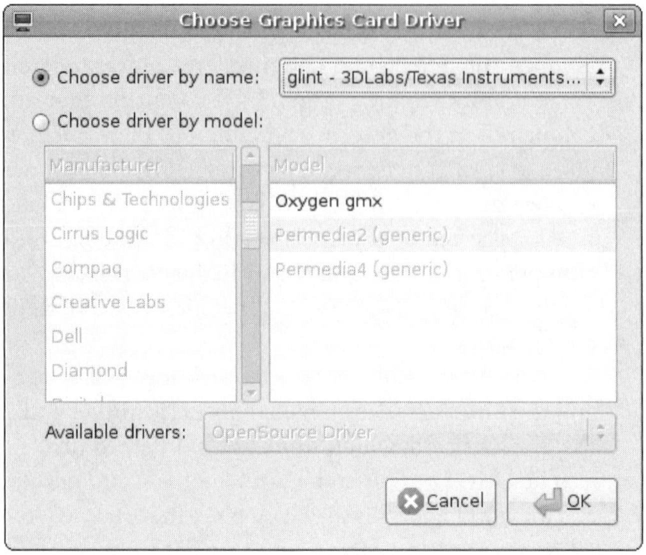

VGA is short for Video Graphics Array, a standard for older cathode ray
tube monitors. VESA is short for the Video Electronics Standards Association,
which provides a number of standards; when cited in Linux, the standard is
associated with Super VGA hardware.

Alternatively, if you select Choose Driver By Model, you can choose from one or
more graphics cards from nearly 40 different manufacturers. After selecting a card,
you may be able to choose the amount of video memory, if the graphics card and
associated Linux driver support this.

Once a graphics card is configured, then it's appropriate to configure a monitor
as described under the Screen tab. To select a monitor, click the text box adjacent
to Model. It opens a Choose Screen window, which supports monitor selection
by make and manufacturer. Widescreen monitors can be configured as needed. If
desired, there's a detect button, which can detect most current monitor hardware
and suggest an appropriate driver.

Once changes are complete and the tool closed, changes are saved to the X server
configuration file, /etc/X11/xorg.conf. The message that suggests that all users must
log off is a prerequisite to restarting the X server, which is when the changes to the
xorg.conf file are applied.

Screen Resolution

To open the Screen Resolution tool on the GNOME desktop, click System |
Preferences | Screen Resolution or run the **gnome-display-properties** command in the
GUI. This opens the Screen Resolution Preferences window shown in Figure 11-15
(while the window appears much different in the Hardy Heron release, it's functionally
almost identical).

The options in this window are straightforward. The Resolution depends on the
capabilities of the graphics card. The Refresh Rate can be changed only if it does not
affect the ability of the monitor to handle it. The Rotation can be useful for systems
such as notebook tablets, as it can change the orientation of the GUI display.

As the Screen Resolution Preferences window is user-specific, I suspect most
administrators and power users would want to limit access to the local system. Once
changes are complete, they are saved to the local user's %gconf.xml configuration
file, in that user's home directory, in the .gconf/desktop/gnome/screen/default/0/
subdirectory.

Manage Screen Resolution from the Command Line

There are two ways to manage screen resolution from the command-line interface.
First, there's the **dpkg-reconfigure** tool, which can be applied to the X server
package, xserver-xorg. And there are also the options associated with the X
command, which can automatically detect most hardware and create a proposed X
Window configuration file, xorg.conf, in the local directory.

FIGURE 11-15

Select a screen
resolution.

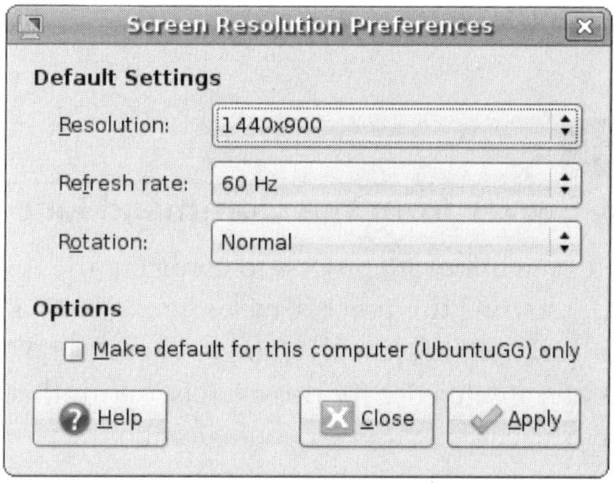

Reconfiguring the X Server

Those of you familiar with other Linux distributions may be familiar with the command-line configuration tool for the X Window System. On older distributions, it was known as **xf86config**; on the latest distributions, it's known as **xorgconfig** (which is not available from the standard Ubuntu repositories). The command shown in the exercise at the end of this section brings the administrator through a similar series of steps as those described in the following exercise.

If you need to stop the tool any time during the process, start a new command-line window and find the process identifier with the **ps aux | grep dpkg-reconfigure** command. The process identifier is shown in the second column; one example when I run the command is

```
root      9628  5.3  0.5  13444 10592 pts/2     S+   08:23
      0:00 /usr/bin/perl -w /usr/sbin/dpkg-reconfigure xserver-xorg
```

In that case, the process identifier is 9628, at which point I can stop the process with the following command:

```
$ sudo kill 9628
```

The process in the following exercise is complex, and includes a substantial number of steps. If you don't want to do all the steps shown in the exercise, include the **-phigh** switch, which limits questions to those which are high priority. In other words, if you want to run the full exercise, run the following command:

```
$ sudo dpkg-reconfigure xserver-xorg
```

Alternatively, if you want to go through fewer steps, run the following command:

```
$ sudo dpkg-reconfigure -phigh xserver-xorg
```

EXERCISE 11-1

Configure the X Server from the Command Line

It's a straightforward process to configure the X server from the command line. But before starting this process, make sure to have a backup of the current X server configuration file, /etc/X11/xorg.conf. In fact, you may want to make a printout of this file, as reference for this exercise. With that in mind, the following command saves the current X server configuration file to the current user's home directory:

```
$ cp /etc/X11/xorg.conf ~
```

Now with that secure, configure the X server from the command line with the following steps:

1. Run the following command to start the configuration utility:

   ```
   $ sudo dpkg-reconfigure xserver-xorg
   ```

2. The previous command opens low-level graphical screens similar to that shown in the following illustration, and depicted in the steps that follow. Be aware that it's not possible to "click" an option with the mouse in these screens; you'll need to select an option using the TAB, ENTER, and arrow keys.

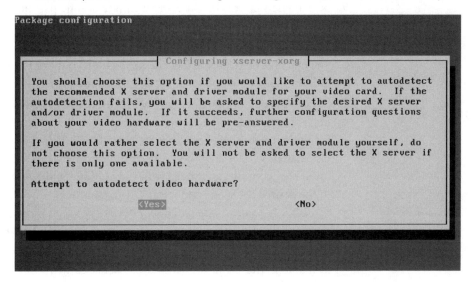

3. Normally, you should attempt autodetection of the graphics card, as it's simpler. But to learn more about the process, avoid autodetection by selecting No to this option.

4. Select a video card driver. Those available on the local system are listed for selection. These drivers are typically associated with a manufacturer; if in doubt, refer to the saved copy of the xorg.conf file for the stanza entitled **Section "Device"**; alternatively, the *vesa* driver will probably at least partially work for most configurations. Then select OK to continue.

5. Include an identifier for the video card. One may be input for you; the words entered at this step do not affect the actual configuration. Make a choice and select OK to continue.

6. Read the notes that follow and select OK to continue.

7. Enter the Video Card's Bus Identifier, normally an address associated with a PCI slot, and select OK to continue. As an example, my identifier is PCI:0:2:0, shown with the **BusID** directive in the saved version of the xorg.conf configuration file.

8. If desired, enter an amount of memory to be used by the video card. This is especially important if the video card shares RAM with the main system, or the video card RAM is not detected. Make a choice or leave this entry blank and select OK to continue.

9. Select whether or not to use a Framebuffer. Some trial and error may be appropriate for optimal performance. Select Yes or No and press ENTER to continue.

10. You can choose to autodetect the keyboard layout; for the purpose of this exercise, select No and press ENTER to continue.

11. Review the description associated with keyboard layouts; normally users of U.S. English keyboards will enter **us**. The ISO codes described in the instructions for alternate-language keyboards are available in the iso_3166.tab file, in the /usr/share/iso-codes directory. Any current setting should be available in the saved xorg.conf file, associated with the **Option "XkbLayout"** directive. Type in the desired ISO code and select OK to continue.

12. Now you can select an X Keyboard Extension ruleset, listed in the menu as XKB. Normally, you should just accept the **xorg** default; other options are well beyond the scope of the UCP curriculum. Any current setting should be available in the saved xorg.conf file, associated with the **Option "XkbRules"** directive. Type in a different selection if desired, and select OK to continue.

13. Read the options associated with the XKB rulesets. (Yeah, I know, this information would be better placed before step 12.) After reading, select OK to continue.

14. Type in the associated keyboard model. A default should be presented. If uncertain of your choice, refer to the saved xorg.conf file, and look for the **Option "XkbModel"** directive. Type in a different selection if desired, and select OK to continue.

15. Review the description of keyboard options, and select OK to continue.

16. If there's a keyboard variant required, enter it in the text box here. If uncertain of a choice, refer to the saved xorg.conf file, and look for the **Option "XkbVariant"** directive. Normally, a variant is not required for a U.S. keyboard.

17. Read the description of additional keyboard options available for options such as "Meta" keys, and select OK to continue.

18. Enter any desired keyboard options, and select OK to continue.

19. Read the description of mouse configuration ports, and select OK to continue.

20. Select an appropriate mouse port. If uncertain of your choice, refer to the saved xorg.conf file, and look for the **Option "Device"** directive in a **Section "InputDevice"** stanza. Older PS/2 and COM port mice *might* prefer /dev/psaux and /dev/ttyS0, respectively. Some trial and error may be required. Make a choice and select OK to continue.

21. Select a mouse protocol. If uncertain of your choice, refer to the saved xorg.conf file, and look for the **Option "Protocol"** directive in the same **Section "InputDevice"** stanza. The so-called "IntelliMouse" uses the ImPS/2 protocol, which is also associated with most USB pointing devices. The ExplorerPS/2 protocol is associated with a mouse with side buttons. Make a choice and select OK to continue.

22. You'll see a question whether to "Emulate 3 Button Mouse." It's generally advisable to do so. Even if you already have a properly configured three-button mouse, this option just simulates the action of the middle mouse button if both left and right buttons are pressed simultaneously. Select Yes and press ENTER to continue.

23. The option here is whether to enable access to local server modules. Select Yes and press ENTER to continue.

24. Now you'll see an option to autodetect a monitor. Normally, you should attempt autodetection, as it's simpler. But to learn more about the process, avoid autodetection by selecting No to this option.

25. Enter an identifier for the monitor. What you enter should be descriptive, as it's included as a comment in the xorg.conf configuration file. But it does not otherwise affect the configuration of the X server. Make any desired entry and select OK to continue.

26. Select the desired video mode(s) for the X server. As shown in the following illustration, available options may include regular and wide-screen modes.

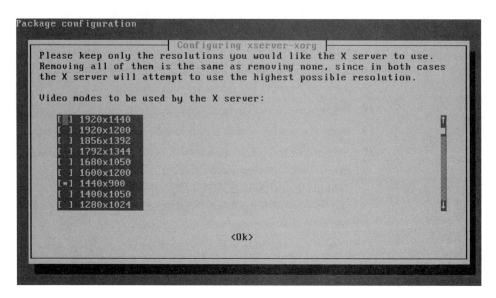

27. Read the descriptions of Simple, Medium, and Advanced options, and select OK to continue.

28. For the purpose of this exercise, select Advanced, and select OK to continue.

29. Enter a range of horizontal sync values, in kHz. BE CAREFUL! Values that exceed the capabilities of your hardware can burn out your monitor. That can be expensive if the monitor is a laptop display. Refer to your documentation if needed. While it's probably OK to accept the suggested defaults, and many modern monitors have fail-safe features, there are no guarantees. When in doubt, choose an appropriate lower value. Remember the option described earlier to kill this process, if needed. Otherwise, enter values as desired and select OK to continue.

30. Enter a range of vertical refresh ranges, in Hz. The same warnings for the previous step apply here. Enter values or accept the defaults as desired, and select OK to continue.

31. If ready, accept the option to write monitor sync ranges to the X server configuration file. Otherwise, select No to continue.

32. Select a desired color depth, in bits. Generally, most users will select full color, by choosing 24 bits. Make a choice and select OK to continue.

33. The configuration will be written to the /etc/X11 directory in an xorg.conf file, with an extension associated with the current date and time. For example, my system includes an xorg.conf.20080131083845 file, written on January 31, 2008, at 8:38 am.

Create a Proposed X Server Configuration

After going through the exercise in the previous section, many would look for an easier way. Well, maybe there is. The **Xorg -configure** command automatically detects appropriate hardware and creates an xorg.conf file in the local directory. Be aware that for older X.org releases, the **X** and **Xorg** commands are, for our purposes, functionally identical. However, in either case, that file isn't automatically written to the /etc/X11 directory, as autodetection may not properly detect all relevant hardware. The output is written to the local directory as the xorg.conf.new file.

The **Xorg -configure** command doesn't work in the GUI; in Ubuntu Linux, the easiest way to make sure of this is to move to runlevel 1 with a command such as

```
$ sudo init 1
```

Whatever you do to create a new X Window configuration file, evaluate the new xorg.conf file. While most details of that configuration file are beyond the scope of this book, detailed information on the contents of this file is available in my *RHCE Red Hat Certified Engineer Study Guide*.

Make Fonts Work for You

The fonts you prefer are as subjective as the art you like. If the Ubuntu Linux system is solely for personal use, feel free to ignore most of the recommendations in this section. However, the UCP curriculum does suggest that you need to know how to install Win32 fonts, which I describe shortly.

Updated Font Tools and Configuration Files

Some of the configuration tools listed in the UCP curriculum are now obsolete; I cover successor tools with similar functionality. The UCP curriculum refers to the **fontconfig** utility, formerly part of the fontconfig package. That package still exists and should be installed. If needed, run the following commands to include appropriate font packages on your system.

```
$ sudo apt-get install fontconfig fontconfig-config
```

Fonts are a more complex issue when associated with different languages. For more information on installing additional languages, see the section "Localize the Operating System" in Chapter 8. While the **fontconfig** utility is now obsolete, the functionality has been taken by the **dpkg-reconfigure** configuration tool. If the preceding command actually installs the **fontconfig-config** package, then you'll see the steps described shortly in the "Reconfiguring Fonts" section.

The fontconfig package also includes the /etc/fonts/fonts.conf configuration file, which calls appropriate font libraries in various directories, including /usr/share/fonts, /usr/share/X11/fonts, /usr/local/share/fonts, and .fonts subdirectories in individual user's home directories. Hidden .fonts.conf files in user home directories are a common method to customize fonts for different languages.

The functionality of the **gnome-font-properties** utility is now part of the **gnome-appearance-properties** tool described earlier.

Adding Microsoft Fonts

There are two packages associated with installing Microsoft fonts on Ubuntu Linux. They can be installed with the following command:

```
$ sudo apt-get install msttcorefonts ttf-xfree86-nonfree
```

These packages are available from the Multiverse repository, which can be enabled as discussed in Chapter 6 in the section "Update and Manage Clients."

Reconfiguring Fonts

Basic font configuration is associated with the fontconfig-config package. To configure fonts on the local system, run the following command:

```
$ sudo dpkg-reconfigure fontconfig-config
```

Fortunately, there are only three steps in this process. The first step refers to "Bitstream Vera (the default in Debian)" fonts. As Ubuntu Linux is a derivative of Debian Linux, this option applies to this book. Be aware that this option also supports proper rendering of Microsoft fonts.

The next step supports "subpixel rendering," which optimizes the view of fonts on flat screens, including LCD and laptop monitors. Select Automatic if you use both LCD and older Cathode Ray Tube (CRT) monitors.

The final step allows the enabling of bitmapped fonts. The recommended default is to disable such fonts, due to the quality. Make a choice and press ENTER to continue.

Changes aren't implemented until the next time the X server is started. They are written to files in the the /etc/fonts/conf.d/ directory. The services that run the X server use the /etc/fonts/fonts.conf file, as well as related files in the /etc/fonts subdirectories.

To customize the look and feel of fonts on the local screen, click System | Preferences | Appearances, or run the **gnome-appearance-properties** command in a GUI, and then select the Fonts tab in the Appearance Preferences window, as shown in Figure 11-16.

FIGURE 11-16

Modifying font appearances

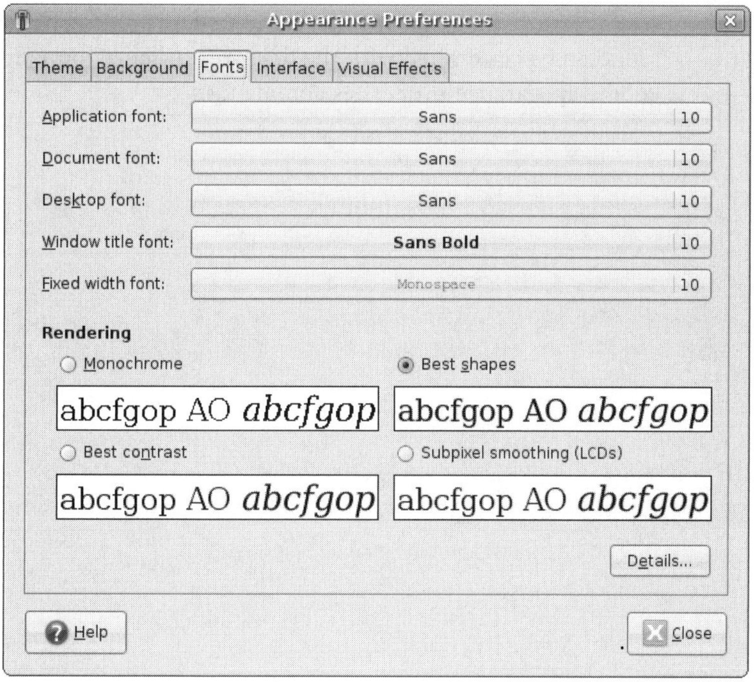

CERTIFICATION SUMMARY

This chapter provided an administrative view of the GNOME desktop environment, with a focus on customization using GConf tools. Default and mandatory settings are stored in the /etc/gconf directory; individually customized settings are stored in each user's home directory, deep in the .gconf/ subdirectory. Changes can be made with the GConf editor or command, accessible with the **gconf-editor** and **gconftool-2** commands, respectively. GNOME includes a variety of custom tools available from the System | Preferences directory, also available with the right commands run at a GUI command line. Changes as customized are incorporated in %gconf.xml files in appropriate directories.

Screen features depend on the X server, as configured in the /etc/X11/xorg.conf configuration file. There are several ways to reconfigure this file, including the **dpkg-reconfigure xserver-xorg**, **Xorg -configure**, **displayconfig-gtk**, and **gnome-display-properties** commands. Fonts are part of the X Window configuration, starting with the /etc/fonts/fonts.conf configuration file. Similarly, fonts can be customized with the **dpkg-reconfigure fontconfig-config** and **gnome-appearance-properties** commands.

✓ TWO-MINUTE DRILL

Here are some of the key points from the certification objectives in Chapter 11.

Configure the Desktop Environment

❑ Detailed settings for GNOME are governed by the GConf daemon, **gconfd-2**, in the /usr/lib/libgconf2-4/ directory.

❑ GConf settings can be default, mandatory, and user-specific, in apps, desktop, GNOME, schemas, and systems categories.

❑ GConf settings can be edited with the GConf editor or the **gconftool-2** command.

❑ GNOME menus can be customized with the Menu Editor, accessible with the **alacarte** command.

❑ Icons that start applications are associated with .desktop files.

❑ Many GNOME customized settings are available through tools available from the System | Preferences menu.

Manage Screen Features and Fonts

❑ Screen resolution can be managed from the GUI with tools that can be started with the **displayconfig-gtk** and **gnome-display-properties** commands.

❑ Screen resolution can be configured from the command-line interface with appropriate **dpkg-reconfigure** and **Xorg -configure** commands, which save changes in xorg.conf files with a suitable file extension.

❑ Fonts can be customized for a variety of configurations such as different monitors or languages.

SELF TEST

The following questions will help you measure your understanding of the material presented in this chapter. Read all the questions carefully, as there may be more than one correct answer. Some questions are "fill in the blank" and normally require an exact answer. Choose all correct answers for each question.

Configure the Desktop Environment

1. If you want to edit the GNOME configuration for the current user, which of the following commands would start the GUI GConf editor appropriately?
   A. sudo gconftool-2
   B. gconftool-2
   C. sudo gconf-editor
   D. gconf-editor

2. Which of the following commands starts another instance of the **GConf** daemon?
   A. sudo /etc/init.d/gconf start
   B. sudo gconftool-2 --spawn
   C. sudo /usr/sbin/gconfd
   D. sudo gconf-editor --spawn

3. If you want to disable the Boolean click setting in the .gconf/desktop/gnome/peripherals/ keyboard directory for the current user, which of the following commands would work?
   A. $ gconftool-2 --set /desktop/gnome/peripherals/keyboard/click \
      --type bool "0"
   B. $ gconftool-2 --set .gconf/desktop/gnome/peripherals/keyboard/click \
      --type bool "0"
   C. $ sudo gconftool-2 --set /desktop/gnome/peripherals/keyboard/click \
      --type bool "0"
   D. $ sudo gconftool-2 --set /desktop/gnome/peripherals/keyboard/click \
      --type bool "0"

4. What command supports access to the menu editor? Do not include the directory path.

   _____

5. Which of the following actions reveals the command associated with an icon on the left side of the top GNOME desktop environment panel?
   A. Right-click on the icon and click Properties in the pop-up menu.
   B. Right-click on the icon and click Command in the pop-up menu.

    C. Right-click on the icon and click Icon in the pop-up menu.

    D. Right-click on the icon and click GNOME in the pop-up menu.

6. What is the path to the directory with custom GNOME settings for user mike? Assume that the user has a standard home directory.

    _____

7. When the GNOME desktop environment is open, it works with mandatory, default, and user settings. Type in the order in which these settings are considered.

    _____

8. What is the command that opens the Sound Preferences window in a GUI command-line interface? Do not include the full path.

    _____

9. Which of the following directories would you delete to restore default GNOME settings for user michael?

    A. /home/michael/gconf

    B. /home/michael/.gconf

    C. /etc/gconf

    D. /usr/lib/gconf

Manage Screen Features and Fonts

10. Which of the following commands would configure the X server? (Two answers are correct.)

    A. sudo system-config-xserver

    B. sudo dpkg-reconfigure xserver-xorg

    C. sudo Xorg -configure

    D. sudo Xorg

11. What is the standard X server configuration file, including the full path?

    _____

12. When running the **Xorg -configure** command, which of the following files contains the output? Assume the local directory is /tmp, and the date is June 17, 2008.

    A. /tmp/xorg.conf

    B. /etc/X11/xorg.conf

    C. /tmp/xorg.conf.20080617103059

    D. /tmp/xorg.conf.new

13. Which of the following commands configures basic font settings on the local system for the current user?

    A. sudo fontconfig-config

    B. sudo dpkg-reconfigure fontconfig-config

    C. sudo font-properties

    D. sudo gnome-appearance-properties

14. Which of the following factors probably requires a different font configuration? (Two answers are correct.)

    A. An upgrade from a CRT system to a LCD monitor

    B. A new version of OpenOffice.org Writer

    C. The installation of Chinese on the local system

    D. A new printer

15. Which of the following runlevels is best suited to running the **Xorg -configure** command?

    A. 0

    B. 1

    C. 2

    D. 6

LAB QUESTIONS

Lab 1

This lab illustrates options associated with a simpler reconfiguration of the X server. The steps should be simpler than those shown in Exercise 11-1. In any case, the first step should be to back up the current X server configuration file. In addition, you should know how to access "Recovery Mode" from the GRUB menu when booting the local system. To open the GRUB menu, you'll need to press a key when prompted during the boot process. Then you can select "Recovery Mode," which boots Ubuntu Linux into runlevel 1, from which you can restore the original X server configuration file.

    1. Back up the current X server configuration file to your home directory with the following command:

```
$ cp /etc/X11/xorg.conf  ~
```

    2. Start the reconfiguration process with the following command:

```
$ sudo dpkg-reconfigure -phigh xserver-xorg
```

3. How many steps did it take to reconfigure the X server? (A ballpark number is sufficient.) Where is the file saved? Is there a significance to the file extension?

4. Save the result to the /etc/X11/xorg.conf configuration file.

5. Start runlevel 1, which should access a text-mode screen associated with the root user, with the following command:

   ```
   $ sudo init 1
   ```

6. Start runlevel 2, which is the default, which should also restart the X server. If the new configuration works, the regular GUI login screen for Ubuntu Linux should appear.

7. If the regular GUI login screen for Ubuntu Linux does not appear (or even if it does), restore the original X server configuration file. Press CTRL-ALT-F1 to access a command-line terminal, and log in normally. You should then be able to restore the original X server configuration file with the following command:

   ```
   $ sudo cp ~/xorg.conf /etc/X11
   ```

   If you can't access a command-line terminal, you might have to restart the local system and start recovery mode as described in the introduction to this lab.

8. Repeat steps 5 and 6. You should see the original GUI login screen, with the original X server configuration.

Lab 2

In this lab, you'll reconfigure fonts using low priority.

1. Start the reconfiguration process with the following command:

   ```
   $ sudo dpkg-reconfigure -plow fontconfig-config
   ```

2. How many steps did it take to reconfigure fonts? Is there any difference with a reconfiguration without the **-plow** swtich? Can you explain why?

SELF TEST ANSWERS

Configure the Desktop Environment

1. ☑ **D.** You do not want to invoke administrative privileges to use **gconf-editor** to edit settings for the local account.
   ☒ The **gconftool-2** command works from the command line and does not open any GConf editor. The **sudo gconf-editor** command edits settings for the root user. Therefore, answers **A**, **B**, and **C** are incorrect.

2. ☑ **B.** The **sudo gconftool-2 --spawn** command starts another instance of the **GConf** daemon.
   ☒ There is no gconf script in the /etc/init.d directory, nor is there a **gconfd** command in the /usr/sbin directory. The **gconf-editor** does not include any option to spawn another instance of the **GConf** daemon. Therefore, answers **A**, **C**, and **D** are incorrect.

3. ☑ **A.** The **gconftool-2** command isn't run with the full directory path; its directories are subdirectories of the .gconf or /etc/gconf directories.
   ☒ The **sudo gconftool-2** command affects settings for the root user. The **gconftool-2** command can't be applied directly to that user's .gconf directory. Therefore, answers **B**, **C**, and **D** are incorrect.

4. ☑ **alacarte.** This command starts the GNOME menu editor.

5. ☑ **A.** The properties for an application icon, such as those in the left side of the top panel, reveal the command-line command that starts the application.
   ☒ The other options don't exist in the pop-up menu when you right-click on the noted icon. Therefore, answers **B**, **C**, and **D** are incorrect.

6. ☑ **/home/mike/.gconf.** Custom settings for the GNOME desktop for user mike are contained in this directory.

7. ☑ **Mandatory, user, default.** GNOME GConf settings are considered in the noted order.

8. ☑ **gnome-sound-properties.** This command, when run in a GUI command line, opens the Sound Preferences window.

9. ☑ **B.** User-specific settings for user michael are stored in the /home/michael/.gconf directory.
   ☒ The /etc/gconf directory does contain both default and mandatory settings. The other directories do not normally exist or contain GConf configuration files. Therefore, answers **A**, **C**, and **D** are all incorrect.

Manage Screen Features and Fonts

10. ☑ **B and C.** The **sudo dpkg-reconfigure xserver-xorg** and **sudo Xorg -configure** commands can be used to create an X server configuration file.

☒ There is no **system-config-xserver** command in Ubuntu Linux, and the **sudo Xorg** command just starts the X server. Therefore, answers **A** and **D** are both incorrect.

11. ☑ **/etc/X11/xorg.conf**. This is the standard X server configuration file.

12. ☑ **D.** The **Xorg -configure** command creates a proposed X server configuration file in the local directory (/tmp), in the xorg.conf.new file.
☒ The **Xorg -configure** command creates a proposed X server file with a .new extension. Answer **C**, which includes the date and time, is what would be created from a **sudo dpkg-reconfigure xserver-xorg** command. Therefore, answers **A**, **B**, and **C** are all incorrect.

13. ☑ **B.** The **sudo dpkg-reconfigure fontconfig-config** command configures, or in this case, reconfigures basic font settings on the local system.
☒ There is no **fontconfig-config** or **font-properties** command. The **sudo gnome-appearance-properties** command configures font details for the root user. Therefore, answers **A**, **C**, and **D** are all incorrect.

14. ☑ **A** and **C.** LCD and CRT monitors render fonts differently. New languages, especially those with non-European alphabets, require different font configurations.
☒ It's possible that a new version of the OpenOffice.org Writer application or a new printer could require new fonts; however, it's unlikely. Therefore, answers **B** and **D** are both incorrect.

15. ☑ **B.** Runlevel 1 does not include the GUI, and is therefore best suited to running the **Xorg -configure** command.
☒ Runlevel 2 is the default for the GUI. If the GUI is installed, and you're in that runlevel, the **Xorg -configure** command does not work. Runlevels 0 and 6 are associated with halting and rebooting the system. Therefore, answers **A**, **C**, and **D** are all incorrect.

LAB ANSWERS

These labs are fairly straightforward. Do remember to make the backups of the configuration files as suggested in the steps.

Lab I

The steps in this lab are designed to illustrate a simple reconfiguration of the X server. The steps towards the end of the lab should restore the original configuration. Even if everything works fine in the lab, and you're unfamiliar with "Recovery Mode," you should learn to boot into that mode during the system boot process.

Lab 2

This lab is designed to illustrate that the **dpkg-reconfigure** command reconfigures the desired package, by default, in low priority.

12

Customizing GNOME

There are two basic topics in this chapter, the GNOME display manager and the Evolution e-mail client. The GNOME display manager is the graphical login screen shown by default in Ubuntu Linux; you'll learn about how this display can be configured in a number of ways. While Evolution is a personal information manager functionally similar to Microsoft Outlook, the focus of the UCP curriculum is on Evolution as an e-mail client. You'll learn about some of the features of Evolution as an e-mail client, including how it can be connected to a Microsoft Exchange server.

Set Up the Display Manager

Most GNOME display manager configuration files are stored in the /etc/gdm directory. The main configuration file is /etc/gdm/gdm.conf; custom settings are stored in the /etc/gdm/gdm.conf-custom configuration file. The GNOME display manager can also be customized with the Login Window Preferences tool, which can be started with the **gdmsetup** command.

GNOME Display Manager File Structure

The configuration files associated with the GNOME display manager are stored primarily in the /etc/gdm directory. The GNOME display manager daemon, **gdm**, can be controlled by a script in the /etc/init.d directory. Log messages are sent to files in the /var/log/gdm directory. In this section, you'll examine these files in more detail.

ⓦatch *Understand the functionality of each of the files in the /etc/gdm directory, as well as what you*	*can configure with the Login Window Preferences tool, which you can start with the gdmsetup command.*

INSIDE THE EXAM

Configure GNOME Display Manager (125.2)

The GNOME display manager is the graphical login screen associated with the GNOME desktop environment, as shown in the following illustration. The screen looks simple. The configuration options are a lot more complex. To understand how the GNOME display manager is configured, you need to understand the configuration files in the /etc/gdm directory and the options available with the **gdmsetup** tool. With these tools, you can "customize the display manager greeting, including the login banner and login screen."

Configure Evolution Mail Client (125.4)

Yes, Evolution is much more than just an e-mail client. But the UCP curriculum specifies that candidates need to know how "to configure Evolution to work with a variety of server types and mail protocols." Evolution filters can help you manage spam and other e-mail. The evolution-exchange package supports a connection from the Evolution e-mail client to the Microsoft Exchange server.

GNOME Display Manager Configuration Files

The primary GNOME display manager configuration file is /etc/gdm/gdm.conf. The first comment at the top of this file is a warning that "this file should not be updated by hand." Any configuration changes should be made to the /etc/gdm/gdm.conf-custom file. In the Gutsy Gibbon release, there was even a backup of /etc/gdm/gdm.conf in the /etc/gdm/factory-gdm.conf file. For more information on the files in the /etc/gdm directory, see Table 12-1. Yes, there are directories in this table, but remember, in Linux, a directory is just a special version of a file.

TABLE 12-1	File in the /etc/gdm Directory	Description
GNOME Display Manager Configuration Files	factory-gdm.conf	Stores the default configuration; should be identical to gdm.conf (may be shown as gdm-cdd.conf; not available in the Hardy Heron release)
	failsafeBlacklist	Specifies graphics card characteristics that don't work with a VESA driver
	failsafeDexconf	Creates an xorg.conf.failsafe configuration file in case of a failure with the X server
	failsafeXinit	Initializes the X Window System in case of a failure with the X server
	failsafeXServer	Starts a failsafe X server, in case of a failure with the current X server configuration
	gdm.conf	Includes the primary GNOME display manager configuration file; changes should be added to gdm.conf-custom
	gdm.conf-custom	Adds custom settings to gdm.conf
	gdmprefetchlist	Loads key libraries to speed GUI login performance
	Init/Default	Includes keyboard and other default GUI settings
	locale.conf	Adds language settings
	modules/*	Incorporates mouse settings for the GUI
	PostLogin/Default	Adds user-defined settings after login, before the GUI desktop is presented to the user
	PostSession/Default	Adds user-defined settings after logout
	PreSession/Default	Adds user-defined settings after login, after PostLogin/Default is run, before the GUI desktop is presented to the user
	XKeepsCrashing	Provides messages even if the BulletProofX files don't work
	Xsession	Configures part of the X Window System during the start process

The BulletProofX system is designed to create a graphical screen even when there are certain serious problems with the configuration of the X server. The files associated with the BulletProofX system were first implemented for Ubuntu Linux Gutsy Gibbon. If there's a complete failure in the X Window System, the BulletProofX files start a minimal graphical screen with the **displayconfig-gtk** utility described in Chapter 11. These configuration files are the **failsafe*** files described in Table 12-1.

on the **job**

With the Hardy Heron release, the X Server is even more resilient. It's more difficult to create a situation where the BulletProofX system calls the displayconfig-gtk utility. The X Server now works even with certain configuration files missing, or fails completely.

The GNOME Display Manager Control Script

The control script for the GNOME display manager is /etc/init.d/gdm. It starts the GNOME display manager, as specified in the /etc/X11/default-display-manager configuration file. Different stanzas are associated with starting, stopping, reloading, and restarting the script. It starts the daemon, **/usr/sbin/gdm**, using the language as defined in the /etc/environment configuration file.

GNOME Display Manager Log Files

Most problems with the GNOME display manager are logged in the /var/log/gdm directory. Problems with the first graphical console are logged in files that start with a **:0**; problems associated with any configured second graphical console are logged in files that start with a **:1**.

GNOME Display Manager Configuration File

The GNOME display manager configuration file is /etc/gdm/gdm.conf. While changes should be made to the /etc/gdm/gdm.conf-custom file, the main file is well commented and is discussed here. As there are over 700 lines in this file, *I only describe a few active directives that are most frequently customized*—and a couple of others of interest. You'll see many more directives in the /etc/gdm/gdm.conf file on the local system.

This configuration file is divided into several stanzas, as described in Table 12-2.

TABLE 12-2	Stanza	Description
Stanzas in the GNOME Display Manager Configuration File	[daemon]	Includes fundamental directives that drive how the display manager starts, operates, and responds to errors
	[security]	Configures basic security settings, Pluggable Authentication Modules (PAM), more
	[xdmcp]	Sets up remote access to the display manager
	[gui]	Configures resource files based on The GIMP Toolkit (GTK+)
	[greeter]	Sets up the title bar, window position, and the face browser, as well as responses to actions in the display manager
	[chooser]	Specifies settings associated with an XDMCP connection
	[debug]	Sets up information sent to the system log file
	[servers]	Configures how displays are run; closely related are the [server-Standard], [server-Terminal], and [server-Chooser] stanzas
	[customcommand]	Reserved for custom display manager commands

Most of the directives that I describe are in the **[daemon]** stanza; in other words, they determine and configure how the GNOME display manager works. The first directives can enable automatic logins for the user as specified. The default settings disable automatic logins:

```
AutomaticLoginEnable=false
AutomaticLogin=
```

I could enable automatic logins, bypassing the login screen for my account, if I changed those directives as follows:

```
AutomaticLoginEnable=true
AutomaticLogin=michael
```

The following directives could be changed for users such as guest on a public terminal:

```
TimedLoginEnable=false
TimedLogin=
TimedLoginDelay=30
```

The next directive specifies the use of a graphical greeting:

```
Greeter=/usr/lib/gdm/gdmgreeter
```

There are directives that set the **PATH** environment variable for regular and default users. These directives do not supersede any default values of **PATH** for any specific user. Note, the value of the **RootPath** variable has been truncated, as it includes more directories than can be shown given the formatting limitations of this book.

```
DefaultPath=/usr/local/bin:/usr/bin:/bin:/usr/bin/X11:/usr/games
RootPath=/usr/local/bin:/usr/local/sbin:/sbin:/usr/sbin:/bin:/usr/bin
```

For access to related applications, the following directives provide access to scripts and files owned by the gdm user and group:

```
User=gdm
Group=gdm
```

The following directives run other scripts in the /etc/gdm directory. These directives all name directories, and run the contents of the file named Default in each of these directories.

```
PostLoginScriptDir=/etc/gdm/PostLogin/
PreSessionScriptDir=/etc/gdm/PreSession/
PostSessionScriptDir=/etc/gdm/PostSession/
DisplayInitDir=/etc/gdm/Init
```

If there are problems, the **gdm** daemon refers to the BulletProofX files with the following directive:

```
FailsafeXServer=/etc/gdm/failsafeXServer
```

If even the BulletProofX files don't work, the following directive provides messages to the user:

```
XKeepsCrashing=/etc/gdm/XKeepsCrashing
```

Assuming the hardware supports it, the following commands should be available from the Options button shown in the lower-left corner. However, the **hibernate** command listed in the following example may only be available in the logout menu shown when you click System | Quit in the GNOME desktop.

```
RebootCommand=/sbin/shutdown -r now "Rebooted via gdm."
HaltCommand=/sbin/shutdown -h now "Shut Down via gdm."
SuspendCommand=/usr/sbin/pmi action suspend
HibernateCommand=/usr/sbin/pmi action hibernate
```

The next directive associates these directives with actual commands in the display manager:

```
SystemCommandsInMenu=HALT;REBOOT;SUSPEND;CUSTOM_CMD
```

A similar directive works with the display manager during the logout process:

```
AllowLogoutActions=HALT;REBOOT;SUSPEND;CUSTOM_CMD
```

There are a few other directives of interest, for example, in the [security] and [servers] stanzas. The following directive specifies the Xsession script:

```
BaseXsession=/etc/gdm/Xsession
```

And the following directive specifies the default.desktop configuration file, which runs user-specific X client scripts:

```
DefaultSession=default.desktop
```

The following directive means you can access the first GNOME display manager terminal by pressing CTRL-ALT-F7:

```
FirstVT=7
```

It's important in my opinion to disable remote root access, and especially automated logins, and that's done with the following directives in the [security] stanza:

```
AllowRemoteRoot=false
AllowRemoteAutoLogin=false
```

The following directive supports PAM authentication for the GNOME display manager:

```
PamStack=gdm
```

Further security-related directives are associated with the [xdmcp] stanza. Naturally, it's disabled by default, and should be enabled only behind a secure firewall:

```
Enable=false
```

The number of logins should be limited to minimize the risk of remote attacks through the GNOME display manager. The following limits the number of GNOME display manager displays per system. Even though the following directive is in comments, it is the default. Larger values have a higher risk of a Denial of Service (DoS) attack.

```
#DisplaysPerHost=2
```

One more directive that limits the size of a file read by the GNOME display manager is the **UserMaxFile**. Larger files may take a long time for a GNOME display manager to read, also increasing the risk of a DoS attack. The following directive is the default, in bytes.

```
#UserMaxFile=65536
```

Finally, the following directive sets up a standard graphical console based in part on the **FirstVT** directive earlier in this file. In other words, it sets up the first GNOME display manager in a console accessible by pressing CTRL-ALT-F7.

```
0=Standard device=/dev/console
```

More consoles can be set up; an example of how this can be done is described in the second lab at the end of this chapter.

The GUI Login Manager Customization Tool

To customize the GNOME login manager, you need to open the Login Window Preferences screen. It can be opened in two ways in the GUI. Either click System | Administration | Login Window, or run the **sudo gdmsetup** command. The Gutsy Gibbon version of this tool is shown in Figure 12-1.

There are six tabs associated with the login window, which support configuration in quite a bit of detail. Older versions of Ubuntu Linux do not have as many options—and it's to be expected that later versions of Ubuntu Linux will include different features in the Login Window Preferences tool. There are already slight modifications from the version included with the Hardy Heron release. As this chapter is based on the Gutsy Gibbon release, do not take this as an exact or complete description of what you can do with the noted tool.

General Login Window Preferences

Configuration options under the General tab relate to basic login options as seen by the user. The options are as follows:

- **Show Visual Feedback (Asterisks) In The Password Entry**   Responds to each keystroke in the password text box with asterisks. (The Hardy Heron version of the GDM Setup Tool rephrases this to **Hide Visual Feedback In The Password Entry**.)

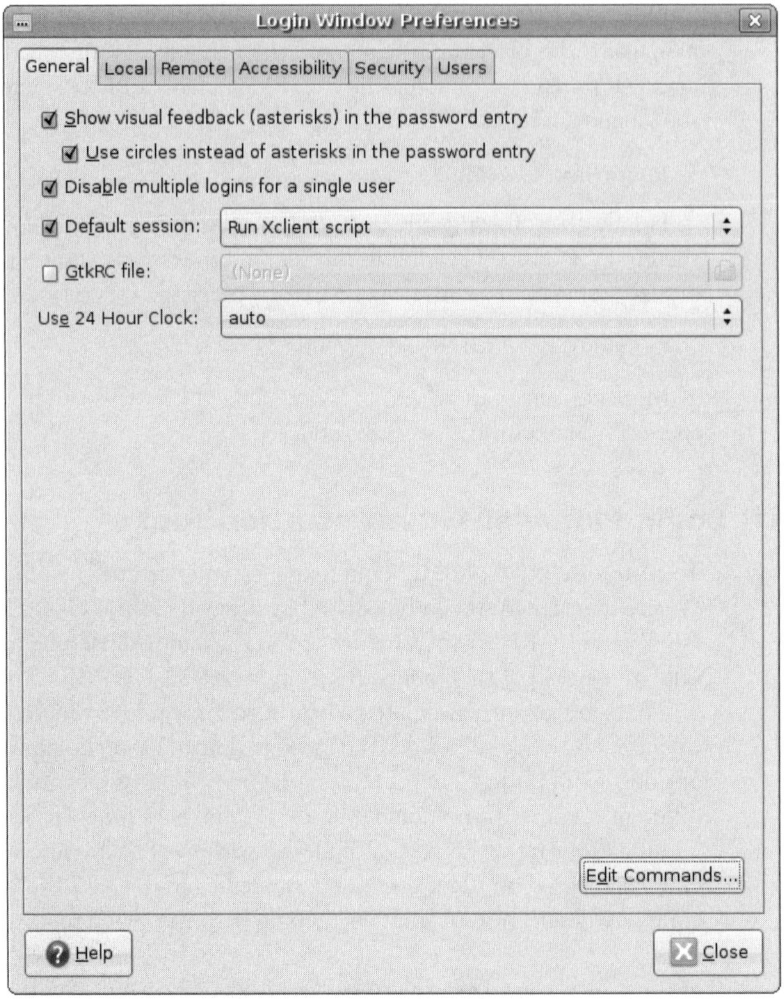

FIGURE 12-1

GNOME
Login Window
Preferences tool

- **Use Circles Instead Of Asterisks In The Password Entry** Replaces asterisks with dark circles for each keystroke.
- **Disable Multiple Logins For A Single User** Allows a user to log in with one account at a time; the user can still access different accounts from within GUI command lines with the **su** command described in Chapter 8 in the section "Set Up More Administrators."

■ **Default Session**   The associated drop-down text box determines the default GUI desktop environment. Additional options may be available; for example, if KDE and Xfce are installed, you'll see those in the drop-down text box as well.

- ■ **Run Xclient Script**   Starts the GNOME desktop environment using settings in a .Xclients configuration file, and the .gconf subdirectory, in the local home directory.

- ■ **GNOME**   Runs the default GNOME desktop environment, using .gconf settings in each user's home directory.

- ■ **Failsafe GNOME**   Starts GNOME without any custom settings.

- ■ **Failsafe Terminal**   Opens a minimal GUI with a command-line terminal.

■ **GtkRC File**   Supports a custom background image and theme.

■ **Use 24 Hour Clock**   Configures an A.M./P.M. or 24 hour time format in the login screen.

For more options, click the Edit Commands button. This opens the Reboot, Halt, Suspend, And Custom Command Preferences window shown in Figure 12-2. The commands configured here affect what's seen and executed from the Options menu shown in the illlustration at the beginning of the chapter and when you click System | Quit from the GNOME desktop.

Each of the options under the Command Type drop-down text box is associated with a different command combination. They may not be quite what's expected. For example, a newer Linux user might expect to see the **halt** command shown when you select the Halt Command in the Command Type text box. However, the command as shown is the original way Linux systems were halted (**shutdown -h now**).

More About the Local Login Window

Configuration options under the Local tab change the display and menu options available from the login screen, as shown in Figure 12-3. As shown in the middle of the screen, several login window themes are available. The other options are as follows:

- ■ **Style**   Allows themed or plain options, with or without a face browser. If a face browser is configured, "faces" associated with allowed users are shown in the login window. Allowed users are configured in the Users tab.

- ■ **Theme**   Supports a specific or random theme. Other themes, which may be available from third parties, can be added with the Add button.

- ■ **Background Color**   Supports a custom background color in the login window.

FIGURE 12-2

GNOME Login
Manager Custom
Command
Preferences
window

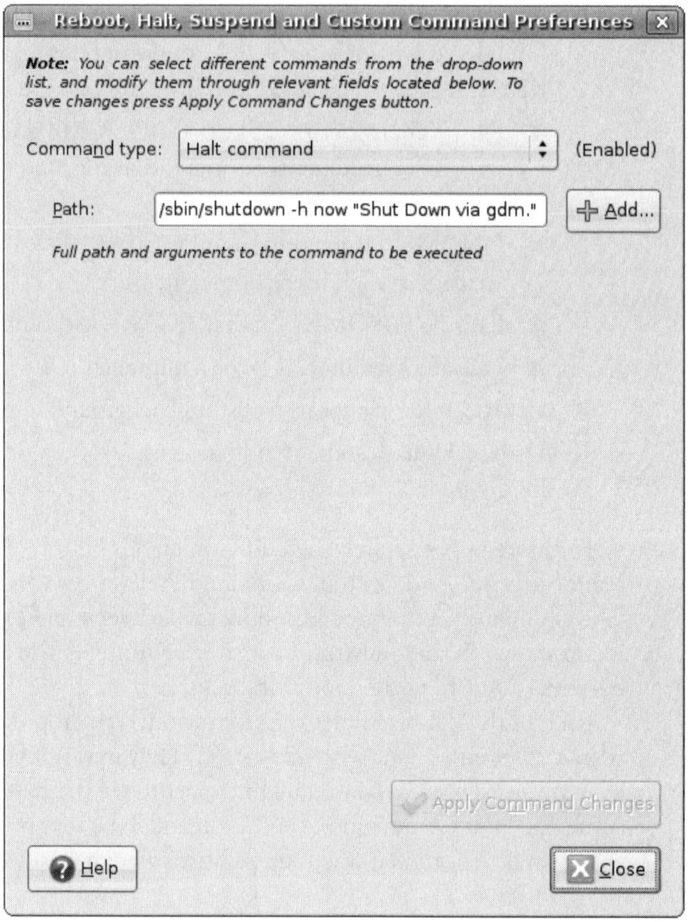

Reboot, Halt, Suspend and Custom Command Preferences

Note: You can select different commands from the drop-down list, and modify them through relevant fields located below. To save changes press Apply Command Changes button.

Command type: | Halt command | ▲▼ | (Enabled)

Path: | /sbin/shutdown -h now "Shut Down via gdm." | + Add...

Full path and arguments to the command to be executed

Apply Command Changes

? Help   ✕ Close

- **Menu Bar**   Allows configuration of actions, including remote access via the X Display Manager Control Protocol (XDMCP).
- **Welcome Message**   Supports a custom welcome message.

Configure Remote Access

Configuration options under the Remote tab change the display and menu theme available when connecting to a remote login screen. For our purposes, the options are essentially the same as those available under the Local tab; however, remote access is disabled by default.

FIGURE 12-3

GNOME Login
Manager Local
Preferences tab

on the

! job *As of this writing, Remote Access has problems when accessing one Gutsy Gibbon system from another, per bug 150193 at http://bugs.launchpad.net. As the problem has been fixed in the Hardy Heron release, with Long Term Support, I do not know if this issue will ever be addressed in the Gutsy Gibbon release.*

Enabling Accessibility

Configuration options under the Accessibility tab support help for sight-impaired users. If enabled, the options are straightforward:

- **Allow Users To Change Fonts And Colors Of Plain Greeter** Allows users to customize the greeter for optimal visibility
- **Login Screen Ready** Supports selection of a sound when the login screen is ready
- **Login Successful** Supports selection of a sound when a login is accepted
- **Login Failed** Supports selection of a sound when a login is not accepted

Configure Login Window Security

Configuration options under the Security tab change the ways logins are allowed through the display manager screen. Options, as shown in Figure 12-4, are as follows:

- **Enable Automatic Login** Allows a specified user to bypass the login screen without entering a password.
- **Enable Timed Login** Configures a login as a specified user (such as guest) if specific user information is not entered for a specific time.
- **Login Retry Delay** Allows a second chance at logins after a fixed number of seconds.
- **Minimal UID** Permits logins for users with at least a certain User ID number, as described in Chapter 8.
- **Allow Local System Administrator Login** Configures access for the root user. This doesn't work unless a root password is configured.
- **Allow Remote System Administrator Login** Configures remote access for the root user.
- **Enable Debug Messages To System Log** Sets up log messages.
- **Deny TCP Connections To Xserver** Disables forwarding of X Window data. This doesn't affect options under the Remote tab.
- **Only Allow Login If User Owns Their Home Directory** Configures user logins to that user's home directory; may also be limited depending on the permissions associated with that home directory.

GNOME Login
Manager Security
Preferences tab

The Configure X Server button opens another window, which allows you to configure more. For example, additional GUI terminals can be configured.

Set Up Users

Configuration options under the Users tab change the ways logins are allowed through the display manager screen. These options work only if the Plain With Face Browser option is selected under the Local tab. As of this writing, it does not work with the Themed With Face Browser option under the Local tab. User preferences are as shown in Figure 12-5 as follows:

- **Include All Users from /etc/passwd** Includes all users from the local authentication database. Does not include remote users, even if the Network Information Service (NIS) is enabled. If this option is disabled, you're allowed to select users to enable and disable.
- **Default Face** Configures a default icon for users.
- **Global Face Dir** Sets a default directory for face files.

FIGURE 12-5

GNOME Login
Manager Users
Preferences tab

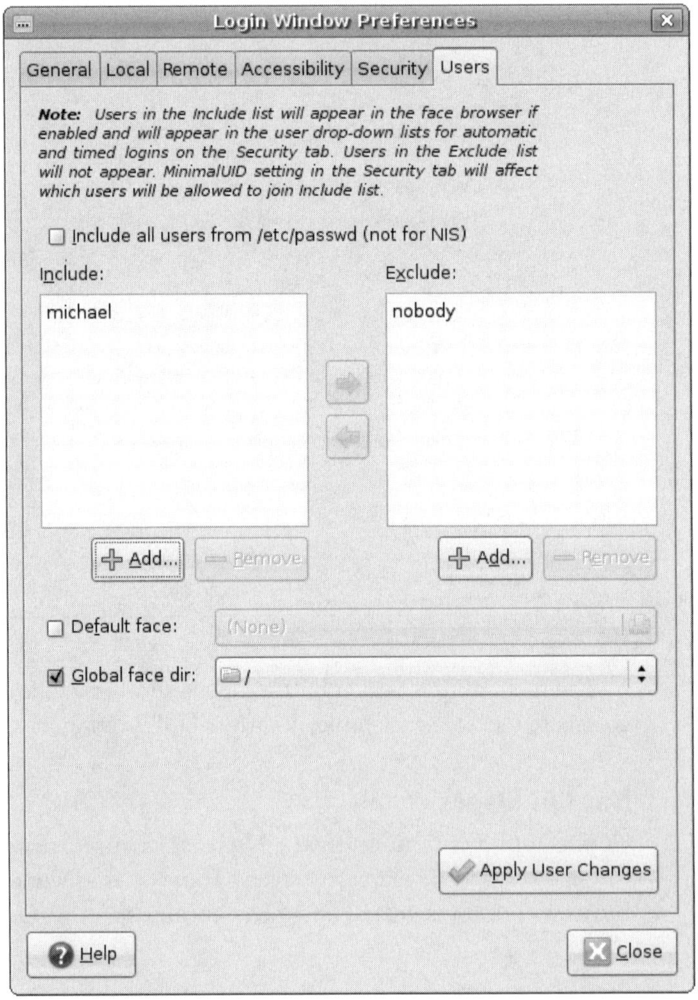

Login Window Preferences

| General | Local | Remote | Accessibility | Security | Users |

Note: Users in the Include list will appear in the face browser if enabled and will appear in the user drop-down lists for automatic and timed logins on the Security tab. Users in the Exclude list will not appear. MinimalUID setting in the Security tab will affect which users will be allowed to join Include list.

☐ Include all users from /etc/passwd (not for NIS)

Include:

michael

Exclude:

nobody

➕ Add...   ➖ Remove   ➕ Add...   ➖ Remove

☐ Default face: (None)

☑ Global face dir: /

✔ Apply User Changes

❓ Help   ✖ Close

CERTIFICATION OBJECTIVE 12.02

Work with the Evolution Mail Client

The Evolution Groupware Suite is more than just a mail client. It's a contact manager, a calendar, a memo manager, and a task scheduler. It's a personal information manager with essentially the same functionality as Microsoft Outlook. With the evolution-exchange package, it can connect to a Microsoft Exchange server, or Novell's replacement for that server, Novell GroupWise.

on the

ⓞob

Evolution is now owned by Novell, the same company that owns SUSE Linux. Both are released under open source licenses, and can therefore be freely used in other open source systems such as Ubuntu Linux.

Evolution supports a wide variety of e-mail protocols, including IMAP, POP, SMTP, Microsoft Exchange, and more. It supports authentication for each of these servers. It can enable encrypted connections using standards such as the GNU Privacy Guard (GPG), the Linux implementation of Pretty Good Privacy (PGP), SSL (Secure Sockets Layer) and its successor, TLS (Transport Layer Security). The Evolution e-mail manager supports address completion as well as Object Linking and Embedding (OLE) of attachments, graphical images, and more.

To address the key terms from the UCP curriculum, the mail client can be started in the GUI command line with the **evolution** command. User files for the client are stored in individual home directories, in the .evolution/ subdirectory. The evolution-exchange package includes a connector setup tool, which can connect a local Evolution client to a Microsoft Exchange or a Novell Exchange server.

e x a m

ⓦatch

Learn how to configure Evolution as an e-mail client. Per the UCP curriculum, candidates should be able to set up filters to manage spam and other e-mail. Technically, UCP topics are fair game on the exam. However, it is difficult to test some skills such as filtering even with a "fill in the blank" question.

Configure an Email Account

The first time the Evolution e-mail manager is opened, it starts the Evolution Setup Assistant. If you open Evolution from the GUI command line, with the **evolution** command, it displays one interesting message at the command line:

```
Loading Spamassassin as the default junk plugin
```

Spamassassin is an e-mail filter, sponsored by the Apache project. It uses a variety of tests to identify e-mail with spam characteristics, and illustrates the power associated with Evolution.

The Evolution Setup Assistant first allows you to restore from a backup. In a second system on Evolution, when I clicked File | Backup settings, it created a suitable backup in the evolution-backup.tar.gz file. The file can be pretty big—nearly a full GB for my personal system. However, if you don't have a backup, you'll be creating accounts on Evolution for the first time. There are also options for importing e-mail from other systems.

on the **Ụob**

When I acquired a new system, I didn't bother creating an Evolution backup file. I just copied the contents of the .evolution subdirectory in my home directory to the new system.

Evolution can work with a wide variety of e-mail servers, as listed in Table 12-3.

EXERCISE 12-1

Configuring an Account in the Evolution Email Manager

The first time you start the Evolution e-mail manager, the Evolution Setup Assistant prompts for the information needed for an e-mail account. Similar steps are available from the Evolution Preferences window. To configure an account in the Evolution e-mail manager, take the following steps:

1. Open Evolution in a GUI command-line interface, with the **evolution** command. If this is the first time you've opened Evolution, it starts the Evolution Setup Assistant. Click Forward to continue.

2. Unless you've already created a backup—or want to use the backup/restore feature, do not select the Restore Evolution From The Backup File option. Click Forward to continue.

Server	Description
Hula	Based on a Novell open source mail project
IMAP	Accesses an Internet Message Access Protocol (IMAP) server
Microsoft Exchange	Creates a connection to a Microsoft Exchange server
Novell GroupWise	Connects to a Novell GroupWise server
POP	Accesses a Post Office Protocol (POP) server
USENET News	Creates a connection to a news server
Local Delivery	Accesses and moves user mail files in the /var/spool/mail directory; contrast with last two options
MH-Format mail directories	Supports access to mail handler (MH) format directories; associated with the Mutt e-mail client
Maildir-Format mail directories	Access and download from individual files in maildir directories; associated with qmail, an option to sendmail
Standard Unix mbox spool directory	Reads but does not unload mail from the /var/spool/mail directory
Standard Unix mbox spool file	Reads but does not unload mail individual files; contrast to Maildir-Format mail directories

Alternatively, if you've already run Evolution, click Edit | Preferences. In the Evolution Preferences window that appears, click Add. In the Evolution Account Assistant window that appears, click Forward. While the window name will be slightly different, the contents will still be the same.

3. In the Identity window that appears, as shown in the following illustration, enter the e-mail address. If desired, enter a different "Reply-To" address; user replies will be sent to that address by default. The Organization is just for information. Click Forward to continue.

4. In the Receiving Email window that appears, click the Server Type drop-down option box. Review the variety of available server types; for more information, see Table 12-1. Select an appropriate e-mail server, and note the text boxes and options that appear. For this exercise, select a POP e-mail server.

5. In the same Receiving Email window, more information now can be entered, associated with the selected e-mail server type, as shown in the following illustration. The options to enter are as follows:

- The server is the fully qualified domain name (FQDN) or IP address of the e-mail server.
- The username is the authentication user account for the server. There are typically two options: a username or a full e-mail address.
- Encryption should be used if the server supports it. Options from the Use Secure Connection drop-down box are: No Encryption, TLS Encryption, and SSL Encryption. TLS is short for Transport Layer Security, the advanced version of SSL (short for Secure Sockets Layer.) Some trial and error may be required.
- Under Authentication Type, click the Check For Supported Types button. An error may indicate an encryption issue; some mail servers do not support TLS encryption.
- The Password drop-down option box may show options for supported authentication schemes. Details are beyond the scope of the UCP exam.

Generally you should activate the Remember Password check box, otherwise, you'll have to enter your password each time e-mail is checked.

Make appropriate choices and click Forward to continue.

6. In the Receiving Options screen that appears, you can configure Evolution to
   - Automatically check for new e-mail periodically, every few minutes.
   - Leave messages on the server.
   - Disable support for POP3 extensions. Depending on the functionality of the e-mail server, you might want to enable this option.

   Make the desired choices and click Forward to continue.

7. In the Sending Email window, the Server Type drop-down option box supports two options. The default is to send e-mail to some SMTP (Simple Mail Transfer Protocol) server; the alternative is to send e-mail to a local sendmail server. As shown in the following illustration , the options are similar to the Receiving Email window shown in step 5.

While the options are configured slightly differently, the same basic information on the e-mail server, encryption, username, and password are required. Enter appropriate information and click Forward to continue.

8. In the Account Management window, enter a descriptive name for the account and click Forward to continue.

   If you're running these steps because you're starting Evolution for the first time, you'll now see a Timezone map—where you should select a current time zone, so e-mail from other time zones is properly converted for where you are. Select your time zone and click Forward to continue.

9. Finally, you're told that you're done! Click Apply to write the changes to the local system.

Creating Mail Filters

In this section, I'll show you how to create an e-mail filter in Evolution for the Ubuntu users mailing list. First, one way to sign up for the Ubuntu users mailing list is to navigate to https://lists.ubuntu.com, scroll to the Community Support section, select the *ubuntu-users* list, and follow the instructions. For the purpose of this section, be sure to use the e-mail account configured for your version of Evolution.

Once you've confirmed through the Evolution mail client that you're receiving e-mail from the Ubuntu users mailing list, it's time to create an e-mail filter. With the following steps, I'll show you how to create a folder, filter information from the mailing list from the inbox, and send that information to that new folder. The following steps describe just one method. Other filters can work just as efficiently.

1. First, open the Evolution Mail manager if it isn't already open. In a command line in the GUI, enter the **evolution** command.

2. To set up a folder, click Folder New. This opens a Create Folder window, as shown in Figure 12-6.

3. Enter a name in the Folder Name text box, and select a location for the folder. As I'm going to filter the messages from the Inbox, I'm going to call it UbuntuUsers and make it a subfolder of the Inbox. Make your choices and click Create.

4. Confirm that the new folder is created as a subfolder of the Inbox. Now click Edit | Message Filters to open the Message Filters window.

FIGURE 12-6

Evolution Create
Folder window

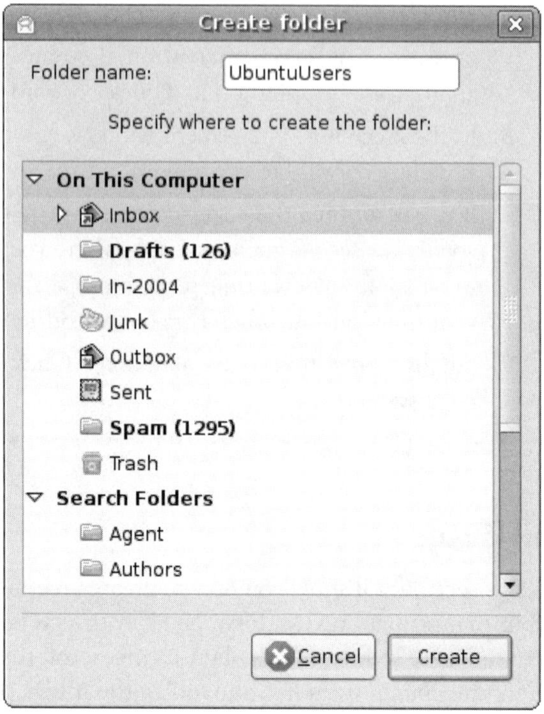

To give you some visual hints on how filters are created, I illustrate my Spam folder configuration in Figure 12-7. Note how I use the *[SPAM]* in the subject, added courtesy of the Spamassassin features used by my ISP. Email with *[SPAM]* in the subject line is removed, as shown in the upper part of the window. That e-mail is then moved to the folder named Spam, and then is deleted from the local Inbox.

5. In the Message Filters window, click Add to open the Add Rule window. Type in the search name of your choice; I use "Ubuntu Users Mailing List."

   The options are extensive. Click the Sender drop-down box to see a wide variety of options. Most are self-explanatory, but they also determine the search options that follow. For example, *Sender* filters by the contents of the e-mail address; the options that follow are logical expressions such as *is*, *contains*, and *ends with*. Other options are shown in Table 12-4.

6. If you want to create additional filters, the Add button can help. For e-mails that match one or more filters, the Then part of the window determines

FIGURE 12-7

Evolution spam
filter example

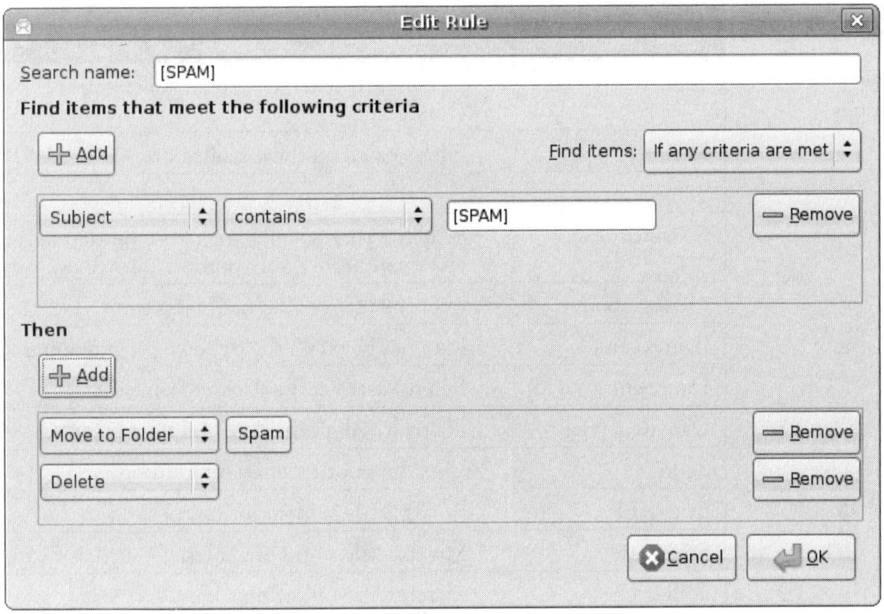

the action. For this section, I select the Move To Folder drop-down box, and
then choose the UbuntuUsers folder created earlier.

7. I then click Add and select Delete to delete messages from the Ubuntu Users
   mailing list from my regular inbox.

8. I click OK to exit from the Add Rule window. I then click OK to exit the
   Message Filters window, to implement the change.

9. The configuration is tested the next time messages are downloaded from
   the Ubuntu Users mailing list. If you see such messages in the UbuntuUsers
   folder, and not in the Inbox, the filter is successful.

Managing Spam

As suggested in Figure 12-7, spam e-mail may have a *[SPAM]* label in the subject
line, and I've used that label to filter spam from my Evolution e-mail client. The
[SPAM] label is added by Spamassassin as configured by my ISP. Other ISPs may not
add the label; however, the spam scores assigned by Spamassassin are given a score
and status.

TABLE 12-4	Filter Option	Description
Email Filter Options	Sender	Searches through the e-mail address in the "From" part of an e-mail
	Recipients	Filters based on the e-mail addresses in the "To" part of an e-mail
	Subject	Uses the contents of the subject line
	Specific Header	Searches through all parts of the header; for more information on an e-mail header in Evolution, click View | All Message Headers
	Message Body	Uses the text of all e-mail messages
	Expression	Matches based on the Scheme programming language
	Date Sent	Filters based on the date and time sent
	Date Received	Filters based on the date and time received
	Score	Uses the priority set by other filters
	Size (KB)	Runs based on the priority in KB
	Status	Matches the status of a message, such as Read, Draft, and Junk
	Follow Up	Matches the follow-up status of a message, flagged or not flagged
	Completed On	Matches the completed status of a message
	Attachments	Filters based on the existence of an attachment
	Mailing List	Uses the mailing list associated with a message
	Regex Match	Uses the header or body of a message
	Source Account	Matches the configured Evolution account
	Pipe To Program	Supports the use of outside programs for filtering
	Junk Test	Uses filters based on e-mail previously marked as junk
	Match All	Supports the use of multiple filters

Without getting into the details on how Spamassassin works, each e-mail is evaluated and may be labeled as spam if it meets certain criteria. To use the status label, create a filter using the steps in Exercise 12-2.

EXERCISE 12-2

Configuring a Filter in the Evolution Email Manager

In this exercise, you'll create a rule associated with spam for the Evolution e-mail manager. The steps in this exercise work only if the e-mail server, perhaps at your

ISP, uses Spamassassin to evaluate each e-mail. To create this spam filter, take the following steps:

1. Open the Evolution e-mail manager. In a GUI command line, use the **evolution** command. If the e-mail manager isn't already open, press CTRL-1.
2. Click Edit | Message Filters to open the Message Filters window.
3. Click Add to open the Add Rule window.
4. Click the Sender drop-down option box, and select Specific Header. Type in **X-Spam-Flag** in the first text box that appears, and then **YES** in the second text box.

5. In the lower part of the Add Rule window, select Move To Folder from the first drop-down box, click the button to the right of it that appears. Select the folder that you want to use for Spam.

   While spam filters are now excellent, there are times when desired e-mails are accidentally classified as spam. I therefore recommend that such e-mail be sent to a local folder in Evolution; as shown in the illustration in step 4, I've created the SpamTest folder for that purpose.

6. This rule may not be complete. If you want to avoid seeing spam e-mails in the Inbox, click the Add button in the lower part of the Add Rule window. In the first drop-down box, select Delete. This part of the rule deletes the spam e-mails from the text box after sending a copy to the SpamTest folder.

7. Click OK to close the Add Rule text box, and click OK to close the Message Filters window. Assuming your ISP uses Spamassassin, the next time you download e-mail, it should filter spam to the folder specified in the Evolution rule configured in this exercise.

Work with Microsoft Exchange

The evolution-exchange package works as a "connector," which allows Evolution to connect to a Microsoft Exchange server as a client. To make Evolution a client, you'll need to install the evolution-exchange package with a command such as

```
$ sudo apt-get install evolution-exchange
```

Once this package is installed, the **exchange-connector-setup-2.12** command (the version number may be different) can start a wizard to connect Evolution to one of the noted servers. The version number may vary, depending on the version of Evolution that's installed on the local system. However, the GNOME project is working to make this tool obsolete. In any case, evolution-exchange is explicitly cited in the UCP curriculum.

So I'll show you another way to create a connection to an Evolution server—which uses the same steps described earlier for creating an account. If you have a working Microsoft Exchange server, you can create a connection with the following steps:

1. Open the Evolution e-mail manager. One method is to run the **evolution** command from a GUI command line.

2. Click Edit | Preferences to open the Evolution Preferences window.

3. Click Add to open the Evolution Account Assistant.

4. Enter information on user identity. Make sure the e-mail address is governed by the Microsoft Exchange server to which you're connecting. Click Forward to continue.

5. In the Server Type drop-down box, select Microsoft Exchange. Enter your username and Outlook Web Access Universal Resource Locater (OWA URL), as assigned by the Exchange server administrator.

CERTIFICATION SUMMARY

In this chapter, you learned how to configure the GNOME display manager. Associated configuration files are in the /etc/gdm directory. Key directives in the gdm.conf configuration file include **AutomaticLoginEnable**, **FailsafeXServer**, **FirstVT**, and **DisplaysPerHost**. The display manager can also be configured with a graphical tool, which you can start with the **sudo gdmsetup** command. Remote access can work using the XDMCP protocol.

This chapter also described how the Evolution Groupware Suite can work as an e-mail client. It described how Evolution supports encryption, as well as a connection to a Microsoft Exchange server. It showed you how to configure e-mail accounts on Evolution using a wide variety of authenticated protocols, including POP, IMAP, and SMTP and also demonstrated how e-mails can be filtered for spam and a variety of other criteria.

✓ # TWO-MINUTE DRILL

Here are some of the key points from the certification objectives in Chapter 12.

Set Up the Display Manager

❑ The GNOME display manager is the default Ubuntu Linux graphical login screen.

❑ Changes to the display manager can be added to the /etc/gdm/gdm.conf-custom configuration file.

❑ Changes to the display manager can also be configured with the Login Window Preferences tool; those changes are written to the /etc/gdm/gdm.conf-custom file.

❑ Other files in the /etc/gdm directory configure other actions such as scripts run during the login and logout process.

❑ The BulletProofX files configure access to a graphical configuration tool if there's a failure in the X server.

❑ GNOME display manager log files are stored in the /var/log/gdm directory.

Work with the Evolution Mail Client

❑ The Evolution e-mail client is just one part of the Evolution Groupware Suite.

❑ Evolution can work with a variety of e-mail and news servers, including Hula, IMAP, Microsoft Exchange, Novell GroupWise, POP, USENET news, MH-Format mail directories, Maildir-Format mail directories, as well as Standard Unix mbox spool directories and files.

❑ Mail filters can help sort spam out of the Evolution Inbox; they can also organize other types of mail such as those from mailing lists.

❑ With the evolution-exchange package, Evolution can work as a Microsoft Exchange (or Novell GroupWise) client.

SELF TEST

The following questions will help you measure your understanding of the material presented in this chapter. Read all the questions carefully, as there may be more than one correct answer. Some questions are "fill in the blank" and normally require an exact answer. Choose all correct answers for each question.

Set Up the Display Manager

1. Which of the following commands configures the GNOME login screen for just the root user?
   A. sudo gdmsetup
   B. gdmsetup --root
   C. sudo /etc/init.d/gdm start
   D. There is no single command that configures the GNOME login screen for just the root user.

2. Name the GNOME display configuration file created for user changes. Do not include the directory path.

   _____

3. Which of the following directives in the gdm.conf configuration file limits the number of logins from a single system if you've enabled remote access?
   A. TimedLoginEnable
   B. DisplaysPerHost
   C. HostLimit
   D. AllowAdd

4. Which of the following commands is not available from the Options menu in the GNOME display manager login screen?
   A. Hibernate
   B. Reboot
   C. Halt
   D. Shutdown

5. Specify the full path of the directory with the GNOME display manager configuration files.

   _____

6. Which of the following protocols allows remote access to a GNOME display manager?
   A. SSH
   B. HTTP

C. XDMCP

D. ICMP

7. If there are problems with the GNOME display manager, where are error messages sent? Name the full path of the target directory.

   _____

8. Which of the following directories contains a script that is executed just after you log out? Assume you logged in via the GNOME display manager.

   A. /etc/gdm/Init

   B. /etc/gdm/PostLogin

   C. /etc/gdm/PostSession

   D. /etc/gdm/PreSession

Work with the Evolution Mail Client

9. Which of the following is an example of an OWA?

   A. http://test.example.net/server

   B. owa://test.example.net/server

   C. michael@example.net

   D. test.example.net

10. Which of the following features is not a part of Evolution?

   A. E-mail manager

   B. Contact manager

   C. POP3 server manager

   D. Task manager

11. For user john, what directory contains that user's e-mails for his Evolution client? Assume user john has a standard home directory.

   _____

12. Which of the following message protocols cannot be configured with Evolution?

   A. IMAP

   B. POP

   C. SMTP

   D. TCP

13. Name the package that connects an Evolution e-mail client to a Microsoft Exchange server.

   _____

14. Which of the following filter criteria is not possible with Evolution?
    A. Recipients
    B. Spam score
    C. Date received
    D. Mailing list

15. Which of the following e-mail protocols can be configured with TLS?
    A. POP3
    B. IMAP4
    C. SMTP
    D. All of the above

LAB QUESTIONS

Lab I

This lab modifies the GNOME display manager to create two login consoles. Remember, changes made to the /etc/gdm/gdm.conf-custom configuration file are integrated into the GNOME display manager service. To set up and verify two graphical login consoles, take the following steps:

1. Open the gdm.conf-custom configuration file in a text editor.

2. Add the following directives in the [**servers**] section:

   ```
   1=Standard device=/dev/console
   2=Standard device=/dev/console
   ```

3. Reread the GNOME display manager configuration files with the following command:

   ```
   $ sudo /etc/init.d/gdm reload
   ```

4. Read the messages; to interpret, there are X sessions currently running, the changes aren't yet in effect. One way to stop and restart all X sessions is to move to runlevel 1 and then back to runlevel 2 with the following commands (starting with Hardy Heron, the **sudo init 1** command leads to a recovery menu; selecting Resume moves back to runlevel 2, also restarting all X sessions.):

   ```
   $ sudo init 1
   # init 2
   ```

5. You should see a GNOME login console. Review available consoles. Press CTRL-ALT-F1. Press ENTER if needed. Note the tty1 in the login message, associated with terminal 1.

6. Repeat step 5 for consoles 2 through 6. For example, to review console 2, press CTRL-ALT-F2.

7. Press CTRL-ALT-F7. Note the graphical login console in terminal 7.

8. Press CTRL-ALT-F8. What do you see here?

9. Press CTRL-ALT-F9. What kind of login screen do you see?

10. Press CTRL-ALT-F10. Do you see a login screen?

11. Return to the /etc/gdm/gdm.conf-custom configuration file, and remove the lines with the **1=Standard** and **2=Standard** directives added earlier.

12. Rerun steps 3 and 4 to restart the GNOME display manager and all X sessions.

Lab 2

In this lab, you'll review the structure of Evolution data files in your home directory. (I assume you're running an Ubuntu Linux system with Evolution installed.) To do so, take the following steps:

1. Open or log in to a command-line interface, preferably in the GNOME desktop environment by selecting Applications | Accessories | Terminal.

2. Based on default settings, you should now be in your home directory, which can be confirmed with a **pwd** command. If necessary, change to your home directory; the most universal method is with the tilde (~), which represents every user's home directory:

```
$ cd /home/michael
```

3. Run the following command to list the contents of your Evolution data directories:

```
$ ls .evolution
```

4. Review available subdirectories. What do they mean?

5. As the focus of this chapter is on Evolution as an e-mail client, review the contents of the mail/ subdirectory:

```
$ ls .evolution/mail
```

6. I assume you've configured an Evolution e-mail account associated with either a POP or IMAP server. In that case, you'll see a pop/ or imap/ subdirectory. Review the contents of that directory. What do you see?

7. Now review the contents of the local/ subdirectory. Cross-check it against the contents of the Evolution e-mail manager. In another command-line terminal, type in the **evolution** command.

8. In the Evolution window, to make sure you're in the e-mail manager, press CTRL+1. Make sure the options associated with On This Computer are expanded. Compare these names with the contents of the .evolution/mail/local/ subdirectory.

SELF TEST ANSWERS

Set Up the Display Manager

I. ☑ **D.** The **gdmsetup** command does not configure display manager settings for individual users.
☒ The **sudo gdmsetup** command starts the Login Window Preferences tool. The **gdmsetup --root** command doesn't work. The **sudo /etc/init.d/gdm start** command starts the GNOME display manager service, but does not configure the display manager. Therefore, answers **A**, **B**, and **C** are all incorrect.

2. ☑ **gdm.conf-custom.** This file contains custom settings and is automatically incorporated in the GDM configuration.

3. ☑ **B.** The **DisplaysPerHost** directive limits the number of displays available via the GNOME display manager. A limit on this directive limits the access available to potential crackers.
☒ The **TimedLoginEnable** directive, if set to true, sets up an automatic login for a predetermined user. There are no **HostLimit** or **AllowAdd** directives. Therefore, answers **A**, **C**, and **D** are incorrect.

4. ☑ **A.** The Hibernate command is not available from the Options menu from the GNOME display manager.
☒ The reboot, halt, and shutdown commands are available from the Options menu in the GNOME display manager. Therefore, answers **B**, **C**, and **D** are incorrect.

5. ☑ **/etc/gdm.** The GNOME display manager configuration files are stored in the /etc/gdm directory.

6. ☑ **C.** The XDMCP protocol supports remote access to the GNOME display manager.
☒ While it's possible to connect remotely over SSH, XDMCP is designed for remote access to the GNOME display manager. HTTP and ICMP are unrelated to remote access to a display manager. Therefore, answers **A**, **B**, and **D** are incorrect.

7. ☑ **/var/log/gdm.** The /var/log/gdm directory contains logs with error messages associated with the GNOME display manager.

8. ☑ **C.** The Default file in the /etc/gdm/PostSession file is a script that's run when a user logs out of a GNOME desktop through the GNOME display manager.
☒ The scripts in the /etc/gdm/Init, /etc/gdm/PostLogin, and /etc/gdm/PreSession directories are run during and after the login through the GNOME display manager. Therefore, answers **A**, **B**, and **D** are all incorrect.

Work with the Evolution Mail Client

9. ☑ **A.** The OWA is a URL, which therefore is a web address, which starts with the **http://**.
☒ As the other answers aren't URLs, answers **B**, **C**, and **D** are incorrect. While text.example.net
may be interpreted as a URL in a Web browser, it's not necessarily so.

10. ☑ **C.** Evolution can't (yet) directly manage POP3 servers.
☒ As Evoution can function as an e-mail, contact, and task manager, answers **A**, **B**, and **D**
are incorrect.

11. ☑ **/home/john/.evolution.** User data from the Evolution mail client is stored in that user's
home directory, in the .evolution subdirectory.

12. ☑ **D.** While e-mail protocols use TCP, the TCP protocol is not an e-mail protocol.
☒ As POP, IMAP, and SMTP are all e-mail protocols, answers **A**, **B**, and **C** are all incorrect.

13. ☑ **evolution-exchange.** The name of the Ubuntu Linux package that makes a connection
possible between the Evolution e-mail manager and a Microsoft Exchange server is evolution-
exchange.

14. ☑ **B.** A spam score is not a criterion for filtering, at least in current versions of the Evolution
e-mail manager.
☒ Recipients, Date Received, and Mailing List are filtering criteria for the Evolution e-mail
manager. Therefore, answers **A**, **C**, and **D** are all incorrect.

15. ☑ **D.** Connections to e-mail servers via POP, IMAP, and SMTP protocols can be encrypted
with TLS.

LAB ANSWERS

These labs are fairly straightforward. Do remember to make the backups of the configuration files as
suggested in the steps.

Lab I

The steps in this lab are designed to illustrate a simple reconfiguration of the GNOME display manager,
and how you can set up multiple GUI desktops on the same system. The steps towards the end of the lab
should restore the original configuration.

Lab 2

This lab is designed to help you understand how the Evolution e-mail manager works by the way its
data is stored in user home directories.

A

About the CD-ROM

T he CD-ROM included with this book comes complete with a MasterExam and the electronic version of the book. The software is easy to install on any Windows 98/ NT/2000/XP/Vista computer, and must be installed to access the MasterExam feature.

While it is possible to install the MasterExam on Linux using WINE (Wine Is Not an Emulator) software, there is no guaranty or warrantee associated with such an installation and no support will be available if you choose to do so. It is known that the Flash code associated with fill in the blank questions will lead to errors. Windows is the only recommended installation.

The MasterExam does not recognize the bolding of commands. In fact, some commands may be inaccurately shown in uppercase. We apologize for this limitation in the MasterExam software.

A paper and pencil version of the exam has been included in the root directory of the CD-ROM in .pdf format. If you are unable to run MasterExam in either Windows or Linux environments, you may still view the exam content by viewing this .pdf on your computer. Our apologies, but you will not be able to print the .pdf.

To register for a second, bonus MasterExam, simply click the Online Training link on the Main Page and follow the directions to the free online registration.

System Requirements

The electronic book requires Adobe Acrobat Reader or an equivalent Linux reader such as Evince.

Installing and Running the MasterExam

On Microsoft Windows, if your computer's CD-ROM drive is configured to AutoRun, the CD-ROM automatically starts when you insert the disc. From the opening screen, you may install the MasterExam by clicking the MasterExam button. This begins the installation process and creates a program group named LearnKey. To run the MasterExam, choose Start | All Programs | LearnKey | MasterExam | LearnKey MasterExam. If the AutoRun feature did not launch your CD, browse to the CD in Windows Explorer and click the LaunchTraining.exe icon. Then click the MasterExam link and follow the prompts.

If it isn't already expanded, click the plus sign next to Ubuntu Certification Study Guide (Exam LPI 199) to show the Quiz and MasterExam options. If you select Quiz, you're prompted to choose up to 48 questions, and are limited to 90 minutes.

If you select MasterExam, you're presented with an exam with only 45 questions and a two-hour time limit. (There are actually 75 minutes allocated for the exam, but the time you take to read the non-disclosure agreement counts against you.)

Taking the MasterExam

The MasterExam provides you with a simulation of the actual exam. The number of questions, the type of questions, and the time allowed, despite the problems just cited, are intended to be an accurate representation of the exam environment. You have the option to take an open-book exam, which includes hints, references, and answers, a closed-book (90 minute) exam, or the timed (120 minute) MasterExam simulation. When you launch the MasterExam, a digital clock display appears in the lower-right corner of your screen. The clock continues to count down to zero unless you choose to end the exam before the time expires.

For the "fill in the blank" questions, you'll need to type in precise answers. A misspelled word is just as wrong as a misspelled command in real life.

Removing an Installation

In Microsoft Windows, for *best* results for removal of programs, use the Start | All Programs | LearnKey Uninstall | Uninstall LearnKey MasterExam option to remove MasterExam.

LearnKey Technical Support

For technical problems with a Microsoft installation of the software (installation, operation, and uninstallation) and for questions regarding online registration, visit www.learnkey.com or e-mail techsupport@learnkey.com. No support is provided for Linux installation of the software.

Obtaining Content Support

For questions regarding the technical content of the electronic book or MasterExam, visit www.mhprofessional.com or e-mail customer.service@mcgraw-hill.com. For customers outside the fifty United States, e-mail international_cs@mcgraw-hill.com.

B

Test Linux
with VMware

When studying for a certification exam, it's helpful to have a virtual machine. You can test commands and more on that machine without affecting actual production systems. With enough RAM and hard drive space, you can even set up virtual machines for several instances of Ubuntu Linux. To that end, this appendix describes how to configure VMware Server, version 1.05, as a virtual machine.

VMware Server is freely downloadable for noncommercial use, and installing it on Microsoft Windows and various Linux distributions is a straightforward process. The interface is easily customizable with a variety of hardware components.

Two of the available major alternatives are available: Xen and the Kernel-based Virtual Machine (KVM). Both alternatives can be run only on Linux. I assume some of you may study for the UCP exam from a Microsoft system. As this is beyond the experience associated with UCP exam candidates, I do not describe how to create a Xen or KVM-based virtual machine here. For more information, I describe the process of creating a KVM-based virtual machine, as well as a VMware Server 2.0 system, in the upcoming *Ubuntu Server Administration*, to be released in late 2008.

While there are several VMware products available, I recommend the use of VMware Server, because it is freely available, supports hardware customization, allows practice with various Linux installation programs, and includes "snapshots," which allow you to restore a working configuration in case you forget the changes you've made.

Before installing VMware Server, make sure there's sufficient RAM and hard drive space on the local system. RAM is required not only for the operating system on the virtual machine, but also to continue to run the local host operating system. Hard drive space is required for the large files used to simulate virtual machine hard drive files. In my experience, 4GB is sufficient for the selected distributions.

on the
ôob

I have a multiboot system on my laptop, with Ubuntu Linux, Red Hat Enterprise Linux, and Microsoft Windows XP. I store my VMware Virtual Machine files on a VFAT partition, accessible to both Linux and Microsoft operating systems. I can run the same virtual machines from any of the operating systems on my laptop.

The steps described in this appendix are basic, and may not answer all of your questions. For more information, VMware has a knowledge base and community discussion forum available at www.vmware.com/support/.

Acquire VMware Server

You can get VMware Server from www.vmware.com. With free registration, VMware provides needed serial numbers, which enable full functionality. Follow these steps (as of this writing) to register and download VMware Server:

1. Navigate to the Download VMware Server page at www.vmware.com/download/server/.
2. Click the "register for your free serial number(s)" link, fill in the required information, and click Submit.
3. Print out the serial number(s) automatically generated from the website.
4. Return to the Download VMware Server page, click the Download Now button for the latest version of VMware Server, accept the license agreement (assuming you're willing), and then download the package as an EXE file for Microsoft Windows or as a "tarball" in tar.gz format for Ubuntu Linux.

I'll describe how I've installed VMware Server on my Microsoft Windows and Ubuntu Hardy Heron (8.04) systems. For your information, when writing this book, I installed Ubuntu Gutsy Gibbon on a VMware Server virtual machine loaded on a Ubuntu Dapper Drake system.

Until the Hardy Heron release, it was possible to install VMware Server from the Ubuntu partner repository. But as it isn't possible on the Ubuntu Hardy Heron release, I limit this discussion to the tarball which can be downloaded from www.vmware.com.

As of this writing, VMware Server has not been updated for the Ubuntu Hardy Heron release. Until this happens, you'll need to install the so-called "any-any" patch. As it's not officially released by VMware or Ubuntu, there are no controls on the integrity of the patch. But a link is available at www.vmware.com/support/reference/linux/prebuilt_modules_linux.html, which may forward to a different URL. In some cases, a later version may be required. However, the source for such patches is not controlled by VMware or Ubuntu, so the security of such patches may not be reliable.

When you install from the tarball, you'll get a directory with the installation files you need. Then you'll be able to install using the same vmware-install.pl script. If you're installing VMware Server on Microsoft Windows, read the section that follows. If you're installing VMware Server on Ubuntu Hardy Heron, skip to the corresponding section.

Install VMware Server on Microsoft Windows

As the UCP exam is designed for *junior*-level Linux administrators, many candidates may still be using Microsoft Windows, at least part time. It may be the only operating system available to many candidates at work or home. In this section, I demonstrate the installation of VMware Server on Microsoft Windows XP Media Center, with Service Pack 2. I have not tested the installation of VMware Server on any other Microsoft operating system, so the steps may vary.

To install VMware Server on Microsoft Windows, take the following steps:

1. Navigate to the directory where the VMware Server executable was downloaded, and run that VMware Server file.

2. The executable should, after a bit of time, start the Installation Wizard. Click Next, read and accept the license agreement (assuming you really do want to install VMware Server), and click Next again.

3. Unless you're strapped for disk space, select Complete for a complete installation of all VMware Server and Client components, and click Next.

4. If you see a warning about the VMware Management Interface being supported only on Server operating systems, just make a note of it and click OK (which is the only choice available).

5. Accept the default location for VMware Server installation, or change it if a different location is preferred. If you've installed different VMware products, you may want to install VMware Server in a different directory. Otherwise, click Next.

6. Click Install to begin the installation. The process may take a few minutes. Click Finish when prompted.

7. Now you should be able to open the installed VMware Server. Click Start | All Programs | VMware | VMware Server | VMware Server Console.

8. To continue, read the steps in "Preparing VMware for Linux Installation," later in the appendix. The steps required to install Ubuntu Linux will be the same.

Install VMware Server on Ubuntu Hardy Heron

This section shows how to install VMware Server on an Ubuntu Hardy Heron system from the aforementioned tarball. This section assumes that you've installed the latest kernel and source code or kernel development packages with kernel modules. It also assumes that you've installed the GNU C Compiler package for your distribution. You should know how to open another virtual console to run other commands as needed. If you've run the noted installation scripts before, you may not have to see all the steps listed in this section. You'll also need to make sure prerequisite packages are installed with a command such as:

```
$ sudo apt-get install build-essential linux-kernel-devel \
linux-headers-generic xinetd
```

To install VMware Server on an Ubuntu Hardy Heron system, take the following steps:

1. Download the tarball. For this example, I've downloaded the file archive named VMware-server-1.0.5-80187.tar.gz, to the /tmp directory. I've also downloaded the "any-any" patch to the same directory.

2. While not covered elsewhere in this book, the way to unpack an archive from a tarball with the .tar.gz or .tgz extension is with the **tar xzvf** command, which extracts (**x**), unzips (**z**), verbosely (**v**) in case of errors, from the filename (**f**) that follows:

```
$ tar xzvf /tmp/VMware-server-1.0.5-80187.tar.gz
$ tar xzvf /tmp/vmware-any-any-update117.tgz
```

3. Navigate to the directory with the VMware server files. Otherwise, the VMware installation script will have errors.

```
$ cd vmware-server-distrib
```

4. Run the **vmware-install.pl** script. The **./** in front of the script specifies the current directory:

```
$ sudo ./vmware-install.pl
```

5. Unless you really know what you're doing, accept the default to install binary files in the /usr/bin directory, by pressing ENTER.

```
Creating a new installer database using the tar3 format.
Installing the content of the package.
In which directory do you want to install the binary files?
[/usr/bin]
```

6. Unless you really know what you're doing, accept the default to set up the **vmware** configuration script in the /etc/rcx.d/ directories, where *x* is between 0 and 6. To do so, press ENTER.

```
What is the directory that contains the init directories
(rc0.d/ to rc6.d/)?
[/etc]
```

7. Unless you really know what you're doing, accept the default to set up the **vmware** service script in the /etc/init.d/ directory. To do so, press ENTER.

```
What is the directory that contains the init scripts
[/etc/init.d]
```

8. Unless you really know what you're doing, accept the default to set up the **vmware** daemon files in the /usr/sbin/ directory. To do so, press ENTER.

```
In which directory do you want to install the daemon files?
[/usr/sbin]
```

9. Unless you really know what you're doing, accept the default to set up the **vmware** library files in the /usr/lib/vmware/ directory. To do so, press ENTER.

```
In which directory do you want to install the library files?
[/usr/lib/vmware]
```

Unless the directory already exists, you'll be prompted to let the installation script create that directory.

10. Unless you really know what you're doing, accept the default to set up the **vmware** manual files in the /usr/share/man/ directory. To do so, press ENTER.

```
In which directory do you want to install the manual files?
[/usr/share/man]
```

11. Unless you really know what you're doing, accept the default to set up the **vmware** documentation files in the /usr/share/doc/vmware/ directory. To do so, press ENTER.

```
In which directory do you want to install the documentation files?
[/usr/share/doc/vmware]
```

Unless the directory already exists, you'll be prompted to let the installation script create that directory.

There's also an uninstallation script available, as suggested by the following message:

```
The installation of VMware Server 1.0.5 build-80187 for
Linux completed successfully. You can decide to remove
this software from your system at any time by invoking the
following command:
"/usr/bin/vmware-uninstall.pl".
```

12. Finally, you're prompted to configure the installed VMware system. Accept the default by pressing ENTER.

    ```
    Before running VMware Server for the first time, you need to
    configure it by invoking the following command:
    "/usr/bin/vmware-config.pl". Do you want this program to
    invoke the command for you now? [yes]
    ```

13. For the given version of VMware Server, the vmware-config.pl script would not work. It will work in the future. If you have a later version of VMware Server and the process ends with an "Unable to build the vmmod module" error, return to the previous step and reply **no**.

    In that case, run the following commands (or something similar, depending on version numbers):

    ```
    $ cd ../vmware-any-any-update115
    $ sudo ./runme.pl
    ```

    You should see messages such as:

    ```
    Updating /usr/bin/vmware-config.pl ... now patched
    Updating /usr/bin/vmware ... No patch needed/available
    Updating /usr/bin/vmnet-bridge ... No patch needed/available
    Updating /usr/lib/vmware/bin/vmware-vmx ... No patch needed/
    available
    Updating /usr/lib/vmware/bin-debug/vmware-vmx ... No patch
    needed/available
    VMware modules in "/usr/lib/vmware/modules/source" has been
    updated.
    Before running VMware for the first time after update, you
    need to configure it for your running kernel by invoking the
    following command:
    "/usr/bin/vmware-config.pl". Do you want this script to
    invoke the command for you now? [yes]
    ```

    Now the command should work, and you'll be able to continue to the next step. If you've already read the End User License Agreement, the script may skip to step 16.

14. VMware then stops any related running processes, with messages similar to Making sure services for VMware Server are stopped.

    ```
    Stopping VMware services:
       Virtual machine monitor                      [  OK  ]
    ```

Now you can read and accept the End User License Agreement:

```
You must read and accept the End User License Agreement to
continue.

Press Enter to display it.
```

15. If you want to read through the agreement more quickly, press the spacebar until you see this question, where you have to type in **y** or **n**.

```
Do you accept? (yes/no) y
```

16. In the next step, VMware runs GTK+ libraries. You can then choose an icons directory; the default is usually good enough, as it is a standard for most Linux distributions:

```
Configuring fallback GTK+ 2.4 libraries.

In which directory do you want to install the mime type icons?
[/usr/share/icons]
```

17. Unless you really know what you're doing, accept the default to set up the VMware menu entry in the directory with .desktop extensions. The default matches the right directory for Ubuntu; unless you've changed the default, accept it by pressing ENTER.

```
What directory contains your desktop menu entry files?
These files have a

.desktop file extension. [/usr/share/applications]
```

18. Unless you really know what you're doing, accept the default to install the VMware icon in the menu entry in the directory with .desktop extensions. The default matches the right directory for Ubuntu; unless you've changed the default, accept it by pressing ENTER.

```
What directory contains your desktop menu entry files?
These files have a

.desktop file extension. [/usr/share/applications]
```

19. In the step that follows, I recommend that you accept the default location for the application icon. To do so, press ENTER.

```
In which directory do you want to install the application's icon?
[/usr/share/pixmaps]
```

20. If appropriate VMware modules don't yet exist, accept the following offer to have them built. It will work if the appropriate GCC compiler is installed, from the gcc package:

```
None of the pre-built vmmon modules for VMware Server is
suitable for your running kernel.  Do you want this program
to try to build the vmmon module for your system (you need
to have a C compiler installed on your system)? [yes]
```

21. The next message looks for C-language header files:

```
What is the location of the directory of C header files that
match your running kernel?
[/lib/modules/2.6.24-16-generic/build/include]
```

This cites the standard location for these files in an Ubuntu Hardy Heron system. If you don't see these specifics, the linux-headers-`uname -r` package may not be installed.

Watch for mismatches in version numbers. The installation may not work if you use kernel code with a different version from the kernel currently running on your system. If the right version is cited, press ENTER to continue.

If everything goes well, the following message eventually appears:

```
The module loads perfectly in the running kernel.
```

22. As the installation proceeds, you should generally accept defaults for networking, a network bridge, and more. Some of the steps may appear to "hang" for a minute or two as the script configures useful private subnets.

23. While the default port for remote connections to a VMware server is 902, it may already be in use. If so, the installation script suggests an alternative. If you're just using a VMware server locally, the port number does not matter. The associated message looks like:

```
Please specify a port for remote console connections to use [902]
```

24. When the following message appears, it may help to change the directory to the virtual machine to a subdirectory of your home directory:

```
In which directory do you want to keep your virtual machine files?
[/var/lib/vmware/Virtual Machines]
```

25. When you see a prompt for a serial number, enter the registration code described earlier in the "Acquire VMware Server" section. Review the following message, which readies VMware for use:

```
Starting VMware services:
 Virtual machine monitor                              done
 Virtual ethernet                                     done
 Bridged networking on /dev/vmnet0                    done
 Host-only networking on /dev/vmnet1 (background) done
 Host-only networking on /dev/vmnet8 (background) done
 NAT service on /dev/vmnet8                           done

The configuration of VMware Server 1.0.5 build-80187
for Linux for this running kernel completed successfully.
```

If you run into problems while the script is running, press CTRL-C. While this stops the script, it allows you to fix problems such as missing packages. You can run the script again.

In addition, you may need to install the gcc-3.4 and gcc-4.2 packages. If you see the error messages similar to

```
/usr/lib/vmware/bin/vmware: /usr/lib/vmware/lib/libgcc_s.so.1/
libgcc_s.so.1: version `GCC_3.4' not found
```

you may need to remove the noted library file, so VMware uses the version supplied and compiled for Ubuntu Linux. I do so carefully with the following command to move the file to my home directory:

```
$ sudo mv /usr/lib/vmware/lib/libgcc_s.so.1/libgcc_s.so.1  ~
```

If something goes wrong, I could then restore the file to the noted location. But if all goes well, the **vmware** command from a GUI-based console will start the VMware Server normally.

Preparing VMware for Linux Installation

In this section, I assume you have downloaded and burned the installation CD/DVD for at least one of the selected distributions. As it is possible (and in my opinion, fairly easy for anyone considering taking the UCP exam) to burn downloaded installation CD/DVD files even on Microsoft systems, I shall not explain that process here.

Start VMware in a GUI. In Linux, one standard method is to run the **vmware** command in a command-line console inside the GUI. When the Connect To Host window appears, click Connect to move to the main VMware Server Console window, shown in the following illustration:

1. To prepare for Linux installation, click Create A New Virtual Machine. This starts the New Virtual Machine Wizard. Click Next, select the Custom configuration, and then click Next to see the operating system options shown

in the following illustration. (The steps are different if a Typical configuration is selected.)

2. Select Linux. Click the Version drop-down text box arrow and review the variety of Linux distributions that VMware Server can handle. Select the distribution that you're planning to install, or at least the latest available version thereof. Make your selection and click Next.

3. Select a name for your system, and a directory for the virtual machine files. I often override the defaults with a name such as UbuntuHH and a directory such as /home/michael/VM/UbuntuHH. As the directory will contain the files for the virtual machine, typically several gigabytes large, make sure the directory is in a partition that can handle such files. After making any desired changes, click Next.

4. For systems with multiple processors (or a multicore CPU), VMware prompts you to set the number of processors allocated to the virtual machine. Select a number and click Next.

5. VMware supports different access rights for the virtual machine. Unless you want to share it, just accept the default to make it private, and click Next.

6. Set the RAM for the virtual machine; just make sure not to take away too much from the host system. A good minimum for a GUI system is 256 MB; a smaller number is practical for most text-based systems. Click Next to see the networking options.

7. Unless there is no networking on the host operating system, retain the default, Use Bridged Networking. The guest Linux system can then connect to the network (even through a Microsoft host) as a separate computer. Click Next to continue.

8. VMware's supports IDE (PATA) and two different SCSI Adapters. Make a selection between SCSI Adapters and click Next.

9. Select Create A New Virtual Disk and click Next.

10. Read the Select A Disk Type window. Most users will want to select a SCSI Virtual Disk Type, which most closely simulates a Linux server. Click Next to see the Disk Size options shown in the following illustration:

11. In my experience, a 4GB disk size is sufficient for a test system. Your experience may vary depending on the packages you want to install with the selected distribution. It's best to select Allocate All Disk Space Now, especially if you're running VMware Server on Microsoft Windows. Fragmentation is a serious problem with VMware Server disk files, especially on compressed NTFS filesystems. Click Next when you've finished changing settings.

12. Assign a name to the disk file. If you've set it to be split into 2GB files, there will be multiple files with names such as UbuntuHH-f001.vdmk and UbuntuHH-f002.vdmk. Click Finish.

13. Assuming that you're installing from a CD/DVD, click Power On This Virtual Machine, and let it boot from that drive. Click inside the virtual machine window, and you should be able to proceed with a normal Linux installation.

VMware Snapshots

One of the main reasons I use VMware Server is the ease with which I can take "snapshots." In other words, when I've configured a Linux system on a VMware virtual machine to my satisfaction, I take a snapshot (which is available as a button command in the top menu bar). I then make changes to test the system to some new configuration. If I make a mistake, I can restore the system from the snapshot, by clicking the Revert button.

Alternatively, select VM | Snapshot and then select Take Snapshot or Revert to Snapshot.

Glossary

A s the Ubuntu Certified Professional (UCP) exam assumes two years of experience with Linux, I limit this glossary primarily to those Linux terms associated with the UCP exam. Many terms that might belong in a regular glossary may not be covered here if they should be common knowledge to basic Linux users.

~   The tilde (~) represents the home directory of the currently active user.

account   The **account** directive in PAM allows or denies access according to the account policies.

ACPI "S" State   ACPI is associated with several power states, known as the "S" states, which describe various states of power consumption for the CPU, RAM, and other components.

Address Resolution Protocol (ARP)   A protocol that maps an IP address to the hardware address of a network card.

Advanced Power Management (APM)   A legacy power management system that works with the BIOS; current systems use ACPI, as the latest BIOSes no longer support APM. Based on the apmd package.

Advanced Configuration and Power Interface (ACPI)   The Advanced Configuration and Power Interface (ACPI) puts the operating system in control of power management. It needs no specialized settings in the BIOS. It supports fine-grained power management of just about every appropriate component.

Alpha release   For most software, the distribution of an Alpha release is limited to testers and developers within the company or organization. For Ubuntu Linux, Alpha releases are publicly available. In fact, most developmental Ubuntu Linux releases are Alpha releases, and are intended for developmental testing.

Alternate CD   The Ubuntu Linux Alternate CD includes installation programs without a Live CD boot option.

Apache web server   The Apache web server provides both normal and secure web services, controlled by the **httpd** daemon.

AppArmor   The default mandatory access control security system, developed by Novell; similar to Red Hat's Security Enhanced Linux (SELinux).

alien   The **alien** command can be used to convert packages between RPM, Debian/Ubuntu DPKG, Stampede, and Slackware package formats.

apt-cache   The simplest way to review available repositories for package information is with the **apt-cache** command. For example, the **apt-cache search apache** command searches all repositories for packages that refer to the Apache web server.

apt-cdrom   The **apt-cdrom** command is designed to add a CD/DVD (or in some cases, a mounted ISO image file) to the repository list in /etc/apt/sources.list.

apt-file   The **apt-file** command uses the repository databases to help search within uninstalled packages.

apt-ftparchive   The apt-ftparchive command can be used to configure a repository for client access.

apt-get   The **apt-get** commands can install and remove packages. Specifically, the **apt-get install** *package* and **apt-get remove** *package* commands install and remove the package of your choice, with all dependencies.

apt-mirror   The **apt-mirror** command can be used to create a local mirror of part or all of the repository of your choice.

aptitude   The **aptitude** command can be used as a front end to many **apt-*** commands.

arp (Address Resolution Protocol)   The **arp** command is used to view or modify the kernel's ARP table, and can detect problems such as duplicate addresses on the network. Alternatively, the **arp** command can be used to add the required entries from your LAN.

at   The **at** command is similar to **cron**, but it allows you to run a job on a one-time basis.

auth   The **auth** directive in PAM establishes the identity of a user.

authentication   The way Linux checks the login rights of a user. Linux and Unix users are normally authenticated through use of a username and password, checked against /etc/passwd and related files.

bash   The current default shell for Ubuntu Linux is the bash shell. The name "bash" is short for the Bourne Again SHell.

Bazaar   Bazaar is a version control system for Launchpad, designed for source code management.

Beta freeze   The Beta freeze is the development milestone after which package changes are further limited to minimize the risk of package dependency issues; comes before the Beta release.

Beta release   A Beta release is a point in the developmental process where features and package changes are frozen and ready for testing on nonproduction systems in real-world situations.

BIND (Berkeley Internet Name Domain)   BIND is the Unix/Linux software that is used to set up a Domain Name System (DNS) service. The associated daemon is **named**.

Blueprints   Blueprints is a specification tracker for Launchpad, designed to document new software features.

Bluetooth   Bluetooth is the low-power low-range standard for wireless communication.

/boot   The directory with the main files required to boot Linux, including the Linux kernel and initial RAM disk. The /boot directory is often mounted on a separate partition.

boot loader   A Linux boot loader loads a configuration file that allows the user to select an operating system during the boot process. Available Linux boot loaders are GRUB and LILO. Also written as bootloader.

BOOTP   A TCP/IP protocol that sends IP address information from a remote DHCP server.

Breezy Badger   The codename for the third release of Ubuntu Linux, version 5.10, released October 2005.

Bugsy Malone   The Ubuntu bug tracker, part of the Launchpad platform, is known as Bugsy Malone. It goes beyond standard user reports to collect information from the system with the bug.

BulletProofX   The BulletProofX system is designed to create a graphical screen even when there are serious problems with the configuration of the X server. The files associated with the BulletProofX system were first implemented for Ubuntu Linux Gutsy Gibbon.

caching-only name server   A caching-only name server that performs many of the functions of a DNS server. It stores the IP address associated with recent name searches, for use by other computers on your LAN.

Canonical   Canonical, Ltd., is the commercial sponsor behind Ubuntu Linux.

ccsm   The ccsm command starts the CompizConfig Settings Manager.

chage   The chage command manages the expiration date of a password.

chattr   The chattr command allows you to change file attributes.

chgrp   The chgrp command changes the group that owns a file.

chmod   The chmod command changes the permissions on a file.

chown   The chown command changes ownership on a file.

CIFS (Common Internet File System)   CIFS is the Microsoft's term for file sharing on a Windows network. It's also covered by the latest version of Samba 3, which is included with Ubuntu Linux.

CNAME (canonical name) The CNAME is a way to assign several different names to a computer in a DNS database. For example, you can set up *www* as an alias for the computer with your web server. CNAME records cannot be assigned to a mail server (MX) or a Start of Authority (SOA) record.

Compiz Compiz is a compositing window manager for the X Window System.

cron A service that runs jobs on a periodic basis. It's configured in /etc/crontab; by default, it executes jobs in the /etc/cron.hourly, /etc/cron.daily, /etc/cron.weekly, and /etc/cron.monthly directories.

crontab Individual users can run the **crontab** command to configure jobs that are run periodically.

CUPS (Common Unix Printing System) CUPS is the default print service for Ubuntu Linux.

cupsaccept The **cupsaccept** command enables a CUPS queue on a specified printer.

cupsaddsmb The **cupsaddsmb** command copies Microsoft drivers from the /usr/share/cups/drivers directory.

cupsdisable The **cupsdisable** *printer* command disables the queue on the noted printer.

cupsenable The **cupsenable** *printer* command enables the queue on the noted printer.

cupsreject The **cupsreject** command disables a CUPS queue on a specified printer.

cupstestppd The **cupstestppd** command can be used to make sure a PPD driver is formatted appropriately.

daemon A process such as the web service (**httpd**) or X Font Server (**xfs**) that runs in the background and executes as required.

Dapper Drake   The codename for the first Long Term Support (LTS) release of Ubuntu Linux, version 6.06, released June 2006.

dash   Ubuntu Linux developers are working toward making the dash shell into the default shell. The name "dash" is short for the Debian Almquist SHell.

debconf   The **debconf** command is a preconfiguration option associated with the Ubuntu Linux installation process. It loads an associated preseed configuration file.

debconf-get-selections   The **debconf-get-selections** command can help create a preseed configuration file from a current installation of Ubuntu Linux.

Debian Foundation   The Debian Foundation is the organization behind the Debian Linux distribution.

Debian import freeze   The Debian import freeze is the point at which new packages are no longer imported from the Debian Linux unstable (development) repository.

Debian Linux   Debian Linux is a distribution based on the work of volunteers. Ubuntu Linux is based on the developmental testing packages of Debian Linux.

depmod   The **depmod** command scans available modules, finds dependencies for installed modules, and maps them out to a file (modules.dep).

.desktop   Configuration files with the .desktop extension are often used as application icons.

/dev   The directory with device files, used to represent hardware and software components.

DHCP (Dynamic Host Configuration Protocol)   DHCP clients lease IP addresses for a fixed period of time from a DHCP server on a local network. The BOOTP protocol allows DHCP clients to get IP address information from a remote DHCP server. The DHCP server daemon may be **dhcpd** or **dhcpd3**.

DHCP Client   DHCP clients lease IP addresses for a fixed period of time from a DHCP server on a local network. The BOOTP protocol allows DHCP clients to get IP address information from a remote DHCP server. DHCP client configuration files include /etc/dhcpc/config and /etc/default/dhcpcd.

diskless client   A diskless client is more than a "dumb terminal," as it requires a network card, and the BIOS on the terminal is enabled with the Pre-boot eXecution Environment (PXE).

display manager   A Linux display manager includes a dialog box for your username and password. The default display manager for Ubuntu Linux is the GNOME display manager.

displayconfig-gtk   The **displayconfig-gtk** command starts the Screen and Graphics Preferences tool for configuring the X Server.

dmesg   The **dmesg** command lists the kernel ring buffer and the initial boot messages. If your system boots successfully, /var/log/dmesg is one place to look for messages if you think you have boot problems.

DNS (Domain Name System)   The DNS service maintains a database of fully qualified domain names such as www.redhat.com and IP addresses such as 206.132.41.202. If the domain name is not in the local database, DNS is normally configured to look to other, more authoritative, DNS servers. The associated daemon is **named**.

Dovecot   The Dovecot service is associated with POP and IMAP e-mail.

dpkg   The **dpkg** command is the Debian package manager. It is analogous to the **rpm** command on Red Hat–based distributions.

dpkg-reconfigure   The **dpkg-reconfigure** command reconfigures the options for a currently installed package.

dumpe2fs   The **dumpe2fs** command provides a lot of information about the format of a partition.

e2label   The e2label command associates a device with a filesystem directory.

Edgy Eft   The codename for the second 2006 release of Ubuntu Linux, version 6.10, released October 2006.

Edubuntu Linux   A release of Ubuntu Linux associated with educational applications, which also uses the GNOME desktop environment.

emacs   The emacs editor is a popular text editor this is run from a text console.

environment   Each user's environment specifies default settings such as login prompts, terminals, the **PATH**, mail directories, and more.

/etc/apt/sources.list   The /etc/apt/sources.list configuration file includes connections to remote repositories for package management.

/etc/bash.bashrc   The /etc/bash.bashrc configuration file is used for aliases and functions, on a system-wide basis.

/etc/bash_completion   The /etc/bash_completion configuration file specifies default actions for certain commands and keyboard actions.

/etc/default/locale   The /etc/default/locale configuration file specifies current language settings.

/etc/dhclient.conf   The /etc/dhclient.conf configuration file specifies DHCP client settings.

/etc/exports   The /etc/exports configuration file defines shared NFS directories.

/etc/fstab   The /etc/fstab configuration file defines default mounted directories.

/etc/ftpusers   The /etc/ftpusers file is commonly used by other FTP servers to configure users who are not allowed access through the server.

/etc/group   The /etc/group configuration file contains information for group accounts.

/etc/gdm   The /etc/gdm directory contains GNOME display manager configuration files. The main configuration file is gdm.conf; the customizable configuration file is gdm.conf-custom.

/etc/gshadow   The /etc/gshadow configuration file contains Shadow Password Suite information for group accounts.

/etc/host.conf   The /etc/host.conf configuration file specifies a search order between /etc/hosts and DNS servers as specified in /etc/resolv.conf.

/etc/lsb-release   The /etc/lsb-release configuration file includes release information for the current distribution.

/etc/network/if-down.d   Scripts in the /etc/network/if-down.d directory are run just as a local network service is deactivated.

/etc/network/if-post-down.d   Scripts in the /etc/network/if-post-down.d directory are run just after a local network service is deactivated.

/etc/network/if-pre.up.d   Scripts in the /etc/network/if-pre-up.d directory are run just before a local network service is activated.

/etc/network/if-up.d   Scripts in the /etc/network/if-up.d directory are run just as a local network service is activated.

/etc/network/interfaces   The /etc/network/interfaces configuration file includes default network settings for the local system.

/etc/nsswitch.conf   The /etc/nsswitch.conf configuration file specifies a search order for domain names, usernames, and more.

/etc/passwd   The /etc/passwd configuration file contains information for user accounts.

/etc/printcap   The /etc/printcap configuration file contains a list of shared printers for the CUPS and LPRng print services.

/etc/profile   The /etc/profile configuration file is used for system-wide environment and startup files.

/etc/rcS.d   The scripts in the /etc/rcS.d directory are started at all runlevels.

/etc/resolv.conf   The /etc/resolv.conf configuration file specifies the IP address of DNS servers to search.

/etc/samba/smb.conf   The /etc/samba/smb.conf configuration file is used for the Samba server.

/etc/shadow   The /etc/shadow configuration file contains information for user accounts, based on the Shadow Password Suite. Passwords in this file are encrypted, and accessible only to the root user.

/etc/sysctl.conf   The /etc/sysctl.conf configuration file contains kernel configuration parameters.

/etc/vsftpd.conf   The /etc/vsftpd.conf configuration file is used for the vsFTP server.

/etc/X11/xorg.conf   The /etc/X11/xorg.conf configuration file is used for the X Window System.

/etc/yp.conf   The /etc/yp.conf configuration file specifies information for an NIS client.

exportfs   The **exportfs** command allows shared NFS directories to be shared with a network.

Evolution   The Evolution personal information manager is functionally similar to Microsoft Outlook. The UCP curriculum only lists requirements associated with the Evolution e-mail manager.

evolution-exchange   The evolution-exchange package is required for systems that need a connection to a Microsoft Exchange server.

ExpressCard   An ExpressCard is the successor to the PC Card/PCMCIA standard. The two standards are not physically compatible, as PCMCIA cards do not fit into ExpressCard slots.

fdisk   A standard disk-partition command utility that allows you to modify the physical and logical disk partition layout.

feature freeze   A feature freeze is the point where developers stop introducing new features, and focus on bug fixes.

Feisty Fawn   The codename for the first 2007 release of Ubuntu Linux, version 7.04, released April 2007.

filesystem (or file system)   Filesystem has multiple meanings in Linux. It refers to mounted directories; the root directory (/) filesystem is formatted on its own partition. It also refers to file formats; Linux partitions are typically formatted to the ext3 filesystem.

Filesystem Hierarchy Standard (FHS)   The Filesystem Hierarchy Standard (FHS) is the official way to organize files in Unix and Linux directories. The top-level directory is known as the root directory (/); users' home directories are configured in /home.

find   The **find** command searches for a desired file through a given directory and its subdirectories.

firewall   A hardware or software system that prevents unauthorized access over a network. Normally used to protect a private LAN from attacks through the Internet.

Fluxbuntu   An Ubuntu Linux derivative that uses the Fluxbox window manager, and limits itself to free software.

fontconfig   The **fontconfig** command is a now-obsolete tool cited in the UCP curriculum for font customization. Fonts can now be configured with the **dpkg-reconfigure fontconfig-config** command.

Freespire   Released by Linspire, formerly known as Lindows. Until recently, Freespire was based on Debian Linux. Now based on Ubuntu Linux.

Freedom Toaster   The Freedom Toaster is a vending-machine-style dispenser of free digital products, including Ubuntu Linux. Part of Ubuntu's technical infrastructure.

Fridge   The Ubuntu Fridge provides "news, grassroots marketing, advocacy, team collaboration, and great original content." Available at http://fridge.ubuntu.com, it's essentially a community news site, detailing release announcements, conference events, hot new features, project reports, and more.

fsck   The **fsck** command checks the filesystem on a Linux partition for consistency. It should never be run on a mounted partition.

FTP (File Transfer Protocol)   The FTP protocol is a TCP/IP protocol designed to optimize file transfer between computers.

gateway   A gateway is a route from a computer to another network. A default gateway address is the IP address of a computer or router that connects a LAN with another network such as the Internet.

GConf   The GConf daemon governs the configuration settings associated with each user's GNOME desktop environment. The daemon is **gconfd-2**.

gconftool-2   The **gconftool-2** command can control and configure GConf settings.

gconf-editor   The **gconf-editor** command opens the Configuration Editor GUI tool, which I find functionally similar to the Microsoft Registry Editor, with effects limited to the GNOME desktop environment.

gdmsetup   The **gdmsetup** command opens the Login Window Preferences tool, to configure the GNOME display manager login screen.

gNewSense   An Ubuntu Linux derivative that uses only free software; endorsed by the Free Software Foundation.

GNOME (GNU Network Object Model Environment)   GNOME is the default GUI desktop for Ubuntu Linux.

gnome-appearance-properties   The gnome-appearance-properties command starts the GNOME Appearance Preferences window.

gnome-control-center   The gnome-control-center command starts a front end to other GNOME tools.

gnome-cups-printer   The gnome-cups-printer command starts the GNOME printer configuration tool in a GNOME desktop environment.

gnome-display-properties   The gnome-display-properties command starts the GNOME Screen Resolution Preferences window.

gnome-font-properties   The gnome-font-properties command is now obsolete; its functionality is now part of the gnome-appearance-properties tool.

gnome-keyboard-properties   The gnome-keyboard-properties command starts the GNOME Keyboard Preferences window.

gnome-keybinding-properties   The gnome-keybinding-properties command starts the GNOME Keyboard Shortcuts window.

gnome-language-selector   The gnome-language-selector command starts the GNOME Language Support tool, where additional languages can be installed and configured.

gnome-mouse-properties   The gnome-mouse-properties command starts the GNOME Mouse Management window.

gnome-sound-properties   The gnome-sound-properties command starts the GNOME Sound Preferences window.

gnome-volume-properties   The gnome-volume-properties command starts the GNOME Removable Drives and Media Preferences window.

gnome-window-properties The gnome-window-properties command starts the GNOME Window Preferences window.

Gnoppix Live CD distribution, based on Debian Linux; similar to Knoppix, except with the GNOME desktop.

Guadalinex An Ubuntu Linux–based distribution, promoted by the autonomous Andalucia community of Spain.

Gobuntu The release of Ubuntu Linux limited to open source software.

GPG (GNU Privacy Guard) GPG is an implementation of the OpenPGP standard included with Ubuntu Linux.

group ID Every Linux group has a group ID, as defined in /etc/group.

groupadd The groupadd command adds local groups.

groupdel The groupdel command deletes local groups.

GRUB (Grand Unified Bootloader) The default boot loader for Ubuntu Linux.

Gutsy Gibbon The codename for the second 2007 release of Ubuntu Linux, version 7.10, released October 2007.

Hardware Abstraction Layer (HAL) Conceptually different from the Microsoft version, the Linux Hardware Abstraction Layer (HAL) provides a constantly updated list of detected components.

Hardy Heron The codename for the second LTS release of Ubuntu Linux, version 8.04, released April 2008.

hdparm The hdparm command can help control a number of settings on CD/DVD and hard drives, including power consumption.

Hoary Hedgehog The codename for the second release of Ubuntu Linux, version 5.04, released April 2005.

home directory The home directory is the login directory for Linux users. Normally, this is /home/*user*, where *user* is the user's login name. It's also represented by the tilde (~) in any Linux command.

htpasswd The **htpasswd** command helps create passwords for accessing your local web site.

ICMP (Internet Control Message Protocol) A protocol for sending online error control messages. Associated with the **ping** command.

i386 The i386 architecture in Ubuntu Linux refers primarily to packages that can be installed on Intel-32 bit CPU systems and clones.

ifconfig The **ifconfig** command is used to configure and display network devices.

ifdown The **ifdown** command is used to activate a network device.

ifup The **ifup** command is used to deactivate a network device.

IMAP (Internet Message Access Protocol) IMAP is an e-mail protocol. It works on port 143; connections to an IMAP server can be configured through the Evolution e-mail client. IMAP4 is the current standard for IMAP servers. IMAP connections can be encrypted with Evolution, if the server supports it.

ImpiLinux A Linux distribution based on Ubuntu Linux, released by a separate company also owned by the owner of Canonical, Mark Shuttleworth.

init The **init** process is the first Linux process called by the kernel. This process starts other processes that compose a working Linux system, including the shell.

Initial RAM Disk Many Linux distributions use an initial RAM disk in the boot process; it's stored as initrd.img-`uname -r`-generic file in the boot directory, where `uname -r` is the version number of the kernel and -generic (or -server) specifies the purpose for which the kernel was built.

Internet Print Protocol (IPP)   The Internet Print Protocol (IPP) is the evolving standard for printers shared over networks. It's being adapted by all major operating systems; the Linux implementation is CUPS.

IP forwarding   IP forwarding occurs when data is forwarded between computers or networks through your computer.

IPv4 (Internet Protocol version 4), IPv6 (Internet Protocol version 6)   IPv4 and IPv6 are different systems of IP addressing. Version 4 is what we use today and is based on 32-bit addresses; version 6 is coming online and is based on 128-bit addresses.

IrDA   IrDA refers to the basic standard of the Infrared Data Association. It's a protocol for data exchange based on infrared light transmission.

ISO   ISO has at least two meanings in Ubuntu Linux. An ISO file is associated with an ISO image, and is based on a standard published by the International Organization for Standardization for disk images, which can be burned to CD or DVD drives. ISO encodings also are associated with language options.

iwconfig   The **iwconfig** command can display current wireless settings, and can configure a specific wireless card with network characteristics such as the ID, channel, encryption, transmitted power, and more.

iwevent   The **iwevent** command monitors the system for other wireless events.

iwgetid   The **iwgetid** command identifies the wireless network ID, also known as the Extended Service Set ID (ESSID).

iwlist   The **iwlist** command lists wireless network interface data, such as channels, transmission power, and authorization keys.

iwpriv   The **iwpriv** command configures detailed parameters associated with a wireless network card.

iwspy   The **iwspy** command measures quality of wireless link information.

KDE   A GUI for Linux and Unix computers. Also known as the K Desktop Environment.

Kerberos 5   Kerberos 5 is a computer network authentication protocol, which provides mutual authentication between client and server. It was developed at the Massachusetts Institute of Technology.

kernel   The kernel is the heart of any operating system. It loads device drivers. You can recompile a Linux kernel for additional drivers, for faster loading, and to minimize the required memory.

kernel module   Kernel modules are pluggable drivers that can be loaded and unloaded into the kernel as needed. Some loaded kernel modules are shown with the **lsmod** command.

Kernel-Based Virtual Machine (KVM)   The Kernel-Based Virtual Machine (KVM) is one virtualization technology native to Linux, similar to Xen.

Kickstart   Kickstart is the automated installation system developed by Red Hat that allows you to supply the answers required during the installation process. When properly configured, a Kickstart floppy can allow you to start your computer and install Ubuntu Linux automatically from a network source.

Kubuntu Linux   A version of Ubuntu Linux, which installs the KDE desktop as the default GUI.

LAMP   LAMP is the Ubuntu Server installation option that installs Linux, Apache, MySQL, and PHP.

Launchpad   Launchpad is Canonical's proprietary platform for hosting open source projects, bug tracking, and more.

LDP (Linux Documentation Project)   The LDP is a global effort to produce reliable documentation for all aspects of the Linux operating system. Its work is available online at www.tldp.org.

lftp   The **lftp** command starts a moderately flexible FTP command-line client, when compared to the **ftp** command client.

Lightweight Directory Access Protocol (LDAP)   The Lightweight Directory Access Protocol allows authentication information on a central networked server.

LILO (Linux Loader)   An older bootloader available for Ubuntu Linux; an alternative to GRUB.

Line Print Daemon (LPD)   The Line Print Daemon (LPD) service is an older print service still available for Ubuntu Linux.

Line Printer, Next Generation (LPRng)   The Line Printer, Next Generation (LPRng) service is an older print service still available for Ubuntu Linux.

Linux Terminal Server Project (LTSP)   The Linux Terminal Server Project (LTSP) supports the creation of diskless clients that connect to an Ubuntu Linux server.

LinuxMint   A derivative of Ubuntu Linux "focused on a more elegant desktop environment."

Linux Terminal Server Project   A system available for Ubuntu Server for thin-client support.

Live CD   A computer operating system that boots directly from the CD/DVD drive, without being installed on the hard drive.

localization   Localization is the way to customize Linux systems for language, dialect, custom, and country-specific formats such as currencies, character sets, and more; spelled *localisation* in the UCP curriculum.

locale   The locale specifies the current localization settings for the system. The **locale -a** command returns available default language options.

locate The **locate** command searches through a default database of files and directories. The database is refreshed daily with the mlocate or slocate scripts in the /etc/cron.daily/ directory.

Long Term Support (LTS) Regular releases of Ubuntu Linux are supported for 18 months. Long Term Support (LTS) releases are supported for three years on the desktop, and five years on the server.

logical extent (LE) A logical extent (LE) is a chunk of disk space that corresponds to a physical extent (PE).

logical volume (LV) A logical volume (LV) is composed of a group of logical extents (LEs).

Logical Volume Management (LVM) Logical Volume Management (LVM) allows you to set up a filesystem on multiple partitions. Also known as the Logical Volume Manager.

lpadmin Members of the lpadmin group in /etc/group are configured by default as print administrators in the Ubuntu Linux implementation of CUPS.

lpc You can use the **lpc** command to scan all configured print devices and queues.

lpinfo You can use the **lpinfo -v** command to display available print devices.

lpq You can use the **lpq** command to view print jobs still in progress.

lpr You can use the **lpr** command to send print requests.

lprm You can use the **lprm** command to remove print jobs from the queue.

lsattr The **lsattr** command lists file attributes.

lshal The **lshal** command lists detected hardware.

lsmod The **lsmod** command lists installed kernel modules.

lspci   The **lspci** command lists detected PCI devices and associated settings. The **lspci -v** and **lspci -vv** commands provide detailed data on each hardware device.

lspcmcia   The **lspcmcia** command lists detected PC Card (PCMCIA) devices.

lsusb   The **lsusb** command lists detected USB buses and devices.

ltsp-build-client   The **ltsp-build-client** command builds the files required for an LTSP client system on an LTSP server.

lvcreate   The **lvcreate** command creates a logical volume (LV) from a specified number of available physical extents (PEs).

lvdisplay   The **lvdisplay** command specifies current configuration information for logical volumes (LVs).

lvextend   The **lvextend** command allows you to increase the physical volume (PV) area allocated to a logical volume (LV).

lvremove   Functionally opposite to the **lvcreate** command.

masquerading   Masquerading enables you to provide Internet access to all of the computers on a LAN with a single public IP address.

main repository   The Ubuntu Linux main repository includes open source packages supported by Canonical.

Malone   Malone, sometimes known as "Bugsy Malone," is the bug tracker for Launchpad.

MBR (Master Boot Record)   The first sector of a bootable disk. Once the BIOS cycle is complete, it looks for a pointer on the boot disk's MBR, which then looks at a boot loader configuration file such as grub.conf to see how to start an operating system.

Microsoft Exchange   The Microsoft Exchange server is a groupware suite associated with Microsoft Outlook. Evolution can be configured to connect to a Microsoft Exchange server.

mirror site   A mirror site is a server that stores the same information as the original server. Mirror sites are commonly used as alternate sites for Ubuntu Linux repositories and downloadable CD/DVD ISO image files.

mkfs   The **mkfs** command can help you format a newly configured partition. Variations are available, including **mkfs.ext3**, which formats to the default ext3 filesystem.

mksmbpasswd   The **mksmbpasswd** command helps prepare a Linux authentication database for use by Samba.

modprobe   You can use the **modprobe** command to control device modules to be installed.

mount   You can use the **mount** command to specify mounted partitions, or attach local or network partitions to specified directories.

mount.cifs and umount.cifs   The **mount.cifs** and **umount.cifs** commands, when properly configured, allow regular users to mount directories shared over a Microsoft Windows network through Samba.

msttcorefonts   The Ubuntu Linux package for Microsoft Windows fonts.

Multiverse repository   The Ubuntu Linux Multiverse repository includes packages not supported by Canonical, and which are also not open source.

Mythbuntu   A Ubuntu-based distribution that incorporates the MythTV application for digital multimedia.

NAT (Network Address Translation)   NAT is a feature associated with firewall commands such as **iptables,** which connects computers inside your LAN to the Internet while disguising their true IP addresses. NAT modifies IP packet headers. The process is reversed for return messages. Closely related to masquerading.

netstat   The **netstat** command displays connectivity information for your network cards. For example, the **netstat -r** command is used to display the routing tables as stored in your kernel.

Network Time Protocol (NTP)   The Network Time Protocol allows you to synchronize your computer with a central timeserver. You can do this by editing /etc/ntpd.conf and activating the ntpd service.

network-admin   The **network-admin** command starts the Network Settings tool in the GUI, which is the Ubuntu Linux tool for administering network cards.

NFS (Network File System)   NFS is a file-sharing protocol originally developed by Sun Microsystems; it is the networked filesystem most commonly used for networks of Linux and Unix computers. The associated Ubuntu server is the NFS kernel server.

NIC (Network Interface Card)   A NIC connects your computer to a network. A NIC can be anything from a Gigabit Ethernet adapter to a telephone modem.

NIS (Network Information System)   NIS allows you to share one centrally managed authorization database for the Linux and Unix systems on your network.

nisdomainname   The **nisdomainname** command finds and can assign a domain name for the local system for a NIS network.

oem-config-prepare   The **oem-config-prepare** command customizes an Ubuntu Linux installation for original equipment manufacturers (OEM).

PAM (Pluggable Authentication Modules)   PAM separates the authentication process from individual applications. PAM consists of a set of dynamically loadable library modules that configure how an application verifies its users before allowing access.

parted   **parted** is a standard disk-partition command utility that allows you to modify the physical and logical disk partition layout. Be careful when using it, as changes are immediately written to the partition table.

partprobe   You can use the **partprobe** command to reread a recently changed partition table without rebooting.

password   The **password** directive in PAM manages other password policies.

passwd The **passwd** command changes the password of the current or specified user.

PATH A shell variable that specifies the directories (and in what order) the shell automatically searches for input commands and files.

pdbedit The **pdbedit** command can also be used to add or delete users for a Windows security accounts manager (SAM) database. Functionally similar to the **smbpasswd** command.

PGP (Pretty Good Privacy) A technique for encrypting messages, often used for e-mail. It includes a secure private- and public-key system similar to RSA. The Linux version of PGP is known as GPG (GNU Privacy Guard).

physical extent (PE) A chunk of disk space created from a physical volume (PV) for Logical Volume Manager (LVM).

physical volume (PV) An area of space for a Logical Volume Manager (LVM) that usually corresponds to a partition or a hard drive.

POP (Post Office Protocol) POP is an e-mail protocol. It works on port 110; connections to a POP server can be configured through the Evolution e-mail client. POP3 is the current standard for POP servers. POP3 connections can be encrypted, if the server supports it.

Postscript Printer Definition (PPD) Postscript Printer Definition (PPD) files are drivers also available for Microsoft Windows systems that can be used for CUPS.

Pre-boot eXecution Environment (PXE) The Pre-boot eXecution Environment boots computers over a network independent of local storage devices.

preseed A preseed file is an answers file that can be configured to automate the Ubuntu Linux installation process.

Primary ATA (PATA) Primary ATA is the media standard associated with older IDE drives, also known as ATA (Advanced Technology Attachment).

Primary Domain Controller (PDC) A PDC is the governing server on a Microsoft Windows NT4 network. You can configure Ubuntu Linux with Samba to function as a PDC or as a member server on more current Microsoft networks.

/proc /proc is the Linux *virtual* filesystem. *Virtual* means that it doesn't occupy real disk space. /proc files are used to provide information on kernel configuration and device status.

public/private key Encryption standards such as PGP, GPG, or RSA are based on public/private key pairs. The private key is kept on the local computer; others can decrypt it with the public key.

pvcreate The **pvcreate** command allows you to configure physical extents (PEs) from a properly configured partition.

pvdisplay The **pvdisplay** command specifies current configuration information for physical volumes (PVs).

resize2fs The **resize2fs** command allows you to increase the size of a filesystem; often used after increasing the space associated with an LVM.

RAID (Redundant Array of Independent Disks) Ubuntu Linux supports software RAID. You can use the installation program to set up software RAID arrays. You can also set up RAID arrays using the **fdisk** or **parted** commands with **mdadm**. Also known as Redundant Array of Inexpensive Disks.

RAID 0 A RAID 0 array requires two or more partitions or hard drives. Reads and writes are done in parallel, increasing performance, filling up all partitions or hard drives equally. RAID 0 includes no redundancy; if any partition or hard drive in the array fails, all data in the array is lost.

RAID 1 A RAID 1 array requires two or more partitions or hard drives. RAID 1 is also known as mirroring, because the same information is written to both partitions. If one disk is damaged, all data will still be intact and accessible from the other disk.

RAID 5 A RAID 5 array requires three or more partitions. Parity information is striped across all partitions. If one disk fails, the data can be rebuilt. It can be automatically written to a spare disk.

RAID 6 A RAID 6 array requires four or more partitions. Parity information is striped twice across all partitions. If one or two disks fail, the data can be rebuilt. It can be automatically written to a spare disk.

recovery mode When you boot Ubuntu Linux in recovery mode, you're automatically logged in as the root user, in runlevel 1, without networking or most services. If your Linux system has boot problems, recovery mode may provide a sufficient quantity of tools to fix the problem.

refresh rate The refresh rate regulates the rate at which the image you see on your screen is redrawn, in hertz (Hz).

release candidate A release candidate is the milestone in the development cycle where a production quality prerelease is made.

repository A repository for Ubuntu Linux is a dedicated part of a server with Ubuntu Linux packages. Repositories available for Ubuntu Linux include main, restricted, Universe, Multiverse, Backports, updates, proposed, security, and partner.

restricted repository The Ubuntu Linux restricted repository includes packages supported by Canonical that are not open source.

reverse (inverse) zone A DNS reverse (inverse) zone can be required by some servers, such as Apache and sendmail, to make sure an IP address points to a real computer. If the reverse zone hostname does not match the IP address, the server might not respond.

Red Hat Certified Engineer (RHCE) Perhaps the elite certification available for Linux systems administrators. Designed to qualify Linux administrators with significant experience in configuring Linux LANs with Red Hat Enterprise Linux. I believe Ubuntu will eventually develop a competitor to this certification.

root This word has multiple meanings in Linux. The root user is the default administrative user. The root directory (/) is the top-level directory in Linux. The root user's home directory, /root, is a subdirectory of the root directory (/).

Rosetta Rosetta is the Launchpad translations tool, available at https:// launchpad.net/rosetta. It's an open source human-language translation tool.

route   The **route** command is associated with routing tables. The command can be used with or without the **-n** switch, and is equivalent to **netstat -r**.

rpcinfo   The **rpcinfo** command reports Remote Procedure Call (RPC) information; commonly associated with NIS and NFS.

rsync   The **rsync** command is used to synchronize local and remote groups of files.

runlevel   Ubuntu Linux includes six available runlevels. Key runlevels include 0, halt; 1, single-user mode; 2, GUI login; and 6, reboot.

run-parts   The **run-parts** directive in many scripts is used to run the scripts in specified directories.

Samba   The Linux and Unix implementation of the Server Message Block protocol and the Common Internet File System (CIFS). Allows computers that run Linux and Unix to communicate with computers that run Microsoft Windows operating systems.

Secure Shell (SSH)   The Secure Shell service is a network protocol that enables secure communication over a network; it's implemented in Ubuntu Linux with the openssh-server package.

secure virtual hosts   You can configure multiple secure virtual hosts on a single Apache server.

sendmail   A standard e-mail server application used by most Internet e-mail. Different from Sendmail, which is a commercial e-mail server application not installed on Ubuntu Linux.

Serial ATA (SATA)   A newer standard on hard drives that facilitates faster communication and more reliable operation. SATA drives have device file labels similar to SCSI; for example, the first SATA drive is known as /dev/sda.

session   The **session** directive in PAM applies settings for an application.

SGID   The SGID bit sets common group ID permissions on a file or directory.

Shadow Password Suite   The Shadow Password Suite creates an additional layer of protection for Linux users and groups in the /etc/shadow and /etc/gshadow files.

Shuttleworth, Mark   Mark Shuttleworth is the founder of Canonical, Ltd, dedicated to promoting certain free software projects, including Ubuntu Linux.

ShipIt   ShipIt is Ubuntu's free CD distribution and shipping service, which allows anyone to request and receive physical copies of the Ubuntu Linux distribution by postal mail. Part of Ubuntu's technical infrastructure.

showmount   The **showmount** command lists the shared directories from an NFS server.

ServerRoot   The **ServerRoot** directive in a CUPS configuration file specifies the default top-level root directory for CUPS configuration files.

services-admin   The **services-admin** command starts the Service Settings tool in the GUI, which is the Ubuntu Linux tool for administering service status during the boot process.

shadowconfig   The **shadowconfig** command can activate or deactivate the Shadow Password Suite.

shares-admin   The **shares-admin** command starts the Shared Folders tool in the GUI, which is the Ubuntu Linux tool for configuring shared directories over Samba and NFS services.

smbclient   The **smbclient** command can browse shared Samba directories.

smbpasswd   The **smbpasswd** command helps you create usernames and passwords for a Samba (Microsoft Windows NT4-style) network.

SMTP (Simple Mail Transfer Protocol)   SMTP is a TCP/IP protocol for sending mail; used by sendmail and Postfix. Can be configured through the Evolution e-mail client, with and without authentication. SMTP connections can be encrypted.

SOA (Start of Authority)   In a DNS database, the SOA record is the preamble to all zone files. It describes the zone, the DNS server computer (such as ns.*your-domain*.com), the responsible administrator (such as hostmaster@your-domain.com), the serial number associated with this file, and other information related to caching and secondary DNS servers.

Soyuz   Soyuz is a tracker for Linux distributions registered in Launchpad.

Squid   Squid is a high-performance HTTP and FTP caching proxy server.

Structured Query Language (SQL)   The basis for several database systems, including some that can be run on Linux, including MySQL and PostgreSQL.

SUID   The SUID bit sets common user ID permissions on a file or directory.

su   The **su** command supports a move to a different user account from the command line.

sudo   The **sudo** command supports administrative access as configured in /etc/sudoers.

sudoedit   The **sudoedit** command edits a specified file based on administrative access rights as configured in /etc/sudoers.

superuser (super user)   The superuser represents a regular user who has taken root user privileges. Closely associated with the **su** and **sudo** commands.

swap space   Linux uses swap space for less frequently used data that would otherwise be stored in RAM. It is normally configured in Linux in a swap partition.

Synaptic Package Manager   The Synaptic Package Manager is a front end to several of the **apt-*** commands, including **apt-get**, **apt-cdrom**, **apt-cache**, and more, and provides a visual overview of available packages.

sysctl   The **sysctl** command can be used to configure kernel parameters, using the /etc/sysctl.conf configuration file; **sysctl -p** rereads changes to that file.

system-config-printer   The **system-config-printer** command starts the Ubuntu Linux printer configuration tool in a GUI desktop.

TCP/IP (Transmission Control Protocol/Internet Protocol)   TCP/IP is a suite of communications protocols for internetwork communication. It is primarily used as the communication system for the Internet.

Telnet   A terminal emulation program that allows you to connect to remote computers.

testparm   The **testparm** command can be used as a syntax checker for the Samba configuration file, /etc/samba/smb.conf.

Trivial File Transfer Protocol (TFTP)   The Trivial File Transfer Protocol (TFTP) is a file-sharing service, similar to FTP.

Ubuntu Certified Professional   The Ubuntu Certified Professional (UCP) exam is targeted at the junior-level system administrator.

Ubuntu Certified Professional Curriculum   The Ubuntu Certified Professional Curriculum specifies the course outline associated with the UCP exam.

Ubuntu Linux   Ubuntu Linux is a Linux distribution released by Canonical, Ltd., which installs the GNOME desktop environment by default.

Ubuntu Studio   The release of Ubuntu Linux with features targeted at the multimedia enthusiast.

Ubuntu Security Notices (USN)   Ubuntu Security Notices (USN) are designed to help the administrator understand whether a security update is needed. The latest USN are available from www.ubuntu.com/usn.

Ubuntu Server   The release of Ubuntu Linux focused on server applications. A GUI is not installed by default in Ubuntu Server.

Ubuntu Wiki   The Ubuntu Wiki at http://wiki.ubuntu.com is an organizational tool for Ubuntu Linux development and documentation. The current version of this wiki illustrates how resources and teams are organized, lists community councils and boards, cites current Ubuntu events, and notes a list of releases.

Universal Resource Identifier (URI) The Universal Resource Identifier (URI) is a superset of the well-known Universal Resource Locator (URL), commonly used for CUPS printer addresses.

umask The **umask** command defines default permissions for newly created files.

Universe repository The Ubuntu Linux Universe repository includes open source packages *not* supported by Canonical.

update-alternatives The **update-alternatives** command configures files in the /etc/alternatives directory. For example, to configure the default editor on my system, I run the **sudo update-alternatives --config editor** command.

update-rc.d The **update-rc.d** command can change the default settings for scripts in specific runlevels.

Update Manager The Update Manager is a GUI tool that takes the current list of packages, and compares it against the local database, which lists available updates.

user ID (UID) Every Linux user has a user ID, as defined in /etc/passwd.

User Interface Freeze The User Interface Freeze is the development milestone when changes to the look, feel, and functionality of the GUI and related applications are frozen.

useradd The **useradd** command adds local users.

userdel The **userdel** command deletes local users.

UTC For our purposes, UTC is the same as Greenwich Mean Time or U.S. military Zulu time. The UTC acronym is based on a political compromise and is not relevant to the UCP exam.

usermod   The **usermod** command modifies different settings in /etc/passwd, such as expiration date and additional groups.

users-admin   The **users-admin** command starts the Users Settings tool in the GUI, which is the Ubuntu Linux tool for administering users and groups.

Very Secure FTP (vsFTP)   The Very Secure FTP service is a commonly used FTP server.

vgcreate   The **vgcreate** command creates a volume group (VG) from one or more physical volumes (PVs) for Logical Volume Manager (LVM).

vgdisplay   The **vgdisplay** command specifies current configuration information for volume groups (VGs).

vgextend   The **vgextend** command allows you to increase the extents or space allocated to a volume group (VG).

vi   The vi editor is a basic Linux text editor. While other editors are more popular, vi may be the only editor you have available in certain rescue environments.

vigr   The **vigr** command edits the /etc/group configuration file in the vi editor.

vipw   The **vipw** command edits the /etc/passwd configuration file in the vi editor.

visudo   The **visudo** command edits the /etc/sudoers configuration file in the vi editor.

virtual hosts   You can configure multiple web sites on a single Apache server by configuring a number of virtual hosts.

virtualization   Virtualization is an abstraction of computer resources; most often associated with platform virtualization, in which you can include one or more virtual machines on a physical system. Two options for virtualization are VMware and KVM.

VMware   VMware is a proprietary system with virtualization products freely available to all. With snapshots, it can help you test a system with less risk. It's available from the partner repository.

volume group (VG)   A collection of physical volumes (PVs) in Logical Volume Manager (LVM).

Warty Warthog   The codename for the first release of Ubuntu Linux, version 4.10, released October 2004.

wildcard   A wildcard is a special character used to substitute for others in an alphanumeric phrase; users and administrators can use wildcards in a single expression to specify multiple filenames and directives.

window manager   The window manager is a special type of X client that controls how other X clients appear on your display.

WINS (Windows Internet Name Service)   WINS provides name resolution on Microsoft networks; it can be activated on Samba.

wpa_action   The **wpa_action** command is used by related scripts to stop and start an interface.

wpa_passphrase   The **wpa_passphrase** command is designed to create a preshared key (PSK), which enables the use of a shared passphrase on both the wireless client and access point.

wpa_supplicant   The **wpa_supplicant** command is designed as a background service that controls the wireless connection. It works only when the wireless network is connected, and an encryption key of some sort is enabled.

WUBI   The Microsoft Windows installer of Ubuntu Linux, also known as *wubi-cdboot.exe*.

wvdialconf   The **wvdialconf** command can be used to detect configured telephone modem ports.

X client   An X client is an application that uses the X server services to display output.

X Display   The X Display is a console and a virtual window. By default, there are six virtual text consoles configured with Linux; the X Display is associated with virtual console number seven.

X server   The X server is the part of the X Window System that runs on your desktop. The X server draws images on your screen, takes input from your keyboard and mouse, and controls access to your display.

X Window System   A GUI for Linux, also known as the X Window System. Unlike other applications, the X Window System is a layered application.

Xen   Xen is one virtualization technology native to Linux. It requires the use of a custom Xen kernel and can support virtual machines in paravirtualized and full hardware virtualized modes.

Xfce   Xfce is the default GUI desktop environment for Xubuntu Linux. Xfce is the full name of the product.

xinetd daemon   The **xinetd** "super-server" daemon controls connections to servers in the /etc/xinetd.d directory such as the **rsync** and Kerberos Telnet servers.

X.org   The X.org server is the default X server for Ubuntu Linux.

Xubuntu   The release of Ubuntu Linux with the Xfce desktop environment.

ypbind   The NIS client service is **ypbind**.

ypserv   The NIS server service is **ypserv**.

Zeroconf   Zero Configuration Networking (Zeroconf) is set up on IP network 169.254.0.0/ 255.255.0.0. It's designed to work where static networking is not configured and a DHCP server is not available. It's also known in the Microsoft world as Automatic Private IP Addressing and the Apple world as Bonjour.

INDEX

S

T

Y

Z